# Praise for *Marketing Strategy*

If you heard that there are four challenges to be addressed by (market customers change, all competitors react and all resources are limit Drucker or Ted Levitt. Think again: attribute that statement to Rob Palmatier and Hari Sridhar. Then get their book, *Marketing Strategy: Based on First Principles and Data Analytics*, read it and you will understand the latest relevant research findings and how those principles apply in our data-intensive world. This book is a great accomplishment and promises to have a profound influence on the teaching and practice of marketing strategy.

> — Dr Gary Lilien, Distinguished Research Professor of Management Science, Penn State, USA, and Research Director, Institute for the Study of Business Markets, USA

With its four marketing principles (All Customers Differ, All Customers Change, All Competitors React, and All Resources are Limited), Palmatier and Sridhar's new book is a welcoming breath of fresh air to the plethora of existing marketing strategy textbooks. Here's a book that in a very pedagogically sound manner lays out what are the consequences of these four marketing principles. The authors accompany their book with a wealth of data analytics techniques, the latest marketing research, and in-depth case studies. I predict this book to become a leading textbook on marketing strategy.

> — Dr Adam Lindgreen, Head of Department of Marketing, Copenhagen Business School, Denmark, and Co-Editor-in-Chief of *Industrial Marketing Management*

The marketing strategy text by Palmatier and Sridhar offers a pragmatic and data-driven treatment on marketing strategy that is rooted in science. Their treatment is accessible and practical while also being highly sophisticated. This text provides a fresh take on many issues that are all the more important in today's increasingly data-driven and analytics-focused business environments.

> — Professor Andrew Stephen, L'Oréal Professor of Marketing, Saïd Business School, University of Oxford, UK

This book is a refreshing change. It offers analytical tools and conceptual frameworks that are decision-specific, not surface-level generalities. At last! A book that I can use with my advanced students, all the way up to the most sophisticated executive MBA audience.

> — Mark B. Houston, PhD, Department Head, Professor of Marketing, Texas A&M University, USA

Most marketing strategy classes are taught using business cases which provide in-depth examples of select marketing problems in select industries. Managers applying these case concepts at work often encounter a lack of generalizability, thereby limiting how case learning extends out to practice. In First Principles, the authors organize the most crucial problems, processes and tools of marketing strategy into one framework that can be applied to all industries. Moreover, the authors stress the role of data, analytics and research-based guidance while executing marketing strategy. Most marketing strategy textbooks and business cases are not sufficiently quantitative to equip managers in today's competitive analytics age. In that sense, this book plugs a major gap, by describing analytical tools for marketing strategy, and providing data-enabled cases to let students practice the tools before they implement them in the real world.

> — Rajdeep Grewal, PhD, JMR Editor-in-Chief, Professor of Marketing, University of North Carolina, USA

This is an excellent, comprehensive, and well-structured marketing textbook, offering a clear in-depth view of the fundamental concepts and tools of marketing strategy. The ideas and frameworks provided are well organized, pragmatically grounded, and based on well-conducted research.

> — Constantine S. Katsikeas, PhD, Associate Dean and Chair of the Marketing Division, University of Leeds, UK

I have used the First Principles approach for many years and I find it a compelling framework for teaching marketing strategy to both undergraduate and graduate students. It provides a compelling way to guide students through the multitude of tools, processes, and concepts in marketing strategy. The book's insights are built on a solid foundation of research findings.

> — Eric Fang, PhD, Professor of Marketing, University of Illinois, USA

# MARKETING STRATEGY

Based on First Principles and Data Analytics

Robert W. Palmatier

Shrihari Sridhar

First published 2017 by
PALGRAVE

Palgrave in the UK is an imprint of Macmillan Publishers Limited, registered in England, company number 785998, of 4 Crinan Street, London, N1 9XW.

Palgrave® and Macmillan® are registered trademarks in the United States, the United Kingdom, Europe and other countries.

ISBN 978–1–137–52623–6 paperback

This book is printed on paper suitable for recycling and made from fully managed and sustained forest sources. Logging, pulping and manufacturing processes are expected to conform to the environmental regulations of the country of origin.

A catalogue record for this book is available from the British Library.

A catalog record for this book is available from the Library of Congress.

Printed and bound in Great Britain by Ashford Colour Press Ltd

# Brief Contents

# Contents

# List of Figures

# List of Tables

# List of Data Analytics Techniques

# Author Biographies

**Robert Palmatier** is Professor of Marketing and John C. Narver Chair of Business Administration at the Foster School at the University of Washington. He founded and serves as the research director of the Center of Sales and Marketing Strategy at the University of Washington. He earned his bachelor's and master's degrees in electrical engineering from Georgia Institute of Technology, as well as an MBA from Georgia State University and a doctoral degree from the University of Missouri, followed by post-doctoral research at Northwestern University's Kellogg School of Management. Prior to entering academia, Professor Palmatier held various industry positions, including president and COO of C&K Components (global electronics company) and European general manager and sales and marketing manager at Tyco-Raychem Corporation. He also served as a US Navy lieutenant on board nuclear submarines.

Robert's research interests focus on marketing strategy, relationship marketing, customer loyalty, marketing channels, and sales management. His research has appeared in *Harvard Business Review*, *Journal of Marketing*, *Journal of Academy of Marketing Science*, *Journal of Marketing Research*, *Marketing Science*, *Journal of Retailing*, *Journal of Consumer Psychology*, *Marketing Letters*, and *International Journal of Research in Marketing*. He has also published the leading textbook *Marketing Channel Strategy*; a monograph entitled *Relationship Marketing*; and chapters in various texts, including *Marketing Channel Relationships*, *Relationship Marketing*, *Anti-Relationship Marketing: Understanding Relationship Destroying Behaviors*, and *Understanding the Relational Ecosystem in a Connected World*. His research has been featured in the *New York Times Magazine*, *LA Times*, *Electrical Wholesaling*, *Agency Sales*, and *The Representor*, as well as on NPR and MSNBC.

Robert is the Editor-in-Chief of the *Journal of Academy of Marketing Science*, which recently ranked second among all marketing journals in its five-year impact factor. He serves as an area editor for *Journal of Marketing*; and also sits on the editorial review boards for *Journal of Retailing* and *Journal of Business-to-Business Marketing*. His publications have received multiple awards, including the Harold H. Maynard, Sheth *Journal of Marketing*, Robert D. Buzzell, Lou W. Stern, MSI Young Scholar, Varadarajan Award for Early Contribution to Marketing Strategy Research, and the American Marketing Association Best Services Article awards. He also has won multiple awards as a teacher of advanced marketing strategy in the doctoral, EMBA, and MBA programs at the University of Washington.

Among the numerous industry and governmental committees on which Robert has served, he chaired proposal selection committees for the National Research Council (NRC), National Academy of Sciences (NAS), and the Wright Centers of Innovation, which awarded grants of $20 million for the development of a new Wright Center of Innovation based on joint academic–industry proposals. He has served on NASA's Computing, Information, and Communications Advisory Group, with the AMES Research Center. This advisory group assesses the current state of technology development within academia, governmental agencies, and industry related to NASA's information technology activities and space exploration requirements; recommends future investment areas; and outlines a sustainable process to ensure optimal investment strategies and technology portfolios for NASA's Space Exploration Enterprise. He also consults and serves as an expert witness for companies including Alston+Bird, Paul Hastings, Microsoft, Telstra, Starbucks, Emerson, Fifth Third Bank, Wells Fargo, Genie, Cincom, World Vision, and Belkin.

**Shrihari Sridhar** is Center for Executive Development Professor, and Associate Professor of Marketing at the Mays Business School at Texas A&M University. He is also the Associate Research Director of the Institute for Study of Business Markets (ISBM) at Pennsylvania State University. He earned his bachelor's degree in mechanical engineering from R.V. College of Engineering in Bangalore, India, and his masters and doctoral degrees from the University of Missouri. Prior to joining Texas A&M University, Hari was a marketing professor at Pennsylvania State University and Michigan State University.

Hari's expertise is in understanding how firms can improve the effectiveness of their marketing spending decisions – a core responsibility of marketing managers. His research spans three main areas: assessing marketing mix spending effectiveness in two-sided media markets; investigating how marketing mix effectiveness varies across firms, products, and industries; and examining the properties of optimal marketing budgeting and allocation policies. He has published more than 25 articles in top-tier national and international peer-reviewed journals and practitioner publications, including *Harvard Business Review, Marketing Science, Journal of Marketing, Journal of Marketing Research, Journal of the Academy of Marketing Science, Journal of Retailing,* and *Marketing Letters*; his work has been cited by researchers in more 30 countries. It also has received national media recognition from outlets such as National Public Radio (NPR), Reuters Inc., FOX News, and Booz & Co.

Hari serves as an area editor for *Journal of the Academy of Marketing Science* and sits on the editorial review boards for *Journal of Marketing, Journal of Marketing Research, Journal of Retailing,* and *Customer Needs and Solutions*. His research won a best paper award for *Journal of Interactive Marketing* and was among the finalists for the best paper award for *Journal of Retailing*. He also was awarded the Marketing Science Institute Young Scholar award and the Varadarajan Award for Early Career Contributions to Marketing Strategy Research.

Hari has served as an analytics coach, consultant, and research advisor to numerous firms, with a focus on business-to-business and media companies. He is also an award-wining teacher, earning multiple teaching awards at the undergraduate and MBA levels at Pennsylvania State University.

# Preface

## Aim of the Book

The primary goal of this book is to create a comprehensive, research-based, action-oriented guide for an international audience of practicing managers and managers-in-training to develop, implement, and evaluate real-world marketing strategies. Many marketing strategy classes rely almost exclusively on business cases that may serve as exemplars of marketing strategy but also offer relatively limited data analytics related to the decision-making process. Thus, students and future managers come away with little insight into situations that differ from the case examples, as well as few analytical tools or processes for developing or implementing effective strategies. They also might develop the mistaken impression that a single firm's successful solution to a marketing problem is evidence that the solution will automatically generalize to other firms.

This book addresses these concerns by adopting a different approach that can be used separately or in conjunction with traditional cases, by:

- Organizing the processes, tools, and chapters around the *First Principles of marketing strategy* to give managers a structured framework for developing effective strategies for diverse marketing problems.
- Integrating state-of-the-art *data analytics techniques* into all aspects of the strategic planning process to allow managers to make more effective data-based decisions.
- Introducing the *latest marketing research* as underpinning for the guidance outlined in this book to give managers evidence-based insights.

This approach – as captured in the title, *Marketing Strategy: Based on First Principles and Data Analytics* – has been applied and refined at multiple universities by multiple professors for undergraduate, MBA, and EMBA students for almost a decade. However, this is the first time the approach has been summarized and offered in a textbook. Accordingly, this text expressly seeks to enable instructors to add the First Principles approach, data analytics, and research-based insights to marketing strategy classes. It also can support classes focused on data analytics as a strategic organizing framework to tackle the challenges of today's big data environments.

## First Principles Approach to Marketing Strategy

To make marketing strategy comprehensible, this book shows that marketing decisions can be organized to solve four underlying "problems" or complexities that all firms face when designing and implementing their marketing strategies. These four problems represent critical hurdles to marketing success; they also define the organization for this book. We refer to them as the *First Principles of marketing strategy*, because they reflect the foundational assumptions on which marketing strategy is based. In short, marketing strategists' most critical decisions must address these First Principles.

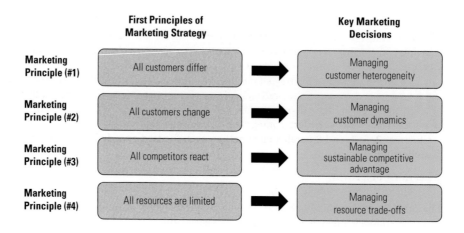

Each First Principle or underlying assumption, when matched with its associated managerial decisions, is a *Marketing Principle* (MP). For example, all customers differ, so firms must make strategic decisions to manage customer heterogeneity, and together these insights constitute MP#1. This First Principle approach to marketing strategy is unique. Its goal is to align the analysis tools, processes, and research techniques offered in many consulting books, together with existing frameworks and insights on the marketing mix (4Ps), competitors, and marketing tasks from traditional textbooks. Their alignment suggests tactics for "solving," or at least addressing, the underlying First Principles. Organizing the varied discussions around four fundamental principles means that every decision appears within its meaningful context, which includes its impact on other decisions. This view and context establishes a guiding purpose for strategic marketing efforts. Thus, it helps answer relevant student questions:

1  What are the real takeaways from a class on marketing strategy?
2  What tools do I have to help me make marketing decisions?
3  When should I use each specific framework or analysis tool?

## Integrated Data Analytics

More firms are relying on customer analytics to improve their marketing decisions. To enable a manager to develop and implement a marketing strategy successfully, strong customer analytic capabilities often are a prerequisite. In response to these trends, and to increase the linkages between data-based decision making and marketing strategy, this book integrates relevant analytical methods and techniques into every chapter's discussion of marketing strategy. The data analytics techniques offered throughout the book provide details and examples of the analytical methods used most frequently by marketers. This book also contains four broad empirical cases, with datasets and step-by-step solution guides. Each case demonstrates one of the four Marketing Principles and relevant analyses and processes, such that students have access to hands-on examples they can analyze, using the tools outlined in the book, in a relevant, real-world context.

The cases and empirical examples often rely on Marketing Engineering (MEXL), an add-on to Microsoft Excel, or Statistical Analysis Software (SAS) to conduct the analyses (see Data Analytics Technique 9.1). Thus, students have a low-cost way to conduct most of the analyses and techniques described in this book. Many professors teaching marketing strategy or data analytics classes already use MEXL software or SAS; however, other software packages can work just as well (e.g., SPSS).

# Structure of the Book

The nine chapters in this book are organized to match the natural temporal ordering of the First Principles, according to how managers address them when developing a marketing strategy. Chapter 1 serves as an introduction to marketing strategy, including its history and definitions, differences between corporate and marketing strategies, evidence of the strong linkage between marketing strategy and firm performance, and the underlying logic of the First Principles approach to marketing strategy. In addition to providing a short summary of each of the First Principles, this first chapter describes how they fit together to generate integrated marketing strategies.

Chapters 2, 3, 4, and 8 parallel one another, each focused on a different First Principle, and provide the following:

- Learning objectives
- Description and rationale for the First Principle
- Evolution and description of approaches used to address the specific Marketing Principle
- Relevant marketing research, concepts, tools, and analyses
- Input, output, and process framework
- Summary
- Takeaways
- Case, with full description, summary, figures and tables, and dataset description

Furthermore, the First Principle that states that *all competitors react*, requiring firms to *manage sustainable competitive advantages* to build a barrier around their business to withstand competitive assault (MP#3), as covered in Chapter 4, requires some further consideration. Building and maintaining sustainable competitive advantage is central to any successful marketing strategy, so this book offers a separate chapter for each major market-based source of competitive advantage: brands, offerings (products/services), and relationships (Chapters 5, 6, and 7). These chapters also employ a parallel structure, outlining theoretical frameworks and research findings on how brands, offerings, or relationships lead to sustainable competitive advantages. Each chapter also provides unique concepts, strategies, metrics, and specific processes for effective management, based on the wealth of research related to brands, offerings, and relationships.

Finally, Chapter 9 pulls it all together by integrating the four Marketing Principles, according to their temporal interconnections and synergies. It also notes key trends that influence marketing today and will do so in the future. In addition, it outlines necessary steps for building data analytics capabilities and key success factors for implementing marketing strategies.

# Unique Features for Instructors

## Rich and Detailed Instructor Materials

To support in-class delivery of content, supporting materials are available to instructors through Palgrave's online web portal, www.palgravehighered.com/palmatier-ms, or from the authors directly. These supporting materials include an instructor's manual, example syllabi, more than 500 PowerPoint slides (for classroom instruction), video supplements to many chapters (to facilitate engagement), as well as a test bank and solution guide (restricted to lecturers). The goal is to reduce the time and effort it takes for an instructor to adopt the book for classroom instruction.

## Broad Analytics Cases

The book contains four broad empirical cases, with datasets and step-by-step solution guides. Each case refers to one of the four First Principles, such that instructors have access to hands-on examples they can analyze, using the tools outlined in the book, in a relevant, real-world context. Each of the cases deals with one of the four fundamental marketing problems:

- "Managing Customer Heterogeneity at DentMax" (Chapter 2) deals with customer heterogeneity, and walks students through segmenting, targeting and positioning.
- "Preempting and Preventing Customer Churn at TKL" (Chapter 3) discusses challenges associated with customer dynamics, and teaches students how to deal with customer churn through a model-based approach.
- "Fighting Competitive Attack at Exteriors Inc." (Chapter 4) deals with the challenges of competitive attack, and walks students through customer-facing new product development.
- "Allocating Dollars Wisely at BRT Tribune" (Chapter 8) discusses the challenges associated with resource allocation, and teaches students how to allocate marketing dollars optimally.

We envision that instructors could use these cases and solutions included at the end of relevant chapters (datasets can be downloaded from the Palgrave website, www.palgravehighered.com/palmatier-ms) as a demonstration of the processes and techniques taught in the book. Thus, they can provide the basis for an in-class example of key processes and techniques discussed in a lecture. We are developing more cases, which we plan to add to the book's website over time.

The structure of the cases parallel one another, each focused on a different First Principle, and provide the following:

- Problem Background
- Problem Statement
- Data
- Solution Process
- Summary of Solution
- Tables and Figures
- Appendix describing the Dataset

## Data Analytics Techniques

The data analytics techniques offered throughout the book are meant to showcase details and provide short examples about the most popular analytical methods used by marketers, to allow instructors to design a student's toolkit in a customizable manner. Each data analytics technique contains four parts; a description, a discussion of when to use the technique, a detailed discussion of how the technique works, and a real-life example of the technique in use. The data analytics techniques provide a short, practical glimpse into how to apply data analytics to marketing decision environments. A list of the techniques discussed in the book is shown in the table below.

| Chapter | Data Analytics Technique | Chapter | Data Analytics Technique |
|---|---|---|---|
| 1.1 | Markstrat: A Tool for Practicing the First Principle Approach to Marketing Strategy | 3.3 | Customer Lifetime Value Analysis |
| 2.1 | Factor Analysis | 4.1 | Marketing Experiments |
| 2.2 | Cluster Analysis | 5.1 | Customer Surveys |
| 2.3 | SWOT and 3C Analysis | 6.1 | Conjoint Analysis |
| 2.4 | Discriminant and Classification Analyses | 7.1 | Multivariate Regression Analysis |
| 3.1 | Hidden Markov Model Analysis | 8.1 | Response Models |
| 3.2 | Choice Model Analysis | 9.1 | Using Data Analytics to Implement Marketing Principles |

## Diverse Examples

Examples are critical to making complex marketing concepts and arguments comprehensible and compelling. This book includes more than 250 diverse marketing examples, reflecting 200 different companies, 25 countries, and most industry segments. The examples reveal how the focal processes, tools, and frameworks apply to various situations. In addition, the international flavor of the book is consistent with globalization trends in most industries and markets. A comprehensive company, country, and industry example index provides an easy way to locate the diverse examples.

## Analytics Case References

In addition to the broad analytics cases, the chapters contain references to cases that were developed by DecisionPro® to be used with MEXL (an add-in module for Excel) or Enginius (a cloud-based version of the software). These cases are often more narrowly defined but provide an excellent way to learn the key marketing processes and analysis tools outlined in the chapter. Each of these cases comes with an associated dataset. These cases and datasets can be accessed at www.decisionpro.biz. In the table below, we list the DecisionPro® cases that are relevant for the book, on a chapter-by-chapter basis.

## DecisionPro Cases

| Chapter | Case | Chapter | Case |
|---|---|---|---|
| 2 | Pacific Brands Case uses cluster analysis to identify and define the segments within the brassiere market and recommend cost-effective advertising and promotional activities. | 5 | Infiniti G20 Case uses a positioning map to understand how the market perceives the Infiniti brand relative to competitors. |
| 2 | FLIP Side of Segmentation Case uses cluster analysis to segment and choose target markets. | 6 | Kirin USA Case uses a conjoint model to understand what new beer Kirin should develop to improve their competitive standing in the US. |
| 2 | Addison Wesley Longman Case uses a GE matrix to allocate resources and support to each of three potential new offerings. | 6 | Ford Hybrid Cars Case uses a Bass forecasting model to understand the sales growth of Ford Hybrid Car. |
| 2 | Suzlon Case uses a GE matrix to allocate resources/support to each of three potential new offerings. | 7 | Convergys Case uses segmentation and GE models to identify best customers for growing business. |
| 2 | ConneCtor PDA 2001 Case uses a perceptual map to help position a product in a key target market. | 7 | ABB Electric Case uses customer choice model to identify which customers should be targeted with a supplementary marketing campaign. |
| 2 | Heineken Case uses a perceptual map to reposition Heineken's beer brands in the Spanish market to increase sales. | 8 | Blue Mountain Coffee Case uses ADBUDG spreadsheet to determine Blue Mountain's advertising budget for the next year. |

*(Continued)*

| Chapter | Case | Chapter | Case |
|---------|------|---------|------|
| 3 | Bookbinders Book Club Case uses a customer choice model to evaluate different methods (RFM, regression or binary logit) that are best for prioritizing customers to target for a campaign. | 8 | Syntex Laboratories (A) Case uses resource allocation model to identify how many sales reps Syntex should hire over the next three years and how the reps should be allocated across products and physician specialty types. |
| 3 | Northern Aero Case uses a customer lifetime value model, to evaluate the value of a typical customer in each segment. | 8 | BrainCell Internet Advertising Case uses Excel Solver to allocate an advertising budget to maximize profits. |

## Integration with Marketing Simulation Software (e.g., Markstrat)

In addition to helping students understand the four First Principles and how they fit together, we discuss market simulation software, such as Markstrat, as a complement and experiential learning tool (see Data Analytics Technique 1.1). This interactive software requires real-time decisions by students that map onto the four Marketing Principles, while using the outputs of the other analyses outlined in this book (e.g., positioning maps, multidimensional scaling, consumer surveys, marketing experiments, regression analysis, conjoint analysis) to inform key marketing decisions. Many professors and students find this experiential-based learning approach effective for understanding and demonstrating the power of the First Principles, as well as the importance of data analysis for real-world development and implementation of effective marketing strategy. Other simulation software packages are also available and work as well, but Markstrat parallels our approach very closely.

## Putting it Together: Syllabi for Marketing Strategy and Marketing Analytics Classes

We view our material as suitable for marketing strategy/management and marketing analytics classes. In both classes we use the First Principles to provide structure, but just change the depth of coverage of material based on the focus of the class. Specifically, each chapter of the textbook is designed to stand on its own. Since each chapter is modular, it can be discussed with examples to demonstrate a specific First Principle, or combined with a discussion of data analytics techniques and cases for a data analytics class.

### Marketing Strategy/Marketing Management Class

We view this course as focusing on strategically analyzing and solving marketing problems from a decision maker's perspective. Specifically, the course has two key learning objectives:

1 Understanding and effectively using the fundamental frameworks, processes, and analysis tools of marketing management.
2 Using the "First Principles" of marketing strategy to solve business problems.

This course builds on the topics explored in earlier courses (e.g., Principles of Marketing, Introduction to Marketing) by helping students frame the business issue or problem confronting their firm (using our frameworks), outlining the steps for solving problems (using our processes), collecting data and applying analysis tools to inform problems, and weighting and integrating information to make choices (using our analytics techniques and broad cases with solutions). The course will emphasize the process of developing and implementing a marketing strategy. Course content can be organized into 14 sessions (w/o quizzes or tests) as shown in the table below (more class syllabi are shown on the book's website).

| Week | Topic | Notes | Chapter |
|------|-------|-------|---------|
| 1.1 | Overview and Benefits of Marketing Strategy | Instructor Slides | 1 |
| 1.2 | Overview of First Principle's Approach (continued) | Instructor Slides | 1 |
| 2.1 | Principle 1: All Customers are Different → Managing Customer Heterogeneity | Instructor Slides | 2 |
| 2.2 | Segmentation and Targeting Concept and Demonstration | Analytics Technique, MEXL (Dentmax Case) | 2 |
| 3.1 | Markstrat Session 1 and/or Case | | |
| 3.2 | Positioning Concepts and Demonstration | Analytics Technique, MEXL (Infiniti Case) | 2 |
| 4.1 | Markstrat Session 2 and/or Case | | |
| 4.2 | Principle 2: All Customers Change → Managing Customer Dynamics | Instructor Slides | 3 |
| 5.1 | Markstrat Session 3 and/or Case | | |
| 5.2 | Choice Models Concept and Demonstration | Analytics Technique, MEXL (TKL Case) | 3 |
| 6.1 | Markstrat Session 4 and/or Case | | |
| 6.2 | Principle 3: All Competitors React → Managing Sustainable Competitive Advantage | Instructor Slides | 4 |
| 7.1 | Markstrat Session 5 and/or Case | | |
| 7.2 | Principle 3 (continued): Managing Brand-based Competitive Advantage | Instructor Slides | 5 |
| 8.1 | Markstrat Session 6 and/or Case | | |
| 8.2 | Principle 3 (continued): Managing Offering-based Competitive Advantage | Instructor Slides | 6 |
| 9.1 | Markstrat Session 7 and/or Case | | |
| 9.2 | Conjoint Concept and Demonstration | Analytics Technique, MEXL (Exteriors Case) | 6 |
| 10.1 | Markstrat Session 8 and/or Case | | |
| 10.2 | Principle 3 (continued): Managing Relationship-based Competitive Advantage | Instructor Slides | 7 |
| 11.1 | Markstrat Session 9 and/or Case | | |
| 11.2 | Principle 4: All Resources are Limited → Managing Resource Trade-offs | Instructor Slides | 8 |
| 12.1 | Markstrat Session 10 and/or Case | | |
| 12.2 | Response Models Concept and Demonstration | Analytics Technique, MeXL (BRT Tribune Case) | 8 |
| 13.1 | Markstrat Session 11 and/or Case | | |
| 13.2 | Integrating the Four Principles | Instructor Slides | 9 |
| 14.1 | Review of Markstrat Performance | | |
| 14.2 | Review of First Principles of Marketing | Instructor Slides | 9 |

### Marketing Analytics Class

The objective of the marketing analytics course will be to show students the benefits of using a systematic and analytical approach to marketing decision making. An analytical approach will enable students to:

1 Understand how the "First Principles" of marketing strategy help firms organize the analytics opportunity and challenge in today's data era in an overarching fashion.
2 Use and execute data analytics techniques to understand how to solve marketing analytics problems in a scientific and process-driven manner.

We argue that most analytic challenges facing marketing researchers, consultants, and managers could be integrated under one umbrella that comprises four fundamental marketing problems. We then emphasize how the "First Principles" of marketing strategy help solve the four fundamental marketing problems, and help students develop analytic competencies pertaining to each of the four First Principles. Overall, by completing this course, students will be on their way to making the return on investment case for marketing expenditures that companies are increasingly asking of their executives. Class syllabi are shown on the book's website.

## Takeaways for Students and Instructors

We are excited that you are considering using our book to better understand marketing strategy. We know you have chosen to invest effort and time in absorbing the material. We have done our absolute best to ensure you have a fulfilling experience. We summarize the key benefits of using our book below.

### Key Benefits for Instructors:

- We have organized marketing processes, tools, and concepts around the *First Principles of marketing strategy* to give you a structured framework for organizing your class.
- We have developed example syllabi, over 500 slides, test banks, and other teaching materials to make adoption of this class as easy as possible.
- We have integrated state-of-the-art *data analytics techniques* and written *four broad analytics cases* to allow you to enforce the message that marketing strategy is more about doing than just learning.
- We have summarized the *latest marketing research* as underpinning for the guidance outlined in the book, so as to let you be up to date with state-of-the-art research in the field.
- We have provided more than 250 *diverse marketing examples* across 200 different companies and 25 countries and most industry segments, showing how various processes, tools, and frameworks apply to many different firms, countries, and situations.
- We have ensured our material integrates with *data analysis* (e.g., MEXL, SAS, SPSS) and *market simulation* (e.g., Markstrat) *software*, to provide hands-on access to marketing strategy through experiential learning tools.
- We have provided *in-depth videos* about key topics from the book, including the First Principles, marketing concepts, real business examples, and data analytical methods.

### Key Benefits for Students/Working Professionals:

- We have organized a multitude of marketing processes, tools, and concepts around the *First Principles of marketing strategy* to help you use one framework to deal with marketing challenges in diverse marketing firms, industries, and environments.
- We use a "tell-show-do" approach to the book, integrating state-of-the-art *data analytics techniques* into all aspects of the strategic planning process to allow you to make more effective data-based decisions.

- We use the *latest marketing research* as underpinning for all our guidance, synthesizing more than 60 years of thought in marketing research in one book.
- We have added numerous *analytics techniques* to provide details and short examples about the most popular analytical methods used by marketers, for you to customize your own toolkit from the book.
- We have ensured that our material is *package agnostic*, and that it could integrate with several *data analysis* (e.g., MEXL, SAS, SPSS) and *market simulation* (e.g., Markstrat) software packages.
- We have provided *solutions to each of our broad cases*, allowing you to learn how to apply the learning from a data analytics problem.

# Overview of First Principles of Marketing Strategy

### MP#1: All Customers Differ →
### Managing Customer Heterogeneity

The most basic issue facing managers making marketing mix decisions (pricing, product, promotion, place) is that all customers differ. Customers vary widely in their needs and preferences, whether real or perceived. Their desires even vary for basic commodity products (e.g., bottled water). Thus, effective marketing strategies must manage this customer heterogeneity, often through segmenting, targeting, and positioning efforts. They allow the firm to make sense of the customer landscape by identifying a manageable number of homogeneous customer groups, such that the firm can meaningfully evaluate its relative strengths and make strategically critical decisions about how to win and keep customers.

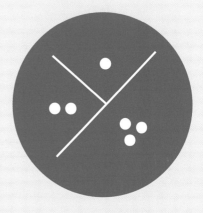

### MP#2: All Customers Change →
### Managing Customer Dynamics

Managers developing their marketing strategies must account for variation as customers' needs change over time. Even within a well-defined segment, members' individual needs often evolve at different rates or directions. At some point in the future, customers who once were part of a relatively homogeneous segment will exhibit widely divergent needs and desires. A firm's marketing strategy must account for customer dynamics to avoid becoming obsolete by identifying and understanding how a firm's customers migrate (i.e., change), triggers of these migrations, differing needs across stages, and, ultimately, desirable positions to appeal to these customers over time.

## MP#3: All Competitors React → Managing Sustainable Competitive Advantage

No matter how well a firm addresses customer heterogeneity and customer dynamics, competitors will constantly try to copy its success or innovate business processes and offerings to match customers' needs and desires better. Since all competitors react, through persistent efforts to copy and innovate, marketing managers must constantly work at building and maintaining barriers to competitive attacks. Managers build sustainable competitive advantages that are relevant for a specific target segment, by building high quality brands, delivering innovative offerings, and developing strong customer relationships.

## MP#4: All Resources Are Limited → Managing Resource Trade-offs

Most marketing decisions require trade-offs across multiple objectives, because the resources available to address these needs often are interdependent and limited. When marketing strategies allocate spending to brand advertising, or innovating new products, or expanding the sales organization to build stronger relationships, they often rely on the same fixed resource pool. A firm only has so many resources so important trade-offs are unavoidable. Managing resources optimally is critical; marketing resources provide the levers to implement what the firm learns from the first three marketing principles.

# Tour of the Book

### Data Analytics Techniques
Easy step-by-step toolkit on using state-of-the-art data analytics for effective decision making.

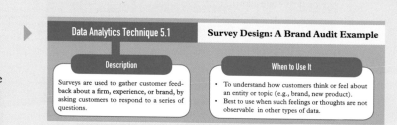

Data Analytics Technique 5.1 — Survey Design: A Brand Audit Example

**Description**

Surveys are used to gather customer feedback about a firm, experience, or brand, by asking customers to respond to a series of questions.

**When to Use It**

- To understand how customers think or feel about an entity or topic (e.g., brand, new product).
- Best to use when such feelings or thoughts are not observable in other types of data.

**Table 2.1** Sources of Customer Heterogeneity

| Source | Description | Examples |
|---|---|---|
| Individual differences | A person's stable and consistent way of responding to the environment in a specific domain | Favorite colors, Big Five personality traits – openness, conscientiousness, extraversion, agreeableness, neuroticism |
| Life experiences | An individual's life experiences capture events and experiences unique to their life that have a lasting impact on the value and preferences they place on products and services, which, in turn, affect preferences independent of individual differences | A child raised closer to the equator, in warmer climates, will typically have a higher preference for spicy foods, as carryover of past periods when spices were used to preserve and help mask the taste of food more likely to spoil in warmer climates |
| Functional needs | An individual's personal decision weightings across functional attributes | What price can they afford to pay (income), how long does the product need to last (quality, |

### Tables and Figures
Summarizing important information, illustrating key concepts visually, and offering checklists.

### Glossary
Key technical terms are marked in bold, blue text throughout and defined in the glossary at the back of the book.

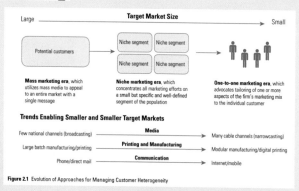

**Figure 2.1** Evolution of Approaches for Managing Customer Heterogeneity

## Glossary

**acquisition, expansion, retention (AER) approach** An approach that grouping existing customers into three stages – those recently acquired, longer term customers, and those lost or at risk of being lost – can offer some insights into customer dynamics.

**acquisition stage** A stage where customers first evaluate and begin to deal with a firm, at or before first contact, where they start to learn about the firm's offerings and how to transact with the firm.

**adoption lifecycle** A model that describes the timeline and pattern of adoption of a new product, service of innovation that generally follows a normal distribution.

**anchoring and adjustment heuristics** A decision-making process where an individual generally uses a prior expectation (anchor) with which to form beliefs, and updates the belief (adjustment) based on new data that changes the prior expectation.

**attribution-based processes** A method for gauging marketing effectiveness that attributes causal economic effect to a marketing investment, in environments where multiple marketing and confounds events may shape an economic outcome.

**Bass model** A model that uses social contagion theories to predict adoption rates of new products, also capturing product-based factors such as pricing and advertising levels.

## Learning Objectives

- Understand and explain why all customers differ.
- Critically discuss why an effective marketing strategy must manage customer heterogeneity (Marketing Principle #1).

### Learning Objectives
What you will learn in each chapter. Helps organize your study and track your progress.

## Key Points

Highlighted throughout the text are key sections, crucial points for learning.

▼

Customers represent the fundamental unit of analysis for marketing strategy, because each individual customer is an independent, decision-making entity.

## References

Full details are provided at the end of each chapter of important articles, books, and research that are cited within the chapters. These references help identify key publications for further understanding.

### References

1 Stevenson, A. (ed.) (2010) *Oxford Dictionary of English*, 3rd edn. Oxford: Oxford University Press.

2 Von Clausewitz, C. (1832) *On War*. Translated by Howard, M. and Paret, P., 1976. Princeton, NJ: Princeton University Press.

3 Chandler, A. (1962) *Strategy and Structure: Chapters in the History of American Industrial Enterprise*. Cambridge, MA: MIT Press; Kerin, R.A., Varadarajan, P.R. and Peterson, R.A. (1992) 'First-mover advantage: A synthesis, conceptual framework, and research propositions,' *Journal of Marketing*, 56(4), pp. 33–52.

4 Porter, M. (1980) *Competitive Strategy: Techniques for Analyzing Industry and Competitors*. New York: The Free Press; Porter, M.E. (1985) *Competitive Advantage: Creating*

7 Gupta, S. and Lehmann, D.R. (2005) *Managing Customers as Investments: The Strategic Value of Customers in the Long Run*. Upper Saddle River, NJ: Wharton School Publishing.

8 Gabriel, B. and Abouwer, T. (2013) 'Case study: Philips: Innovation and change management in global organizations: the case study of.' Available at: www.adaptivecycle.nl/index. php?title=Case_study:_Philips_:_Innovation_and_change_ management_in_global_organizations:_the_case_study_of (accessed 23 September, 2015).

9 Johnson, G. and Scholes, K. (1999) *Exploring Corporate Strategy*, 5th edn. New York: Prentice Hall.

10 Bell, D.R., Chiang, J. and Padmanabhan, V. (1999) 'The decomposition of promotional response: An empirical

## International Examples

Over 30 more detailed international examples are highlighted to show marketing strategy in action. Examples are drawn from household brands to innovative new startups.

▼

Finally, another way to view the impact of ma and profits can be broken down into compone many different factors, each of which has a role profit. For example, the sales revenue ($) chain demand (units) × market share (%) × average products or advertise extensively grow their ow competitors; they also influence growth in the o product category. That is, a marketing strategy af ratio equation.

**Example:** Apple (US)
. . . . . . . . . . . . . . . . . . . . . . . . . . . . . . . . . . . . .
Consider the launch of Apple's innovative iPhone. It c smartphone market. For example, the overall smartph more than 486 million five years later, an increase of 3 the market increased from 3.3% to 18.4%. Apple has a price over its competitors' average selling prices. In a insight, Apple's sales revenues from unit sales of iPho $1.8 billion in its first year (3% market share × 109 mill $55.3 billion after five years (18% share × 486 million u increase in sales revenue of more than 2,900%.[18]

## Analytics Driven Cases

Each Part includes one longer case that is specific to the Four Marketing Principles. Cases are accompanied by online datasets and step-by-step solution guide.

▼

### Analytics Driven Case

#### Managing Customer Heterogen

##### Problem Background

Orthodontists rely on dental imaging tec oral diseases in patients. In the last two de than analog-) based intraoral sensors for compared to their analog counterparts, images on the screen, computerized archiv exposure to radiation, and rapid acquisiti a result, the global market for dental X-ra $2.44 bn by 2017, where 66% of the curre for the lion's share of the sales coming fro

[1] Williamson, G.F. (2016) "Best practices and patient c articles/print/volume-30/issue-10/features/best-pract

## Takeaways

Key points summarized in easily digestible bullets at the end of each chapter.

▼

### Takeaways

- The second underlying challenge that fir customers change. This principle can be eit the firm understands and manages it.
- Customer dynamics arise from five source move through typical lifecycles as they ag knowledge about a product category. Lear level. Finally, each customer is situated in filled with outside entities trying to change works simultaneously and cumulatively to cr
- Due to rapid technological and communi change and their expectations about firms' r
- There are three approaches to managing cu tation, and customer lifetime value approac
- The lifecycle approach predicts that custom cles that can be used to inform marketing d lematic though, because it assumes an avera
- The customer dynamic segmentation app occurs when customers are just beginning t sion is when the firm tries to cross-sell or up

## Companion Website

Visit the companion website, www.palgravehighered.com/palmatier-ms, for professional video features outlining each of the Four Principles from the authors, four large cases with datasets, and Microsoft PowerPoint slides for lecturers and students. Instructor-only access to instructor's handbook, 10- and 15-week sample syllabi for marketing strategy and data analytics courses, and test bank.

▼

### Companion website

Please visit the companion website, **www.palgravehighered.com/palmatier-ms**, to access summary videos from the authors, and full-length cases with datasets and step-by-step solution guides.

# List of Abbreviations

| | |
|---|---|
| AER | acquisition, expansion, retention |
| B2B | business-to-business |
| B2C | business-to-consumer |
| BOR | brand, offering, relationship |
| CEO | chief executive officer |
| CIO | chief information officer |
| CLV | customer lifetime value |
| CPG | consumer packaged goods |
| CRM | customer relationship management |
| GE | General Electric |
| HMM | hidden Markov models |
| IMC | integrated marketing communications |
| MDA | multiple discriminant analysis |
| MP | Marketing Principle |
| OEMs | original equipment manufacturers |
| P&G | Procter & Gamble |
| PC | personal computer |
| PR | public relations |
| R&D | research and development |
| RM | relationship marketing |
| SCA | sustainable competitive advantage |
| STP | segmentation, targeting, and positioning |
| SWOT | strengths, weaknesses, opportunities, and threats |
| UK | United Kingdom |
| US | United States |
| VoIP | voice over Internet protocol |
| WOM | word of mouth |

# Acknowledgments

Robert Palmatier thanks his colleagues and doctoral students whose ongoing insights into marketing strategy and data analytics have helped inform this book in multiple ways: Todd Arnold, Joshua T. Beck, Alexander Bleier, Abhishek Borah, Kelly Chapman, Fred C. Ciao, Kenneth R. Evans, Eric Fang, Shankar Ganesan, Srinath Gopalakrishna, Dhruv Grewal, Rajdeep Grewal, Colleen Harmeling, Conor Henderson, Mark B. Houston, Brett Josephson, Frank R. Kardes, Jisu Kim, Irina V. Kozlenkova, V. Kumar, Jongkuk Lee, Ju-Yeon Lee, Gary L. Lilien, Mehdi Nezami, Kelly Martin, Jordan Moffett, Stephen Samaha, Lisa K. Scheer, Arun Sharma, Jan-Benedict E.M. Steenkamp, Lena Steinhoff, George Watson, T.J. Weiten, Stefan Worm, and Jonathan Zhang. Robert also appreciates all the help that the research assistants from the Center of Sales and Marketing Strategy have provided by researching material for this book: Jamie Koffman, Ben Yan, Wu Yifan, and Sydney Zeldes. His debt to numerous past MBA, EMBA, and PhD students is unbounded; they were instrumental in shaping many of the insights in this book. He is also very grateful to Charles and Gwen Lillis for their generous support of the Foster Business School and his research, which helped make this book possible. Finally, Rob would like to acknowledge with gratitude the support and love of his daughter, Alexandra, which made this effort worthwhile.

Shrihari Sridhar thanks his wife, Akshaya, and son, Virat, without whom none of his work would even be meaningful. For all the discussions on marketing strategy, which helped inform this book, he is indebted to his colleagues and doctoral students: Sönke Albers, Min Ding, Xiaodan Dong, Jason Garrett, Manpreet Gill, Frank Germann, Srinath Gopalakrishna, Rajdeep Grewal, Conor Henderson, Brett Josephson, Thorsten Hennig-Thurau, Mark B. Houston, Charles Kang, Ju-Yeon Lee, Gary L. Lilien, Murali Mantrala, Prasad A. Naik, Sriram Narayanan, Adithya Pattabhiramaiah, Debika Sihi, Raji Srinivasan, S. Sriram, Kalyan Raman, Huanhuan Shi, Yihui Tang, Esther Thorson, and Clay Voorhees. He appreciates the research assistance provided by Qian Chen and Mayank Nagpal, which added color and richness to the book. He is also thankful to all his undergraduate, MBA, EMBA, and PhD students, whose class participation and engagement added context to the material. Finally, he is grateful to Texas A&M University and Pennsylvania State University for their support and encouragement, which have made this book possible.

Both authors offer thanks and their appreciation to Elisabeth Nevins for rewriting many chapters to make the book friendlier to the reader and Colleen Harmeling for her contributions to the graphics, figures, and examples throughout the text. Finally, we are indebted to the vast number of authors whose work we cite throughout this text. Without their efforts, we could not have written this book.

Robert W. Palmatier
Seattle, Washington

Shrihari Sridhar
College Station, Texas

Chapter **1**

# Marketing Strategy: A First Principles Approach

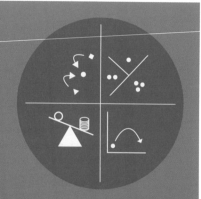

## Learning objectives

- Define marketing strategy.
- Identify and evaluate the similarities and differences between corporate and marketing strategy.
- Critically assess the importance of marketing strategy to a firm's success.
- Identify and describe the importance of the underlying complexity associated with each First Principle.
- Understand and critically discuss the logic behind the First Principle approach to marketing strategy.
- Review and analyze the major approaches for managing each marketing principle.
- Outline the key inputs and outputs for each marketing principle.
- Understand how to integrate the four Marketing Principles of marketing strategy.

# Introduction

As the marketing discipline evolves, managers are being overwhelmed with more and more analysis tools, processes, and research techniques for evaluating business phenomena and implementing new marketing strategies (e.g., customer centricity, big data, net promoter scores). After the success of each new startup, a flood of articles follows, offering unique marketing insights into how to duplicate its results (e.g., Freemium pricing! Crowdsourcing! Big data!). Although many of these new approaches offer some value, a marketing strategist is left with unanswered questions:

1 *When* should I use each specific approach?
2 *How* does each new marketing approach improve my firm's performance?
3 *Which* approaches are worth my firm's time and investment to implement?

Marketing strategy texts integrate new techniques into their existing structures, typically organized around discrete chapters for each of the *4Ps of the marketing mix* (product, price, place, promotion), suggesting ways for dealing with competitors or executing specific marketing tasks (segmenting, branding). This functional or task perspective on marketing strategy leaves managers with a wealth of frameworks and processes, distributed across different marketing domains. But it offers little overall guidance on *when* to use the various frameworks, *how* they work, *which* ones are most valuable, or *how* they all fit together.

> **First Principles:** The fundamental concepts or assumptions on which a theory, system, or method is based (*Oxford Dictionaries*, 2015).[1]

This book takes a very different approach to marketing strategy. Rather than adding to its complexity, we attempt to simplify it by arguing that managers' marketing decisions should focus on solving four underlying "problems" or "complexities" that all organizations face when designing and implementing their marketing strategies. These four problems represent the most critical hurdles to marketing success; they also define the organization for this book. We refer to them as the *First Principles of marketing strategy*, because they reflect the foundational assumptions on which marketing strategy is based.[2] In short, marketing strategists' most critical decisions must address the following First Principles of marketing strategy:

1 All customers differ.
2 All customers change.
3 All competitors react.
4 All resources are limited.

This First Principle approach to marketing strategy is unique, because its goal is to align the analysis tools, processes, and research techniques offered in many consulting books, together with existing frameworks and insights on the marketing mix (4Ps), competitors, and marketing tasks from traditional textbooks. Their alignment in turn suggests tactics for "solving," or at least addressing, the underlying First Principles. Organizing the varied discussions around four fundamental principles means that every decision appears within its meaningful context, which includes its impact on other decisions. This view and context establishes a guiding purpose for strategic marketing efforts.

For example, segmentation and customer centricity both attempt to deal with a First Principle: *all customers differ*. By taking the First Principle approach, we offer marketing strategists a toolbox for dealing with a broad range of marketing challenges, rather than learning unique techniques for each specific marketing event. That is, the guiding framework can solve a wide range of marketing problems. Conceptually, the application is similar to using Newton's laws of motion (i.e., First Principles of physics) to solve a multitude of physics problems, rather than learning different process steps for each type of problem.

This chapter therefore begins with a short, historical overview and definition of marketing strategy, to place it in an appropriate temporal context and set the boundaries of the domain relative to corporate strategy. We offer arguments for why marketing is so critically important to a firm's success and provide evidence for why managers should invest the time and effort to develop effective marketing strategies. In turn, we present the logic behind the First Principle approach to marketing strategy. With an overview of each of the four First Principles, we prepare readers to dive deeper into the concepts, analyses, and decisions addressed in the rest of this book. Finally, this chapter integrates the four First Principles of marketing strategy to derive insights into how they fit together in a natural sequence that allows organizations to develop effective marketing strategies.

## Brief History and Definition of Marketing Strategy

To appreciate the First Principle approach to marketing strategy, we first have to define marketing strategy: What are its key elements and its scope? We note five key elements that have been identified as its conceptualizations have evolved over time:

1 Decisions and actions
2 Differential advantages over competitors
3 Sustainability
4 Ability to enhance firm performance
5 Customer perspective.

Next, we trace how these five elements have emerged over time, resulting in our current definition of marketing strategy. The strategy concept arose from a military context, where a strategy represents the pursuit of situational superiority over an enemy. Karl von Clausewitz, in *On War* (1832, p. 196), describes strategy as follows: "Consequently, the forces available must be employed with such skill that even in the absence of absolute superiority, relative superiority is attained at the decisive point."[3] From these military roots, the notion of using resources skillfully, to create decisive positions of superiority over competitors, began to be applied in business in the 1950s and 1960s. A variety of forces (e.g., rapid, unpredictable changes in customer, competitor, technical, and economic environments) were beginning to challenge the "lumbering corporations" of the time, whose size presented an obstacle to operational dexterity. A new way of thinking – generally described as formal strategic planning – was needed. Thus, a typical definition of business strategy from the 1960s described "the determination of the basic long-term goals and objectives of an enterprise, and the adoption of courses of action and the allocation of resources necessary for carrying out these goals" (p. 13).[4] Management scholars and practitioners from this era retained two elements of military strategy, focused on how *decisions and actions* could lead to *differential advantages over opponents* (or competitors).

Over the next few decades, though, thought leaders added two elements that they regarded as necessary to apply the strategy concept to a business: the need to make the differential advantage *sustainable* and the idea that the objective of any business strategy is to *enhance firm performance*.[5] Even more recently, marketing strategists have suggested a refined view in which both the sustainable differential advantage and its objective should be evaluated from the *perspective of the customer*, such that the central approach is "strategy from the outside-in."[6]

As adopted in this book, this viewpoint argues that crafting the most effective long-term strategy begins by creating value for the customer, because the customer ultimately determines the strategy's success or failure. Working backward from a desired position of advantage among customers, strategy can be crafted purposefully, to make such a position a reality and deliver it with a business model that provides attractive returns to the firm. This customer-centric view contrasts with that of economists who tend to take an industry-level perspective, or of management scholars who often adopt a firm-centric perspective.[7] But the objective of a marketing strategy cannot be to focus only on the firm's goals (capturing the needs of shareholders, managers, and employees/stakeholders); it must also include the goals of another key stakeholder, the customer. Any strategy that fails to generate customer value in the long term ultimately is unsustainable. Therefore, this customer-centric perspective represents a key difference between a corporate strategy and a marketing strategy.

The shift in focus that involves explicitly incorporating the customer's perspective also represents a natural, long-term progression. Academics and managers continue to search for ways to explain variation in firms' performance by addressing smaller and smaller units of analysis: from a focus on industries, to firms, to individual customers. Each new level of analysis provides another set of variables that help explain more variation in firm performance. Ultimately, however, customers represent the fundamental unit of analysis for marketing strategy, because each individual customer is an independent, decision-making entity. Industries and firms instead represent aggregations of customers, and aggregation is always accompanied by a necessary loss in precision and insights.

> Customers represent the fundamental unit of analysis for marketing strategy, because each individual customer is an independent, decision-making entity.

The customer-centric perspective is therefore an important foundation for this book, as reflected in later chapters that describe marketing strategy frameworks and analysis techniques designed to capture, evaluate, and act on individual, customer-level data (versus treating all customers the same way or grouping customers into a few segments based on some demographic characteristic). For example, customer lifetime value (CLV) analyses attempt to assign discounted cash flow values to each customer based on future sales and costs, such that they offer the potential for marketing decisions that are optimized for each individual customer.[8]

On the basis of this brief history of the evolution of marketing strategy, we can capture the five key elements in a summary definition of marketing strategy.

> ***Marketing strategy*** consists of decisions and actions focused on building a sustainable differential advantage, relative to competitors, in the minds of customers, to create value for stakeholders.

With this perspective, a marketing strategy can be equally meaningful for any entity with "competitors" focused on some group of "customers." It is just as applicable to countries competing for the right to host a future Olympic Games, to competing industry trade groups or sales regions, and to firms or individual product lines. However, as time progresses, organizations must innovate their marketing strategy in order to remain competitive and adapt to customers' changing needs.

**Example:** Philips (the Netherlands)

Philips, the Netherlands-based technology company, has become a global leader in consumer technology over the past 125 years. Over this time, Philips has innovated its marketing strategy many times to stay competitive. Philips is working to become more customer-centric. Philips builds a strong physical presence in each market it is active in, and uses these teams to understand the local market and its consumers' desires. But as customers' needs are not static, it needs to innovate to continually sustain its competitive advantage. To this end, Philips has nine research centers around the world that have competencies in various domains and can remain connected to local markets. But innovation on existing offerings is not enough. To stay ahead of the competition, it has also created a "technology incubator" that provides an environment where Philips can create technologies new to both the firm and customers. Through market and technical innovation and a consumer-centric focus, Philips has managed to gain and hold global and regional leaderships in many product categories.[9]

## How Marketing Strategy Differs from Corporate Strategy

The larger the organization, the more likely its corporate-level strategic plan is distinct from any marketing strategy. Although the two levels of strategy should have consistent goals (i.e., marketing strategy aligns with corporate strategy), the marketing strategy focuses specifically on the interplay of the firm with its customers. Consider the primary questions to answer to define an entity's marketing strategy:

- Who are your customers?
- What value do you provide your customers (e.g., product, service, experience, status)?
- How are you building a differential advantage relative to competitors for these customers?
- What value do you earn from your customers due to this differential advantage (sales, profits, referrals)?
- How will you sustain this differential advantage into the future?

A marketing strategy must answer these questions, then use the answers to inform the development and implementation of action steps required to achieve firm and stakeholder objectives. However, the implementation of a marketing strategy requires resources and a stable organizational platform from which to operate. Thus, additional questions arise, regarding other aspects of the business, such as cash flow plans, tax considerations, and legal and personnel policies. These queries are the domain of the corporate strategy, defined as "the direction and scope of an organization over the long term: which achieves advantage for the organization through the configuration of resources within a changing environment, to meet the needs of markets and fulfill stakeholder expectations" (p. 10).[10]

Figure 1.1 summarizes key questions for corporate and marketing strategies, such that it illustrates the differences in emphasis and relevant decisions. Although certain domains are primarily associated with corporate (taxes, legal) or marketing (promotions, pricing) strategic decisions, other domains may be influenced by both corporate and marketing strategies (human resources, operations, R&D). As reflected in Figure 1.1, all questions must be answered appropriately. If the questions addressed by the marketing strategy are answered incorrectly or insufficiently, the business's enduring success will be in doubt.

## Importance of Marketing Strategy

Multiple perspectives highlight the importance of an effective marketing strategy for a firm's success. Academic studies provide evidence of the strong links between marketing actions (brand and selling expenditures) and intermediate marketing metrics (customer satisfaction, loyalty, market share) with a firm's financial performance.[11] For example, improving customer satisfaction is not just a "feel-good"

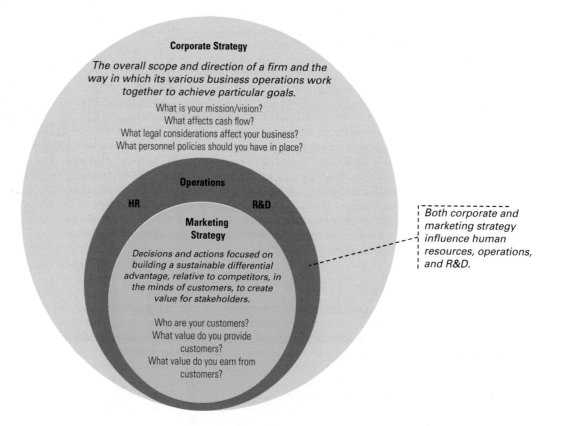

**Figure 1.1** Differences Between Corporate Strategy and Marketing Strategy

tactic but is associated with positive financial outcomes, including enhanced cash flows with reduced variability, sales growth, improved gross margins, and total shareholder returns. Strong evidence also describes when, how, and where brand advertising pays off; how price promotions affect short- and long-term outcomes (e.g., causing current customers to stock up versus attracting new customers); and how other elements of the marketing mix interact to drive performance.

However, research also notes some important nuances: not every strategy pays off every time. For example, the relationship between market share and profitability is not a direct function. Some strategies that might succeed in increasing market share actually can damage profitability. A variety of brand, customer relationship, and other factors conspire to determine the ultimate outcome of a market share strategy.[12]

In addition, business trends help determine marketing strategies. Some trends, especially in developed markets, highlight the importance of market-based barriers (i.e., barriers erected through marketing strategic actions) to help a company withstand competitive assaults. For example, globalization and reduced trade barriers have increased the prevalence of low-cost competitors in many industries that offer similar, "me-too" products at low prices.[13] In response, firms might increase their investments in brand building or relationship marketing strategies, or they might launch a range of loyalty programs to differentiate their "total offering" through intangible factors that are harder for low-cost, copycat firms to duplicate. Today, firms spend as much on customer relationship management and brand building as they do on new product and service introductions.[14] The business trend of building strong brands appears to have caught on in developing countries too. Simply manufacturing world-class products at a low cost is not the only path to success, so new paths for brand building (e.g., tapping into the country's indigenous qualities and culture) are being cut.[15]

In another trend, firms are outsourcing product manufacturing, because the actual production of a product often offers little differential advantage over competitors. As the examples of the personal computing, shoes, and clothing industries reveal, just a few firms have distinctive manufacturing capabilities that create meaningful incremental value for customers, beyond what they can access with products produced by high-capability, subcontracted manufacturers. In response, senior managers shift their emphases, from operations to marketing, with the recognition that strong brand, channel, or customer relationships are more difficult to duplicate than virtually any tangible product. John Stuart, the long-serving CEO of Quaker Oats, explains: "If this business were to be split up, I would be glad to take the brands, trademarks and goodwill and you could have all the bricks and mortar – and I would fare better than you" (p. 8).[16] Empirical evidence similarly shows that marketing capabilities have a greater impact on improving firm performance than either R&D or operations capabilities.[17]

Finally, another way to view the impact of marketing strategy is by considering how sales revenues and profits can be broken down into component parts. Marketing strategy simultaneously affects many different factors, each of which has a role in determining an organization's sales revenue and profit. For example, the sales revenue ($) chain ratio equation in Figure 1.2(a) comprised of market demand (units) × market share (%) × average selling price ($). Firms that launch innovative new products or advertise extensively grow their own market share and receive a price premium versus competitors; they also influence growth in the overall market by creating spillover awareness for the product category. That is, a marketing strategy affects all three components of the sales revenue chain ratio equation.

**Example:** Apple (US)

Consider the launch of Apple's innovative iPhone. It catalyzed the explosive growth of the overall smartphone market. For example, the overall smartphone market grew from 109 million units to more than 486 million five years later, an increase of 345%. During that time, iPhone's share of the market increased from 3.3% to 18.4%. Apple has a remarkable ability to maintain a premium price over its competitors' average selling prices. In aggregate, using the chain ratio for insight, Apple's sales revenues from unit sales of iPhone (not counting accessories) grew from $1.8 billion in its first year (3% market share × 109 million unit market × $558 unit selling price) to $55.3 billion after five years (18% share × 486 million unit market × $620 unit selling price) – an increase in sales revenue of more than 2,900%.[18]

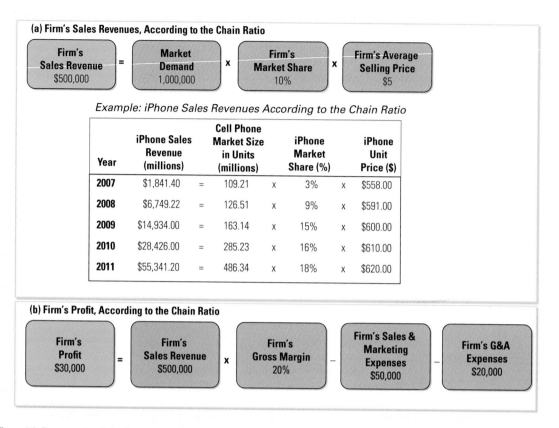

**Figure 1.2** Decomposing Sales Revenue and Profit with the Chain Ratio

Building a powerful brand image or strong relational bonds with customers also can have a strong effect on average selling prices of a firm's products. Price premiums are normal for strong consumer brands, such as Tiffany & Co., Nordstrom, or BMW. Such forces also affect business-to-business (B2B) firms. For example, B2B customers will pay, on average, a 4–5% premium to deal with their favorite salesperson rather than buy the same product from a different salesperson.[19] The price a firm can charge depends hugely on which customers the firm chooses to target and how it implements its targeting strategy. A firm that builds a customer portfolio using price discounting promotions often ends up with a customer base that is highly price sensitive and deal prone, such that it constantly must defend against other firms' price discounts.[20] Thus, all components of the sales revenue chain ratio (demand, market share, and price) stem from a firm's marketing strategy, which in turn has a strong multiplier effect on net sales.

A similar analysis is possible for a firm's profit, as represented in the chain ratio equation in Figure 1.2(b). A new factor in this equation deserves special attention: sales and marketing expenses. These expenses, incurred to execute marketing strategies, can be accounted for as direct reductions to profit, but they also should be recognized as investments that affect all three components of the sales revenue chain ratio. Moreover, effective marketing strategies that build a strong, loyal customer base can affect profitability directly, by significantly *reducing sales and marketing expenses*. First, having loyal customers is less expensive than launching new programs to retain current customers or convincing defectors to come back. Even recognizing the significant cross-industry variation, the cost of acquiring a new customer is generally 5–10 times more than simply retaining an existing customer.[21]

Second, strong loyalty among current customers can reduce new customer acquisition costs, because current customers engage in positive word of mouth, which effectively persuades other customers to try or switch. Jonah Berger, in his book *Contagious*, attributes the effectiveness of word of mouth to its credibility (i.e., fellow customers are objective and candid) and its targeted nature (i.e., customers share news that they believe is relevant to the listener). For example, Ben Fischman, founder of Rue La La (ruelala.com), which sells overstock and clearance high-end fashion products, notes that member word of mouth was far more effective than the firm's early ad campaigns at attracting new members, because: "When a friend tells you you've gotta try Rue La La, you believe them. And you try it" (p. 53).[22] Accordingly, loyal customers can be worth up to three times their individual value, because of their referrals of new customers.[23]

## The Logic for a First Principle Approach to Marketing Strategy

If marketing strategy consists of key decisions that result in certain actions that ultimately lead to enhanced performance, then the path to success seems obvious. Shouldn't a manager simply look at past marketing strategies, identify those that generated the highest performance, and implement those same strategies, again and again? Some firms can follow this approach to generate success in the short run. But, as customers, competitors, and conditions continue to evolve, strategies that created success in the past may become inappropriate, especially if circumstances change. In some cases, past successes using a particular strategy can even hinder a firm's ability to develop the necessary capabilities and strategies to address new conditions.[24] Copying the successful strategies of a competitor also might fail to yield the same results, because each firm has different capabilities.

We want to state this inconvenient truth plainly – no single marketing strategy is ever going to be consistently effective in all conditions or for all firms. As vast research and practical examples demonstrate, the effectiveness of a marketing strategy depends on a multitude of underlying customer, competitor, and contextual factors that are both interdependent and time varying.[25]

A key requirement for making good marketing decisions – which is part of the essence of a marketing strategy – is to identify underlying factors on which the decisions depend. Without such information, a firm might copy the successful marketing actions of a competitor, only to find that those actions work only for certain segments of customers, only at particular points in the customer's lifecycle, only in response to specific competitive actions, or only in certain conditions. Identifying the underlying factors or complexities that determine the efficacy of marketing decisions also requires digging deeper than reading about the most recent consulting fad in a business article. By definition, these fads tend to apply only for a short period of time or in certain situations.

For example, many Silicon Valley firms have been sorely tempted to launch new software products by using, instead of their traditional direct sales forces, a "freemium" or "viral" strategy (e.g., giving away a basic model in the hopes that users will like the product and upgrade to a paid premium version). With a few prominent exceptions, this temptation is likely to lead to ruin. As *Bloomberg Businessweek* noted: "For every Yammer, a social networking company that attracted corporate users initially by giving the product (bought by Microsoft for $1.2 billion), there are hundreds of companies that fail"[26] – in part because consumers and potential adopters are inundated by the thousands of new business apps, all trying to catch their eye with a free version.

Thus, marketing strategy effectiveness requires decisions congruent with four underlying assumptions or complexities that are inherent, at least to some degree, to all businesses interactions:

1 All customers differ.
2 All customers change.
3 All competitors react.
4 All resources are limited.

Of course, you will recognize these four assumptions as the *First Principles of marketing strategy*, or the foundational assumptions on which any marketing strategy is based. As Figure 1.3 indicates, this approach to marketing strategy involves grouping or aligning key marketing decisions with these four assumptions, in such a way that managers can understand and account for their interdependencies and temporal ordering when making decisions. Each First Principle or underlying assumption, when matched with its associated marketing decisions, is a **Marketing Principle (MP)**. For example, all

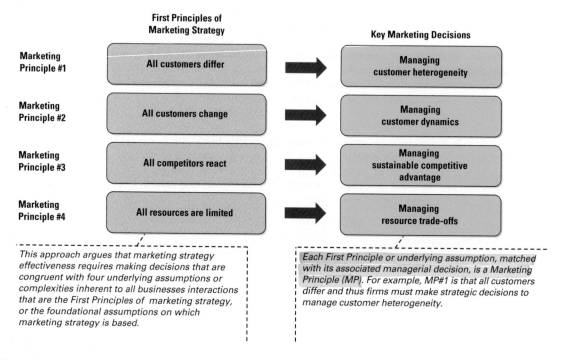

**Figure 1.3** Four Marketing Principles: Aligning Key Marketing Decisions with the First Principles of Marketing Strategy

customers differ, so firms must make strategic decisions to manage customer heterogeneity, and these combined statements constitute MP#1.

Each First Principle or underlying assumption, when matched with its associated marketing decisions, is a **Marketing Principle (MP)**.

With this approach, firms can effectively manage these four inherent business complexities when developing and implementing their marketing strategies. It does not imply removing or preventing underlying complexities; it recognizes that in most cases, the First Principles are given, so firms need to understand and effectively manage each of them.

In support of this approach, we develop guiding frameworks for each of the four MPs, identifying specific tools and analysis techniques that are relevant to the specific principle and can support effective decision making. Then we can integrate the four frameworks to detail the interdependencies and natural causal ordering among the four MPs, such that any firm can generate its overall marketing strategy.

The chapters of this book focus on each Marketing Principle in detail. In the remainder of this chapter, we offer short overviews to help readers understand just what we mean by the four MPs, available tactics for making decisions relevant to that MP, and a graphical input–output framework, all according to a First Principle approach.

# MP#1: All Customers Differ → Managing Customer Heterogeneity

## First Principle: All Customers Differ

The first, foundational, and most basic issue facing managers making marketing mix decisions (pricing, product, promotion, place) is that *all customers differ*. Customers vary widely in their needs and preferences, whether real or perceived. Their desires even vary for basic commodity products, such as salt and bottled water. Customers' desire for variety is evident in the tens of thousands of products offered by most large grocery stores, in their effort to match each individual customer's preference.

Various factors lead customers to differ in their preferences, including: basic, personal differences; varying life experiences; unique functional needs for the product; distinct aspirational self-identities; and previous persuasion-based activities focused on changing their preferences. These different sources all work together to drive substantial variation in customers' preferences.

If firms ignore this first principle of customer differences and offer a single product, they may gain sales in the short term, particularly if competition is weak or the product is scarce. The well-known example in this case is the Ford Model T. As long as Ford was virtually the only company able to provide vehicles, it could get away with making all its cars black. But as competition grew and automobiles became more widely available, Henry Ford's maxim – customers can have any color they want, as long as it is black – flipped on its head. Today, customers can have any color they want in their car's finish, and any company that tried to limit its offerings would find itself in trouble quickly. As demand for any new offering grows, competitors recognize opportunity and begin supplying differentiated products that match the preferences expressed by targeted subsegments of the overall market. If an incumbent firm fails to respond with refined offerings, customers move. The firm thus loses sales revenue. In addition, because competitors likely have targeted the fastest growing or most profitable subsegments, the incumbent firm is left with customers in less desirable, slow growing, and less profitable segments. Failing to manage **customer heterogeneity** – defined as variation among customers in terms of their needs, desires, and subsequent behaviors – has been the death knell for many firms.

## Marketing Decision: Managing Customer Heterogeneity

The different sources of individual variation work together in multifaceted ways. Although customer heterogeneity is a fundamental challenge that all firms must address when developing an effective marketing strategy (MP#1), the ways to do so are not particularly clear. That is, how should each firm manage customer heterogeneity?

First, it could ignore customer heterogeneity and provide an offering that matches the average customers' needs. Many customers will be dissatisfied, but in a large enough market, average customers could be numerous enough to keep the firm profitable – at least temporarily. If the market keeps growing, though, a competitor likely will seek to appeal to some subgroup of customers who are interested in a better fitting solution. The original firm then is left with an oversized infrastructure and associated costs. Combined with lost sales and profits, this situation greatly erodes its financial performance.

Second, a firm could offer a range of products and services to satisfy the needs of many different customer segments. This strategy can be highly effective; it also can be very costly and difficult. A single firm rarely can meet the needs of all these different customers simultaneously. Imagine, for example, trying to appeal to high-end markets, as Four Seasons hotels and Neimen Marcus retailers do, while also marketing to low-end markets, as Motel 6 and Walmart do. From brand and infrastructure perspectives, such efforts seem virtually impossible.

Third, firms might embrace the notion that customers will sacrifice desired product attributes if the price is low enough. With a classic low-cost strategy, firms attempt to identify core, must-have attributes that will satisfy consumers' functional needs, then focus all their efforts on reaching the lowest cost for an offering that meets those needs. Here again, the strategy can be viable, depending on the size of the low-cost segment and the firm's ability to gain differential cost advantages over its competitors.

Fourth, to deal with customer heterogeneity, a firm might select a specific segment of customers and target them by positioning its offering as the best solution, compared with those available from any competitors, for that particular segment (i.e., segmentation, targeting, and positioning, or an **STP approach**). The result is often a strong brand that customers in the segment know and respect. Despite its effectiveness for dealing with customer heterogeneity, an STP approach can limit a firm's future growth. Therefore, it often is combined with a **customer-centric approach** or strategy, in which the firm recognizes the long-term value of its core customer segment and puts it at the center of all major internal business processes and decisions.

**Example:** Godiva (Belgium)

Godiva wants to sell you more chocolate, but the Belgian-based chocolate confectionary needed an effective global marketing strategy. Godiva addressed MP#1 by developing different products for different consumers, or consumers who are looking to purchase their chocolate for different reasons. It realized that there are three basic reasons why people buy premium chocolate: to give to others as a gift, to share with a group, and to eat by oneself. Having identified the three basic reasons, it targeted each category of consumer with a different offering. For example, rather than just offering boxed chocolate for gift-givers to exchange on holidays, Godiva expanded its product line to include new products like boxed brownies or chocolate-fondue baskets. For consumers who want to share their chocolates with a group, Godiva determined that its delicate truffles were not appropriate for candy dishes and so prepared individually wrapped candies. In the case of those who were looking for self-indulgence, Godiva came up with products that worked for "chocolate emergencies." As such, Godiva created lines of large candy bars and individually wrapped Godiva Gems for sale through supermarkets across the world. This strategy has paid off, Godiva has increased its sales by more than 10% per year for many years.[27]

## Input–Output Framework for Managing Customer Heterogeneity

Figure 1.4 contains the input–output framework for managing customer heterogeneity. It captures the approaches, processes, and analyses that aid managers' decision making. The three key inputs to the framework are required to conduct segmentation, targeting, and positioning of potential customers. The first input focuses on all potential customers in the industry or product category; it involves their needs, desires, and preferences (i.e., segmentation); perceptions of specific firms and brands in the marketplace across key attributes (i.e., targeting); and information to determine segment attractiveness, such as their growth rate or price sensitivity. Market segment attractiveness information often comes from multiple sources, such as customer surveys, marketing industry reports, and other secondary sources.

The second and third inputs are similar, but whereas one focuses on the focal company, the other involves the company's competitors. Inventories of the company's and its competitors' strengths and weaknesses are needed to evaluate the focal firm's relative competitive strength in each segment, in support of targeting and positioning processes. Company and competitor strengths and weaknesses should span all relevant domains (i.e., manufacturing, technical, financial, marketing, sales, research) that can be leveraged into a relative competitive advantage. Company and competitor strengths and weaknesses should be collected in conjunction with opportunities and threats in a classic SWOT

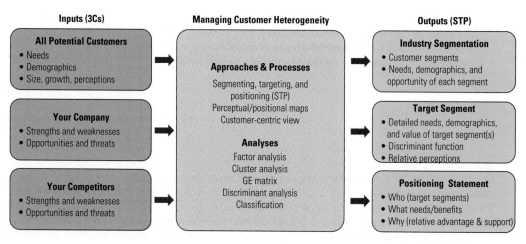

**Figure 1.4** Marketing Principle #1: All Customers Differ → Managing Customer Heterogeneity

(strengths, weaknesses, opportunities, and threats) analysis, because all four factors might facilitate the firm's targeting and positioning efforts.

The inputs to managing customer heterogeneity thus entail the 3Cs of situation analysis: customers, company, and competitors, Together, they provide the contextual background for the firm's strategy. A firm's marketing strategy is embedded in this background and must both "fit" and "leverage" customers' preferences and perceptions, market trends, and the firm's relative strengths.

In turn, the framework generates three outputs, which then provide the inputs for the subsequent Marketing Principles. To start, this framework maps key customer segments for an industry or product category, according to customer preferences. This critical output describes the potential customer landscape by addressing two key questions: Can the marketplace be subdivided into homogeneous groups? What does each group of potential customers want?

A second output then moves from the overall market landscape to the specific segment(s) of interest to the firm, providing detailed descriptions of each segment. These descriptions include the value or attractiveness of each segment and the firm's relative strength. Thus, the second output addresses two additional questions: What segment will the firm pursue? How can the firm identify each group of target customers?

Finally, the third output is a *positioning statement*, which encapsulates three key questions in a single, concise statement that firms can use to direct their internal and external marketing mix activities. The three questions ask:

- Whom should the firm target?
- What needs and benefits are being fulfilled?
- What are the relative advantages of this offering versus competitive offerings?

A position statement should be developed for the firm overall, as well as for each key target segment that the firm addresses. A positioning statement captures the essence of the positioning strategy for a target segment.

## Summary of Marketing Principle #1

The process of converting customer, company, and competitor (3Cs) input into a representation of the firm's environment through industry segmentation, target segments, and positioning statement (STP) outputs is a critical first step in developing a marketing strategy. It allows the firm to make sense of the customer landscape by identifying a manageable number of homogeneous customer groups, such that the firm can meaningfully evaluate its relative strengths and make strategically critical decisions about how to win and keep customers. Almost all other decisions build on this critical first step, according to how it accounts for customer heterogeneity, customer attractiveness, and the company's relative advantage.

> The process of converting customer, company, and competitor (3Cs) input into a representation of the firm's environment through industry segmentation, target segments, and positioning statement (STP) outputs is a critical first step in developing a marketing strategy.

# MP#2: All Customers Change → Managing Customer Dynamics

## First Principle: All Customers Change

In addition to accounting for inherent differences in customers (MP#1), managers developing their marketing strategies also must account for variation as customers' needs change over time (MP#2). These changes might occur at the individual customer level, reflecting specific customer, product market, and contextual factors. At any point in time, customers might be grouped and targeted on the basis of how well their needs and desires match or resonate with a particular product or service. Soon thereafter, though, customers' needs start to evolve. Even within a well-defined segment, members' individual needs often evolve at different rates or directions. At some point in the future, customers who once were part of a relatively homogeneous segment will exhibit widely divergent needs and desires and no longer fit neatly into a market segment.

Consider, for example, the relatively homogeneous segment of new college graduates. Companies like Toyota and GM frequently design automobile incentives targeted to these well-educated consumers on the cusp of launching their professional lives. Fast forward just two or three years, and the distinct paths that members of the "new college graduate" segment follow are numerous. Some have invested totally in their career success. Others have gotten married and are raising or contemplating having children. Another group has returned to an academic setting by entering graduate school. Some are buying their first homes, others rent, and still others have moved back into their parents' houses. The underlying needs and buying preferences that were fairly consistent a short time ago thus have splintered in various, distinct directions. The processes by which customers' desires and needs change over time are **customer dynamics**.

The changes also can be market-level evolutions in customer preferences that accompany technological innovations. In these cases, nearly all customers eventually change, albeit at different rates, so the firms that lag suffer a risk of extinction, along with the old technology. Blockbuster, a US-based video rental company, was a strong market leader when watching a movie at home required the rental of physical VCR tapes, and it shifted effectively to the rental of physical DVDs when that technology emerged. But it struggled to adapt to the flexibility and convenience offered by rental kiosks (e.g., Redbox) and rentals-by-mail (e.g., Netflix). When video streaming entered the fray, it simply could not compete any more and suffered a fatal blow.

Let's look more systematically at these changes in individual customer needs and preferences over time. Why do they occur? The different sources and drivers of customer dynamics combine to make change inevitable. Most of these drivers can be grouped into five categories:

- **Seminal events**: The needs and preferences of individual customers may change due to discrete life events, whether anticipated or not, such as a car accident, graduation, a major promotion, or a new job.
- **Life stages**: People tend to progress relatively steadily through typical lifecycle stages as they mature (e.g., single → married → children → parent of teens → empty nesters → retirement), which influence many of their product and service priorities.[28]
- **Knowledge/expertise**: The attributes most critical to customers often vary systematically, according to their experience with and knowledge about a product or service category, which has been termed a **learning effect**. For example, the choice criteria of a first-time guitar buyer (e.g., price, color, "looks like the one Slash plays") get replaced over time as the musician's knowledge of the attributes that affect playability and sound quality (e.g., neck width, fret board material, tone woods used) grows and expands.
- **Product category maturity**: The changes brought on by this learning effect operate at both the individual customer level and the product market level. For example, when it comes to digital photography, even novice consumers buying their first camera likely consider attributes, like pixels and zoom rates, which were once the domain of only the most expert professional photographers.
- **Regular exposure to relevant information**: Each customer makes decisions in an environment filled with the constant bombardment of information that arrives through varied communication media and sources, from many marketers and organizations (e.g., government, industry trade groups, nonprofit organizations), or from friends or acquaintances – all intending to impact the person's needs and preferences. Think about the number of messages you received in the past week regarding healthy living for example: admonitions to eat more vegetables and fewer desserts, stop smoking, and get exercise, as well as advertisements for exercise equipment or healthy recipes sent by friends. You likely ignored some of those messages, but others might spur some change, in one direction or the other. A public service announcement to get 30 minutes of exercise might encourage you to take a walk after dinner; a recipe from your mom for a vegetable casserole instead might leave you feeling nagged, such that you rebel by ordering the large portion of fries at the drive-through.

Because all customers change over time, unless a firm's time horizon is extremely short, a failure to understand and address customer dynamics ultimately will undermine virtually any marketing strategy.

Because all customers change over time, unless a firm's time horizon is extremely short, a failure to understand and address customer dynamics ultimately will undermine virtually any marketing strategy.

## Marketing Decision: Managing Customer Dynamics

Marketing strategies often take a significant amount of time to implement and begin producing results. Therefore, waiting for the evidence that customers have begun their inevitable change, such as in the form of financial reports that indicate lagging customer sales, before responding is not an effective plan. So how should a firm manage customer dynamics?

There are three main approaches firms can use to respond quickly to change and manage it effectively for a segment of consumers. First, a firm can gain insight into customer dynamics by applying lifecycle perspectives to customers, products, or industries. A **customer lifecycle** refers to the average change or migration among customers as they age, independent of any product or industry differences. These methods thus capture the first two or three sources of customer dynamics we listed previously. A **product or industry lifecycle** approach instead captures typical user experiences and industry developmental effects that can be observed as the product category matures. It ignores individual sources of customer dynamics. In this sense, it mainly captures the fourth and fifth sources of change. These lifecycle approaches are simple and easy to use, which probably explains why they remain predominant in many marketing courses and textbooks.

However, suggesting that all customers or products follow some predetermined lifecycle curve, such that organizations can identify an optimal marketing strategy at each stage, is problematic. Because these approaches use averages across all customers or all products, they assume all customers and products evolve in the same way. Furthermore, the different lifecycles capture effects at different levels but often ignore or provide little insight into other sources of customer dynamics that might be operating simultaneously at different levels. Yet every source of customer dynamics, specific to the firm's customers and products, is critical for understanding and developing the marketing strategy.

Second, some of the insights from MP#1 can apply to the customer dynamics problem, such that firms might segment their *existing customers* according to where they expect to find similar migration patterns. To get a handle on customer dynamics, firms might use the **acquisition, expansion, retention (AER) approach**, which we explain in detail in Chapter 3. Briefly, grouping existing customers into three stages – those recently acquired, longer-term customers, and those lost or at risk of being lost – can offer some insights into customer dynamics, as well as their needs and preferences, so that the firm can compile a descriptive "persona" for each group. Even without the specific AER framework, naming and describing important personas (i.e., prototypical customer groups within a firm's target market), describing their needs and migration paths, and developing visual representations that capture these insights can help managers understand and manage customer dynamics, as well as communicate customer dynamics throughout the organization.

Third, enhancing the dynamic segmentation across AER stages, a **customer lifetime value (CLV)** approach attempts to capture the financial contribution of each customer by determining the discounted value of the sales and costs associated with them, according to their expected migration path over the entire relationship with the firm. Thus, CLV accounts for customer heterogeneity (MP#1), in that it is calculated at the individual customer or segment level, rather than assuming that all customers in the firm's portfolio are the same. It also accounts for customer dynamics (MP#2) by discounting the cash flows (sales and costs) across the acquisition and expansion stages and then integrating the expansion and retention expectations for any specific customers' or segments' expected migration trajectory. As its greatest advantage, CLV provides guidance for making optimal trade-offs and resource allocation decisions across stages and market mix investments.

## Input–Output Framework for Managing Customer Dynamics

The organizing framework for managing customer dynamics is shown in Figure 1.5. Whereas MP#1 focuses on the market as a whole, MP#2 narrows the scope to the firm's existing customers, challenging the firm to understand how its customers change over time.

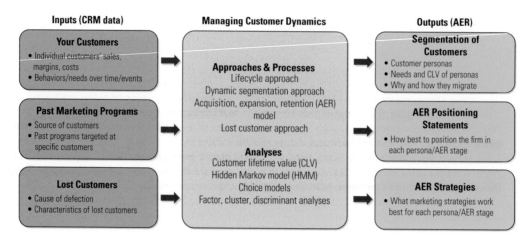

**Figure 1.5** Marketing Principle #2: All Customers Change → Managing Customer Dynamics

There are three categories of inputs for managing customer dynamics. The first category, data about the existing customer portfolio, is arguably the most important. A firm's customer relationship management (CRM) system should provide detailed, customer-level data, such as financial accounting (sales, margins), product purchase (timing, frequency, product migrations), and demographic (zip code, family size, age) information, over time. More advanced and rarer data capture what customers are thinking and feeling at different points in their lifecycle. Such information rarely is available in a CRM database and instead requires additional primary data collection (e.g., surveys, focus groups, observations).

The second category of inputs consists of data that link past customer responses to specific marketing programs (e.g., advertising, new customer promotion, price discounts, reward program gifts), as well as the costs of those programs. If a firm lacks data to connect programs to individual customers, it can instead run small "A/B" experiments. Splitting customers randomly into equally sized groups, it would offer a marketing program to one group but not the other, then track its performance with both groups over time. Such experiments also can compare a program's effectiveness across different customer segments. Properly designed experiments provide robust evidence of the effects of a program and how its impact may vary across customer groups at various points in their lifecycle (see Chapter 4, which describes the experimental methods in more detail).

A third category of inputs for this framework comes from *lost customer analysis*. The careful analysis of customers who have stopped doing business with the firm, or are at a high risk of doing so (e.g., customer complaints), can provide insights into the causes of customer defection, where lost customers go (e.g., stopped using the category, switched to low-cost competitors, upgraded to a competitor with more features), and potential recovery strategies. It also can uncover ineffective strategies, such as those that lead the firm to acquire customers who are not in its target market, promote poorly fitting products or services to target customers, or fail to help customers form relational bonds with its brands or employees to minimize churn.

These inputs in turn produce three categories of outputs. First, a thorough segmentation of the firm's own customer portfolio can reveal how those customers evolve over time. By describing customer personas, their needs and preferences, and how and when customers migrate among those personas, the strategist gains answers to crucial questions:

1 What critical triggers lead to migration among stages.
2 What products and services customers buy in different stages in their lifecycle migration, and why.
3 When they stop buying, and why.
4 The customer lifetime value (CLV) associated with customers in each persona.

The second and third outputs are closely interrelated, namely, acquisition, expansion, retention (AER) positioning statements and strategies. They represent key strategic decisions to make in the effort to manage customer dynamics. This process of identifying aspirational positions for specific personas/segments, then designing strategies to achieve these positions, parallels the decisions that firms make to determine their positioning in the overall market. However, the MP#2 framework is unique, in that it *focuses on a firm's existing customers*, captures differences across their personas and stages, and incorporates insights from lost customers. The AER positioning statements thus need to be congruent with the firm's overall positioning in the marketplace to be effective. However, when firms first start to be proactive in managing customer dynamics, they may find that the relevant data they need to conduct specific analyses and define specific strategies are missing or too general. Over time, firms should track and acquire richer data, which will enable managers to address any gaps and missed opportunities, using more robust strategies that also provide critical input to specific marketing decisions (e.g., acquisition strategies, branding activities, sales approaches).

### Summary of Marketing Principle #2

Because customers' needs and preferences are always changing, for a wide range of underlying causes, a firm's marketing strategy must account for customer dynamics to avoid becoming obsolete. Firms that fail to respond to emerging needs will be replaced by competitors that produce solutions that better meet customers' evolving needs. This First Principle acknowledges that customers change and offer a framework for managing customer dynamics, by identifying and understanding how a firm's customers migrate (i.e., change), triggers of these migrations, differing needs across stages, and, ultimately, desirable positions to appeal to these customers over time. Whereas MP#1 recognizes diverse customer needs across the market and seeks to select appropriate target segments, MP#2 looks at the customers within each target segment to understand how to win and keep them, even as they change over time, by accounting for their evolving diversity.

## MP#3: All Competitors React → Managing Sustainable Competitive Advantage

### First Principle: All Competitors React

The first two marketing principles are focused on potential and existing customers, because understanding and managing customer heterogeneity and dynamics allows a firm to develop a positioning strategy that matches its targeted customers' needs and manage these needs as the firm engages with those customers over time. The selection of target markets and positioning strategies is based on the firm's relative strengths compared with existing competitors'; the firm's long-term success and financial performance also depend on how competitors react now and in the future. No matter how well a firm addresses MP#1 and MP#2, competitors will constantly try to copy its success or innovate business processes and offerings to match customers' needs and desires better. The persistent effort by other firms to copy and innovate, such that *all competitors react*, is the third principle marketing managers must address, by building and maintaining barriers to competitive attacks, which together constitute MP#3.

**Example:** General Electric (US)

The ubiquity of competitors' reactions may seem self-evident, yet history shows that few firms can maintain a leadership position forever. Of the original Dow 30 companies in 1928, only one remains on the list: General Electric (GE), which has repositioned itself during multiple drastic, company-wide initiatives. From 1929 to 2013, the Dow Jones top firms were replaced 56 times due to bankruptcy, poor performance, or other reasons, reflecting their failures to respond successfully to market changes and competitive threats.[29]

Competitors have many avenues for undermining a focal firm's market position. First, technical innovations provide platforms for launching new offerings, such that the firm's existing products or services become obsolete (e.g., transistor radios). Second, customers' desires may change when cultural, environmental, or seemingly random factors cause the firm's brand to appear no longer relevant or even harm the firm's performance directly (e.g., US-based, market share leader Wonder Bread suffered reversed fortunes when consumers started seeking healthier, whole grain, or fresh breads). Third, the entrepreneurship and creativeness of diverse actors are constantly being leveraged to find different, better, alternative solutions to problems and offer new products and services (e.g., Uber replacing taxis). In some cases, these creative efforts replace the market leader; in others, they completely redefine the marketplace. Fourth, competitors can generally copy the firm's offering but also be better at executing its strategy. Marc, Alexander, and Oliver Samwer, three German brothers, have generated billions of dollars by copying the success formula of firms like Pinterest, Groupon, and Airbnb.[30]

Thus, technology, customers, and business environments keep changing, and among these changes, a firm's competitors are constantly trying to create new ways to satisfy customers' needs and desires. Those efforts have great potential to disrupt the firm's market position. The more successful a firm is, as reflected in its sales, profits, and stock prices, the more effort its competitors expend to attack its financially successful position.

> The more successful a firm is, as reflected in its sales, profits, and stock prices, the more effort its competitors expend to attack its financially successful position.

## Marketing Decision: Managing Sustainable Competitive Advantage

Because competitors are always attacking the firm's marketing position, managers developing marketing strategies cannot solely focus on customers' unique needs now (MP#1) and manage the changes in these needs over time (MP#2) but also must anticipate future competitors' reactions, then build barriers to withstand the never-ending competitive onslaught (MP#3). These barriers arise when a firm builds **sustainable competitive advantage (SCA)**. A firm should develop SCAs that are relevant for a specific target segment, if those customer needs change then the firm has to adapt its SCA to protect that segment or evaluate moving to a different customer segment. Accordingly, firms often spend much of their discretionary expenditures on marketing activities to shore up their SCA, relying on the three key marketing-based sources of SCA, which are brands, offerings, and relationships:

- **Brands** as sources of SCA often are most effective in large consumer markets (e.g., soft drinks, beer, fashion, automobiles). Firms invest heavily in advertising, public relations, and celebrity sponsorships to build brand awareness and brand images in customers' minds and match the firms' own positioning strategy. Brands create SCA through multiple mechanisms, but in the simplest form, strong awareness can cause customers to buy on the basis of recognition and habit, which reduces their cognitive effort. When brands have a strong, unique meaning, customers might purchase them, out of a desire for status, to enhance their self-identity, or because of their strong positive attachment to the brand. Customers feel attracted to a brand if its perceived image matches their needs and desires. If the firm's brand aligns better with customers' desires than other, competitive brands, it provides a sustainable relative advantage.
- **Offerings**, such as innovative products or services, can be effective sources of SCA in many markets, because new and innovative products and services have the potential to disrupt most market segments. Firms allocate large budgets to research and development (R&D) in an effort to achieve the newest or most innovative product, as well as reduce their costs, add supplementary services, or fundamentally change customers' experiences. Offerings create SCA if they meet customers' needs better or provide more value than existing offerings. This route also requires that customers care about the new feature, innovation, or value proposition established by the new offering.

- **Relationships** are especially effective sources of SCA in business-to-business (B2B), service, or complex business settings. Building strong relationships between customers and the firm's salespeople or other boundary-spanning employees can bar customer defection, prompt enduring customer loyalty, and ensure superior financial performance.[31] Most B2B transactions are fairly complex, require significant two-way communication, and span long periods, so strong interpersonal relationships between buyers and sellers can help establish the necessary trust, cooperation, and flexibility for these business exchanges. Relationships thus lead to SCA through multiple mechanisms, including greater trust, commitment, and interpersonal reciprocal bonds, which help the exchanges adapt to changing circumstances and give buyers confidence that future outcomes will be fair.

These three sources of sustainable competitive advantage are additive, so they can be evaluated from a *customer equity perspective*, which indicates that customers should be treated like other important assets – measured, managed, and maximized just as the firm would its land, buildings, or equipment. *Customer equity* for a firm is "the total of the discounted lifetime values of all of its customers" (p. 4).[32] When a firm focuses its advertising on building strong brands, makes R&D investments to develop new innovative products, and devotes resources to hiring, training, and incentivizing salespeople to build enduring customer relationships, the results should be brand, offering, and relational equities that combine to increase its customer equity.[33]

The additive nature of these three equities can be captured by the **brand, offering, relationship (BOR) equity stack**. If summed across all the firm's customers, this stack represents the firm's overall customer equity. At an individual customer level, customer equity is analogous to the customer lifetime value (CLV). In turn, a customer equity perspective is well suited to the application of a CLV analysis approach, such that each equity in the BOR equity stack can be analyzed as an addition to the customer's discounted cash flow over time. Similar to tangible assets, BOR equities generate a return on assets, can be built with investments, and depreciate over time if not maintained. We outline this framework in detail in Chapter 4, in which we implement the customer equity perspective according to the BOR equity stack. However, effectively building sustainable competitive advantage using specific BOR strategies is a critical element of marketing strategy, so we also address the strategic management of brands (Chapter 5), offerings (Chapter 6), and relationships (Chapter 7) in more detail in separate chapters, to understand how to manage BOR strategies in a way that leads to sustainable competitive advantage. Thus, Chapters 4–7 are all focused on MP#3, which reflects the importance and key role that marketing strategy plays in a firm's SCA and ultimate financial performance.

## Input–Output Framework for Managing Sustainable Competitive Advantage

We provide an organizing framework for managing sustainable competitive advantage (SCA) in Figure 1.6. Of the three key inputs for this framework, two are outputs from MP#1 and MP#2, and the third captures long-term environmental trends that might disrupt a firm's existing and future SCA. Probably the most important input for this framework is the *positioning statements* derived from the first two marketing principles. Specifically, the positioning statement from the segmenting-targeting-positioning (STP) process identifies the product or service features that the firm will use to appeal to this target segment (e.g., status, price, performance) better than its competitors. It provides guidance about where the firm needs to invest to build and maintain its SCA. The acquisition, expansion, retention (AER) positioning statements, an output of MP#2, answer similar questions but focus only on the firm's existing customers and describe who, what, why, and when details for each customer persona in the firm's portfolio, as they develop over time. The two positioning statements in combination provide insights into what aspects of a brand, offering, relationship (BOR) equity stack are key for *winning* customers in the marketplace and *keeping* these customers as they change over time.

A second input for this framework is the AER strategies from MP#2. The AER strategies are developed and organized by stage and persona, to provide guidance into how a firm should invest to acquire and keep various customers. Thus, AER strategies provide a granular summary of how to win/acquire

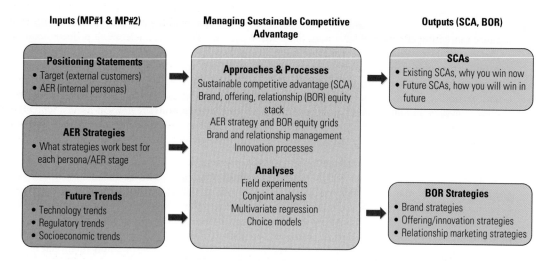

**Figure 1.6** Marketing Principle #3: All Competitors React → Managing Sustainable Competitive Advantage

and keep/retain customers. However, the strategies must be aggregated and reorganized by brand, offering, and relationship categories to match marketers' methods for building SCA, which reflect the firm's BOR equity stack, captured in a BOR equity grid (see Chapter 4 for details).

The third input comes from long-term environmental (e.g., technology, regulatory) trends, which may disrupt an organization's SCA. This input helps counteract the known weaknesses of focusing only on existing customers and competitors. That is, managers who do so often fail to recognize long-term trends or discontinuous changes in the environment.[34]

Two outputs result from the managing SCA framework. The first is a description of the firm's SCA, now and in the future. This description offers a high-level statement of how the organization will win in the competitive marketplace. The aggregation, across all individual target segments and personas, helps ensure compatibility and requires the firm to recognize the core foundation of its long-term success.

The second output is the brand, offering, relationship (BOR) strategies, reflecting an aggregation and reorganization of each targeted customer and persona need (accounting for customer heterogeneity) and the most effective strategies over time (accounting for customer dynamics), according to the brand, offering, and relationship categories. Marketing programs often spill over to multiple personas and stages, so a high-level strategy is needed to provide consistent brand strategies that remain effective for multiple customer groups.

Both of these outputs (SCA and BOR strategies) thus aggregate insights gained from more fine-grained analyses, combining and reorganizing them to support more effective macro-level decision making. The micro–macro duality is critical to a successful marketing strategy, because true customer understanding occurs at micro levels (which avoid aggregation bias), but most strategic and resource-oriented decisions occur at macro levels (advertising, R&D, sales force strategies and expenditures).

> The micro–macro duality is critical to a successful marketing strategy, because true customer understanding occurs at micro levels (which avoid aggregation bias), but most strategic and resource-oriented decisions occur at macro levels (advertising, R&D, sales force strategies and expenditures).

## Summary of Marketing Principle #3

MP#1 focuses on understanding what customers in the overall marketplace want and how the firm should position itself in this space, and MP#2 addresses the firm's own customers to understand what AER strategies are most effective when customers change over time. Then MP#3 reflects a natural next step, building and maintaining strong barriers to withstand competitive attacks on these identified and high value customer segments. These barriers, or sustainable competitive advantages, result because marketing efforts build them, in the form of brand, offering, and relationship (BOR) equities.

The three BOR equities combine into customer equity. That is, customers can be viewed as similar to other firm assets, measured and managed to improve firm performance. The natural ordering for making BOR strategic decisions leads to the firm's customer equity stack. First, the firm should make brand decisions, which are highly influenced by its overall positioning objectives (MP#1 and MP#2). Second, the firm should make choices about its offering, because product and service innovation and R&D efforts must align with both brand strategies and the firm's positioning. Third, relationship strategies normally get determined last, because they involve delivery and the experiential aspects of the offerings.

# MP#4: All Resources Are Limited → Managing Resource Trade-offs

## First Principle: All Resources Are Limited

The final issue is perennial for managers: *all resources are limited.* Most marketing decisions require trade-offs across multiple objectives, because the resources available to address these needs often are interdependent. Allocating thousands of square feet of retail shelf space to products that serve a wrongly targeted consumer segment could lead to substantial losses, such as the obsolescence that would result if a retailer stocked pallets full of skinny jeans, just as wide-legged styles were coming back into fashion. When marketing strategies allocate spending to brand advertising, or innovating new products, or expanding the sales organization to build stronger relationships, they often rely on the same fixed resource pool. A firm only has so many resources so important trade-offs are unavoidable. Managing resources optimally also is critical, because marketing resources create the levers to implement what the firm has learned from MPs#1–3.

Multiple factors impact these complex resource trade-offs, though five are perhaps the most critical:

- **Resource slack** refers to the usable resources a firm has that enables it to initiate changes in its marketing strategy. Firms differ substantially in how much they choose to emphasize marketing, but for most firms, their amount of resource slack generally depends heavily on the economy and the firm's financial performance.
- **Changes in customers' needs** result in the size and attractiveness of segments changing over time, as well as the number of targeted segments the firm addresses, which can cause the firm to reallocate resources to match the firm's ongoing commitment to the various segments.
- As the **lifecycle stages of a firm's product portfolio** evolve, a firm might try to balance its product portfolio to include various products that span multiple lifecycle stages and serve varied target segments.
- Changes in the **product market landscape** result from the entry and exit of competitors. When the firm moves into an advantageous market position, competitors quickly make countermoves, which could negate the impact of the incumbent's advantage, often leading to jostling for secondary demand. That is, firms steal market share from one another. These competitive actions and reactions often require resource allocations to be revised.
- The **effectiveness of marketing activities** also varies, because customer segments, values, and tastes change as products age, as do the competitive landscape and economic conditions. The same amount of well-targeted resources thus could be rendered more or less effective due to changes in the effectiveness of the marketing activity. Trading off resources in such environments can be very challenging, and firms must constantly vary their allocations over different planning horizons; in some cases, they even must reverse their seemingly stable allocation rules.

These different sources work together to create the powerful need for complex trade-offs when firms execute their marketing strategy, representing another First Principle.

Firms that ignore the complexity of making resource allocation adjustments may gain sales in the short term, particularly if they operate in a monopoly (e.g., daily newspapers from the 1960s to the

1990s). But it rarely works in the longer run. Trading off among multiple marketing options is inevitable in a dynamic business environment where multiple factors simultaneously influence firm performance. If firms do not develop effective methods to manage these complex trade-offs, they risk losing whole customer segments or significant market share to competitors that have become more effective at allocating their resources.

## Marketing Decision: Managing Resource Trade-offs

The assumption that *all resources are limited* and that an effective marketing strategy must *manage resource trade-offs* is the fourth and final marketing principle. A firm's resource trade-off strategies, defining how much it allocates to each target market segment, AER strategy, and SCA strategy, should be developed to be relevant to the firm's current target segments (MP#1), to maintain the firm's current AER strategy (MP#2), and to support its stated SCA (MP#3). If any of these factors (e.g., changes in the composition of a firm's customer segments or product portfolio, changes in the effectiveness of marketing activities) induce additional resource trade-offs, the firm also must adapt its strategy to acclimate to these changes. A firm's resource allocation decision framework can be informed by two broad approaches.

First, firms use **heuristic-based processes** to make resource trade-offs when they lack hard data about the attractiveness of each resource option. Managers solve the resource trade-off problem by using simple rules of thumb, driven by intuition and judgment. Such easy-to-use heuristics might suggest allocating a percentage of sales to marketing, an approach that also can be adapted quickly, such that it is appealing in a complex situation. However, most heuristics are incorrect. They lack any scientific basis for the decisions, relying instead on managers' gut feelings about what the right resource allocations are. For example, keeping the average percentages allocated in the past to set advertising budgets for all segments would violate MP#1; it assumes advertising pays off equally across all customer groups, ignoring the principle that all customers differ. If the firm instead sets advertising expenditures as a percentage of sales, it violates MP#2 and ignores the principle that all customers change, because it assumes that advertising pays off equally well today and in the future.

To improve on these methods, firms can continually adjust their heuristics, in a process known as "anchoring and adjusting." For example, managers might make resource allocations based on an initial heuristic (i.e., anchors), then adjust their decisions every period, after observing the outcomes of their prior choice. For a heuristic that suggests spending 1% of sales on advertising, in each period, the firm can conduct "business as usual" and set advertising at 1% of sales, or it might "adjust" the heuristic upward or downward. In relatively stable markets, these methods might be acceptable; however, in highly unstable markets with substantial heterogeneity and sales volatility, simple decision rules often lead to poor trade-off decisions.

Second, the use of **attribution-based processes** is more popular for making resource trade-off decisions, especially as modern managers capitalize on their improved computing power and advances in statistics and data management. Firms are in a better position to review their historical data and measure the impacts of various marketing resource allocations on outcomes such as sales and profits. Historical data contain insightful information about whether and how much marketing resources truly increase economic outcomes. With a well-executed attribution approach, marketing managers can answer critical resource allocation questions, such as: How much would our financial outcomes change if we increased marketing efforts by 1% (i.e., marketing elasticity)? If marketing managers use more than one marketing resource (as is almost always the case), they can discern the relative impact of each resource, which is crucial to their optimal allocation.

In summary, all resources are limited, and a firm's marketing strategy must effectively allocate resources to maximize its business performance over time. Chapter 8 is dedicated to expanding on this discussion of heuristic- and attribution-based approaches to effective resource trade-offs.

---

All resources are limited, and a firm's marketing strategy must effectively allocate resources to maximize its business performance over time.

---

## Input–Output Framework for Managing Resource Trade-offs

In the organizing framework for managing resource trade-offs in Figure 1.7, the three key inputs reflect the outputs of the three preceding First Principles. That is, MP#1 (what customers want and how the firm should position itself) yields a positioning statement that captures information to enable several trade-offs, including: the key customer segments to target; the key products to invest in or discontinue; the key regions to target; and the key relative differences to build and maintain. Thus, this output serves as a starting point for the resource trade-off framework, because it provides the working bounds for executing the firm's positioning statements.

Next, MP#2 yields AER positioning statements and strategies that describe who, what, why, and when information for each key customer persona in the firm's customer portfolio as well as the most effective AER strategies across customer personas and stage. The combined outputs from MP#1 and MP#2 thus narrow the key trade-offs (across segments, products, regions, and relative differences) in the resource allocation decision. That is, these inputs restrict the decision to those trade-offs that are key to *winning* customers in the marketplace and *keeping* these customers as they change over time.

Finally, MP#3 focuses on how to build and maintain strong barriers around customers to withstand competitive attacks, so its output captures the firm's BOR strategy, describing the key objectives of branding, offering, and relationship investments – and their many trade-offs – to build and maintain the firm's SCA.

Then this managing resource trade-off framework produces two outputs: plans and budgets, and marketing metrics.

The first set of outputs is based on the specific resource allocation decision that the manager makes (captured in the firm's annual marketing plans and budgets). It consists of three sub-decisions:

- **Budget per marketing activity**, or the size of the commitment the firm makes to the marketing activity.
- **Allocation across categories**, which reflects the percentage split of the marketing budget for a specific activity across categories.
- **Time horizon** of the budget, involving the timespan for which the firm commits to this marketing budget.

The appropriate metrics that a firm needs to manage its resource allocation activities can determine whether it is successful in achieving its goals. For example, financial metrics based on financial ratios can be converted easily into monetary outcomes such as net profit or returns on investments. Marketing metrics reflect customers' attitudes, behaviors, and mindsets about a firm's products, measured with variables such as awareness, satisfaction, loyalty, and brand equity. Mindset metrics also can

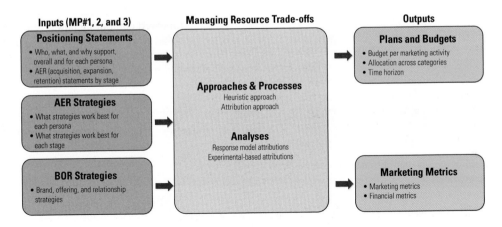

**Figure 1.7** Marketing Principle #4: All Resources Are Limited → Managing Resource Trade-offs

answer questions about exactly why marketing has paid off. Chapter 8 provides an exhaustive list of marketing and financial metrics pertaining to various marketing functions.

As market segments change, due to changes in customers or the competitive landscape, the metrics and resource allocation decisions need to be adapted continually too. Chapter 8 therefore outlines a five-step process for using the framework to transform inputs into outputs.

## Summary of Marketing Principle #4

With MP#4, the focus is on tackling the perennial issue of resource limitations. Managing resources optimally is critical; marketing resources provide the levers to implement what the firm learns from the first three marketing principles. First, to *manage customer heterogeneity* (MP#1) effectively, managers must develop a segmenting and targeting approach, but then they need good systems and processes to allocate resources appropriately to these identified segments. Second, to *manage customer dynamics* (MP#2) effectively, managers design acquisition, expansion, and retention strategies to be able to serve customers through their lifecycles. In this case, they need an adequate marketing budget to refine their resource allocation policies and cater to any changes in the customer landscape. Third, to *build sustainable competitive advantages* (MP#3), managers devote various resources to building brands, introducing new products, and maintaining organizations that ensure strong customer relationships, which demand astute resource allocation policies across BOR strategies.

Chapter 8 describes two approaches for managing resource trade-offs in more detail. With a heuristics-based approach, managers use an "anchor" as a base decision rule, then adjust the anchor every period. An attribution-based approach is more scientific, relying on a mathematical assessment of the effectiveness of marketing activities according to past data to optimize resource trade-off decisions.

# Implementing the Four Marketing Principles

We close this chapter with a brief discussion of how to implement the four Marketing Principles (MPs) in practice. Each principle is a stand-alone entity, with its own input–output structure. But to make effective marketing decisions, firms must consistently take actions that reflect their strategy for building relative advantages over competitors, making this relative advantage salient to customers, and sustaining this advantage over time, even as customers change and competitors react. Thus, to successfully implement the four MPs, managers need to integrate them into their day-to-day practices, build strong marketing capabilities to effectively conduct the individual steps, processes, and analyses, and continuously iterate to improve the execution of each principle.

## Integrating the Four Marketing Principles

The solution to the four principles is *hierarchical.* Solving some principles requires knowledge of the solution to other principles. Figure 1.8 illustrates how the four MPs are connected in operation. The gray boxes represent the overarching marketing principle; the blue ovals represent its solution (or output). Imagine a firm faced with developing a sustainable competitive advantage (SCA) by devising a set of brand and offering strategies for its customer base. The brand and offering strategy needs to address three conditions:

1 Customers must care about what the SCA offers.
2 The firm must do "it" (whatever "it" is) better than competitors, leading to a relative advantage.
3 The SCA must be hard to duplicate or substitute.

However, it would be impossible to build an effective set of brand and offering strategies unless the firm knows what customer segments it wants to pursue and how it can uniquely fulfill their needs and benefits (relative to other offerings). That is, it would need the output of MP#1 to even begin building an SCA ("Positioning statement" in Figure 1.8). Moreover, to build SCAs that thwart competitive attacks, it needs to account for how customers might change over time and understand when customers might start or stop buying from it or competitors. The output of MP#2, which captures

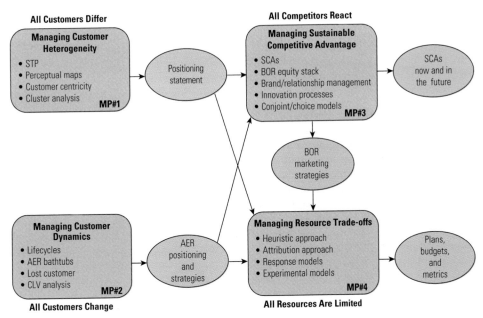

The four Marketing Principles (gray boxes) can be integrated according to the key output (blue oval) of each principle that serves as an input for each subsequent principle.

**Figure 1.8** Integrating the Four Marketing Principles

critical triggers of migration across stages, thus represents a critical input to the problem of building SCA ("AER positioning and strategies" in Figure 1.8). The same intuition applies to the solution of MP#4, because making resource trade-offs requires a clear understanding the first three MPs.

## Building Marketing Analytics Capabilities

A key enabler to implementing the four Marketing Principles framework successfully is for a firm to develop customer analytics capabilities. Customer analytics can be defined as a technology-enabled, model-supported approach to harnessing customer and market data to understand and serve customers. Firms using customer analytics rely on data and methods to test and improve their marketing decision frameworks. The effective use of customer analytics requires building both data capabilities and methodological capabilities. A firm can increase its data capabilities by building databases that improve three forms of intelligence. First, economic data help a firm understand the trading environment and changes in business conditions. Second, customer data capture customers' needs and behaviors. Lastly, competitive data reveal the competitive landscape in terms of threats and opportunities. A firm also needs to build methodological capabilities by mastering the analytical tools that we describe in the process boxes of each of the four Marketing Principles' frameworks. Both data and methodological capabilities are required to successful implement the four MPs.

## Continuously Iterating and Improving

Finally, a firm cannot solve all the First Principles simultaneously, because of their complex and inter-related nature. Instead, firms need an iterative approach to integrate the principles. An ideal solution would optimize all the key First Principles simultaneously, but firms likely lack the required time, resources, and skills to implement an ideal solution. Instead, they can gradually improve their overall marketing functions by improving one principle at a time, maintaining an existing (even if suboptimal) approach to the other principles.

# Putting it All Together Using Markstrat Simulation

In order to understand the four Marketing Principles and how they fit together, we recommend "gaining practice" using market simulation software such as Markstrat. Markstrat simulation software is an interactive learning tool that requires real-time decisions. Teams of students or business-people, assigned to different virtual companies, compete by making a series of marketing decisions. After each decision round, each team submits its marketing decisions. The simulation platform then determines the sales, profits, and market share of each firm, using an empirical model derived from the historical performance of many real businesses. Teams observe the impact of their decisions before making another set of decisions to compete in the simulated business environment. With this decision environment, participants can review marketing reports, analyze data, make actual decisions, and then see the results of their decisions. Customers and markets shift over the years in each decision round, such that participants can observe five to ten years of market evolution in just a few weeks.

The decisions that each team makes map onto the four Marketing Principles and parallel many of the tools and analyses described in this book. Each team makes STP decisions: targeting customer segments, evaluating perceptual maps to determine their positioning strategies (MP#1, all customers differ, so teams must manage customer heterogeneity). Customer segments evolve over time due to alterations in their desired attributes (performance, price), channel preferences, and size or importance (MP#2, all customers change, so teams need to change their strategy to manage customer dynamics). In addition, the business environment includes mature and emerging product markets, with varying lifecycles. Because each team can observe the actions (targeting, advertising, new product launches) and results (sales, share, stock price) of all other teams, a real-time competitive environment results. The teams need to build sustainable competitive advantage (SCA) through their brands, offerings, and sales channels to withstand competitive onslaughts by the other teams (MP#3, all competitors react, so teams need to manage their SCA). Finally, in each decision round, teams have a budget. Therefore, they must make resource allocation decisions across advertising, new products, and sales organizations in each decision round (MP#4, all resources are limited, so teams need to manage resource trade-offs).

In addition to participating in a simulated environment that encompasses many aspects of the four Marketing Principles, the software offers a range of reports and analysis tools. Participants can see how marketing research reports (positioning maps, surveys) and analysis techniques (experiments, conjoint analysis) inform key decisions – reinforcing many of the key aspects of the approach promoted in this book.

The Markstrat simulation software is described in more detail in Data Analytics Technique 1.1. Although this simulation software is an excellent companion to this book, it is not required and there are many other simulation packages available, including Interpretive Simulation's PharmaSim and StratSim*Marketing* programs, Cesim's SimBrand, and Marketplace Simulation's Strategic Marketing and Advanced Strategic Marketing.[35] We focus on Markstrat, because it mirrors our approach for this book, but the other simulation packages are also very effective for integrating the concepts, approaches, and techniques offered herein.

# Summary

Marketing strategy texts typically integrate the growing numbers of marketing analysis tools, processes, and research techniques available for evaluating business phenomena around the 4Ps (product, price, place, promotion) of the marketing mix, for dealing with competitors, and for executing specific marketing tasks (segmenting, branding). This functional perspective provides a wealth of frameworks and processes, yet it offers little overall guidance on *when* to use those tools, *how* they work, *which* ones are most valuable, or *how* they all fit together.

This book proposes a simplifying approach to marketing strategy, arguing that marketing decisions primarily should involve solving the basic underlying problems or complexities that all entities face when designing and implementing a marketing strategy. Central to this First Principles approach is

# Markstrat: A Tool for Practicing the First Principle Approach to Marketing Strategy

## Description

Markstrat simulation software is an interactive learning tool that requires "real-time" decisions, such that users gain a better understanding of the four Marketing Principles.

## When to Use It

- To practice implementing the four Marketing Principles for developing effective marketing strategies.
- To test the effects of a marketing action in a simulated environment, before implementing the action in the real world.

## How It Works

Markstrat is a supplement to the material covered in this book that can increase intuition for marketing strategy through the practice and implementation of the four Marketing Principles. It is available online, for a subscription fee, at web.stratxsimulations.com.

**MP#1:** Target products to meet the needs of different customer segments and manage customer heterogeneity.

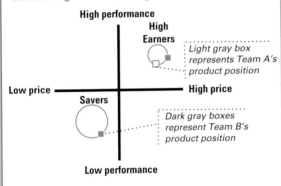

**MP#2:** Adjust strategies over time to adapt to changing customer needs.

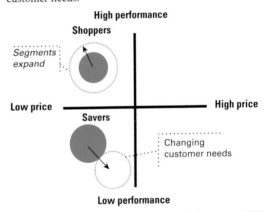

**MP#3:** Introduce new products to create a sustainable competitive advantage (SCA) as a barrier to other teams attacking your position.

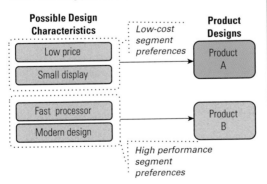

**MP#4:** Manage limited resources by making resource trade-offs among marketing mix categories and brands.

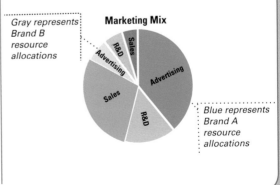

the assumption that firms build sustainable differential advantages by evaluating how they are seen by customers. Thus, marketing strategy is a set of decisions and actions, focused on building a sustainable differential advantage, relative to competitors, in the minds of customers, to create value for stakeholders. With this view of marketing strategy, this book outlines and details four fundamental problems and critical hurdles to marketing success, termed the *First Principles of marketing strategy*, which constitute the foundational assumptions on which marketing strategy is based.

The first and most basic issue facing managers as they make marketing mix decisions (pricing, product, promotion, place) for their firm is that *all customers differ*. Many factors cause customers to differ in their preferences for a product or service, including basic differences across people, varying life experiences, unique functional needs for products, differing aspirational self-identities, and the results of previous persuasion-based activities focused on changing customer preferences. Thus, customer heterogeneity is a fundamental problem that all firms must address when developing an effective marketing strategy (MP#1).

The second underlying complexity for managers as they make short- and long-term marketing decisions is that *all customers change*. The multitude of different sources or drivers of customer dynamics include seminal events in customers' lives, life stages, knowledge changes, product category maturity, and new exposures in customers' lives. A key question is how a firm can manage those customer dynamics. Thus, whereas MP#1 focuses on the market as a whole, to understand which consumers or businesses to target in the overall marketplace, MP#2 narrows the scope to just the *firm's own customers* and challenges firms to understand how their existing customers change over time.

Persistent efforts by other firms to copy and innovate, or the premise that *all competitors react*, is the third principle that marketing managers must address, by building and maintaining barriers to competitive attacks (MP#3). Barriers that can withstand competitors' actions are *sustainable competitive advantages* (SCAs). A firm's SCA should resonate with a specific customer target segment. If those customer needs change, then the firm has to adapt its SCA to protect the segment, or else evaluate whether it should shift to a different customer segment.

Finally, a perennial issue facing managers as they make strategic marketing decisions is that *all resources are limited*. Many factors create complex resource trade-offs for firms, such as changes in resource slack, a firm's customer segments, a firm's product portfolio, the product landscape, or the effectiveness of a firm's marketing activities. A firm's resource trade-off strategy, or how much it allocates to each target market segment, AER strategy, and SCA strategy, must be relevant for the firm's current target segments, maintain the firm's current AER strategy, and reinforce its stated SCA.

Thus, to make effective marketing decisions, firms must consistently address and optimize their plans for building a relative advantage over competitors, making their relative advantage salient to customers, and sustaining this advantage over time as customers change and competitors react. Managers need to integrate the four MPs fully into their day-to-day practice, build marketing analytics capabilities, and constantly iterate to improve.

## Takeaways

- Marketing strategy is the set of decisions and actions focused on building a sustainable differential advantage, relative to competitors, in the minds of customers, to create value for stakeholders.
- This book takes a simplifying approach to marketing strategy, arguing that marketing decisions should focus on solving the four underlying problems or complexities that all entities face when designing and implementing a marketing strategy.
- The first and most basic issue facing managers in their marketing mix decisions (pricing, product, promotion, place) for the firm is that *all customers differ*. Customer heterogeneity is a fundamental problem that all firms must address when developing an effective marketing strategy (MP#1).
- The input–output framework for managing customer heterogeneity captures the approaches, processes, and analyses that can aid managerial decision making. The inputs include customers, the

company, and competitors, which together constitute the contextual background in which a firm's strategy must operate. The output identifies key industry segments, the firm's target segment(s), and positioning statements, which reveal the relative advantage of the firm's offering for the target segment.

- A second underlying complexity for both short- and long-term marketing decisions is that *all customers change*. Therefore, with a focus on the firm's own customers, MP#2 challenges firms to understand how their existing customers change over time.

- The input–output framework for managing this customer dynamism emphasizes the firm's existing customer portfolio and data that link past customer responses to specific marketing programs as inputs. The outputs are acquisition, expansion, retention (AER) positioning statements and strategies, which help the firm effectively manage dynamics.

- The idea that *all competitors react* is the third principle that marketing managers must address, by building and maintaining barriers to these competitive attacks and thereby ensuring a sustainable competitive advantage (MP#3).

- The input–output framework for managing competitive reactions cites three inputs: the outputs from MP#1, the outputs from MP#2, and long-term environmental trends. Its outputs are a firm's brand, offering, relationship (BOR) strategies, which aggregate and reorganize the needs of each targeted customer and persona, as well as the most effective strategies over time, in terms of brands, offerings, and relationships.

- The fourth marketing principle holds that *all resources are limited*, so firms must develop resource trade-off strategies that are relevant for their current target segments (MP#1) and maintain their current AER strategy (MP#2) and stated SCA (MP#3), which together constitute MP#4.

- In the input–output framework for managing resource trade-offs, the inputs include the outputs from the first, second, and third marketing principles; the outputs are the metrics that firms need to manage their resource allocation activities, as well as the specific resource allocation decision that managers make for that period.

# References

1 Oxford Dictionary (2015) Available at: https://en. oxforddictionaries.com/definition/first_principles (accessed 28 October 2016).

2 Stevenson, A. (ed.) (2010) *Oxford Dictionary of English*, 3rd edn. Oxford: Oxford University Press.

3 Von Clausewitz, C. (1832) *On War*. Translated by Howard, M. and Paret, P., 1976. Princeton, NJ: Princeton University Press.

4 Chandler, A. (1962) *Strategy and Structure: Chapters in the History of American Industrial Enterprise*. Cambridge, MA: MIT Press; Kerin, R.A., Varadarajan, P.R. and Peterson, R.A. (1992) 'First-mover advantage: A synthesis, conceptual framework, and research propositions,' *Journal of Marketing*, 56(4), pp. 33–52.

5 Porter, M. (1980) *Competitive Strategy: Techniques for Analyzing Industry and Competitors*. New York: The Free Press; Porter, M.E. (1985) *Competitive Advantage: Creating and Sustaining Competitive Performance*. New York: The Free Press; Hamel, G. and Prahalad, C.K. (1990) 'The core competence of the corporation,' *Harvard Business Review*, 68(3), pp. 79–91.

6 Day, G.S. and Moorman, C. (2010) *Strategy From the Outside In: Profiting From Customer Value*. New York: McGraw-Hill.

7 Kozlenkova, I.V., Samaha, S.A. and Palmatier, R.W. (2014) 'Resource-based theory in marketing,' *Journal of the Academy of Marketing Science*, 42(1), pp. 1–21.

8 Gupta, S. and Lehmann, D.R. (2005) *Managing Customers as Investments: The Strategic Value of Customers in the Long Run*. Upper Saddle River, NJ: Wharton School Publishing.

9 Gabriel, B. and Abouwer, T. (2013) 'Case study: Philips: Innovation and change management in global organizations: the case study of.' Available at: www.adaptivecycle.nl/index. php?title=Case_study:_Philips_:_Innovation_and_change_ management_in_global_organizations:_the_case_study_of (accessed 23 September, 2015).

10 Johnson, G. and Scholes, K. (1999) *Exploring Corporate Strategy*, 5th edn. New York: Prentice Hall.

11 Bell, D.R., Chiang, J. and Padmanabhan, V. (1999) 'The decomposition of promotional response: An empirical generalization,' *Marketing Science*, 18(4), pp. 504–26; Hanssens, D.M. (2009) *Empirical Generalizations about Marketing Impact: What we have learned from Academic Research*. Cambridge, MA: Marketing Science Institute; Morgan, N.A. and Rego, L.L. (2006) 'The value of different customer satisfaction and loyalty metrics in predicting

business performance,' *Marketing Science*, 25(5), pp. 426–39; Sethuraman, R., Tellis, G.J. and Briesch, R.A. (2011) 'How well does advertising work? Generalizations from meta-analysis of brand advertising elasticities,' *Journal of Marketing Research*, 48(3), pp. 457–71; Tellis, G.J. (2003) *Effective Advertising: Understanding When, How, and Why Advertising Works*. Thousand Oaks, CA: Sage; Van Heerde, H.J., Gupta, S. and Wittink, D.R. (2003) 'Is 75% of the sales promotion bump due to brand switching? No, only 33% is,' *Journal of Marketing Research*, 40(4), pp. 481–91.

12  Szymanski, D.M., Bharadwaj, S.G. and Varadarajan, P.R. (1993) 'An analysis of the market share–profitability relationship,' *Journal of Marketing*, 57(3), pp. 1–18.

13  Slywotzky, A., Weber, K. and Wise, R. (2003) *How to Grow When Markets Don't*. New York: Warner Business Books.

14  CMO (2014) 'CMO survey report: Highlights and insights.' Available at: http://cmosurvey.org/results/survey-results-august-2014/ (accessed 23 September, 2015).

15  Kumar, N. and Steenkamp, J.B.E. (2013) *Brand Breakout: How Emerging Market Brands Will Go Global*. New York: Palgrave Macmillan.

16  Rivkin, S. and Sutherland, F. (2004) *The Making of a Name: The Inside Story of the Brands We Buy*. New York: Oxford University Press.

17  Krasnikov, A. and Jayachandran, S. (2008) 'The relative impact of marketing, research-and-development, and operations capabilities on firm performance,' *Journal of Marketing*, 72(4), pp. 1–11.

18  Seitz, P. (2014) 'Sorry, cheapskates, apple iPhones to remain pricey,' *Investor's Business Daily*, 26 February; Apple, Inc. (2015) *Financial Information*. Available at: http://investor.apple.com/financials.cfm (accessed 23 September, 2015).

19  Palmatier, R.W., Scheer, L.K. and Steenkamp, J.B.E.M. (2007) 'Customer loyalty to whom? Managing the benefits and risks of salesperson-owned loyalty,' *Journal of Marketing Research*, 44(2), pp. 185–99.

20  Lodish, L.M. and Mela, C.F. (2007) 'If brands are built over years, why are they managed over quarters?,' *Harvard Business Review*, 85(7/8), pp. 104–12.

21  Daly, J.L. (2002) *Pricing for Profitability: Activity-Based Pricing for Competitive Advantage*. New York: John Wiley & Sons.

22  Berger, J. (2013) *Contagious: Why Things Catch On*. New York: Simon & Schuster.

23  Kumar, V., Petersen, J.A. and Leone, R.P. (2007) 'How valuable is word of mouth?,' *Harvard Business Review*, 85(1), pp. 139–46; Reichheld, F.F. and Markey, R. (2011) *The Ultimate Question 2.0: How Net Promoter Companies Thrive*

in a Customer-Driven World. Boston: Harvard Business Review Press; Wiesel, T., Skiera, B. and Villanueva, J. (2008) 'Customer equity: An integral part of financial reporting,' *Journal of Marketing*, 72(2), pp. 1–14.

24  Leonard-Barton, D., Schendel, D. and Channon, D. (1992) 'Core capabilities and core rigidities: A paradox in managing new product development,' *Strategic Management Journal*, 13(S1), pp. 111–25.

25  Zeithaml, V.A., Varadarajan, R.P. and Zeithaml, C.P. (1988) 'The contingency approach: Its foundations and relevance to theory building and research in marketing,' *European Journal of Marketing*, 22(7), pp. 37–64.

26  Pfeffer, J. (2013) 'A deadly Silicon Valley habit: Chasing the latest fad.' Available at: www.bloomberg.com/bw/articles/2013-01-08/a-deadly-silicon-valley-habit-chasing-the-latest-fad (accessed 23 September, 2015).

27  Holmes, E. (2011) 'Breeding a nation of chocoholics,' 30 November. Available at: www.wsj.com/articles/SB10001424052970204262304577068191047284320 (accessed 13 August, 2016).

28  Keller, K.L. and Kotler, P. (2014) *Marketing Management*, 14th edn. Upper Saddle River, NJ: Prentice Hall.

29  S&P Dow Jones Indices (2013) *Dow Jones Industrial Average Historical Components*. New York: McGraw Hill Financial.

30  Ekekwe, N. (2012) 'When you can't innovate, copy,' 24 May. Available at: https://hbr.org/2012/05/when-you-cant-innovate-copy (accessed 23 September, 2015).

31  Palmatier, R.W., Dant, R.P., Grewal, D. and Evans, K.R. (2006) 'Factors influencing the effectiveness of relationship marketing: A meta-analysis,' *Journal of Marketing*, 70(4), pp. 136–53.

32  Rust, R., Zeithaml, V. and Lemon, K. (2000) *Driving Customer Equity: How Customer Lifetime Value is Shaping Corporate Strategy*. New York: The Free Press.

33  Vogel, V., Evanschitzky, H. and Ramaseshan, B. (2008) 'Customer equity drivers and future sales,' *Journal of Marketing*, 72(6), pp. 98–108.

34  Christensen, C.M. (2006) *The Innovator's Dilemma*. New York: First Collins Business Essentials.

35  Interpretive Simulations, *PharmaSim*. Available at: www.interpretive.com/rd6/index.php?pg=ps4&sid=0 (accessed 8 October, 2015); Cesim SimBrand, *Marketing Management Simulation Game*. Available at: www.cesim.com/simulations/cesim-simbrand-marketing-management-simulation-game/ (accessed 8 October, 2015); Marketplace Live, *Compare Marketing Simulations*. Available at: www.marketplace-simulation.com/compare-marketing (accessed 8 October, 2015).

## Companion website

Please visit the companion website, **www.palgravehighered.com/palmatier-ms**, to access summary videos from the authors, and full-length cases with datasets and step-by-step solution guides.

# Part 1

# ALL CUSTOMERS DIFFER

The most basic issue facing managers making marketing mix decisions (pricing, product, promotion, place) is that all customers differ. Customers vary widely in their needs and preferences, whether real or perceived. Their desires even vary for basic commodity products (e.g., bottled water). Thus, effective marketing strategies must manage this customer heterogeneity, often through segmenting, targeting, and positioning efforts. It allows the firm to make sense of the customer landscape by identifying a manageable number of homogeneous customer groups, such that the firm can meaningfully evaluate its relative strengths and make strategically critical decisions about how to win and keep customers.

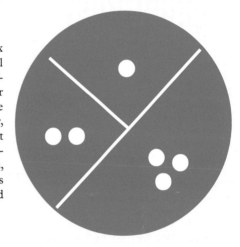

Visit www.palgravehighered.com/palmatier-ms to watch the authors provide an overview of the *All Customers Differ* First Principle and the relevant tools, analyses, and cases in either an executive summary or a full-length, pre-recorded video lecture format.

Chapter **2**

# Marketing Principle #1:
# All Customers Differ
# → Managing Customer
# Heterogeneity

**ALL
CUSTOMERS
DIFFER**

## Learning objectives

- Understand and explain why all customers differ.
- Critically discuss why an effective marketing strategy must manage customer heterogeneity (Marketing Principle #1).
- Analyze the differences among mass, niche, and one-to-one marketing.
- Explain why niche and one-to-one marketing often have an advantage over mass marketing.
- Outline in detail the STP (segmentation, targeting, positioning) approach to managing customer heterogeneity.
- Explain why segmenting should not be based solely on demographic factors but rather should include customer needs and desires.
- Critically analyze the criteria for an ideal target segment.
- Describe the importance of a positioning strategy (including a positioning statement) to a firm's long-term success.
- Outline the pros and cons of a customer-centric approach.
- Explain the synergy between STP and customer-centric approaches to managing customer heterogeneity.
- Describe the objectives of factor, cluster, and discriminant analyses.
- Recognize the three inputs and outputs for the framework for managing customer heterogeneity.
- Understand the four-step process for managing customer heterogeneity (MP#1).

# Introduction

## All Customers Differ

The first and most basic issue facing managers, as they make strategic marketing decisions for their firms, is that *all customers differ*. It is a foundational assumption that customers vary widely in their needs and preferences, whether real or perceived. This may seem *too* basic to warrant mention, but consider the magnitude of the effects of this issue. From product or service categories in which customers exhibit a careful choice process (e.g., there are over 19,000 mutual fund[1] offerings for investors) to more routine purchases (e.g., a grocery store may offer over 50,000 different stock-keeping units), firms try to match their offerings to different customers' preferences.[2] Consumers' desires vary even for so-called "commodity products," such as bottled water, as evidenced by the dozens of configurations on store shelves involving different brands, sizes, bottle types, fizzy versus still, and so on.

Some firms assume away customer differences by offering a single product to the entire target market. This approach may work in peculiar circumstances, particularly if competition is weak or scarce, but it rarely works in the long run. Consider a stalwart model from the early days of the automotive industry. Ford found great success with the one-size-fits-all Model T, with its philosophy of "you can have any color you want, as long as it is black." This approach worked at the beginning stages of the automobile's product lifecycle, but as demand soared, competitors began offering differentiated products that better matched fragmenting customer desires,[3] and it became obvious that Ford had to adapt.

Ford's experience with the Model T is not unique. Across industries, as a category grows in size, competitors recognize untapped opportunity, identify niches of customers whose needs are poorly served by an incumbent product, and then target those customers with a tailored offering that is better aligned with those needs. Moreover, customers begin to express unique preferences for various forms of the product, after they come to understand its value. If the incumbent company fails to respond with new or refined offerings, then customers have a compelling reason to migrate to the competitor's product. Would Ford still be a successful automotive manufacturer if it offered only black cars today?

**Example:** Sears & Roebuck (US)

Sears & Roebuck, a large US retailer, once had a very successful broad-line catalog operation, printing 75 million catalogs every year that resulted in more than 180,000 daily orders at a peak moment, totaling annual sales of over $250 million.[4] Through the iconic Sears "Big Book," the company offered seeds and tools to rural farmers, household appliances to families, sports equipment and toys to kids, as well as clothing and shoes for virtually everyone. However, over subsequent years, other firms identified and attacked profitable subsegments of Sears' customer base with more narrowly focused catalogs that were well targeted to smaller, more homogeneous customer groups, undermining Sears' business. For example, Hammacher Schlemmer offered a catalog that specialized in tools and other innovative home products, Spiegel sold fashionable women's clothes and accessories for stay-at-home moms and later businesswomen, and L.L. Bean sold clothes and supplies to outdoors enthusiasts.[5] Not only did Sears lose sales revenue in these segments, but the competitors often went after the best and most profitable customer segments. This left Sears with a broad portfolio of diverse customers in less desirable segments that were often slow growing and less profitable. Furthermore, Sears found it hard to serve the remaining unprofitable customers, whose lower sales volume also prompted higher inventory and acquisition costs.

Sears found itself stuck between a rock and a hard place. If it stopped serving a category, it lost even more revenue, but if it continued to serve that category, it often had to do so at a net loss. This no-win situation, similar to situations faced by many firms, arose because Sears did not effectively manage its customer heterogeneity, or variation among customers in terms of their needs, desires, and subsequent behaviors. Ultimately, Sears stopped issuing its "Big Book" catalog, which was no longer profitable. Although this example focused on Sears' catalog business, the situation parallels what has happened in its retail stores too.[6]

Thus, firms' marketing strategies must cater to differences in customers' preferences in a product category, or else a competitor ultimately will take these customers away by satisfying their unmet needs, at least for some valuable customer segments (i.e., those that are large, growing, and profitable). However, a key question emerges from these examples: Why are customer preferences so different? Why doesn't every customer want the same coffee, car, or clothes? Understanding the underlying sources of customer heterogeneity is important, because it provides compelling insights into the ways that customers differ in their real and perceived preferences. Identifying and exploiting customer heterogeneity is key to developing effective marketing strategies.

Identifying and exploiting customer heterogeneity is key to developing effective marketing strategies.

## Sources of Customer Heterogeneity

Customer preferences for one among multiple competing products or services are usually driven by the aggregation of that customer's desires across various product or service attributes (e.g., price, time savings, durability). Customers make trade-off decisions (consciously or not) across differentially important attributes, resulting in a purchase choice. Variations in preferences (needs, desires, and subsequent choices) across customers for any product or service stem from several underlying sources. The different sources of customer heterogeneity combine and interact to generate widely diverging preferences across consumers, as summarized in Table 2.1.

**Table 2.1** Sources of Customer Heterogeneity

| Source | Description | Examples |
|---|---|---|
| Individual differences | A person's stable and consistent way of responding to the environment in a specific domain | Favorite colors, Big Five personality traits – openness, conscientiousness, extraversion, agreeableness, neuroticism |
| Life experiences | An individual's life experiences capture events and experiences unique to their life that have a lasting impact on the value and preferences they place on products and services, which, in turn, affect preferences independent of individual differences | A child raised closer to the equator, in warmer climates, will typically have a higher preference for spicy foods, as a carryover of past periods when spices were used to preserve and help mask the taste of food more likely to spoil in warmer climates |
| Functional needs | An individual's personal decision weightings across functional attributes based on their personal circumstances | What price can they afford to pay (income), how long does the product need to last (quality, warranty), when will they use the product (battery powered, size), and are there any special usage features that they need (waterproof)? |
| Self-identity/ image | Customers actively seek products that they feel will support or promote their desired self-image | Motorcycle riders often wear leather (functional and image driven), and Goths like the color black because of their desire to identify with the image of a specific user or social group |
| Marketing activities | Firms' attempts to build linkages between their brands and prototypical identities or meanings | BMW paid $25 million to have James Bond drive a BMW in the movie *Skyfall*, based on the belief that Bond's image would be aspirational to many potential target customers – men aged 30–50 years |

First, probably the most fundamental source of customer heterogeneity is basic **individual differences** across people, defined as each person's stable and consistent way of responding to the environment in a specific domain.[7] There are innumerable ways in which people differ psychologically; one popular typology sums up these differences as the "Big 5" traits: openness, conscientiousness, extraversion, agreeableness, and neuroticism. Another example is consumers' preference for color, a basic design feature of many products. Research shows that men's favorite colors break down as 45% blue, 19% green, 12% black, and 12% red, while women's favorite colors are 28% green, 25% blue, 12% purple, and 12% red.[8] Ford thus could not maintain its cost-effective black-only color strategy; it would be matching the preferences of only 12% of all men and not even rank among the top five colors for women. Similarly, people vary in their favorite flavors, textures, sounds, and smells. Many individual difference preferences are ingrained at birth, due to random or genetic variation, such that this key source of customer heterogeneity applies even to the most homogeneous of product offerings.[9]

Second, a person's **life experiences** capture events and experiences that are unique to their life and have a lasting impact on the value and preference the person places on products and services, affecting preferences independently of the individual differences. Some geographic and cultural environmental factors have systematic impacts; other factors have an impact but unclear directional effects. For example, a person's exposure to certain television shows, events in the local neighborhood, or books by certain authors at an early life stage could have dramatic impacts on their worldview, propensity to take risk, or proclivity for consuming certain luxury goods. Furthermore, some individual difference-based psychological factors likely interact with characteristics of an individual's environment to cause varying reactions.[10] Thus, life experiences are a source of customer heterogeneity, but their actual linkages to preferences are often difficult to predict.

Third, perhaps the most straightforward source of heterogeneity in preferences is an individual's **functional needs** for a specific offering. These differences capture the weights a person applies in a decision, across functional attributes based on personal circumstances: What price can they afford to pay (income), how long does the product need to last (quality, warranty), when will they use the product or service (battery powered, size), and are there any special usage features that they need (waterproof)? Higher quality, more features, and additional capabilities are almost always desired, but they often come with a higher price or other physical trade-offs in size or weight, which prevent firms from making any single, "ideal" product that could match every customer's preference. In addition, customer preferences for any attribute vary continuously across a range of values (price, battery life, weight), yet firms usually manufacture products at specific levels ($100, 3 hours, 4 oz.), so the firm cannot perfectly "match" many customers' preferences with a reasonable assortment of products.

Fourth, consumers often want their purchases to support their actual or aspirational **self-identity** or **image**.[11] Some sources of heterogeneity operate below the level of consciousness (e.g., individual differences, life experiences); consumers' desire to buy products and services that match their self-identity or image instead tends to entail a more proactive, conscious decision process. Consumers actively seek products that they believe will support or promote their desired self-image and fulfill their need for uniqueness. A product's image can come from a linkage to an iconic figure or celebrity or what is popular in a peer or aspirational social group. Some people instead search out products that are not popular but rather are noticeably unique, to match their desire for distinctiveness.[12] The wide variety in consumers' choices in fashion, housing, electronics, and cars is often driven by individuals' desires to enhance or support their self-image or status. Thus, for example, motorcycle riders often wear leather (which may be both functional and image driven), and Goths like the color black, reflecting their desire to identify with the image of a specific and distinctive user or social group.[13]

Fifth, the last source of customer heterogeneity, persuasion from **marketing activities**, often results from firms' attempts to build linkages between their brands and prototypical identities or meanings. By building a strong association between their product and a specific identity, marketers increase the likelihood that a consumer will purchase an offering that matches their aspirational self-image. For example, BMW paid $25 million to have James Bond drive a BMW in the movie *Skyfall*, based on the belief that Bond's image would be aspirational to many potential target customers (e.g., men aged 30–50 years).[14] In other cases, rather than linking to a popular or prototypical image (James Bond), marketers work to develop a new and unique brand identity or extend an existing brand image to help differentiate their offering from other firms' products. J. Walter Thompson launched diamonds as a "token of love" after many years of failure to penetrate the Asian market by developing a brand image that represented a break with an Eastern past, in advertising that showed couples dressed in Western clothing and involved in Western pastimes.[15] The resulting image of diamonds – as modern and Western rather than traditional and Eastern – appealed to many consumers in that market.

To the degree that marketing efforts are successful in persuading consumers that some unique characteristic is specific to their identity or is an important purchase attribute, customer heterogeneity increases. For example, Volvo's advertising about automobile safety increased the weight that many consumers placed on safety when buying a car, which supported Volvo's positioning strategy. A few decades ago, bottled still water was mostly an undifferentiated commodity (low heterogeneity); after millions of dollars of marketing, bottled water is now linked to a range of attributes, as in the examples of Aquafina's "Pure Water, Perfect Taste," Arrowhead's "Born Better & 100% Mountain Spring Water," Crystal Geyser's "Naturally Good!," Fiji Water's "Natural Artisan Water," or Evian's "Live Young."

Thus, marketing strategies not only attempt to match natural sources of variation in customer preferences (e.g., individual differences, life experiences, functional needs, self-identity) but also serve as significant sources of customer heterogeneity themselves. Marketers work to make "natural differences" in preferences more salient to consumers, as well as persuade consumers of the importance of new attributes (e.g., environmentally safe or green, blood diamonds, Made in the USA), to build new purchase preferences. Greek yogurt went from a 1% to a 36% share of the yogurt market between 2007 and 2013, largely because marketers made the health aspects of Greek yogurt more salient to US consumers.[16]

The growing heterogeneity of customer preferences in response to marketing that focuses on new or differentiated attributes also has been accelerated by technological advances. Modern marketers can communicate unique messages to smaller customer groups, account for geographic location or unique purchase situations, and offer more differentiated products in new and cost-effective ways.[17] Mobile marketing technology means that geographic marketing can go beyond the zip code level to identify locations by latitude and longitude, then send push notifications according to users' exact locations. Both Starbucks and 7-Eleven (a large convenience store chain) use this technology to integrate customer preferences and location information. Chinese companies spend 28% of their overall marketing budgets on modern mobile technologies.[18]

These effects of technology are nothing new though. Returning to the Sears catalog example, advances in technology doomed the retailer's strategy of mailing the same 600-page catalog to all its customers. Economies of scale from printing large batches of the same catalog were overwhelmed by small-run printing equipment that supported more low volume, cost-effective catalogs. Changes in print and manufacturing technology allowed niche firms to address narrow segments; the availability of detailed customer data supported more refined targeting; and easily searched online catalogs enabled small firms to serve very small, specialized customer segments while bypassing multiple middlemen (i.e., retailers and wholesalers).[19]

## Customer Heterogeneity: A Fundamental Assumption of Marketing Strategy

As summarized in Table 2.1, there are multiple factors that work together in multifaceted ways to make all customers differ in their preferences for products and services, and thus, customer heterogeneity is a fundamental "problem" that all firms must address when developing an effective marketing strategy. Assuming all customers are the same is a recipe for failure, at least in the long term, as competitors will better satisfy subsegments with more aligned offerings, leading to a downward spiral in which the firm has fewer, less profitable customers that are more costly to serve (e.g., Sears). The variation in customers' preferences that firms must account for in developing an effective marketing strategy represents an underlying assumption of marketing strategy, or a *First Principle* – one of "the fundamental concepts or assumptions on which a theory, system, or method is based."[20] The assumption that all customers differ and that an effective marketing strategy must manage ever-present customer heterogeneity is the first of the four Marketing Principles (MP#1).

> The assumption that *all customers differ* and that an *effective marketing strategy must manage ever-present customer heterogeneity* is Marketing Principle #1.

Still, some situations allow marketers to ignore some elements of customer heterogeneity, such as electrical utilities' one-size-fits-all offerings. The utilities can ignore differences in customers' preferences due to their monopoly power. The government typically gives utilities the sole right to provide electrical services in a specific region, so by law, no competitor may encroach on their business, and they do not need to match their offerings to customers' preferences. However, when a firm loses monopolistic power, it often finds it very difficult to start managing customer heterogeneity. The result tends to be a significant loss in both customers and sales.

**Example:** AT&T (US)

In 1984, AT&T lost its US government-granted monopoly as the sole telecommunication provider, so direct competition began, and within just two years, AT&T had to cut 27,400 employees and lost $3.2 billion in profits. By 1991, the company had lost 83% of its sales revenue.[21] Although AT&T's subsidiary Western Electric had already moved beyond offering only the classic black rotary handset (the Model T Ford of phones), launching a new handset design about once every decade, the deregulation of this market allowed for the entrance of many new competitors, determined to satisfy customer needs better. Western Electric came to an end in 1995. This pattern, in which a transition from a public to private enterprise means an increasing focus on customers after breaking up a monopoly, has been replicated in many countries around the world, including Egypt in 2015.[22]

Uber's move into the highly regulated taxi market (regulated by city versus federal governments in the US) might prove to offer a similar example. However, some firms can adapt after losing their monopoly position by increasing their focus on customers' needs. Telstra, Australia's largest telecommunications company, successfully turned around its struggling business in 2005 by implementing market-based management, as opposed to its previous product-based management. This effort involved a deeper understanding of its customers by adopting a multiple-segment approach based on consumer needs and providing offerings targeted to each segment.[23]

These examples reinforce an important point. In some markets, customer heterogeneity may be latent or hidden. Customers vary on some underlying preferences, but no firms are supplying offerings that fit their desires, so those preferences are not evident. In some cases, customers might not even know of their diverse preferences, because they have no options to evaluate. This latent customer heterogeneity, defined as potential differences in desires that are unobserved and have not yet become manifest in customer purchase preferences or behaviors, may stem from legal (government regulations, patents), economic (prohibitive prices, due to the size of market or the costs of providing), technological (only way known to make something), or innovative (no firm has yet identified and satisfied the need) constraints. Starbucks innovatively identified that customers had a wide assortment of latent needs, in terms of both coffee and the settings in which they could consume or experience it. By carefully identifying and matching customers' heterogeneous needs, it developed a $56 billion company in a category that previously sold a seemingly low-cost, commodity product.[24] If firms hope to ignore latent customer heterogeneity, their long-term success is contingent on the constraints that keep the latent needs from emerging – a reliance that history suggests is a risky strategy.

If we agree that all customers are different, even if sometimes these differences are latent, then we need to consider the ramifications for firms' marketing strategies too. First, if a firm ignores customer heterogeneity by providing offerings that fail to match customers' varying needs, then as soon as the market grows large enough, legal or technical barriers break down, or an innovative competitor provides a better fit, customers will shift to the new solution. This shift often leaves the firm with an oversized infrastructure and costs that erode its financial performance even further, on top of the losses of sales and profits. As expected, competitors first target the most profitable, fastest growing customer segments that are being poorly served, which makes losing those customers especially painful.

Second, a firm might work to deliver a range of products and services to satisfy the needs of as many different customer segments as is practical, targeting the "best" customer segments. This marketing strategy certainly can be effective, but there are typically costs and barriers to a single firm simultaneously meeting all the different customer needs. In many situations, the manufacturing process restricts a firm to certain price and performance profiles, the location and design of its stores aligns a firm with specific segments, or the effective positioning of brands across divergent segments is too difficult. When Toyota wanted to target the luxury automotive segment, it realized it could not stretch the Toyota brand image sufficiently to compete with BMW or Mercedes, so it launched Lexus, with different showrooms and a very different image, to address these customers' needs. Procter & Gamble (P&G) captures about one-third of the global market in fabric and home care products, but it does so with a vast range of brands (e.g., Ace, Ariel, Cheer, Dawn, Downy, Duracell, Gain, Tide), each with its own brand image and set of product attributes to match customers' heterogeneous needs.[25] Purposefully, P&G does not highlight for customers that it owns all of these brands, which supports stronger product differentiation than might be possible if consumers realized the products often are made in the same factory.

Third, to deal with customer heterogeneity, a firm might select a single, fairly homogeneous subgroup of customers and target just them. A true niche strategy may still require multiple offerings, but it allows firms to build a strong brand that customers in this segment know and respect. This focus can turn the firm into an expert for this type of customer, such that it can predict changes and adapt faster than firms focused more broadly on multiple segments. This customer-centric approach or strategy implies that the firm recognizes the long-term value of its customers by putting them at the core of all major business decisions. Such a niche approach is an effective way to deal with customer heterogeneity, but often limits the firm's future growth, because it is restricted to customers in just one or two segments. A market size limitation on future growth is one of the primary reasons that both Toyota and Honda launched new brands to expand from economy to luxury automotive segments (Lexus and Acura, respectively).

Another way firms try to deal with customer heterogeneity is by assuming that most customers will sacrifice many product attributes if the price is low enough, parallel to a classic low-cost strategy. These firms attempt to identify what are likely the core, must-have attributes – normally, ones that satisfy the consumer's functional needs – and then focus all of their efforts on achieving the lowest cost offering in that category. Walmart often offers only two to three products in a category and strips away many other factors that add cost (e.g., sales support, store atmospherics, location). Its success with price-sensitive consumers and in non-status product categories suggests it is a viable marketing strategy (i.e., price value and price-sensitive affluent shoppers are two of Walmart's key target segments).[26] In contrast, many other shoppers are willing to pay a significant premium to gain extra services or different product assortments. Apple deemphasizes price while striving to increase perceived quality. Moreover, Walmart has grown to the point that other firms target subsegments of its price-sensitive customer segment. As a 2014 Goldman Sachs report cautioned:

> customers are abandoning the big-box pioneer in droves ... With $469 billion in annual sales, Walmart isn't quite going out of business, but the retailer has seen sales slip for five straight quarters ... customers are looking for better deals on a more narrow assortment of goods available at stores like Costco and dollar stores.[27]

In summary, customers all differ in their preferences, and even when customer heterogeneity remains latent, in the long term, changes in the legal, economic, technological, or innovation landscape allow customers to find the products and services that best match their underlying preferences. Thus, a firm's marketing strategy must account for customer heterogeneity, or its business performance will suffer over time. The rest of this chapter focuses on the approaches, processes, and analysis tools that can help firms manage this customer heterogeneity.

# Approaches for Managing Customer Heterogeneity

## Evolution of Approaches for Managing Customer Heterogeneity

Looking back over the past 60–70 years provides insights into the evolution of approaches for managing customer heterogeneity. The general approach of grouping customers into segments, selecting target segments, and using marketing activities to improve a firm's positioning in the target segment (or STP analysis) has been around since the 1950s, and firms have targeted smaller and smaller customer segments over time. Simultaneously, the segmentation criteria have been refined, starting with demographic factors, progressing in the 1960s to include geographical and behavioral factors, and adding psychological factors in the 1970s. Today, all three types of data generally are merged, and firms' "big data" efforts provide highly refined targeting information.

As a demonstration of these trends, much of the twentieth century can be broken down into three overlapping eras, according to the most popular, if not the most prevalent, approach to managing customer heterogeneity at the time: mass marketing, niche marketing, and one-to-one marketing. Figure 2.1 describes the evolution of these approaches for dealing with customer heterogeneity.

### Mass Marketing Era

**Mass marketing (undifferentiated marketing)**, which uses mass media to appeal to an entire market with a single message, is a marketing strategy in which a firm mostly ignores customer heterogeneity, with the assumption that reaching the largest audience possible will lead to the largest sales revenue. Mass marketing became popular with the emergence of radio and television media outlets, which had the potential to deliver the same message to a larger number of consumers than was ever possible before. For example, television advertising was $12.3 million in 1949; two years later it had grown tenfold. By 1960, televisions approached 90% household penetration.[28] However, mass marketing is not individualized; it assumes everyone's preferences are the same. Typically, mass marketing generates relatively lower profit margins and response rates, and it is often accompanied by high competitive intensity. In the 1950s and 1960s, companies such as P&G, Coca-Cola, McDonald's, General Motors, and Unilever Group were all dedicated mass marketers, but as the twentieth century came to a close, most of them were shifting to more targeted approaches. James R. Stengel, P&G's global marketing officer, argues that the company no longer mass markets any of its brands, "whether it's Tide or Old Spice or Crest or Pampers or Ivory. Every one of our brands is targeted."[29]

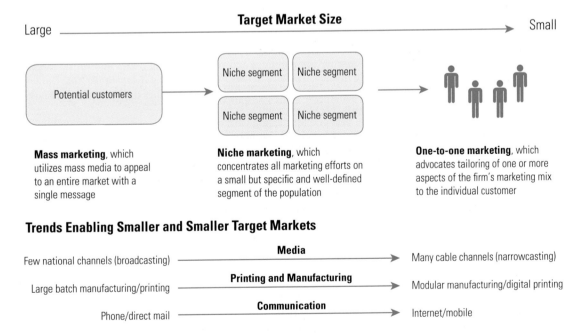

**Figure 2.1** Evolution of Approaches for Managing Customer Heterogeneity

## Niche Marketing Era

**Niche marketing** focuses marketing efforts on well-defined, narrow segments of consumers, and by specializing, this method seeks to give the firm a competitive advantage. Coming up against the limitations they confronted when they ignored customer differences, marketers recognized that a niche marketing strategy (micro-marketing) could be more effective for driving profits and withstanding competition, especially if they deployed a niche strategy against a mass marketing firm. Niche firms often receive a price premium, because they offer a "scarce" product relative to mass marketers but target a segment that a mass marketer is serving only with a general offering, instead of something that matches the subgroup's preferences. For example, Eurosport Soccer targets soccer enthusiasts with their favorite team's jersey, cleats, and even custom gear for local club teams, an assortment that is not available in department stores or even sports-focused chains like Sports Authority and Big Five Sports. Sports channels such as Fox Soccer Channel provide firms like Eurosport with an excellent medium to target a relatively homogeneous group of customers (at least as compared with NBC News or even ESPN) with advertisements for their offerings. Shifting from broadcast to cable television, with its ability to provide hundreds of channels, better supports niche communication strategies or "narrowcasting." Similar advances in printing technology and modular manufacturing processes also have enabled firms to execute niche marketing. In turn, some firms try to merge the benefits of mass marketing and niche marketing strategies. Department stores like Nordstrom and Galeries Lafayette carry a large assortment targeted to diverse, high-end customer preferences, but then they add "shop-within-a-shop" areas in their large department store formats to promote niche brands to specific customer subsegments.

Many firms successfully employ niche marketing strategies, such as Airwalk focusing on skaters in Southern California; Lululemon Athletica selling athletic wear and accessories to women; and Zumiez targeting young consumers interested in surfing, skateboarding, and snowboarding. In many cases, finding and accessing specific customers who use Internet and online searches has enabled online retailers to target relatively small niche markets quite effectively.

## One-to-one Marketing Era

The present era is marked by a shift towards one-to-one marketing, such that firms attempt to apply marketing strategies directly to specific consumers. **One-to-one marketing** tailors one or more aspects of the firm's marketing mix to the individual customer, which is an extreme form of segmentation, with a single customer in the target segment.[30] Amazon.com attempts to be a one-to-one marketer by remembering each customer's preferences and recommending books and music targeted to their tastes. In a book predicting this era, *The One to One Future: Building Relationships One Customer at a Time*, Peppers and Rogers suggest that in this new business model, rather than the share of market, firms will focus on the share of customer, one at a time.[31]

Theoretically, this strategy is the best one for dealing with customer heterogeneity, because it recognizes that all customers are different and provides a unique product or service to match each customer's preference. Continued technological advances make this approach far more feasible, but for most offerings, the added costs of providing a truly one-to-one solution, reflected in the higher price to the consumer, outweigh the added benefits that the consumer receives from an optimally aligned offering, compared with a firm that targets a subgroup of multiple similar customers with a relatively well-targeted offering. Continuing the soccer example, the extra cost of a *completely custom* jersey or cleat designed for an individual, versus the *semi-custom* offering of selecting colors and printing applied to a range of existing products, likely is not worth the benefits of complete customizability.

However, technological developments continue to enable and advance this approach. The Internet provides a powerful platform for one-to-one marketing, because each customer can be separately targeted and retargeted on the basis of their browsing history. It also allows very small firms with very small marketing budgets to cover a large geographic area. Advanced search engines permit a single customer to find a unique offering from an unknown firm. Changes in media, communication, and logistics technologies are also enabling this approach. Comcast's Spotlight service has the capability to deliver a unique advertisement to a specific user's cable box; experimental cable boxes can even detect the number and body mass of people in the room to better differentiate messaging between children and adults. As Comcast puts it: "Reaching and engaging customers today means going beyond airing a traditional ad on television … target your ideal customers … inviting viewers to connect with you one-to-one."[32] One-to-one marketing techniques are also the focus of Amazon's and Netflix's "suggestions for you" campaigns, for which they collect, store, and analyze customers' histories to make specific book and movie recommendations.

Across all three eras, the underlying method for dealing with customer heterogeneity is the same: focus on smaller and smaller groups of customers, such that the needs of each group are more similar as they get subdivided into smaller units, until the focus reaches an individual customer. Why has this trend continued? First, it delivers a product or service that better matches a customer's intrinsic preference (i.e., gives customers what they want). All else being equal, the smaller the target segment, the more closely a targeted offering will match the needs of the members of that segment.

Second, by focusing on a subsample of the overall market with mostly homogeneous customers, firms can better anticipate future needs and detect emerging trends, which allows them to respond with well-targeted solutions before their more broadly focused competitors do. For example, if one equipment supplier deals with customers that operate in multiple markets (medical, financial services, manufacturing), an emerging trend in one market (e.g., a new medical regulation) will be harder to detect and address, because this one type of customer is obscured by the large group of varied customers. However, if all of a firm's customers are in this one segment, the firm can identify the emerging issue quickly, as it affects most of its customers, and thus can address it more quickly. The launch of its new offering also might be easier and more successful, because it will appeal to most of its customers, whereas broadly focused firms might change some aspect that is not desired by many other customers. Firms do not need to focus their entire organization on one customer group to gain these benefits though. A firm can consist of business units, each of which is focused on one customer segment (customer-centric structure), then further subdivide the business unit into multiple product market groups, each focused on a relatively narrow customer group.[33]

> By focusing on a subsample of the overall market with mostly homogeneous customers, firms can better anticipate future needs and detect emerging trends, which allows them to respond with well-targeted solutions before their more broadly focused competitors do.

In many markets, in an ongoing competitive race, firms target smaller and smaller segments, limited only by the trade-off in costs against the benefits associated with providing better aligned solutions. As technology and cost trade-offs advance, marketers have responded by targeting the smallest groups feasible for a given cost–benefit ratio. Thus, for example, McDonald's is shifting from mass marketing to micro-targeting, cutting its US television advertising spending in half and moving those resources to micro-targeted campaigns, such as those using "closed-circuit sports programming piped into Hispanic bars … ads in *Upscale*, a custom-published magazine distributed to black barber shops … [and] Foot Locker Inc.'s (FL) in-store video network."[34]

## Segmenting, Targeting, and Positioning (STP) Approach

Segmenting, targeting, and positioning (STP) have been offered as a way to manage customer heterogeneity since the 1950s. However, the mechanics and analyses for executing STP have advanced significantly. In the earliest and most basic form, managers would describe each customer group according to their impressions after meeting potential and existing customers, often with a focus on the most observable customer demographics (segmenting). With this information, managers would select the segment they felt would produce the most sales and profits (targeting), then make product, pricing, channel, and promotion decisions (positioning) in relation to this target segment.

This process captures the essence of the STP approach, but it also has several weaknesses. If based on managers' beliefs rather than empirical analyses, it may be biased:

- Often, it is based on what managers want to be true versus what is actually true.
- It is weighted more toward past customer preferences, reflecting when managers developed their beliefs, rather than present or trending preferences.

- It assumes customers are more similar than is often the case.
- It focuses on firms' own customers while ignoring large, untapped groups of customers who the managers encounter less often.
- It uses customer demographics (gender, age, income) or purchase history as primary segmentation variables, because these data are more readily observable by marketers.

## Segmenting

Over time, techniques have evolved to deal with many of these potential sources of bias across each step in the STP process. Segmenting is the process of dividing the overall market into groups, such that potential customers in each group have similar needs and desires for a particular product or service category (e.g., high preference for quality and service warranties, low need for large assortments), but the differences across groups are maximal. The importance of segmentation is rarely questioned, but the mechanics of conducting a useful segmentation study also are poorly understood. The common use of demographic characteristics to describe customer segments (e.g., that TV show captures the desirable 21- to 45-year-old viewer, large versus small industrial customers in B2B markets) makes it easy to assume, mistakenly, that demographic groups *are* segments, rather than descriptors of the customers within those segments.

It is important never to lose sight of a key point though; the core goal of segmentation is to identify groups of customers who have similar needs, desires, and subsequent behaviors. These customers are similar enough that marketers can design a solution targeted to win them. For some markets, customer needs align closely with demographic characteristics; if you sell baby formula, a simple lifecycle stage segmentation likely will be useful. But for most products, any single demographic characteristic fails to clarify who does or does not have the need or desire for that product. Customers in a specific age group thus might share some preferences for clothing, but the differences in their preferences – driven by personal tastes, experiences, functional goals, and so on – so far outweigh the shared preferences that age alone is of little use as a segmentation variable. In the same way, business customers (i.e., firms) in the same industry share some common preferences, due to industry standards and similar end-customer expectations. But one business customer's unique strategy and context might cause it to emphasize cost control over all other attributes, whereas a second firm might make choices based on customer service, and a third focuses on the depth of its supplier relationship. Again, it is not that industry is unimportant, but the differences in preferences across firms within an industry far outweigh their similarities. The *initial* focus of segmentation therefore should be differentiating consumers according to their unique needs and desires (the basis of segmentation), not demographic characteristics (the descriptor of a segment).

---

The core goal of segmentation is to identify groups of customers who have similar needs, desires, and subsequent behaviors.

---

But how can firms that recognize this demand go to market through media and distribution channels that are structured to reach and serve demographically defined slices of the customer population? The ideal process follows a sequential set of steps. True customer segments are groups of customers with similar preferences (needs, desires, behaviors). Customer research thus might identify segments according to these preferences, such as through cluster analysis (i.e., a data-driven partitioning technique to segment large sets of heterogeneous customers into a few homogeneous groups). However, in the real world, firms rarely have the luxury, prior to making a sales pitch, of surveying every customer to determine their individual preferences. Instead, they might be able to capture a range of potentially relevant demographic characteristics. Once the "true" segment membership of each customer is known, a multivariate discriminant analysis can often predict segment membership reliably using just a few demographic characteristics.

Although a single, demographic variable alone cannot predict segment membership, a small set of variables might be able to do so, at least better than chance. If a useful model can be developed to classify respondents into the correct segment using only demographic factors, a little bit of magic can happen. If the research study is based on a sample of customers who truly represent the market, the researcher can have confidence applying the classification formula to real customers who were not part of the original research study. Demographic characteristics often can be observed or obtained from research vendors. With such data, firms can predict true segmentation membership, *without* surveying or reading the minds of their customers.

Several key points in this process need to be highlighted:

1  Segmentation must start with a random sample of *potential customers* in the market, not just the firm's *existing customers*, because that is the only way to understand what customers in the overall market for this product or service category want, and it is key to uncovering emerging or untapped markets.

2  Customers should be divided into groups on the basis of their *needs and desires* in the product category, not demographic variables (age, gender) or size (annual sales revenue). Knowing customers' preferences is critical to matching their needs to a solution. In many cases, demographics provide a poor indicator of a customer's true preferences and are used only because they are readily observable.

3  It is important to ensure that customers in one group have similar preferences, but it is also ideal to *maximize the differences between segments*, to help the firm offer more clearly differentiated products, without facing spillover competition from other firms that are targeting neighboring segments.

Cluster analysis refers to the primary, data-driven partitioning technique that can identify and classify a large set of heterogeneous consumers or companies into a few homogeneous segments. Although cluster analysis can rely on various attributes, here we can imagine a two-dimensional space. Let's say a sports nutrition company determines that customers of nutrition bars care about protein content and taste. Some customers trade off taste for better performance; others prioritize taste over performance, and still others prefer to balance the two. Cluster analysis uses customer preferences to cluster individual customers into a given number of groups within this two-dimensional space by simultaneously minimizing the distance from each individual customer to the center of a cluster and maximizing the distance between the centers of all clusters. In the real, more complex world, the grouping process occurs in a multidimensional space, determined by the number of purchase attributes or preferences used (price, quality, size). With a completed cluster analysis, we can consider the segmentation results, to determine whether the derived clusters make intuitive sense.

Statisticians will point out that the results of any cluster analysis are influenced (i.e., weighted more heavily) by the inclusion of multiple attributes that capture the same underlying factor. Thus, an important preceding step for any cluster analysis, depending on the number of items included in a research study, is to conduct a factor analysis of all measures of customer preferences. For example, potential customers of a new shopping center may respond to survey questions about the importance of several factors, such as the number of parking spaces, distance from their homes, late shopping hours, and the number of retailers in the shopping center. If the results of all four questions were included in the cluster analysis, more weight might be given to the higher level factor of "convenience," as captured in the first three questions, relative to the number of retailers. However, if the marketer first performed a factor analysis on all the attributes, the results might show that the first three questions are really capturing just one independent factor: convenience. In this case, just the two factors of convenience and number of retailers can be used in the cluster analysis to group potential customers into segments. The value of reducing potential customer preferences into smaller sets of independent factors, prior to conducting additional analyses, is that this step removes a potential source of bias by combining similar questions. It also makes the results more useful to managers, because the key factors become clear and are unlikely to be redundant.

Then, multiple discriminant analysis (MDA) can classify respondents into appropriate segments, using a set of demographic characteristics as predictors. If a prediction formula of sufficient accuracy can be developed, this classification process increases the overall utility of the segmentation exercise, because prospects – about whom the researcher only knows demographic characteristics – can be classified into appropriate need-based segments, using more visible demographic data. In turn, a more effective, likely to be chosen solution can be presented to the targeted customer.

In summary, the factor analysis groups similar questions (purchase attributes) together to avoid biasing the further analyses; the cluster analysis groups similar customers together into segments; and the classification analysis (MDA) predicts true segment membership using demographic variables to facilitate targeting and positioning decisions. Data Analytics Technique 2.1 offers more details about the factor analysis; Data Analytics Technique 2.2 gives a more detailed description of cluster analysis.

## Description

Factor analysis is a data reduction technique that can be used to identify a small number of latent "factors" that explain the variation in a large number of observed variables.

## When to Use It

- To condense a large pool of potential customer needs, wants, and preferences into a short set of similar characteristics.
- To reduce high correlation among predictors.

## How It Works

We begin with a large number of measured variables (e.g., 30) of customer survey measures. The factor analysis algorithm synthesizes the large number of measured variables into smaller sets (e.g., 3–4) of latent "factors" that capture the essence of the meaning in the larger number of measures. To choose the total number of factors to retain, we observe how many factors have an Eigenvalue greater than 1. The strength of the association between a measure variable and its factor is called the "factor loading." When a measured variable has a factor loading greater than 0.3, it is generally associated with a factor. We categorize the measured variable with a factor where it has the highest loading (e.g., if a measured variable has factor loadings of 0.01 and 0.8 with Factors 1 and 2, we would associate the measured variable with Factor 2). Finally, we interpret what each latent factor represents, by surmising the conceptual commonality underlying the measured variables' loading on the factor.

## Example

The manager of an online website collected customer satisfaction data from a survey of 1,000 customers on eight aspects of the company's focal product. The table shows the factor loadings of a few variables after conducting a factor analysis with three factors. Factor 1 is highly associated with product diversity, specialty, and price; thus, it can be interpreted as the "product" factor. Factor 2 is associated with cash back and discounts, and is thus labeled the "promotion" factor. For Factor 3, the "service" factor, delivery service and customer service have the highest factor loadings. The factors can be used as data input for segmentation analyses. The figure shows the focal attributes associated with each factor.

| Attribute | Factor 1 | Factor 2 | Factor 3 |
|---|---|---|---|
| Product Diversity | **0.665** | −0.016 | 0.017 |
| Product Specialty | **0.681** | −0.056 | 0.006 |
| Product Price | **0.638** | 0.284 | 0.173 |
| Cash Back | −0.042 | **0.712** | 0.051 |
| Discount | 0.216 | **0.781** | 0.103 |
| Delivery Service | −0.007 | 0.178 | **0.752** |
| Customer Service | 0.155 | 0.199 | **0.739** |

**Focal Attributes Associated with Factors**

Diversity
Specialty
Price
— Factor 1 (Product)

Cash Back
Discount
— Factor 2 (Promotion)

Delivery Service
Customer Service
— Factor 3 (Service)

## Targeting

After segmenting potential customers into homogeneous groups on the basis of their purchase preferences for a specific product or service category, a marketer needs to select segments to *target*. If segmenting is like cutting the market into slices of pie, then targeting is deciding which slice you want to eat. Specifically, each market segment is rated on two dimensions to aid the choice: market attractiveness and competitive strength. **Market attractiveness** captures external market characteristics that make a given segment strategically and financially valuable to serve, such as size, growth rate, and price sensitivity. Generally speaking, an attractive segment is equally appealing to all firms competing in that market. **Competitive strength** captures the relative strength of a firm, versus competitors, at securing and maintaining market share in a given segment. Thus, this dimension is specific to each firm's competitive situation. The two dimensions account for the three key Cs (customers, competitors, and company), which are central to a situational analysis. By evaluating the market attractiveness and competitive strength of each segment of potential customers, a manager can weigh their desirability against the firm's ability to win them, then select the segment or segments to target. An ideal target segment should meet six criteria:

1 Based on customer needs – customers care.
2 Different than other segments – little crossover competition.
3 Differences match firm's competencies – firm can execute within resource constraints.
4 Sustainable – can keep customers from switching to the competition.
5 Customers are identifiable – can find targeted customers.
6 Financially valuable – valuable in the long term.

> If segmenting is like cutting the market into slices of pie, then targeting is deciding which slice you want to eat.

Firms often target multiple segments simultaneously with different offerings to match different customer preferences and gain access to a larger market space. In some cases, a firm can use similar or related brands with different offerings and price points. For example, Marriot targets price-sensitive, frequent business travelers with Courtyard Marriott properties but goes after high-income vacationers with Marriott Resort Club properties. In other situations, two segments might be mutually exclusive, making it difficult for one firm or brand to address them, as the failed example of Gallo Winery's attempt to enter the high-end wine segment showed. Targeting helps a firm manage customer heterogeneity by purposely focusing its efforts on customers that are more similar and aligned with its own capabilities.

The **GE matrix** is one analysis tool designed to help managers visualize and select target segments. Figure 2.2 provides an example of an analysis by an athletic wear firm, in which the y-axis indicates market attractiveness, the x-axis indicates the competitive strength of each segment, and the size of each "bubble" reflects the size of the market segment. Large segments in the upper-right corner of the graph are the "best," and those in the lower-left corner represent the "worst" segments for this firm.

## Positioning

The last step in the STP approach involves the process of improving a firm's relative advantage in the minds of its targeted customers. Positioning entails changing both the actual offering (innovating products or reducing manufacturing costs) and the perceived offering (building a new brand image). Nearly every marketing mix decision, including product, price, place (channel), and product activities (often termed the 4Ps), that managers make affects the positioning of the firm's offering in customers' minds.

> Nearly every marketing mix decision, including product, price, place (channel), and product activities (often termed the 4Ps), that managers make affects the positioning of the firm's offering in customers' minds.

### Description

Cluster analysis is a data-driven partitioning technique that can be used to identify and classify a large set of heterogeneous consumers or companies into a small number of homogeneous segments.

### When to Use It

- To demystify customer heterogeneity by understanding preference commonalities across subsets of customers.
- To discover how consumers naturally differ and cater to the unique needs of chosen target customer segments.

### How It Works

Cluster analysis usually consists of two steps: segmenting and describing. To perform these two steps, we need to collect two kinds of variables: bases and descriptors. Bases, such as desired product features or pricing requirements, provide the foundations for segmenting consumers according to their differences. Descriptors, such as demographic and geographic information, serve to profile and eventually target the derived segment.

1 In the *segmentation step*, we identify underlying subsamples of customers that are homogeneous in their bases (e.g., ratings on product preferences) and markedly different from other subsamples. For example, customers in one cluster might have very high preferences for quality and do not mind paying a high price, but customers in another cluster may be very value conscious and refuse to pay high prices.

2 In the *describing step*, we use descriptor variables to explain how the subsamples differ and thereby can derive efficient targeting strategies, tailored to each subsample. For example, customers in the quality cluster might be mostly men in their early forties, whereas those in the price cluster are mostly women in their early twenties. Using both bases and descriptor variables, we can discover how customers differ, which customers to target, and what marketing program to use.

Marketing Engineering, SAS, and SPSS software packages are tools that can help conduct the segmenting step; and K-means and hierarchical clustering are approaches to enable cluster analyses.

After the cluster analysis is done, a review of the segmentation results should determine whether the derived clusters make intuitive sense. Evaluations of the validity of the segmentation results and corresponding targeting strategy should consider the following important criteria:

- *Identifiability*: Do the derived segments represent real segments of customers, and can they be profiled using descriptors?
- *Stability*: Are the derived segments likely to change rapidly over time?
- *Responsiveness*: Will each targeted segment respond to the planned marketing strategies?
- *Viability*: Can the company achieve its desired financial objectives with the segmentation scheme?

**Example 1**

Imagine there are five customers, rated on their intention to purchase (1–15 scale). A hierarchical clustering procedure, based on Ward's minimum variance criteria to minimize the sum of the square of errors, starts by assuming each customer is its own cluster. However, combining customers 3 and 4 seems intuitive since they have similar purchase intentions and it results in limited loss of information (0.5 on the dendogram). Similarly, combining customers 1 and 2 results in limited loss of information (4.5). Thus, five customers could be combined into three segments (1,2), (3,4), and (5). If we then try to combine (3,4) and (5) as one customer, the loss of information (25.8) is prohibitive. Thus, we stop at three segments (1,2), (3,4), and (5).

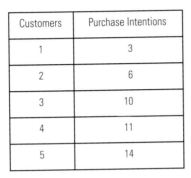

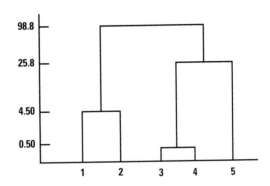

| Customers | Purchase Intentions |
|-----------|---------------------|
| 1 | 3 |
| 2 | 6 |
| 3 | 10 |
| 4 | 11 |
| 5 | 14 |

**Example 2**

A company conducted an annual customer satisfaction survey for an advertised product, collecting perceptions of the product's price, quality, and distribution (on a 5-point scale). To improve customer satisfaction and design more efficient targeting strategies, the company conducted a partition-based clustering analysis of the data and thereby identified three segments: consumers who are dissatisfied on all three attributes (Segment 1), consumers who are highly satisfied on all three attributes (Segment 2), and consumers who are highly satisfied on quality and distribution but dissatisfied on price (Segment 3). The table gives the mean statistics for each segment.

|  | Price | Quality | Distribution |
|--|-------|---------|--------------|
| Segment 1 | 1.82 | 1.97 | 2.95 |
| Segment 2 | 4.31 | 4.05 | 4.57 |
| Segment 3 | 2.75 | 4.45 | 4.32 |

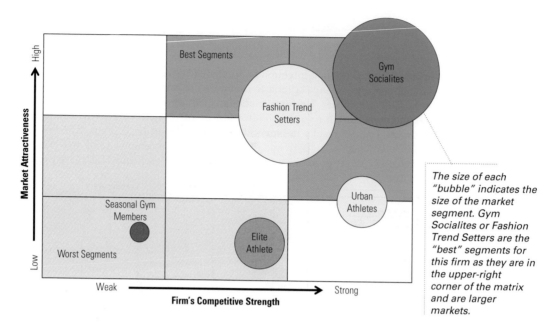

**Figure 2.2** GE Matrix: Analysis Tool for Targeting

Product design and performance represent perhaps the most straightforward way to change an offering's position. Firms like Apple and Bose have large R&D budgets to achieve the high-performance, cool images they strive for and that their target customers prefer. When Samsung wanted to shift the image of its electronics upmarket, it removed its products from Kmart stores, because its target customers' perceptions of Kmart likely were inconsistent with the desired positioning strategy. Many high-end retailers (Gucci, Tiffany) never or infrequently have sales on their products; they want to maintain a brand image of exclusivity. Although they are often less tangible, promotional activities (e.g., advertising, public relations) also can change an offering's position in customers' minds, by informing customers of specific product attributes and changing customer perceptions of the product. For example, a tagline for an advertising campaign that Clairol ran in the 1950s asked: "Does she ... or doesn't she? Hair color so natural only her hairdresser knows for sure." The campaign not only expanded the hair coloring market significantly (eightfold sales growth in a short period) and changed people's perceptions about their own and others' hair color, but it also positioned Clairol strongly in customers' minds, a dominant position it continues to enjoy today.[35]

Positioning also helps a firm manage customer heterogeneity because it can use the marketing mix variables to position or reposition both tangible and intangible elements of its offering to align with the target segment's preferences. A well-positioned product should offer target customers the best fitting solution, relative to competitors; in many cases, it therefore provides a robust barrier to future competitive attacks. In essence, targeting is a coarse selection process: firms select a customer segment that roughly matches their offering and existing brand image. But positioning is the fine-tuning adjustment process that firms can use to adjust perceptions of their own offering and change customers' actual preferences or decision criteria to best align their offerings with the target segment's preferences. Positioning strategies are implemented over time and may take years to achieve.

To visualize and develop effective positioning strategies, many marketers use **perceptual maps**, which depict customer segments, competitors, and a firm's own position in a multidimensional space, defined by the purchase attributes identified during the segmentation process. Figure 2.3 is an example of a firm's perceptual map, before and after a repositioning effort. **Repositioning** refers to the process by which a firm shifts its target market. Consider, for example, how Abercrombie & Fitch had repositioned itself by 2012:

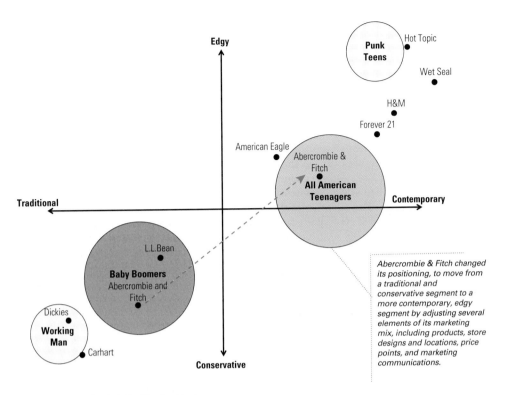

**Figure 2.3** Perceptual Map: Analysis Tool for Positioning

As a baby boomer, I remember Abercrombie & Fitch. It was a very traditional, outdoorsy, hunt club oriented brand. It felt a little bit like L.L. Bean or Orvis. Today, it is a completely different brand. It is hot and sexy and targets teens. In fact, not too long ago it was in the news for the controversy around its featuring semi-nude models at the entrances to its mall stores.[36]

Faced with more recent sales declines, this retailer again is repositioning: removing logos from its clothing, turning up the lights in stores, and putting more clothing on models.[37]

Firms often find it helpful to write a **positioning statement,** to capture the key marketing decisions to appeal to customers in the firm's target segment. Three questions should be addressed in a positioning statement:

1 *Who* are the customers?
2 *What* is the set of needs that the product or service fulfills?
3 *Why* is this product/service the best option to satisfy customer needs (relative to the competition or a substitute)?

Thus, a succinct template for a positioning statement might be: "*For [target segment] the [product/concept] provides [benefit], which [compelling reasons for buying versus competition].*" This statement then becomes the roadmap for a plethora of implementation decisions involved in marketing a product or service, both inside and outside the company. In larger firms, different groups of employees design, implement, or affect customer perceptions, so a clear positioning statement is critical to aligning everyone's decisions and actions. Inconsistency across sales organizations, advertising materials, channel members, and product management has the potential to undermine the effectiveness of an otherwise well-designed positioning strategy. As a powerful external and internal communication tool, the positioning statement instead provides clear guidance to everyone involved, thereby minimizing the potential that any employee or outside vendor will make decisions incongruent with the firm's positioning strategy.

For Kellogg's Nutri-Grain cereal bars, the positioning statement reads: "For people on the go who want to eat healthy, Nutri-Grain is the cereal bar that is a healthy snack you can eat on the run. That's because Nutri-Grain is made with real fruit and more of the whole grains your body needs and comes in individually wrapped packages that you can eat anywhere."[38] It addresses the three key questions: Who – "For people on the go who want to eat healthy." What – "Nutri-Grain is the cereal bar that is a healthy snack you can eat on the run." Why – "Nutri-Grain is made with real fruit and more of the whole grains your body needs and comes in individually wrapped packages that you can eat anywhere."

Thus, the STP approach allows a firm to address MP#1 by first segmenting potential customers into relatively homogeneous groups based on individual preferences. In so doing, firms understand how customers' preferences vary in the marketplace and develop a map of customer heterogeneity. The number and size of customer segments determines the precision and resulting complexity of this map. The firm then selects segment(s) that are attractive to target, because the firm can build a strong position there. The selection of this relatively homogeneous segment to target means the firm does not need to address customer preferences in other, non-targeted segments. Such focus enables the firm to deal effectively with customer variability. As an alternative, the firm could group all potential customers together and try to develop and launch an offering that matches the average needs of all customers' preferences, although in this case, no single customer segment is well served. Finally, the firm develops and executes a positioning strategy that aligns all marketing activities surrounding the offering to match customers' preferences and influence customers' decision criteria. This final refinement ensures that the firm's offering is the best fitting solution for targeted customers. Firms often start with relatively simple maps, which then become more precise and complex over time. The Royal Bank of Canada (RBC) started with just three segments in 1992. Today, it has more than 80 segments that are updated monthly and guide nearly all marketing and business decisions.[39]

The STP process can also be conducted at different levels of analysis within a firm. For example, a firm can undertake the process to define its position in the overall marketplace. It also can perform it for each of the firm's major products or service categories, although these more detailed, lower level STP analyses must be consistent and supportive of the firm's overall position. For example, Honda should have an overall positioning strategy relative to all other automotive manufacturers, and it should have a positioning strategy for its minivan lines.

## Customer-centric Approach

A more continuous, ongoing approach for managing customer heterogeneity, compared with conducting an STP analysis, is the customer-centric approach. The customer-centric approach is a company-wide philosophy that places customers' needs at the center of an organization's strategic process and uses the insights to make decisions. Being customer centric requires a firm to align multiple aspects of its organization to be consistent with this philosophy, including leadership, structure, culture, metrics, processes, and strategy. The critical first step is for senior leadership to adopt this perspective and make customer-centric decisions. Next, the firm organizes around homogeneous customer groups (i.e., customer-centric structure) and uses the relatively homogeneous input from customers to drive marketing decisions within each customer-centric business unit.

Whereas the STP approach promotes the notion that firms' offerings should match customer preferences (external alignment), it does not address whether the firm's internal organizational design enables or supports actions that align with target segments' needs or positioning strategies. In essence, the customer-centric approach constitutes an enabler or execution step, promoting customer preferences throughout the organization in the aftermath of the STP process. It promotes *internal* alignment after the STP approach has established *external* alignment. The benefits from linking these two approaches – that is, aligning external and internal perspectives – is captured by an RBC executive: "While lots of companies claim they're customer-centric, RBC is one of just a handful of organizations that segment customers based on customer needs, not their own. And by focusing its operations on

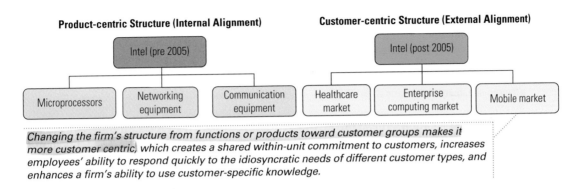

Figure 2.4 Restructuring for Customer Centricity

addressing those needs, RBC has grown its market capitalization from $18 billion almost six years ago to close to $50 billion today."[40]

Accordingly, the use of customer-centric structures among Fortune 500 firms has grown by more than half.[41] As shown in Figure 2.4, Intel made the shift in 2005, with the promise that "rather than relying on a structure focused on the company's discrete product lines, Intel's reorganization will bring together engineers, software writers, and marketers into five market-focused units: corporate computing, the digital home, mobile computing, healthcare, and channel products – PCs for small manufacturers."[42] Customer-centric firms not only structure themselves around customers but also use customer-focused metrics (e.g., net promoter score, customer satisfaction) and seek to build processes to link customer data to all aspects of the firm. Andy Taylor, the CEO of Enterprise Rent-A-Car, argues that by measuring and reporting monthly net promoter scores across the company's 5000 branches and regions, it maintains a customer-centric focus.[43]

Customer centricity offers both benefits and some disadvantages. A customer-centric approach aligns each business entity with a specific customer group, which increases the firm's knowledge of and commitment to each customer segment. Shared customer-specific knowledge positions the firm favorably to identify any unmet needs and enables it to adapt quickly and effectively to changing needs.[44] In contrast, organizations that lack alignment find it difficult to sense changes that might affect a targeted customer segment, which can reduce their speed in responding to emerging trends. Because customer-centric organizations develop richer customer knowledge and greater commitment to each targeted customer segment, they achieve improved customer satisfaction and loyalty. However, customer-centric organizations also need more resources to support their communication and decision-making processes, because of the complex internal organization and the loss of economies of scale. Furthermore, the detrimental effects of duplication and complexity in customer-centric organizations usually lead to higher internal costs.

Successful customer centricity depends on a strong **market orientation** – the organization-wide generation of market intelligence, dissemination of the intelligence across departments and organization-wide responsiveness to it. Market orientation is a popular way to capture an aspect of a firm's customer centricity that enhances firm performance.[45] According to one conceptualization, a market orientation comprises three dimensions:

1 Intelligence generation – "We often meet with customers to understand their future needs"
2 Intelligence dissemination – "There is a high level of communication among our employees about customers"
3 Responsiveness – "We respond quickly to customer needs."[46]

Thus, a market orientation implies that a firm can capture customer preferences, communicate these needs throughout the organization, and use the information to target their needs, all of which allows the firm to match customer needs better.

**Example:** Sainsbury's (UK)
..........................................................................................................

By talking to customers and employees, Sainsbury's, the UK's second largest supermarket, realized that customers' purchase decisions were based on three key factors: product quality, ease of shopping, and access to multichannel interfaces. The supermarket was then able to respond appropriately, by investing in R&D to improve product quality, store location as a key driver to shopping convenience, and IT infrastructure to improve customers' seamless transition across channels.[47]

In summary, customer centricity grants an organization deep knowledge about and commitment to a relatively homogeneous group of customers, supporting faster detection and responses to changing market conditions. This continuous and real-time responsiveness is built into the organization's structure, culture, and processes, and customer-centric metrics provide quick feedback to any misalignments. But focusing on a narrow customer group means that other changes, beyond this customer segment, often are not visible. A customer-centric organization even may grow so committed to a market segment that it becomes unable to evaluate alternative customer segments objectively. Along with the higher internal costs, these aspects constitute the clear weaknesses of this approach. With the STP approach, the firm instead gains a more holistic view and can better weight the pros and cons of targeted versus non-targeted market segments. Conducting an externally focused STP analysis every few years across customers and non-customers, then allowing for continuous and rapid internal adjustments by a customer-centric organization, represents a balanced way to manage customer heterogeneity.

## Framework for Managing Customer Heterogeneity

Figure 2.5 contains an organizing framework for managing customer heterogeneity, which integrates the preceding approaches and analyses. Three key inputs to the framework are needed to conduct segmentation, targeting, and positioning on potential customers. The framework also generates three outputs, which then are used as inputs to the last two marketing principles. Specifically, this framework maps out the key customer segments for an industry or product category based on customer preferences, the firm's selected target segments, and the positioning statement that defines its positioning strategy for each target segment. Finally, this section outlines a step-by-step process and example for using this framework to transform inputs into outputs.

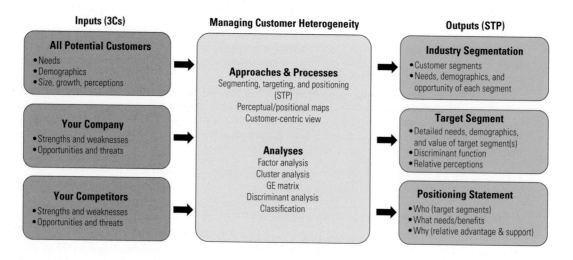

**Figure 2.5** Marketing Principle #1: All Customers Differ → Managing Customer Heterogeneity

## Inputs to the Managing Customer Heterogeneity Framework

The first input refers to *needs, desires, and preferences across customers* in an industry, geographic region, market segment, or product category. Firms often survey potential customers to capture customer preferences across relevant purchase attributes (the basis for segmentation). When entering new markets or after dramatic market turbulence, firms should start with qualitative approaches (focus groups, interviews, market observations) to identify all relevant decision attributes, before capturing more detailed input about the importance of the various attributes. *Demographic information* (gender, age, income, zip codes) and descriptors of a segment then can identify targeted customers during the implementation of acquisition strategies (see Chapter 3). In larger markets or industries (e.g., cell phones, automotive, retail), market research consultants conduct generic segmentation analyses and sell the results to multiple industry participants.

Customers also might provide their *perceptions of specific firms and brands in the marketplace across key attributes*, for use in perceptual maps. Segmentation focuses on customer preferences for attributes, independent of specific firms or brands; perceptual maps capture customers' perceptions of existing brands on the same key attributes. Finally, customer input helps the firm determine segment attractiveness, such as growth rate and price sensitivity information. Such attractiveness information often comes from multiple sources, including customer surveys, marketing industry reports, and other secondary sources.

The next sets of inputs are similar, but whereas one focuses on the focal company, the other pertains to its competitors in the relevant category or industry. In both cases, an *inventory of the company's and competitors' strengths and weaknesses* is needed to evaluate the firm's relative competitive strength, in support of the targeting and positioning processes. Company and competitor strengths and weaknesses should span all relevant domains – manufacturing, technical, financial, marketing, sales, research, legal, or any other domain that could be leveraged as a relative competitive advantage. Company and competitor strengths and weaknesses should be collected together with *opportunities and threats in a classic* **SWOT analysis** (strengths, weaknesses, opportunities, and threats). All four factors can inform a firm's targeting and positioning efforts. (Data Analytics Technique 2.3 describes the SWOT and 3Cs analysis frameworks.) For example, if a firm sells in the consumer package goods market, it may prefer to rate market segments smaller than $250 million higher than larger segments in the targeting process, recognizing the increased threat posed by the market leader P&G if it were to enter the larger segments.

Overall, the inputs to the managing customer heterogeneity framework represent the *3Cs of situation analysis*. Customers, company, and competitors together represent the key contextual background in which a firm's strategy must operate. A firm's marketing strategy is embedded in this background and must both "fit" and "leverage" customers' preferences and perceptions, market trends, and the firm's relative strengths to be effective.

## Outputs of Managing Customer Heterogeneity Framework

The managing customer heterogeneity framework applies one or more different approaches to the three inputs to generate three outputs (see Figure 2.5 above). The first output, *industry segmentation*, describes industry segments and includes, for each named segment, salient purchase preferences, demographic variables, and potential demand opportunities. This output is critical; it maps the potential customer landscape according to two key questions:

1 How can the marketplace be described using homogeneous groups?
2 What does each group of potential customers want?

The second output moves from the overall market landscape to the specific segment(s) of interest, such that it extends the first output by providing a very detailed description of each *target segment*. In so doing, it provides insight into the value or attractiveness of the focal segment and the firm's relative strength, as well as how each target group perceives the firm and its competitors. Targeted customers can be identified on the basis of a detailed description of preferences and demographics, and this

# SWOT and 3C Analyses

## Description

SWOT appraises the *strengths*, *weaknesses*, *opportunities*, and *threats* that affect a company's success. The 3C analysis evaluates customers, competitors, and the company itself.

## When to Use It

- To assess strategic marketing decisions by identifying critical internal and external environmental factors that will contribute to the success or failure of the strategy.
- A SWOT analysis assesses the internal and external nature of the business, looking at current and future situations.
- The 3C analysis emphasizes the need to focus on these three perspectives to gain competitive advantages.

## Inputs

- **External (Environmental) Factors**: relevant legal structure, competitor's core competencies and market share, changes in customer demographics
- **Internal (Company-level) Factors**: core competencies, market share, competitive advantages

## How It Works

### SWOT Analysis

| Internal | Explanation | Strategy Implications |
|---|---|---|
| Strengths | Current strengths, such as a strong financial performance or a reputed brand | The firm can develop new products to leverage these strengths |
| Weaknesses | Current weaknesses, such as a slow customer response rate | Strategies need to be implemented to eliminate these weaknesses |

| External | Explanation | Strategy Implications |
|---|---|---|
| Opportunities | Future opportunities, such as environmental factors that may work in the company's favor | Strategies need to be devised to take advantage of the potential opportunities |
| Threats | Future threats, such as increasing competition | Strategies need to be devised to overcome the threats, such as lowering prices or increasing promotions |

### 3C Analysis

Company
- Competencies
- Aspirations
- Resources

Customers
- Who are the customers?
- What are the needs of various customer segments?

Competitors
- What are competitors offering?
- What can we offer that competitors cannot?

**Strategy implications for 3C analysis**

- What can the company offer to meet the needs of customers?
- How can the company position itself beneficially against competitors?

**Example**

The managers of a bakery wish to open a new store in a neighborhood across town. They perform a SWOT and 3C analysis of the environment to assess the obstacles they may face.

**SWOT Analysis**

| **Strengths**<br>Differentiated by well-known, house-baked sourdough | **Weaknesses**<br>New store location has limited parking |
| --- | --- |
| **Opportunities**<br>Grocery store opening next to bakery, drawing in many new potential customers | **Threats**<br>Competition is well established and has a loyal, local customer base |

**3C Analysis**

| Company | Customers | Competitors |
| --- | --- | --- |
| The *company* itself is known for its house-baked sourdough bread. Production costs are very high though | Potential *customers* in the new neighborhood are primarily high-income families with small children | *Competitors* in the neighborhood include a donut shop and a café with a selection of locally baked goods |

"story" transforms the customer segment into more than a list of statistics. Thus, the second output addresses two additional questions:

1 What set of segments will the firm pursue?
2 How does the firm identify each group of target customers?

Discriminant and classification analyses provide an empirical approach for identifying target customers, using publicly available data versus surveys or other techniques that are not viable for acquiring new customers (due to their lack of purchase history).

Discriminant analysis uses the same segmentation sample to build a model and evaluate the firm's ability to identify a customer's cluster or segment on the basis of accessible demographic variables. Segmentation relies on customer purchase preferences; discriminant analysis tries to identify a customer's segment according to a model of demographic variables. The technique

## Data Analytics Technique 2.4

# Discriminant and Classification Analyses

### Description

Discriminant and classification analyses are multivariate statistical techniques used to determine how segments of consumers differ in their characteristics.

### When to Use It

- To classify a large set of customers into small subgroups that have different characteristics.
- To predict or classify which subgroup a new customer belongs to, so as to better target marketing activities.

### How It Works

Discriminant function analysis is commonly used to describe which predictor variables help differentiate two or more segments of customers. Let us assume that through a prior cluster analysis, the firm has a good understanding of how many segments of customers they deal with every day. By doing cluster analysis, the firm can also classify which segment each customer belongs to; every customer can be assigned either to the quality segment or the value segment. However, discriminant analysis usually follows cluster analysis. Managers using discriminant analysis collect numerous variables about customers (e.g., demographics, often used marketing channels) to describe why a customer falls in a certain segment.

Thus, the dependent variable for discriminant analysis is a categorical variable (i.e., the segment number of a customer), and the independent variables are customer characteristics (e.g., demographics, often used marketing channels). Written as an equation, discriminant analysis is given as:

$$Y_1(x) = \beta_{11} \cdot x_1 + \dots \beta_{1k} x_k$$
$$Y_h(x) = \beta_{h1} \cdot x_1 + \dots \beta_{hk} x_k,$$

In the above equations, the firm has a total of $h$ segments and any $Y_i(x)$ is a binary variable equal to 1 if a customer belongs to the $i^{th}$ segment, and 0 otherwise. Next, the firm uses a total of $k$ profiling variables, and hence every $x_i$ denotes an independent variable. The outputs of the analysis are the weights $\beta_{ij}$, which captures the influence the $j^{th}$ independent variable has in categorizing a customer into the $i^{th}$ segment. If we have $h$ total segments and $k$ total independent variables, we will have $h \times k$ total weights.

produces an estimated percentage of accuracy for predicting a customer segment with a given set of demographic variables. If that accuracy level is acceptable, the discriminant function can be applied to the same demographic variables among other, non-surveyed customers to predict their segment in a **classification analysis**. This process is critical to effective acquisition strategies (see Chapter 3). Data Analytics Technique 2.4 provides an overview of discriminant and classification analysis techniques.

The third output is *positioning statements*, which encapsulate the three key questions into one concise statement that firms use to direct their internal and external marketing activities: Who should the firm target? What needs and benefits are being fulfilled? Why does this offering provide a relative advantage over competitive offerings? Position statements should be developed for the firm overall, as well as for each key target segment it addresses. A positioning statement captures the essence of the firm's positioning strategy for a target segment.

The weights can be interpreted as similar to regression weights; the higher the value of a certain weight $b_i$, the stronger the association between the corresponding predictor $x_i$, and the segment membership. The real usefulness of discriminant analysis is when a firm encounters a customer on whom they did not conduct cluster analysis. The firm observes $x_i$, and knowing that some $x$s are more likely to be associated with certain membership in certain segments lets a firm classify a customer into a segment, even without doing a cluster analysis again.

### Example

A company conducted cluster analysis using a sample of 2,000 customers with regard to the product's price and quality. The company found two dominant segments in their customer base; customers in one segment (quality segment) might have very high preferences for quality and do not mind paying a high price, but customers in another cluster may be very value conscious and refuse to pay high prices (value segment).

To further examine how to profile these derived segments, the company conducts a discriminant analysis using two measures: number of years in business with the customer $(X_1)$ and market value $(X_2)$. The estimated linear score functions for each segment are:

$$\text{Quality segment: } 0.52x_1 - 0.58x_2$$
$$\text{Value segment: } -0.12x_1 + 1.25x_2$$

By conducting discriminant analysis, the company now is able to interpret what each segment stands for. The quality segment represents customers that have small market value (given the negative coefficient $-0.58$) and have been in business with the company for a long time (given the positive coefficient 0.52). The value segment represents customers that have large market value (given the large positive coefficient 1.25) and is associated with customers that have been in business with the company for a short time (given the negative coefficient $-0.12$). The company would now know how to identify Segments 1 and 2, and therefore classify customers into two segments by simply observing their market value as well as their length of relationship with the customer.

The process of converting the customer, company, and competitor (3Cs) input into industry segmentation, target segments, and positioning statement (STP) outputs is critical for developing a marketing strategy. It allows firms to make sense of the customer landscape by identifying a manageable number of homogeneous customer groups, such that the firm can meaningfully evaluate its relative strengths and make strategically critical decisions about how to win these customers. Almost all subsequent decisions build on this first step, because it accounts for customer heterogeneity, customer attractiveness, and the company's relative advantage.

The STP approach mirrors Sun Tzu's ancient guidance in the *Art of War*: segmenting, targeting, and positioning is the process for "finding" the best approach (target segment) to navigate the terrain (all customer segments) to fight the enemy (competitors) and gain relative advantage (differential advantage).[48]

## Process for Managing Customer Heterogeneity

To convert the inputs into outputs, marketers conduct a series of process steps. We describe each step in detail here, but various trade-offs and analysis options make the process less straightforward than it might appear. A trade-off that occurs at each step is the need to balance precision with simplicity. Virtually every customer segment can be divided further into more subsegments, but at some point, doing so makes the overall STP analysis very complex to understand and communicate, such that it hinders the firm's ability to develop feasible, executable marketing strategies. An initial STP analysis therefore should lean toward simplicity. Once the strategy is operating smoothly, a marketer can go back and refine it iteratively.

Furthermore, some steps in the STP and customer-centric processes for managing customer heterogeneity can be skipped, depending on the firm's specific situation. The process also can be applied at multiple levels (firm, geography, product), throughout the organization. In this section, we outline the process for a firm competing in a single product category; larger organizations can duplicate this process for multiple business units or categories as needed. Figure 2.5 above provides a visual depiction of the first three steps of the process.

### Step 1: Segmenting

To initiate the segmentation, managers need to *identify the key purchase attributes*, that is, the needs and desires that a potential customer evaluates when making a purchase decision for this category. It is important to focus not primarily on existing customers but rather on all potential customers of this product. The ideal approach depends on the stability of the category and the firm's existing knowledge in it. If customer needs are constantly in turmoil or it is a new market, conducting focus groups with potential customers, interviews, or observational approaches can help ensure that no attributes or newly emerging preferences are missed, due to the firm's preconceived ideas about what customers care about.

With the list of purchase attributes in hand, the manager should start collecting *responses from a random sample of potential customers about the importance of these attributes* to their purchase decision. In consumer and some B2B markets, this data collection often relies on an online survey, but it also can be done with face-to-face structured interviews or intercept surveys, depending on the type and availability of potential customers. The sample must be random and representative of the overall marketplace to ensure that the results can be generalized. If the sample is biased toward a firm's existing customers or other types of respondents (e.g., certain incomes, ages, or gender), the results will not reflect the true marketplace. In B2B markets, responses from multiple decision makers in a buying center must be integrated to gain an overall picture of the purchase process.

Next, managers should *analyze the data by grouping similar questions (factor analysis)* and *grouping similar customers (cluster analysis)*, which will often reveal three to eight homogeneous customer groups. The number of segments ultimately depends on the results and the firm's ability to understand and communicate with multiple segments. Recall that Data Analytics Techniques 2.1 and 2.2 provide detailed descriptions of factor and cluster analyses. These analyses pertain to customers' needs and desires, not on demographic variables, but when completed, the demographics of each segment need

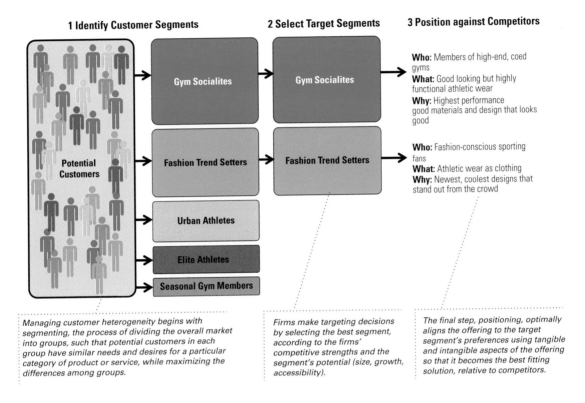

**Figure 2.6** Example of Managing Customer Heterogeneity

to be evaluated to describe them comprehensively. This step also helps the firm name each segment, which makes it easier to communicate the category segmentation throughout the organization. In Figure 2.6, we provide a visual representation of how the athletic wear firm from Figure 2.2 groups its potential customers in five segments: Gym Socialites, Fashion Trend Setters, Urban Athletes, Elite Athletes, and Seasonal Gym Members.

Firms can collect and analyze customer data themselves, or they might engage an outside market research firm to design the instrument, collect data, and analyze customer responses. However, "outsourcing" the segmentation process creates some concerns:

1  Some market research firms specialize in specific industry or product markets, which allows them to spread the cost of their research across multiple firms. But they also offer the same results to competitive firms at the same time, so no single firm gains unique or timelier insights into customer segments or trends, relative to competitors.

2  Market research firms have little insight into the trade-offs or potential subsegments that may not appear in aggregate reports but could be critical to a firm's existing or future marketing strategy.

3  Lack of access to a good sample of potential customers is a key reason that firms outsource segmentation studies, but market research firms face the same challenge. Because it is not in the interest of these firms to acknowledge the poor quality of their sample or results, they might not weight the robustness of the findings properly.

4  Good marketing strategies typically require multiple iterations over time as the firm learns and integrates key insights into its strategy, then collects feedback on the effects of its new strategic initiatives, over and over again. This iterative learning process comes to a halt if the firm only receives packaged reports from a market research firm on different customer segments every few years.

## Step 2: Targeting

The targeting process follows naturally from segmentation, to *identify which segments the firm wants to sell to, based on the attractiveness of each segment and the firm's competitive strength in each segment.* The firm must choose the factors and weights of each factor to determine a rating of the attractiveness and competitive strength of the segments. In some cases, the ratings can be mined from secondary sources (e.g., census data on size and growth of certain groups); in other cases, questions in the segmentation survey aid the targeting (e.g., price sensitivity, growth rate, relative perceptions of firm's brand). An average of managers' rating of factors across each segment also might be informative. In turn, these ratings can be analyzed in the GE matrix described earlier (see Figure 2.2 above).

Firms often want to select multiple segments to target, to access a larger share of the market, but the number of segments a firm can effectively target often is limited:

1 Customers' preferences may be mutually exclusive, such that one segment wants low prices and few features (value segment) and another segment wants high status and exclusivity (status-seeking segment). It would be hard for a firm to develop a brand image consistent with each group's preferences.
2 Firms may be limited by their core competencies and available resources. A firm that has always been a follower in an industry and offers very good service and support may find it hard to become a technology leader, because it simply lacks the internal R&D capabilities to innovate radically.
3 Firms can lose focus if they attempt to satisfy too many market segments; they end up not committed to or knowledgeable about any one segment, because they simultaneously target too many different segments. The ultimate judges of whether a firm is effectively targeting a segment are customers in that segment, who choose the firm's product over a competitor's. But it can be difficult to compete in multiple segments against multiple different firms, each of which might focus solely on that one segment.

Returning to the visual representation of the athletic wear firm in Figure 2.6, we find that the firm targets two segments: Gym Socialites and Fashion Trend Setters. These segments were selected on the basis of their attractiveness, as well as the firm's relative strengths versus competitors'.

## Step 3: Positioning

The separation between targeting and positioning is often blurry. Many of the factors used to evaluate competitive strengths to select a target segment also impact the difficulty of executing an effective positioning strategy for that segment. In its simplest form, positioning involves adjusting a firm's offering (tangible and intangible factors) to match the targeted segment's preferences, so *a key first step is to identify any existing gap between desired attributes and perceived attributes.* If the gap is too large or too difficult to overcome, the firm may not want to target the segment, even if it seems very attractive. If it decides to target this segment, the firm must recognize that significant resources and time will need to be devoted to the execution of this strategy.

A positioning analysis can be facilitated by visual representations of customer perceptions. *Perceptual maps are an excellent tool for visualizing* both gaps in the offerings for a target market and the firm's relative position (see Figure 2.3 above). Some of the data for perceptual maps can come from the data collection used in the segmentation analysis, but they often require additional input. For example, critical purchase attributes are not known or refined until after the factor and cluster analyses, so new surveys need to be designed and executed. Additional data collections also can increase the sample size in the targeted segment. Ideally, only customers in a specific target segment should appear in the perpetual map for that segment. With additional data collections, it also is possible to keep the initial survey short, which should improve response rates, because it is often difficult to get enough people to complete very long surveys that attempt to perform segmentation, targeting, and positioning all at once.

To draw positioning maps, marketers need to ask the customers in a targeted segment about their perceptions of how well firms in this segment satisfy important attributes, and their overall preferences for purchasing from each firm. With this information, managers can draw perceptual maps and thereby

1 identify key competitors,
2 determine how much to change key product attributes to move products into more favorable positions, and
3 visually determine the impact of their communications programs on market perceptions.

Positioning or repositioning involves moving the firm or its offering to the center of the target segment, using marketing activities such as the 4Ps. Firms should account for both the benefits (i.e., moving closer to customers' ideal points) and costs (i.e., resources spent to move) of repositioning. A firm that seeks to be positioned as a "young" brand may have to expend significant resources to advertise to customers, over months of time. In a final step, *writing a positioning statement* for each target segment encapsulates the essence of the segmenting, targeting, and positioning process, by addressing who customers are, what needs the offering satisfies (key purchase attributes), and why this offering or firm is best at satisfying the need (relative advantage). The three key points for the positioning statement for both target segments of the example athletic wear firm also appear in Figure 2.6 above.

### Step 4: Building Customer Centricity

Building a customer-centric organization is different from executing an STP process, in that it requires top-down, enduring commitment from senior leaders to institute a customer-centric philosophy across the firm's entire organization. For a customer-centric philosophy to be authentic, lead to transformational change, and affect day-to-day decisions, it must be instilled throughout the firm's organizational elements, including leadership, culture, structure, metrics, processes, and compensation/rewards. In each element, the guiding criteria should focus on target customers, aligning decisions to continuously improve customer solutions and experiences. A firm might start with an internal audit of each design element, to identify where the firm has failed to focus on or align with its targeted customer segments.

> Building a customer-centric organization is different from executing an STP process, in that it requires top-down, enduring commitment from senior leaders to institute a customer-centric philosophy across the firm's entire organization.

One of Jeff Bezos' letters to Amazon's shareholders captures the essence of a customer-centric organization, as well as some of its benefits:[49]

> it is a fact that the customer-centric way is at this point a defining element of our culture. One advantage – perhaps a somewhat subtle one – of a customer-driven focus is that it aids a certain type of proactivity. When we're at our best, we don't wait for external pressures. We are *internally* driven to improve our services, adding benefits and features, before we have to. We lower prices and increase value for customers before we have to. We invent before we have to. These investments are motivated by customer focus rather than by reaction to competition. We think this approach earns more trust with customers and drives rapid improvements in customer experience – importantly – even in those areas where we are already the leader.

As described in this letter, a customer-centric approach makes a firm "internally driven" to satisfy target customers, synergistic with the STP approach that "externally focuses" the firm on the right customers (i.e., target customer segment). Together, these two approaches allow firms to manage customer heterogeneity by disaggregating customers into homogeneous groups, then narrowly *focusing* and *motivating* the total organization to address the needs of these select customer segments. The goal is to focus the vision of the firm on the specific needs of customers (rather than products). Improvements in the firm's products and services over time then result from listening to the voice of the customer. Many firms pay consultants massive sums to conduct STP analyses – and then put the beautifully designed slides on a shelf in the market manager's office, with little effect on day-to-day decisions. The STP process aims the marketing "gun," but authentic customer centricity helps the firm pull the "trigger" in its everyday decisions. As Amazon's famous CEO explains, the firm's "investments are motivated by customer focus rather than by reaction to competition."

## Summary

The first, most basic issue facing managers as they make strategic marketing decisions is that *all customers differ* in their preferences. Assuming all customers are the same is a path to failure, at least in the long term, because customers will migrate to more focused competitors that target customer segments with better fitting offerings, which leaves the initial firm with only those customers that are not valuable for competitors to target (e.g., smaller, more price-sensitive groups). Many factors cause customers to differ in their preferences. The most fundamental source of customer heterogeneity is the basic individual differences across people. Another source, which builds on the first, is a person's life experiences, accumulated over time. The person's functional needs for a specific offering also change preferences. Consumers often want their purchases to support their actual or aspirational self-identity or image too, which can drive them to specific brands, independent of functional needs. Finally, marketing activities work to change customer preferences to match the firm's offering and brand image. All these different sources then drive the high degree of variation in customers' preferences, which firms must account for when developing an effective marketing strategy. This underlying assumption of marketing strategy, or First Principle, holds that *all customers differ, so an effective marketing strategy must manage the ever-present customer heterogeneity* (MP#1).

Two synergistic approaches for managing customer heterogeneity are available to managers. The *STP approach* defines customer groups according to their needs and desires (segmenting), and then managers select the segment they believe will produce the most future sales and profits (targeting). Managers then make product, pricing, channel, and promotion decisions (positioning) that are well suited to this target segment, to capture market share. Many tools work to make the STP process more accurate and objective. For example, cluster analysis allows firms to identify groups of customers with similar needs and desires; discriminant analysis helps identify customers that belong to a target segment, using demographic or other observable predictors. The GE matrix enables managers to visualize and select target segments on the basis of the customers' attractiveness and the firm's competitive strengths. Perceptual maps also can lead to effective positioning strategies by depicting customer segments, competitors, and the firm's own position in a multidimensional space defined by the purchase attributes identified during the segmentation process. As segmentation and targeting have progressed over three eras (mass marketing, niche marketing, and one-to-one marketing), firms focus on smaller groups of customers in which their needs are more similar. By targeting smaller segments, firms are better able to satisfy customers' needs and withstand competitive pressures.

A second approach for managing customer heterogeneity is more continuous and ongoing. The *customer-centric approach* requires a company-wide philosophy that places customers' needs at the center of an organization's strategic process and uses the resulting insights to make all decisions. The STP approach implies that firms' offerings should match customer preferences (external alignment), but it does not address whether the firm's internal organizational design can support actions aligned with the target segments' needs or positioning strategies (internal alignment). Customer centricity instead helps the organization gain deeper knowledge about and commitment to a relatively homogeneous group of customers, such that it can detect and react quickly to changing market conditions. However, when firms focus solely on a narrow customer group, changes beyond this segment often are not visible; over time, the focal segment may not be the most attractive, or other segments may emerge that offer new opportunities. These weaknesses come along with higher internal costs. Therefore, an externally focused STP analysis every few years across all potential customers in combination with continuous, rapid adjustments through customer centricity may be the best, most balanced way to manage customer heterogeneity.

Figure 2.5 provides an organizing framework for managing customer heterogeneity, integrating all these approaches and analyses. The three key inputs to the framework are needed to conduct segmentation, targeting, and positioning with potential customers. The three outputs then provide inputs for the last two marketing principles. Specifically, this framework maps out key customer segments for an industry or product category, on the basis of customer preferences, the firm's selected target segments, and the positioning statement that defines its positioning strategy for each target segment.

## Takeaways

- A foundational assumption in marketing strategy is that all customers differ in their needs and preferences. A successful marketing strategy must manage and exploit customer heterogeneity, because if competitors identify niches of customers whose needs are poorly served and target them with a better offering, the incumbent firm risks losing its best customers.

- Sources of customer heterogeneity include customers' individual differences, life experiences, functional needs, and self-identity or image, as well as persuasion through marketing. These factors work together to create divergent preferences.

- The STP approach allows a firm to manage customer heterogeneity by segmenting potential customers into relatively homogeneous groups, based on individual preferences and needs. Then the firm selects attractive segment(s) in which it can build a strong position. Finally, the firm develops and executes a positioning strategy that aligns all marketing activities to move the offering such that it can match customers' preferences.

- The evolution of approaches to managing customer heterogeneity indicates that firms have targeted smaller and smaller customer segments over time (mass marketing → niche marketing → one-to-one marketing)

- Company and competitor strengths and weaknesses are collected in conjunction with opportunities and threats in a classic SWOT analysis; all four factors can inform a firm's targeting and positioning efforts.

- A customer-centric approach to managing customer heterogeneity is more continuous and ongoing. This approach implies a company-wide philosophy that places customers' needs at the center of an organization's strategic process and uses the related insights to make decisions. The customer-centric approach promotes internal alignment; an STP approach promotes external alignment. Firms with customer-centric organizations develop richer customer knowledge and greater commitment to each targeted customer segment.

- Factor analysis groups similar questions (purchase attributes) together to avoid biasing further analyses; cluster analysis groups similar customers together into segments; and classification analysis uses discriminant models to predict segment membership using only demographic variables.

- There are three key inputs and three key outputs of the framework for managing customer heterogeneity. The three inputs reflect the 3Cs of a situation analysis: customers (needs and desires), company, and competitors (strengths and weaknesses). The outputs are industry segmentation, target segments, and a positioning statement.

## Analytics Driven Case

## Managing Customer Heterogeneity at DentMax

### Problem Background

Orthodontists rely on dental imaging technology to obtain dental radiographs, which help evaluate oral diseases in patients. In the last two decades, dentists appear to increasingly rely on digital- (rather than analog-) based intraoral sensors for dental diagnosis. Digital sensors have many advantages compared to their analog counterparts, which medical journals summarize as "the ability to view images on the screen, computerized archiving of images, ability to enhance acquired images, reduced exposure to radiation, and rapid acquisition of images without the need for chemical processing."[1] As a result, the global market for digital X-ray equipment was almost $2.12 bn in 2012 and set to reach $2.44 bn by 2017, where 66% of the current sales for the category comes from US. Part of the reason for the lion's share of the sales coming from the US is that most educational conventions for dentists

---
[1] Williamson, G.F. (2016) "Best practices and patient comfort with digital intraoral radiography", accessed at: www.rdhmag.com/articles/print/volume-30/issue-10/features/best-practices-and-patient-comfort-with-digital-intraoral-radiography.html, 4/19/2016.

(where dentists are informed about how to use digital X-ray imaging) are held in the US, and peer influence among dentists gradually increased the popularity of the products.

The four key qualities of a good intraoral digital X-ray sensor include:

- image quality: the ability to provide bold, crisp and clear images
- diagnostic flexibility: the ability to reach every area of the oral cavity
- software integration: the ability to send the images to an easy-to-use graphic interface that can be shared with the patient
- technical support: the ability of the firm to clarify usage-related questions about intraoral radiography.

Founded in 1973, DentMax is a major player in the market for digital dental X-ray sensors. In 2004, DentMax was considered the unparalleled leader in the category, with a market share of 32%. DentMax's dominance in the market arose because its products were widely considered to be of the highest quality. DentMax's two key rivals are DentMed and OxyMax, who claim that their X-ray sensors have high image quality and diagnostic flexibility, but have not been able to match DentMax yet. Indeed, as third-party rankings summarize in Table 1, DentMax is ranked first in image quality and diagnostic flexibility. DentMed is considered a medium to high-quality firm in image quality but not diagnostic flexibility, while OxyMax is considered a medium to high-quality firm in diagnostic flexibility but not image quality. Consequently, DentMax had positioned itself as the premier-quality firm, and did not worry about lower price and lower quality competitors. As Table 1 shows, dentists did not rate DentMax as being price competitive.

**Table 1** Product Perceptions across Firms

|  | DentMax | DentMed | OxyMax |
|---|---|---|---|
| Rank for Image Quality | 1 | 2 | 3 |
| Rank for Diagnostic Flexibility | 1 | 3 | 2 |
| Rank for Low Price | 3 | 1 | 2 |

However, in 2014, DentMax was convinced that it needed to revisit its marketing fundamentals. Several trends prompted anxiety within the management ranks. First, perusing through the market share figures over the previous decade (see Figure 1), it realized that it had lost nearly 10% of its market share. The 10% loss in market share appeared to be a gain for its two key competitors (who

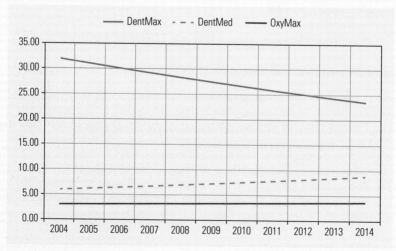

**Figure 1** Market Share Trend

gained about 5%), but also a gain for a multitude of small lower price players in the market (who gained about 5%). Second, it was worried about the smaller players' growth since these competitors mainly offered lower quality, smaller lifetime products, aimed at capturing the "volume" business in the market. Third, it was bemused by the fact that its market share had declined alarmingly over the previous decade even though it was always rated as the highest quality player. Did this mean that DentMax was missing out on providing some other product needs that customers were receiving from competitors? Or that not all the customers in the market wanted high image quality and diagnostic flexibility? DentMax was not quite sure.

As DentMax pondered through its current issue, it was clear it needed a systematic approach to revisit the current state of the industry, its customers, and its competitors, given the changes in the past decade.

## Problem Statement

DentMax's problem appears to fit the first fundamental marketing problem that all firms face while formulating marketing strategy, that is, multiple factors were working together in multifaceted ways to make all dentists differ in the market. So DentMax had to step back to understand how the needs, desires, and preferences across dentists differed in the entire industry. Consequently, it needed to select attractive segment(s) in which it could build a strong position, and develop and execute a positioning strategy that aligns all marketing activities to move the offering such that it could match dentists' preferences. Thus, DentMax launched a strategic initiative aimed at answering the following questions:

- How to effectively segment the market for dental X-ray intraoral sensors, based on the differing needs of dentists?
- What segment(s) of the market are we drawing our customers from? How can we position ourselves even more strongly in these segments?
- Given the needs that we can (and cannot) fulfill, are there segments we could be going after? How do we position ourselves to compete strongly in these new segments?

In 2015, DentMax decided to employ a segmentation and targeting project to answer the questions above, and manage customer heterogeneity. Through segmentation, it sought to determine the key purchase attributes, that is, the *needs and desires* that a potential dentist evaluates when making a purchase decision. Moreover, it sought to identify heterogeneity in the needs and desires in the population of dentist. Thus, it realized that it is important to focus not primarily on existing customers but rather on all potential customers of this product. Thus, it wanted to learn about heterogeneity in the entire market for dental X-ray intraoral sensors, not just its customers. The challenge therefore was in how it was going to build a database that represented the entire market.

## Data[2]

Interestingly for DentMax, the trade show DENTEXPO-2015 was scheduled three months later, in Chicago. DENTEXPO has historically been the premier annual marketing event for dentists, and firms serving the dental industry. Since 1982 DENTEXPO has been organized by the American Dental Association (ADA), with the aim of educating dentists about a variety of issues related to their professional development (including the best products in the market, the latest breakthrough techniques), while serving as an opportunity for dentists to engage in professional networking. Surveys in the past revealed that dentists primarily visited DENTEXPO to learn about new products, network with other dentists, improve their knowledge about state-of-the-art dental procedures, and meet exhibitors with whom they shared a good business relationship. DENTEXPO has also been the marquee event for firms operating in the dental industry, to demonstrate their new products, build corporate image, train dentists, gather competitive information, and boost employee morale.

---

[2] These analyses were performed using MEXL software as described in Data Analytics Technique 9.1 using data from the DentMax Case dataset.

DentMax collected data from three different sources to enable segmentation. First, it obtained data from the trade show organizer, DENTEXPO. Using RFID technology, DENTEXPO could track the whereabouts of each of the visiting dentists whenever they were in the exhibition hall. This tracking technology could therefore let exhibitors know the total amount of time each visitor spent at their booth, as well as a rival's booth. DENTEXPO believed that this data would be useful to exhibitors to better understand who visited their booth, and how long visitors spent at their booth. This would also help exhibitors devise strategies to maximize the time visitors spent at the booth, and thereby stay more engaged with the exhibitor. DentMax was aware that DentMed and OxyMed would also be exhibiting their X-ray imaging products this year, as they always did. Since 35% of the dentists in the city visited DENTEXPO for at least one day of the three-day event, and Chicago was representative of the average market for DentMax's products, DentMax wished to capitalize on the opportunity offered by DENTEXPO to obtain a snapshot of the entire market. From the RFID-enabled technology, DentMax obtained the following variables for each of the show attendees ($n = 2,300$):

- Time Spent at DentMax Booth captured by the minutes spent by each attendee at the DentMax booth
- Time Spent at DentMed Booth captured by the minutes spent by each attendee at the DentMed booth
- Time Spent at OxyMax Booth captured by the minutes spent by each attendee at the OxyMax booth.

Second, DentMax collected the first and last name of the dentist, and the dental practice location for the subsample of DENTEXPO dentists that visited its booth. It matched these details up with its own sales database, to obtain the sales records of the dentists that visited its booth. From this, it could determine whether a dentist who visited its booth had purchased from them in the past, and if so, how much they had purchased. DentMax collected the following variables:

- *% Buying* from DentMax in the past, coded as 1 if the dentist has ever bought from DentMax, 0 otherwise
- *Historical Sales Index*, coded as a scaled number from 0 to 100, where 100 represents the largest sales in dollars
- *Sales Frequency*, coded as the yearly number of orders from DentMax
- *Length of Relationship*, coded as 2016– earliest transacted year
- *Number of Referrals*, coded as the total number of times the dentist provided a key referral for another sale.

Third, using the first and last name of the dentist for the subsample of DENTEXPO dentists who visited its booth, DentMax surveyed the dentists one week after the show. In the survey, it obtained answers to the following questions about the dentists. For each of the questions, 1 was scored as the lowest, 7 being the highest. The questions were as follows:

- *Importance of Image Quality*
- *Importance of Diagnostic Flexibility*
- *Importance of Software Integration*
- *Importance of Technical Assistance*
- *Importance of Price*
- *Trust in TV Ads*
- *Trust in Radio Ads*
- *Trust in Internet Ads*
- *Trust in Dental Magazine Ads*
- *Trust in Peers*

Table 2 describes all of the variables and their definitions.

**Table 2** Variables in the Model

| | Variable | Definition |
|---|---|---|
| Trade Show Floor Behavior | Time Spent at DentMax Booth | Minutes spent at the DentMax booth |
| | Time Spent at DentMed/OxyMax Booth | Minutes spent at the DentMed/OxyMax booth |
| | Total Time Spent at Show | Total minutes spent at the ADA convention |
| Past Purchase Behaviors | % Buying from DentMax in the Past | Coded as 1 if the dentist has ever bought from DentMax, 0 otherwise |
| | Historical Sales Index | A scaled number from 0 to 100, where 100 represents the largest sales in dollars |
| | Sales Frequency | Yearly number of orders from DentMax |
| | Length of Relationship | 2016– Earliest Transacted Date with DentMax |
| | Number of Referrals Offered | Total number of times the dentist provided a key referral for another sale |
| X-Ray Imaging Product Needs | Importance of Image Quality | Stated importance of dimension (1 being the lowest, 7 being the highest) |
| | Importance of Diagnostic Flexibility | Stated importance of dimension (1 being the lowest, 7 being the highest) |
| | Importance of Software Integration | Stated importance of dimension (1 being the lowest, 7 being the highest) |
| | Importance of Technical Assistance | Stated importance of dimension (1 being the lowest, 7 being the highest) |
| | Importance of Price | Stated importance of dimension (1 being the lowest, 7 being the highest) |
| Media Trust | Trust in TV Ads | Stated trust in information source (1 being the lowest, 7 being the highest) |
| | Trust in Radio Ads | Stated trust in information source (1 being the lowest, 7 being the highest) |
| | Trust in Internet Ads | Stated trust in information source (1 being the lowest, 7 being the highest) |
| | Trust in Dental Magazine Ads | Stated trust in information source (1 being the lowest, 7 being the highest) |
| | Trust in Peers | Stated trust in information source (1 being the lowest, 7 being the highest) |

## Industry Segmentation Exercise

The first question that DentMax sought to answer through the data was: "How to effectively segment the market for dental X-ray intraoral sensors, based on the differing needs of dentists?"

### Cluster Analysis Overview

DentMax used cluster analysis to perform an industry segmentation, that is, it tried to identify underlying subsamples of dentists who are homogeneous in their behaviors and preferences and markedly different from other subsamples.

### Number of Clusters

Accordingly, the results of the cluster analysis DentMax performed with the data are described. The first task is to decide the number of clusters. The model first considers each customer as a separate segment. Subsequently, it finds the two segments/customers that, if grouped together, would lead to the lowest loss of information. The model continues to merge segments/customers until such merging would lead to an unacceptable loss of information. The dendogram shown in Figure 2 shows the loss of information associated with grouping the data into different numbers of clusters ranging from two to eight. It appears that the most loss of information occurs when going from four to five clusters, therefore DentMax retained a four-cluster model. An alternative to clustering using all of the variables in the dataset would be to use only the survey data capturing preferences and then using sales and booth behavioral data as descriptors of the segments.

### Description of Clusters

Having grouped all the dentists into one of four clusters, DentMax turned to profiling the clusters. By profiling, we mean that DentMax attempts to create a "picture" of the members of the clusters using

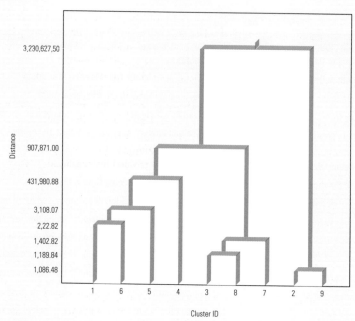

**Figure 2** Dendogram

all the variables of interest; dentists' behaviors in the booth, their past sales histories with DentMax, and their answers on the survey. The profile of each cluster is best seen by the variable means in each cluster in Table 3. Next, we describe each of the clusters.

**Table 3 Cluster Analysis Results**

| | | Loyalists | Switchables | Generalists | Apathetics |
|---|---|---|---|---|---|
| | **Segment Size** | **12%** | **22%** | **49%** | **17%** |
| Trade Show Floor Behavior | Time Spent at DentMax Booth | 45 | 36 | 12 | 6 |
| | Time Spent at DentMed/OxyMax Booth | 26 | 78 | 21 | 11 |
| | Total Time Spent at Show | 130 | 180 | 150 | 60 |
| Past Purchase Behaviors | % Buying from DentMax in the Past | 100% | 45% | 32% | 6% |
| | Historical Sales Index | 58 | 64 | 21 | 9 |
| | Sales Frequency | 5.8 | 4.4 | 3.1 | 0.8 |
| | Length of Relationship | 8.2 years | 8.8 years | 4.3 years | 8.6 years |
| | Number of Referrals Offered | 12 | 2.3 | 0.5 | 0.03 |
| X-Ray Imaging Product Needs | Importance of Image Quality | 6.6 | 6.1 | 5.1 | 3.8 |
| | Importance of Diagnostic Flexibility | 6.8 | 5.5 | 5.2 | 3.8 |
| | Importance of Software Integration | 4.4 | 6.4 | 4.8 | 4.2 |
| | Importance of Technical Assistance | 5.5 | 5.8 | 6.3 | 6.8 |
| | Importance of Price | 4.4 | 5.9 | 6.7 | 6.9 |
| Media Trust | Trust in TV Ads | 5.1 | 4.4 | 4.6 | 3.8 |
| | Trust in Radio Ads | 4.2 | 4.6 | 4.5 | 3.6 |
| | Trust in Internet Ads | 3.6 | 6.1 | 3.8 | 2.8 |
| | Trust in Dental Magazine Ads | 6.5 | 5.8 | 5.4 | 4 |
| | Trust in Peers | 6.1 | 6.8 | 5.6 | 5.3 |

Dentists that comprised Cluster 1 (12%) spent a little over two hours on the trade show floor (130 minutes), but also spent nearly one-third of their time in DentMax's booth (45 minutes), and only about 20% of their time at competitors' booths (26 minutes). Thus, these dentists appear to be favorable to DentMax. Observing their sales records revealed that all the dentists in Cluster 1 had purchased from DentMax in the past, and the historical sales index for these dentists was very high (58), and so was their sales frequency (5.8). Moreover, the relationship between dentists in Cluster 1 and DentMax was 8.2 years on average, indicating that they were both loyal and strong customers. Turning to the survey results, dentists in Cluster 1 highly valued image quality (6.6), diagnostic flexibility (6.8), but only moderately valued software integration (4.4), technical assistance (5.5) and price (4.4). These dentists appeared to trust dental magazine ads (6.5) and peer feedback (6.1) more than TV (5.1), radio (4.2) and the Internet (3.6), for product information. Based on the strong sales records, fit with DentMax's positioning in the marketplace, and the revealed information about time spent at the booth, DentMax named this cluster "Loyalists."

Dentists that comprised Cluster 2 (22%) spent three hours on the trade show floor (180 minutes), but only spent 20% their time in DentMax's booth (36 minutes), and about 43% of their time at competitors' booths (78 minutes). Thus, these dentists appear to be favorable to competitors. Observing their sales records revealed that only 45% of all the dentists in Cluster 2 had purchased from DentMax in the past, but the historical sales index for these dentists was very high (64), and so was their sales frequency (4.4). Moreover, the relationship between dentists in Cluster 2 and DentMax was 8.8 years on average, indicating that they were also strong and loyal. Turning to the survey results, dentists in Cluster 2 highly valued image quality (6.1), and software integration (6.4), and perhaps price (5.9) but only moderately valued diagnostic flexibility (5.5), technical assistance (5.8). Like Cluster 1 dentists, these dentists also appeared to trust dental magazine ads (5.8) and peer feedback (6.8) more than TV (4.4), and radio (4.6), but did trust the Internet highly (6.1), for product information, unlike Cluster 1. Based on the strong sales records, fit with DentMax's positioning in the marketplace, but revealed information about time spent at competitors' booths, DentMax named this cluster "Switchables."

Dentists that comprised the largest cluster, Cluster 3 (49%), spent 150 minutes on the trade show floor, but only spent 8% their time in DentMax's booth (12 minutes), and 14% of their time at competitors' booths (21 minutes). Thus, these dentists appear to be favorable to neither DentMax nor the competitors. Observing their sales records revealed that only 32% of all the dentists in Cluster 3 had purchased from DentMax in the past, the historical sales index for these dentists was moderate (21), and so was their sales frequency (3.1). Moreover, the relationship between dentists in Cluster 2 and DentMax was only 4.3 years on average, indicating that they were not very loyal or strong customers. Turning to the survey results, dentists in Cluster 3 highly valued technical assistance (6.3), and price (6.7), but not image quality (5.1), software integration (4.8), or diagnostic flexibility (5.2). Like Cluster 1 dentists, these dentists also appeared to trust dental magazine ads (5.4) and peer feedback (5.6), but not TV (4.6), radio (4.5), or the Internet (3.8), for product information. Based on the lukewarm sales records, moderate fit with DentMax's positioning in the marketplace, but revealed information about time spent at the booths, DentMax named this cluster "Generalists."

Dentists that comprised the last cluster, Cluster 4 (17%), spent only 60 minutes on the trade show floor, spending 10% of their time in DentMax's booth (6 minutes), and 18% of their time at competitors' booths (11 minutes). Thus, these dentists appear to be favorable to neither DentMax nor the competitors. Observing their sales records revealed that only 6% of all the dentists in Cluster 4 had purchased from DentMax in the past, the historical sales index for these dentists was poor (9), and so was their sales frequency (0.8). Moreover, the relationship between dentists in Cluster 4 and DentMax was 4.8 years on average, indicating that they were not loyal or strong customers. Turning to the survey results, dentists in Cluster 4 highly valued technical assistance (6.8), and price (6.9), but did not value image quality (3.8), software integration (3.8), or diagnostic flexibility (4.2). Cluster 4 dentists only appeared to trust peer feedback (5.3) for product information. Based on the poor sales records, low fit with DentMax's positioning in the marketplace, and revealed information about time spent at the booths, DentMax named this cluster "Apathetics."

## Targeting and Positioning for Competitive Advantage

After segmenting potential dentists into homogeneous groups on the basis of their trade show booth behaviors, past purchase behaviors, and product preferences, DentMax needed to select which current segments to retain, and which new segments to potentially target. DentMax used two broad criteria to target each of the four market segments. First, it assessed the market attractiveness of each segment, that is, whether the segment appeared strategically and financially valuable to serve, based on dentists' past purchase data. Second, it considered the competitive strength of each segment, which represented the relative strength of DentMax, versus competitors, at securing and maintaining market share in a given segment. Based on these two broad criteria, it assessed the value of each segment.

### Loyalists

The Loyalists segment scored highly for DentMax on market attractiveness. Not only had Loyalists purchased from DentMax in the past, they also appear to purchase larger amounts than most segments, purchase at fairly frequent intervals, and maintained a long-standing relationship with DentMax. The Loyalists also scored highly for DentMax on competitive strength. Loyalists appear to spend more time at DentMax's booth than competitors', and valued image quality and diagnostic flexibility, the strengths of DentMax, more than other product attributes. How could DentMax further strengthen its positioning with Loyalists? It reasoned that it could further correspond with dentists through magazine journals, and use peer feedback to further strengthen its ties with Loyalists. However, the small segment size of Loyalists (12% of the market) meant that DentMax had to target other segments.

### Switchables

One of the options to grow market share was to target the Switchables. Switchables also scored highly for DentMax on market attractiveness. Not only had Switchables purchased from DentMax in the past, they also appear to purchase larger amounts than most segments, purchase at fairly frequent intervals, and maintained a long-standing relationship with DentMax. However, Switchables also scored poorly for DentMax on competitive strength. Switchables appear to spend more time at competitors' booth, even though they valued image quality and diagnostic flexibility, the strengths of DentMax, more than other product attributes. How could DentMax further strengthen its positioning with Switchables to win some of these customers back from competitors? First, DentMax noticed that Switchables valued software integration and technical assistance highly. While DentMax provided these attributes in its products, it reflected on the notion that it never mentioned these attributes in its product messages to dentists. Thus, one way to attract more Switchables would be to stress these qualities to dentists. Second, it realized that Switchables cared more about information from Internet-based sources, and hence DentMax decided to use these channels to attract more Switchables.

### Generalists

The Generalists presented a potentially attractive, but tricky opportunity. Generalists scored moderately for DentMax on market attractiveness. While a moderate percentage of Generalists had purchased from DentMax in the past, they did not purchase large amounts, or purchase at frequent intervals, and maintained a fleeting relationship with DentMax. They also scored moderately on competitive strength. Generalists appear to spend more time at competitors' booths, and did not value image quality and diagnostic flexibility, the strengths of DentMax, more than other product attributes. How could DentMax further strengthen its positioning with Generalists? First, DentMax noticed that Generalists valued price and technical assistance highly. While DentMax could mention technical assistance, it did not want to lower its price and compete on price in the marketplace. Thus, one way to attract more Generalists would be to stress technical assistance to dentists. Second, it realized that Generalists did not trust any of the information sources very highly, and perhaps DentMax needed to use personal selling to attract more Generalists.

### Apathetics

Finally, DentMax decided to avoid the Apathetics. Apathetics scored poorly both on market attractiveness and competitive strength. They did not purchase large amounts, purchased infrequently and maintained a fleeting relationship with DentMax. They did not spend time at any booth, and did not value image quality and diagnostic flexibility, the strengths of DentMax, more than other product attributes. Finally, they value price heavily, which was not the focus of DentMax's products in the marketplace.

## Summary of Solution

The analytics exercise enabled DentMax to obtain a better grip of its current standing in the marketplace, by better understanding the needs of its customers:

1 The market was currently serving four types of customers who differed in their purchase behavior, needs and preferences for products, and trust in a variety of product information sources.
2 It had captured a strong loyal majority in the market (Loyalists, making up 12% of the market), who not only purchased regularly from it, but wanted exactly what DentMax was offering. It also uncovered tangible ideas to further strengthen its position in this market space.
3 It could potentially target a promising segment (Switchables) that wanted the same products DentMax was offering, but was currently interested in competitors' products due to competitors offering better technical assistance and software integration. DentMax reasoned that the digital X-ray category was still fairly new, and spending more emphasis on educational efforts could help it win some customers back from DentMed and OxyMax. Moreover, it better understood the drop in 5% of their market share, and could devise strategies based on being the top player when it comes to providing technical assistance and software integration, to win back some of its customers.
4 Some of the customers in the Switchables segment were using the Internet as an important source of information and hence, it knows it could provide the right product message, to the right customer, through the right channel.
5 Apathetics and the Generalists represent the source of heterogeneity that they need not go after; these customers did not appear to stress quality over price, and also did not show any interest or product fit with DentMax's mission in the market. So, DentMax learnt that it could potentially avoid sinking resources into segments that did not fit its core value proposition.

Thus, analytics-oriented efforts helped DentMax solve the first fundamental marketing problem, that all customers differ.

## Appendix: Dataset Description

### General Description of the Data

The dataset is a simulated dataset, aimed at mimicking similar datasets that the authors have used in the past while working with companies. The data contain 19 columns and 2,300 rows. The first column contains the names of the respondents (anonymous), and the 18 other columns pertain to the data to be used by the students in the segmentation exercise.

## Description of Variables in the Data

The 18 variable dataset contains three types of variables. The first three variables contain the following information about each of the show attendees (using RFID trackers):

- Time Spent at DentMax Booth captured by the minutes spent by each attendee at the DentMax booth
- Time Spent at DentMed Booth captured by the minutes spent by each attendee at the DentMed booth
- Total Time Spent at Show captured by the minutes spent by each attendee at the OxyMax booth.

The next five variables contain historical data about the dentists (DentMax's customers), from DentMax's CRM database, by matching the trade show data on dentist IDs with those from DentMax's CRM database:

- *% Buying* from DentMax in the Past, coded as 1 if the dentist has ever bought from DentMax, 0 otherwise
- *Historical Sales Index*, coded as a scaled number from 0 to 100, where 100 represents the largest sales in dollars
- *Sales Frequency*, coded as the yearly number of orders from DentMax
- *Length of Relationship*, coded as 2016– earliest transacted year
- *Number of Referrals*, coded as the total number of times the dentist provided a key referral for another sale.

The last ten variables were obtained by DentMax using the first and last name of the dentist for the subsample of DENTEXPO dentists who visited its booth. DentMax surveyed the dentists one week after the show. The variables include:

- *Importance of Image Quality*
- *Importance of Diagnostic Flexibility*
- *Importance of Software Integration*
- *Importance of Technical Assistance*
- *Importance of Price*
- *Trust in TV Ads*
- *Trust in Radio Ads*
- *Trust in Internet Ads*
- *Trust in Dental Magazine Ads*
- *Trust in Peers*

The variable description and means are presented in Table 3 in the case. To obtain the cluster analysis results, the student can directly load the data in Excel, and use the MEXL add-in pertaining to segmentation analysis. The student should select a five-cluster solution. Depending on the type of analysis chosen, the student might see that some of the variables are highly correlated with each other, and might have to drop one or two variables in the data. The output should be as presented in Table 3.

# References

1  *The Wall Street Journal* (n.d.) 'Mutual Fund Screener.' Available at: http://online.wsj.com/public/quotes/ mutualfund_screener.html (accessed 12 December, 2014).

2  Olster, S. and Kowitt, B. (2010) 'Inside the secret world of Trader Joe's,' *Fortune*, 23 August.

3  TheHenryFord.org (n.d.) *The Innovator and Ford Motor Company.* Available at: www.thehenryford.org/exhibits/hf/ The_Innovator_and_Ford_Motor_Company.asp (accessed 23 September, 2015).

4  Hendrickson, R. (1981) *The Grand Emporiums: The Illustrated History of America's Great Department Stores.* New York: Stein and Day; Hoge, C.C. (1988) *The First Hundred Years Are the Toughest: What We Can Learn from the Competition Between Sears and Wards.* Berkeley, CA: Ten Speed Press; Brisco, J. (n.d.) 'Sears Roebuck catalog.' Available at: www.encyclopedia. com/doc/1G2.3401803785.html/ (accessed 23 September, 2015).

5  Hammacher Schlemmer (n.d.) 'History of Hammacher Schlemmer.' Available at: www.hammacher.com/Editorial/

History (accessed 12 December, 2014); Spiegel (n.d.) 'About Us – Spiegel.' Available at: www.spiegel.com/info/About_Us (accessed 12 December, 2014); L.L. Bean (n.d.) 'LL Bean – Our Story.' Available at: www.llbean.com/customerService/aboutLLBean/images/110408_About-LLB.pdf (accessed 12 December, 2014).

6  Sears (n.d.) 'History of the Sears Catalog.' Available at: www.searsarchives.com/catalogs/history.htm (accessed 12 December, 2014); Lutz, A. (2013) 'The irreversible decline of Sears can be blamed on one thing.' Available at: www.businessinsider.com/sears-gave-up-on-customer-service-2013-2 (accessed 23 September, 2015); Sharf, S. (2014) 'Sears CEO: Retailer's loss, revenue decline "unacceptable".' Available at: www.forbes.com/sites/samanthasharf/2014/08/21/sears-ceo-retailers-loss-revenue-decline-unacceptable/ (accessed 23 September, 2015).

7  Anderson, S., Pearo, L.K. and Widener, S.K. (2008) 'Drivers of service satisfaction,' *Journal of Service Research*, 10(4), pp. 365–81.

8  Ellis, L. and Ficek, C. (2001) 'Color preferences according to gender and sexual orientation,' *Personality and Individual Differences*, 31(8), pp. 1375–9.

9  Reed, D.R., Bachmanov, A.A., Beauchamp, G.K., Tordoff, M.G. and Price, R.A. (1997) 'Heritable variation in food preferences and their contribution to obesity,' *Behavior Genetics*, 27(4), pp. 373–87.

10  Scarr, S. (1992) 'Developmental theories for the 1990s: Development and individual differences,' *Child Development*, 63, pp. 1–19.

11  Puntoni, S. (2001) 'Self-identity and purchase intention: An extension of the theory of planned behavior,' *European Advances in Consumer Research*, 5, pp. 130–4.

12  Chan, C., Berger, J. and van Boven, L. (2012) 'Identifiable but not identical: Combining social identity and uniqueness motives in choice,' *Journal of Consumer Research*, 39(3), pp. 561–73.

13  Chan, C., Berger, J. and van Boven, L. (2012) 'Identifiable but not identical: Combining social identity and uniqueness motives in choice,' *Journal of Consumer Research*, 39(3), pp. 561–73.

14  Felix, S. and Stampler, L. (2012) 'The evolution of James Bond movie product placement.' Available at: www.businessinsider.com/heres-how-james-bonds-relationship-with-product-placement-has-changed-2012.10?op=1#ixzz3Lv7X4vvq (accessed 23 September, 2015); Epstien, E. (2011) 'The stealthy world of brands,' *Ad Week*, 52(34), p. 22; Dudovskiy, J. (2013) 'BMW segmentation targeting and positioning.' Available at: http://research-methodology.net/bmw-segmentation-targeting-and-positioning/ (accessed 23 September, 2015).

15  Epstein, E.J. (1982) 'Have you ever tried to sell a diamond?,' *The Atlantic*, 249, pp. 23–34.

16  Polis, C. (2013) 'Greek yogurt food invasion continues as product is added to cream cheese, hummus and more,' 5 March. Available at: www.huffingtonpost.com/2013/03/05/greek-yogurt-food-product_n_2807818.html (accessed 15 December, 2015).

17  Omogbadegun, Z. (2010) 'Emerging technologies (ICTs) & our businesses,' Women in Technology in Nigeria (WITIN) Conference.

18  Moth, D. (2014) '20+ stats that show the state of mobile marketing in China.' Available at: https://econsultancy.com/blog/65895-20-stats-that-show-the-state-of-mobile-marketing-in-china/ (accessed 5 October, 2015).

19  El-Ansary, A., Palmatier, R. and Stern, L. (2014) *Marketing Channel Strategy*. New York: Pearson Higher Education.

20  Stevenson, A. (ed.) (2010) *Oxford Dictionary of English*, 3rd edn. Oxford: Oxford University Press.

21  *LA Times* (1995) 'AT&T breakup II: Highlights in the history of a telecommunications giant,' *LA Times*, 21 September; Celtnet (2014) 'The history of AT&T.'. Available at: www.celtnet.org.uk/telecos/AT&T-Bell-4.php (accessed 24 December, 2015).

22  Ali & Partners (n.d.) *Telecommunications in the Middle East*. Available at: www.mideastlaw.com/article_telecommunications_in_the_middle_east.html (accessed 9 July, 2015).

23  Cansfield, M., Daley, E. and Ashour, M. (2009) 'Case study: Telstra's telecom marketing excellence,' 26 March. Available from: www.forrester.com/report/Case+Study+Telstras+Telecom+Marketing+Excellence/-/E-RES47557 (accessed 4 August, 2016).

24  Schultz, H. and Gordon J. (2011) *Onward: How Starbucks Fought for its Life without Losing its Soul*. New York: Rodale; Forbes (n.d.) *Starbucks*. Available at: www.forbes.com/companies/starbucks/ (accessed 8 December, 2014).

25  Procter & Gamble (2010) *2010 Annual Report*. Available at: www.pg.com/fr_FR/downloads/annual_reports/PG_2010_AnnualReport.pdf (accessed 23 September, 2015); McCoy, M. (2009) 'The greening game,' *Chemical and Engineering News*, 87(4), p. 13.

26  GFK Custom Research (n.d.) *The Walmart Segmentation Lens*. Available at: www.knowledgenetworks.com/wmsl/ (accessed 27 December, 2014).

27  Brody, B. (2014) 'Walmart: "Going to a very dark place",' *CNN Wire*, 30 July.

28  Tedlow, R. (1990) *New and Improved: The Story of Mass Marketing in America*. New York: Basic Books.

29  Bianco, A., Lowry, T., Berner R., Ardnt, M. and Grover, R. (2004) 'The vanishing mass market,' *Business Week*, 3891, pp. 60–8.

30  Arora, N., Dreze, X., Ghose, A., Hess, J.D., Iyengar, R. et al. (2008) 'Putting one-to-one marketing to work: Personalization, customization, and choice,' *Marketing Letters*, 19(3), pp. 305–21.

31  Peppers, D. and Rogers, M. (1996) *The One to One Future: Building Relationships One Customer at a Time*. New York: Currency Doubleday.

32  Comcast Spotlight (n.d.) *Experience the Power of Comcast Spotlight*. Available at: www.comcastspotlight.com (accessed 27 December, 2014).

33  Lee, J.Y., Kozlenkova, I.V. and Palmatier, R.W. (2015) 'Structural marketing: Using organizational structure to achieve marketing objectives,' *Journal of the Academy of Marketing Science*, 43(1), pp. 73–99.

34  Bianco, A., Lowry, T., Berner, R., Ardnt, M. and Grover, R. (2004) 'The vanishing mass market,' *Business Week*, 3891, pp. 60–8.

35  Klara, R. (2013) 'How Clairol hair color went from taboo to new you: Hair dyeing shifts from shameful secret to $1 billion bonanza,' 28 February. Available at: www.adweek.com/news/advertising-branding/how-clairol-hair-color-went-taboo-new-you-147480 (accessed 22 January, 2016).

36  Van Auken, B. (2012) 'Success and radical brand repositioning.' Available at: www.brandingstrategyinsider.com/2012/06/success-and-radical-brand-repositioning.html#.VJ8ffAz4 (accessed 23 September, 2015).

37  Kapner, S. and Lublin, J.S. (2015) 'Abercrombie & Fitch dials back the sex,' *The Wall Street Journal*, 24 April.

38  Brand And Package The Product (2011) 'Nutri-Grain by Kellogg's.' Available at: https://brandandpackagetheproduct.wordpress.com/tag/brand-positioning-statement/ (accessed 23 January, 2016).

39  Dragoon, A. (2005) 'Customer segmentation done right,' 1 October. Available at: www.cio.com/article/2448413/it-organization/customer-segmentation-done-right.html (accessed 23 September, 2015).

40  Dragoon, A. (2005) 'Customer segmentation done right,' 1 October. Available at: www.cio.com/article/2448413/it-organization/customer-segmentation-done-right.html (accessed 23 September, 2015).

41  Lee, J.Y., Sridhar, S., Henderson, C.M. and Palmatier, R.W. (2015) 'Effect of customer-centric structure on long-term financial performance,' *Marketing Science*, 34(2), pp. 250–68.

42  Edwards, C. (2005) 'Shaking up Intel's insides,' *Business Week*, 3918, p. 35.

43  Reichheld, F. (2003) 'The one number you need to grow,' *Harvard Business Review*, 81(12), pp. 46–55.

44  Lee, J.Y., Kozlenkova, I.V. and Palmatier, R.W. (2015) 'Structural marketing: Using organizational structure to achieve marketing objectives,' *Journal of the Academy of Marketing Science*, 43(1), pp. 73–99.

45  Kohli, A.K. and Jaworski, B.J. (1990) 'Market orientation: The construct, research propositions, and managerial implications,' *Journal of Marketing*, 54(2), pp. 1–18.

46  Jaworski, B.J. and Kohli, A.K. (1993) 'Market orientation: Antecedents and consequences,' *Journal of Marketing*, 57(3), pp. 53–70.

47  Vizard, S. (2014) 'Sainsbury's unveils new marketing plans as sales and profits drop.' Available at: www.marketingweek.com/2014/11/12/sainsburys-unveils-new-marketing-plans-as-sales-and-profits-drop/ (accessed 23 September, 2015).

48  Tzu, S. (5th century BC) *The Art of War*. Translated by Griffith, S.B., 1963. Oxford: Clarendon Press.

49  Bezos, J. (2013) *Letter to Amazon's Shareholders*. Available at: www.sec.gov/Archives/edgar/data/1018724/000119312513151836/d511111dex991.htm (accessed 23 September, 2015).

## Companion website

Please visit the companion website, **www.palgravehighered.com/palmatier-ms**, to access summary videos from the authors, and full-length cases with datasets and step-by-step solution guides.

# Part 2

# ALL CUSTOMERS CHANGE

Managers developing their marketing strategies must account for variation as customers' needs change over time. Even within a well-defined segment, members' individual needs often evolve at different rates or directions. At some point in the future, customers who once were part of a relatively homogeneous segment will exhibit widely divergent needs and desires. A firm's marketing strategy must account for customer dynamics to avoid becoming obsolete by identifying and understanding how a firm's customers migrate (i.e., change), triggers of these migrations, differing needs across stages, and, ultimately, desirable positions to appeal to these customers over time.

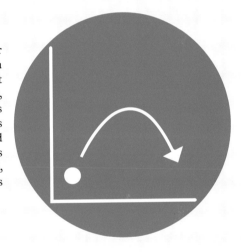

Visit www.palgravehighered.com/palmatier-ms to watch the authors provide an overview of the *All Customers Change* First Principle and the relevant tools, analyses, and cases in either an executive summary or a full-length, pre-recorded video lecture format.

ALL
CUSTOMERS
CHANGE

Chapter **3**

# Marketing Principle #2: All Customers Change → Managing Customer Dynamics

## Learning objectives

- Understand why an effective marketing strategy must manage customer dynamics.
- Define customer dynamics.
- Understand that all customers change and that customer dynamics require careful management (Marketing Principle #2).
- Discuss in detail trends that increase the importance of customer dynamics.
- Describe different sources of customer dynamics.
- Give an example of each source of customer dynamics.
- Critically analyze the three main approaches for managing customer dynamics.
- Provide the pros and cons of lifecycle, dynamic segmentation (AER model), and customer lifetime value (CLV) approaches.
- Describe hidden Markov models (HMM), choice models, and customer lifetime value (CLV) as tools for managing customer change.
- Explain the strengths and weaknesses of using lost customer analysis as a way to understand customer dynamics.
- Identify the three inputs and three outputs to the framework for managing customer dynamics.
- Outline the five-step process for managing customer dynamics.

# Introduction

## All Customers Change

A second underlying challenge facing firms that make short- and long-term marketing decisions is the basic principle that all customers change. Events in people's lives – graduation, marriage, new jobs, the birth of children – change their existing routines and buying habits. Some firms recognize and internalize this marketing principle in their growth strategies; Target, a US retailer, even uses its customers' shopping data to develop a "pregnancy prediction" score and estimate people's due dates within a small window, to enable effective weekly campaigns matched to each stage of the pregnancy. Gregg Steinhafel, Target's president, has suggested that a "heightened focus on items and categories that appeal to specific guest segments such as mom and baby" helps explain Target's above-average growth in the competitive retail industry.[1]

Not all customer change is event driven though; it also results from changes in customers' underlying needs and desires. Laura Ashley, the apparel company known for its "English ladies" image, saw its sales drop throughout its network of more than 500 shops in the 1970s as more women entered the workforce. This slow-moving cultural change gradually encouraged Laura Ashley's target customers to shift to more practical, professional attire rather than romantic floral dresses. Ultimately, Laura Ashley sold all of its North American retail shops in a management buyout for $1.[2] Thus, this First Principle that *all customers change* can represent either an opportunity or a threat, depending on how the firm understands and manages it.

Managers developing marketing strategies in turn must account for both *static* variation in customers' needs, due to their inherent differences (MP#1), and the *dynamic* variation that arises as customer needs change over time (MP#2). At any particular point in time, customers can be segmented into various groups, according to their needs and desires for a particular product or service – the common approach for dealing with customer heterogeneity, as we outlined in Chapter 2. Even after customers are assigned to a segment, their needs continue to evolve, at different rates and in different directions, so at some point in the (near) future, the customers in a once homogeneous segment will develop very different preferences. To devise approaches to address this customer dynamics problem, it can be helpful to understand what causes individual customers to migrate in different directions and at different rates. That is, by identifying sources of customer dynamics, defined as changes in customer preferences that occur over time, it becomes possible to understand and manage these dynamics.

> Even after customers are assigned to a segment, their needs continue to evolve, at different rates and in different directions, so at some point in the (near) future, the customers in a once homogeneous segment will develop very different preferences.

## Sources of Customer Dynamics

Customers' changing needs arise from various sources, often operating at different levels and rates (Table 3.1). First, individual customers change due to discrete life events, such as their graduation, a new job, a marriage, parenthood, or retirement, that have immediate impacts on many aspects of their purchase decisions. Even relatively small events in a customer's life – like a change in the amount of television they watch or eating out more than usual – are associated with shifts in their brand preferences.[3] After a painful divorce, a person might avoid specific brands that were their ex-spouse's favorites, to avoid the psychological distress associated with such reminders.[4] Recent college graduates change their store and brand preferences, because their shopping focus alters when they transition from the role of being a student to becoming an employee.[5]

Second, people progress relatively slowly through a **typical lifecycle** as they mature, which also influences many of their product and service priorities. To meet customers' evolving desires as they age, marketers have identified various psychological and sociological changes over time. Most consumers shift in their willingness to take risks or try new things, and lifecycle frameworks in

**Table 3.1** Sources of Customer Dynamics

| Description | Rate of Change | Examples |
|---|---|---|
| ***Individual level*** | | |
| Discrete life events | Immediate | A first-time parent often changes their preference for cars, vacations, and restaurants |
| Typical lifecycle or maturation as people age | Slow | As people age, they become more focused on risk reduction, less willing to change, and more focused on comfort and health |
| Product learning effects | Medium | Customers might learn, after using a product for a time, that there are certain specialized or high-tech features they would like |
| ***Product market level*** | | |
| Product lifecycle | Medium | During early stages, consumers may purchase more new features, in later periods, they may get more price sensitive |
| ***Environmental level*** | | |
| Changes in economy, government, industry, or culture | Slow to immediate | As the culture around "healthy food" changes, consumer preferences in response to dietary concerns (e.g., calories, sodium, carbohydrates, gluten, fat) also change |

marketing effectively describe some of these general trends. For example, young and single consumers often focus on products and services that promise to make them attractive to potential mates (cologne, salon and exercise services, designer clothing); as they age, they start to focus more on financial safety and security. In the final stages of people's lives, they tend to become fixed in their brand purchases, fairly conservative in their decision making, and more focused on their relationships with sellers.[6] Although these generalizations can offer a broad sense of average changes, assuming that these life changes are constant across all consumers is deeply problematic.

Third, the attributes that customers consider most critical often vary systematically, depending on their experience with and knowledge about a product or service category, which constitutes a learning effect. The customer learning effect is the process by which customers become familiar with the product by using it, which changes their weighting of the relative importance of different attributes due to their enhanced knowledge and experience.[7] Experience with brands similarly influences future choices.[8] For example, a consumer who has grown accustomed to using Apple products regularly might weight the user interface more important and exclude a new version of a Samsung smartphone, even if it offers improved capabilities, from their consideration set. In response to these effects, some firms work diligently to influence the initial "burn-in" or "onboarding" periods. That is, to encourage new customers to come on board and start using their brands, they design programs that ensure some interaction with the customer within the first 90 days after they adopt. These relationship programs make customers more likely to express greater satisfaction, purchase additional products, and recommend the provider to friends.[9] However, sometimes the learning effect can undermine a customer's repurchase intentions if they learn about a brand's feature and decide it offers little value.

Fourth, changes due to learning and experience operate at both the individual customer level, as we just described, and the product market level. The product lifecycle is a well-recognized phenomenon that captures prototypical changes in customers' purchase criteria and marketers' actions as the product category matures. Right after a new product is introduced, for example, most of its sales represent trial purchases, so marketers often offer free samples. As the product begins to take off, with a faster growth rate, consumers begin to rebuy and influence one another through word of mouth. Therefore, firms likely drop their free sample offers, focus more on customer retention, launch loyalty programs, and develop a more competitive pricing plan. This notion is the foundation for the strategies of many apps and video games, which allow consumers to play for free for some limited time, until the mature game becomes so central to their leisure time that consumers agree to pay to continue playing and earning special status within the game.

Fifth, customer decisions take place in a **constantly changing environmental context**. Governments, industry trade groups, nonprofit organizations, and marketers always are working to change perceptions and regulations, using various communication media. Some slow-changing cultural events take generational labels or descriptions (baby boomer, millennial) that seek to capture the vast differences between people born in different eras. These influential factors can affect a person's development trajectory, whether directly or indirectly, by interacting with the other sources of change. Thus, for example, millennials have always functioned in an environment marked by ubiquitous technology, but at the same time, many people in this age cohort currently are experiencing discrete life events such as parenthood. The interaction of these sources then should have notable implications for marketers who seek to sell high-tech products to young parents to help them keep their children safe or entertained. Furthermore, consumer segments with similar preferences at one point may diverge greatly over time, even though they are subjected to similar environmental factors. Firms such as Chipotle recognize the effects of changes driven by multiple sources of change, noting, for example, that:

> Changes in customer tastes and preferences, spending patterns and demographic trends could cause sales to decline ... Our sales could be impacted by changes in consumer preferences in response to dietary concerns, including preferences regarding items such as calories, sodium, carbohydrates or fat. These changes could result in consumers avoiding our menu items in favor of other foods.[10]

Each of these five sources of customer dynamics operates simultaneously and cumulatively to determine how a customer's needs and desires change over time. As Table 3.1 shows, some sources have immediate effects (e.g., first child, well-publicized product failures); others take decades to exert an influence (e.g., personal net worth, society's norms on smoking, cultural trends regarding housing sizes). In addition, some sources have opposing effects, such that the net results on any individual customer are difficult to determine.

## Customer Dynamics: A Fundamental Assumption of Marketing Strategy

Imagine you are starting a business. After spending time and effort to understand the marketplace, you effectively target a new, homogeneous segment of customers with a "perfectly" suited product and a well-designed positioning strategy. Your sales grow quickly because your offering is the best fitting solution for this emerging segment, and other established suppliers are not targeting this segment. To meet rising demand, you build more factories, develop sales channels, and invest in brand building, all based on your well-targeted positioning strategy.

However, as the wide-ranging sources of change impact the customers in your target segment, they start migrating in different directions. A few increase their wealth and want a higher priced, more exclusive product, so they stop purchasing your widely popular product. Others discover, after using your product for a while, that they would prefer to have a few specialized, high-tech features that a smaller, niche supplier offers. You might consider adding these extra features, but your company has grown so much that this small segment is just not worth your firm's time, nor are your factories equipped to manufacture these unique features. But a greater concern emerges when you realize that the average age of your existing customers is increasing. Your product, once perceived as new and cool, is starting to lose some cachet, and some category members seem to think your firm's brand image is not what they want.

One day it dawns on you. You have become the established firm, and customers, both your own and in general, have changed. Smaller firms focused on small emerging segments are targeting your existing customers. Your sales revenue has peaked and is starting to decrease, but it is not obvious which of your customers or customer groups you should follow. Your various investments in facilities and brand building mean that barriers and switching costs (brand image, sales channel conflict) will make following some customers more difficult.

The scenario is quite common. Only monopolies or firms in markets with huge entry and exit barriers can ignore changes among their existing customers. Rather, most firms must understand, anticipate, and adapt to retain existing customers and address new needs in the future. In this sense, consider the outcomes for two automobile manufacturers.

**Example:** General Motors (US)

General Motors failed to manage the customer dynamics for its Buick brand. As customer needs changed, many existing customers moved to other suppliers, leaving behind a smaller and smaller portfolio of older customers, which is a sure sign of a problem in managing customer dynamics. Buick's brand ultimately became associated with the elderly. Even after significant repositioning efforts, its average customer age only decreased from 62 to 59 years – the second highest average customer age of all automobile brands. Its sales also dropped to half of those from a decade earlier.[11] Overall, Buick failed to manage its customer dynamics.

In contrast, Honda realized that as some of its customers grew older and increased their net worth, they sought more expensive, prestigious cars. Even though these customers indicated their high satisfaction with Honda, they were not rebuying the brand; instead, they were migrating to luxury or high-end options. A good understanding of how customers' needs were changing was the impetus Honda used to develop and launch its Acura line: a higher priced luxury car targeted to existing Honda customers with different needs. Rather than take advantage of its existing dealer network, Honda even launched 60 new dealers in North America to support its Acura automobile division, with the high-end amenities and image that customers wanted. As a result, Acura grew to become one of the best-selling luxury brands in the US within just a few years.[12]

Customers change; failing to understand and address these dynamics will lead to poor business performance. A marketer therefore needs to analyze customers' needs now, to segment and target customers in the overall marketplace with an effective positioning strategy (MP#1). But this *static* segmentation must expand to embrace the *dynamics* that emerge as existing and potential customers change. Some business or marketing strategies take years to implement, so waiting until the effects of customer dynamics show up in the firm's financial reports is not an acceptable option. Rather, variation in customers' preferences over time is an inherent condition, facing all marketers, and it represents a First Principle of marketing strategy; all customers change, and an effective marketing strategy must manage these customer dynamics (MP#2). The rest of this chapter focuses on approaches, analysis tools, and guiding frameworks for managing customer dynamics.

> *All customers change* and an *effective marketing strategy must manage customer dynamics* is Marketing Principle #2.

## Approaches to Managing Customer Dynamics

### Evolution of Approaches to Managing Customer Dynamics

Looking back over the past 30 years provides insights into the evolution of approaches to managing customer dynamics. The fast pace of technology turbulence, increases in the speed and breadth of communication, and the erosion of many traditional cultural barriers to change have increased the speed with which customers change. For example, when telephones were new in the early 1900s, it took decades for them to enter 50% of homes; cell phones reached the same level of adoption in less than five years at the end of the same century.[13]

> The fast pace of technology turbulence, increases in the speed and breadth of communication, and the erosion of many traditional cultural barriers to change have increased the speed with which customers change.

**Example:** Keurig (US)

Just 14 years after Keurig, the primary producer of single-cup coffee brewing systems, was founded, 29% of the US market had adopted such a system. This very rapid diffusion is particularly notable because it occurred in the already well-developed market of coffee drinkers.[14]

The entry barriers to starting a new business that targets an emerging customer segment or need also have decreased. As customers change more quickly than before, expectations about firms' response times also have shortened. Many startups compete to find the customer migration points or changes that will provide them with an entry point. When Uber was founded in 2009, its goal was to "crack the horrible taxi problem in San Francisco," but in five short years, it already had expanded to more than 200 cities and was valued at approximately $41 billion.[15]

Overall, the approaches for managing customer dynamics fit into three categories. Each advancement in these approaches seeks faster responses to change and promises a better fit with the needs of smaller groups of customers – two key trends in marketing practice. Figure 3.1 summarizes the different approaches and the pros and cons of each.

## Lifecycle Approach

In the 1950s and 1960s, researchers proposed the lifecycle as a way to understand customer, product, and industry dynamics. It extends the lifecycle concept from its biological roots – all living things go through stages of growth, and an organism's position in this migration determines many aspects of its existence. A lifecycle perspective has been applied to many levels of analysis to generate customer, product, and industry lifecycle models, depending on the focus of the research.[16] Specifically:

- **Customer lifecycle**: Marketers using the lifecycle perspective in the 1960s attempted to predict shopping behavior and consumer decision making;[17] economists started using it as a determinant of household spending.[18] This perspective attempts to capture how individuals *typically* change as they age and reach common age-related milestones (e.g., school, marriage, retirement). A marketing strategy then can be designed to cater to an average individual in each stage.

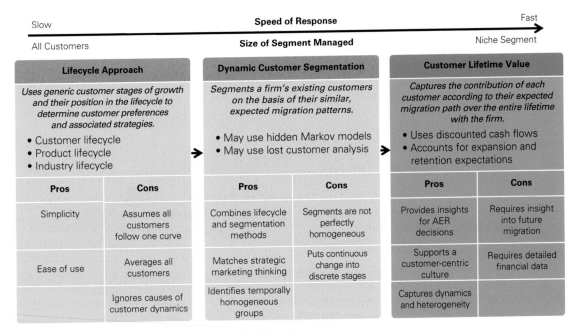

Figure 3.1 Evolution of Approaches for Managing Customer Dynamics

- **Product lifecycle**: The most popular of the three lifecycle models, the product approach proposes that various products go through four typical stages in relation to their acceptance by society: introduction, growth, maturity, and decline. The firm's marketing strategy for each product therefore should reflect where the product is in its developmental process. In the introduction stage, a company might offer free trials to early users and opinion leaders, to help increase word of mouth and accelerate the diffusion process, but in the decline stage, it likely starts pulling back on its marketing expenditures to reduce the costs dedicated to the dying product.
- **Industry lifecycle**: Industry lifecycles comprise five stages:
  1 Early establishment of its range and boundaries.
  2 An innovation stage to set a "dominant design".
  3 The shakeout stage, marked by economies of scale, such that smaller players get forced out.
  4 Maturity, when firms focus on market share and cash flows.
  5 The decline stage, when sales decay for the industry as a whole.[19]

Economists often investigate industry lifecycles, but marketers tend to ignore them, because most of these effects can be captured in product lifecycles, with faster detection and responses. In addition, marketers typically define their budgets at the product level (e.g., advertising, discounts), although some industry trade associations do make investments. In the "Got Milk?" campaign, the US dairy industry has worked hard to increase consumers' purchases and reverse the decline in the industry due to changing consumer preferences.[20]

Each lifecycle model deals with customer dynamics in a similar way but at different levels of aggregation. For example, in a customer lifecycle, customers across multiple products and firms can be aggregated to identify an average change or migration that customers follow as they age, independent of product differences. Different age ranges usually serve to capture this variation over time. Customer lifecycles mainly capture the first two sources of customer dynamics (discrete life events, typical lifecycle stage) shown in Table 3.1 above, due to typical life events and aging effects, but they are ambivalent about the specific learning, product, and environmental effects that operate on different and potentially opposing "cycles."

The learning effect can capture both customer and product lifecycle effects. For example, when a consumer buys their first computer, they might want a machine with average performance, sold by a full-service retailer that offers sales clerks who can explain the product, along with guarantees of after-sales service. As this consumer becomes more experienced and uncovers unique needs, according to how they use the computer and what features are helpful, they might opt for a customized computer ordered from an online retailer to ensure that they get exactly what they want, at a lower price. Such a migration is typical of learning and experience effects at the individual level in any product category.

When learning occurs at the level of society, the effect is captured in the product lifecycle. That is, the product lifecycle captures typical user experiences and industry developmental effects as the product category matures. However, it ignores individual and product-specific sources of customer dynamics (i.e., focuses on the third and fourth but ignores first and second sources of customer dynamics). For example, at the product market level, nearly all PCs sold during the entry stage of this product required a high degree of sales support, as was provided by clerks in retail stores such as Radio Shack.[21] But as this product "matured," even new customers felt knowledgeable and confident enough to buy even their first PC online and make design decisions with little sales support (e.g., Dell online shopping experience). Customers who gain even more expertise might purchase the separate components and build their own computers. In turn, the need for Radio Shack-level assistance largely disappeared, as did the retailer when it was unable to keep pace with these customer dynamics.

One of the greatest advantages of using the lifecycle approach to managing customer dynamics is its simplicity and ease of use – which probably explains why it is still so prevalent in beginning marketing courses and textbooks. Figure 3.2 describes a generic customer product lifecycle as well as each of its four stages.

However, suggesting that all customers or products follow a predetermined lifecycle curve, and then offering guidance about the optimal marketing strategy at each stage, is problematic for several reasons. In particular, it uses the average of all customers or all products, with the implicit (and inaccurate) assumption that all customers and products evolve in the same way. If different customers in

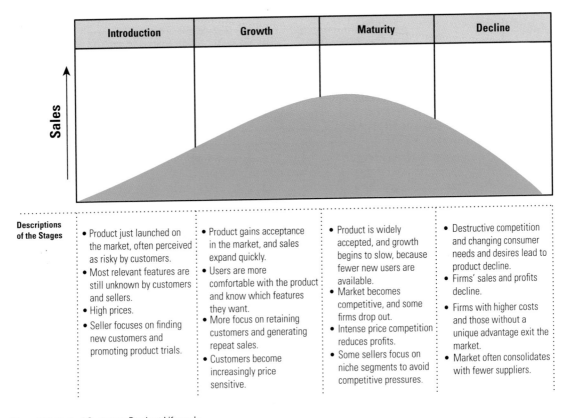

**Figure 3.2** Typical Customer Product Lifecycle

the firm's portfolio migrate in different directions – such that some people are advancing in their careers and want more expensive, feature-rich products bought in high-touch environments, while members of the other group recently started having children and are trying to reduce costs, save time, and buy with low-touch experiences – then the "average" would inaccurately predict demand for a medium-priced product sold with medium touch. This average would not appeal to either emerging segment and might match few customers in reality.

With a generic lifecycle method, managers might average across a large number of different people, product, and industry categories, which may give a general sense of how things are changing. But it cannot offer actionable guidance for any specific customer or product market. For example, millennials (born between 1977 and 2000) are the most diverse generation in history, but some researchers suggest just six segments to describe them. Using responses to survey questions about technology, cause marketing, media habits, and their general outlook on life, these studies identify the following segments: hip-ennial, millennial mom, anti-millennial, gadget guru, clean and green millennial, and old-school millennial.[22] However, marketers are often disappointed when they assume that such broad age- and preference-based groupings will define customers' desires for their firm's specific products.

Each lifecycle also provides little insight into other sources of customer dynamics that operate simultaneously. In truth, the various sources of dynamics among a firm's specific customers and products all are critical to developing an effective marketing strategy.

## Customer Dynamic Segmentation Approach

A natural evolution from the classic lifecycle approach is to apply some of the insights from MP#1 to a customer dynamics problem, segmenting a firm's existing customers according to a criterion that defines migration patterns that are expected to be similar. For example, we might anticipate that

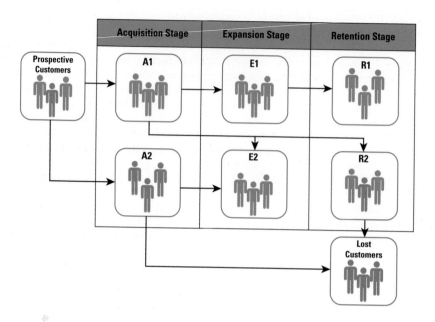

**Figure 3.3** Customer Dynamic Segmentation Approach (AER Model)

customer dynamics will be similar for customers in three different stages of dealing with a firm, as shown in Figure 3.3. This dynamic-based segmentation is sometimes called the acquisition, expansion, retention (AER) model, because it captures customers entering the firm's portfolio and accumulating over time, even as other customers slowly leave. It also has been referred to casually as the "bathtub model," with the notion that customers flow like water into and out of a bathtub.

When customers first evaluate a firm, they are just starting to learn about its offerings and how to interface with this firm. Thus, the acquisition stage begins with the first contact, typically before the first purchase occurs, when prospects and early customers have similar needs. These customers are relatively more homogeneous than all the potential customers in a specific product market category. They already have self-selected offerings from one or a few firms, so the variation in their individual differences is smaller (i.e., first two sources of customer dynamics). Customers who shop at a Porsche dealership are more similar than shoppers across all car dealerships, for example, so their future dynamics should be more similar too.

The firm's dealings with customers immediately after this acquisition stage involve **customer onboarding**, defined as the planned process of introducing new customers to a firm to improve their long-term satisfaction and loyalty. It begins when the customer first interacts with the firm and may continue for up to three to six months, depending on the complexity of the interaction. Successful onboarding lowers costs, enhances cross-selling, and increases retention rates.[23] As one Seattle-based bank manager reported in an MBA class, for its new online banking customers, an outbound "health check" in the form of a call to check on them dramatically increased their retention rates one year later. However, after six months, the same call had little effect on retention. Onboarding research also suggests that good customer service during the initial evaluation phase (while customers are still evaluating the offering) has a more significant effect on the customer's future trajectory, whereas it is less effective later, after customers already have chosen their course of action.[24]

Next, after customers transact with the firm for some period of time, their needs and desires continue to change. Segmenting them into different groups on the basis of their migration patterns or evolving needs can help the firm respond to the changes in an effective way. In this middle, expansion stage, firms are trying to upsell or cross-sell to expand their sales and engagement with existing customers. When the online UK retailer ASOS saw that 50% of orders were placed on mobile, it increased marketing expenditures by over 5% of sales to expand its digital marketing and mobile marketing activities to specifically engage this existing customer group to build loyalty and expand sales.[25] However, expansion strategies cannot focus solely on growing sales and profits; they also need to adapt and anticipate customers' future migration paths. With this approach, they can help prevent a maturing customer from considering a competitor's offering, even when different product attributes become more salient. For example, the financial service industry has identified a typical migration path in which a new customer acquired in their senior year of college with an "easy signup" credit card often requires more financial services and personal interactions when they start their first job, including automobile financing and checking accounts. This expansion stage is critical; if the credit card provider fails to offer other services when this recent graduate starts shopping for them, competitors can use the opportunity to convert them to their credit card business too.

Finally, after customers have been with a firm for a long time, even if they are using an offering that best fits their need, their relationship may grow stagnant. Especially when it comes to consumer goods or experiential services, consumers often want to try something just because it is different (e.g., restaurants, vacation destinations, clothes, coffee shops).

Even when the firm has expanded the depth and breadth of its interaction with customers, without strong relational bonds, customers may become available to competitors. The retention stage therefore deals with customers who migrate because of a mismatch in the core offering or a life event or just because they have a basic propensity to switch, in pursuit of "greener pastures." Some retention strategies aim to increase the switching costs required to move to a competitor (e.g., contracts for service with high cancellation costs, custom data formats), which often work in the short term but then can lead to strong reactions from customers. Their uncomfortable feelings of dependence and "lock in" ultimately undermine their attitudinal loyalty, giving customers reasons to spread negative word of mouth and leave if the opportunity arises. Cell phone and cable television providers currently are facing the negative repercussions of the contracts and bundled deals they established years ago to lock customers into an exchange. Suffering low levels of satisfaction and attitudinal loyalty, customers have actively sought to "cut the cord" and find alternatives to these providers.

Other options for retaining customers include enhancing brand loyalty that links the product to a person's self-identity (Harley-Davidson, BMW) or building relational ties between customers and firm employees to make the interaction seem like more than a business exchange (e.g., family doctor, hair stylists). Relational ties with a firm's brand and frontline employees (e.g., salesperson) often generate the strongest barriers to customer switching.[26]

Segmenting customers according to the acquisition, expansion, and retention (AER) stages offers several key advantages:

1 In many ways, this approach represents a natural second-order approximation of the lifecycle perspective, in that it applies the segmentation solution for managing differences in customers (MP#1) to the problem of customer dynamics (MP#2).
2 Managing customer dynamics by dividing customers into the three stages in Figure 3.3 matches the way that firms often think about and execute marketing actions in each area. For example, some firms assign a separate group to customer retention, dedicating people, budgets, and metrics to keeping existing customers.
3 Relative to other segmentation criteria for identifying groups with homogeneous migration patterns, customers' temporal position in the firm's customer portfolio is often relatively effective.[27]

Despite the significant improvements achieved from dynamically segmenting a firm's customers, rather than assuming all customers across all firms migrate the same way, many of the same disadvantages noted for segmenting customers in MP#1 and for the basic lifecycle approach apply here too, if to a somewhat lesser degree. For example, no matter how many segments a firm generates in each stage, some customers grouped together will be different. The three AER stages also involve an approach that takes customer change, a process that is continuous across time, and assesses it only according to three discrete temporal stages.

## Hidden Markov Model Analysis

Empirical modelers have developed a technique to help overcome some of the disadvantages associated with using the three AER temporal stages, which a firm can use if it has data reflecting customers' behavior over multiple periods of time. Specifically, a **hidden Markov model (HMM)** uses changes in past customer behavior to identify customer "states" and model the probability of transitioning among those various states.[28] States in HMM describe different types of behavior (e.g., large spending, frequent spending) that consumers might exhibit at different points of time; transitions among states capture the notion that consumers (or groups of consumers) can switch from one state to another at any point in time. This method is agnostic with regard to the number of states and the specific migration paths that emerge from an analysis of a firm's customer portfolio. Data Analytics Technique 3.1 provides an overview of HMM, including a description, when to use it, how it works, and a hypothetical example.

We offer a different example of dynamic segmentation here, using results obtained from a longitudinal panel of 346 B2B customers who provided six years' worth of responses about their relationships with a Fortune 500 supplier.[29] In research that applied the HMM approach, the goal was to identify changes in the supplier's relationship with its channel partners over time, as well as the drivers of relationship migrations across different states. With these data and this method, the study derived the four relationship states shown in Figure 3.4.

First, in the **transactional state**, the relationships indicate low levels of customer trust, commitment, dependence, and relational norms. For this supplier, half of its customer relationships are sitting in this state, offering only moderate cooperation, profits, or sales growth. In addition, about half of them simply remain in this state over time, although 35% shift to stronger relational states, whereas 13% move to weaker or damaged states. Like a first date, the transactional state gives customers some value and an opportunity to evaluate the relationship, but it also leaves them open to consider other alternatives that might provide even more value.

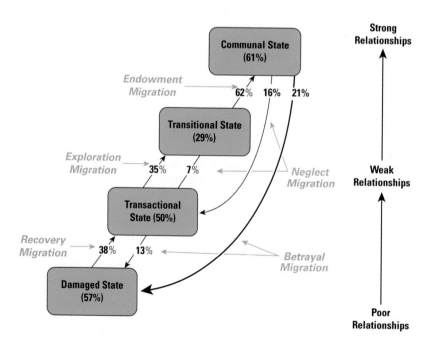

**Figure 3.4** Hidden Markov Model Analysis: Relationship States and Migration Paths

*Note:* Percentages represent how many customers migrate or remain in a relationship state each year.

*Sources:* Zhang, J., Watson, G., Palmatier, R.W. and Dant, R. (2013) 'Integrating relationship marketing and lifecycle perspectives: Strategies for effective relationship migrations,' *Marketing Science Institute Working Paper Series*, 13-121, pp. 1–48; Zhang, J., Watson, G., Palmatier, R.W. and Dant, R. (2016) 'Dynamic relationship marketing,' *Journal of Marketing*, 80(5), pp. 53–75.

### Description

Hidden Markov models (HMM) can uncover "states" of customer behaviors, as well as how those states evolve. Because each state describes the common behaviors exhibited by some groups of customers at some point in their relationship with a firm, HMM is a form of dynamic segmentation.

### When to Use It

- To understand the dynamic states of a customer's relationship with a business.
- To dynamically segment the customer base.
- To predict when a customer might change states, which may imply more or less value for the firm.
- To determine when to proactively seek to build customer relationships.

### How It Works

A customer's relationship with a firm exists in one of several possible unobserved (or hidden) states, each with finite probability. Customer behavior varies depending on the state, such that a "stronger" state customer likely buys more than one in a "weak" state. In HMM, customers also have a finite probability of transitioning from any one state to another, partially as a function of marketing efforts. For example, advertising might cause customers to shift from a weaker to a stronger state.

Customer behaviors (e.g., purchases) and firm actions (e.g., marketing) serve as inputs to the HMM, which estimates five outputs:

1. the number of feasible states (or dynamic states) in the data
2. initial probability that a customer is in each state
3. transition probabilities, or the probability that customers move from one state to another
4. the conditional probability of a behavior, given customers' hidden state
5. the effect of marketing in moving customers across states.

### Example

To dynamically segment alumni donation behavior and investigate which of its marketing activities prompt donors to give money, ABC University conducted an HMM analysis that identified three hidden states: dormant (corresponds with no donation), occasional (corresponds with infrequent donation), and active (corresponds with frequent donation). With low marketing effort, dormant customers remain dormant in the next period with a 90% probability; active customers have a 33% chance of becoming occasional in the next period. With high marketing effort, the dormant customers become occasional donors with a 57% probability, and active customers exhibit only a 25% chance of becoming occasional, both of which are good for ABC.

|  | Dormant | Occasional | Active |
|---|---|---|---|
| Dormant | 0.90 | 0.10 | 0.00 |
| Occasional | 0.08 | 0.55 | 0.37 |
| Active | 0.02 | 0.33 | 0.65 |

**Transitions: Low Marketing Effort**

|  | Dormant | Occasional | Active |
|---|---|---|---|
| Dormant | 0.40 | 0.57 | 0.03 |
| Occasional | 0.03 | 0.50 | 0.47 |
| Active | 0.00 | 0.25 | 0.75 |

**Transitions: High Marketing Effort**

Second, if customers follow a positive migration path and move to the **transitional state**, they do so only briefly. That is, in each year, approximately two-thirds of customers leave this state. Still, it represents a separate category, because while they remain here, customers exhibit higher profit potential, cooperation, and sales growth. The notable change in their relational norms – three to five times greater than any other changes – implies that in this state, specific relational exchange rules guide the interactions, rather than contracts. Following our dating metaphor, this state is like being engaged. The parties have identified each other as promising candidates for future benefits, offered some commitment, and are heading toward closer connections, but they still have some options available for switching if necessary.

Third, we get married. That is, in the **communal state**, the levels of trust, commitment, dependence, and relational norms are higher than in any other state, and the relationship produces good cooperation and profit. This state is also "sticky": 61% of customers remain in it each year. However, if a change occurs, and especially if one partner perceives a relationship transgression, the parties do not return to an earlier, weaker state; they move instead directly to the damaged state.

Fourth, this **damaged state**, similar to a "separation" or pre-divorce, produces low levels of trust and commitment and very low relational norms and cooperation, although customer dependence tends to stay high. Recovery is difficult, such that more than half of the customers in this state remain there year after year. If they do recover, they tend to move only into the transactional state. The relationships are not so much undeveloped as damaged; if not for their high dependence, many of the relationships would likely end, similar to people who want a divorce but still must interact to raise their children.

The data underlying this example further identify five "prototypical" paths that account for migrations across the four states of customer relationships with the firm. The HMM results in Figure 3.4 thus clarify that the relationships might improve (exploration, endowment, recovery) or decline (neglect, betrayal). Consider, for example, the migration from the transactional to the transitional state. It entails exploration, because the partners are exploring the potential for value creation and also demonstrating their normative willingness to share rewards fairly. In addition to identifying value opportunities and building norms, communication and competency strategies can increase the effectiveness of this exploration migration mechanism.

However, for the migration to a communal relationship, the mechanism needs to ensure greater trust, customer commitment, and relational norms, so that the relational bonds get stronger. This endowment migration also suggests a substantial increase in dependence (two to three times greater than the other variables), associated with the powerful relational bonding of the partners and their growing dependence, stemming from their non-recoverable investments in the exchange. In a business relationship, performance reaches its highest level, and **relationship investments** are critical here, reflecting the time, resources, and effort the partners devote. Such investments enable both parties to leverage their value creation capabilities.[30]

Finally, both transitional and communal to transactional state changes indicate neglect. In this pattern, the state variables decay due to passive inattention, often in the form of an absence of communication. Neglect increases the chances that the relationship returns to a transactional state. If instead of passive neglect, the relationships suffer purposeful actions to harm the relationship, such as conflict or injustice, it means betrayal. The emotionally resonant effects of this path combine to cause extreme damage to the relationship.

This real-life example using HMM demonstrates many of the benefits of a dynamic segmentation that focuses on states and state change in a customer–seller relationship. Buyer–seller relationship states may be more generalizable than behavioral data from a firm's relationship management database (e.g., purchase amounts, frequency, product selection) in terms of understanding customers' purchase states and common triggers of migrations. However, the approach and format remain similar.

## Lost Customer Analysis

Lost customer analysis is a powerful, after-the-fact diagnostic tool. In the simplest form, a firm contacts customers who have migrated away, to identify the cause for this change, then works backward to fix the problem and ensure other customers don't leave for the same reason. These data from past customers are rich in information, because the customers know the firm and its products, services, and people, unlike potential or non-customers who have never adopted the firm's offerings and have little knowledge of its actual performance. Existing customers also tend to provide biased answers, worried that any negative evaluations might harm the ongoing relationship. But lost customers already have invested the time and effort to make a change, which suggests they also might be motivated to share details about the problems they encountered.

> Lost customer analysis is a powerful, after-the-fact diagnostic tool. In the simplest form, a firm contacts customers who have migrated away, to identify the cause for this change, then works backward to fix the problem and ensure other customers don't leave for the same reason.

However, by the time the firm collects data from lost customers, those customers are already gone, and typically, it takes a significant number of lost customers before a firm recognizes that it isn't just normal customer churn but rather an indication of an underlying problem. Depending on the problem and its characteristics, a firm's response time may be fairly long, and the risk is that many customers would be lost before the firm even begins to resolve the problem. Finally, the only migration observed in a lost customer analysis is the customer leaving (exit migrations). Many other customer changes and firm actions would remain unobserved, even though they may have significant impacts on the firm's sales and profits (e.g., onboarding in the acquisition stage, cross-selling in the expansion stage).

Still, these analyses are appealing in their straightforward three-step process, which provides insights into both strengths and weaknesses:

1 Firms set regular intervals for contacting lost customers to identify the cause of their transition, where they went, and potential recovery strategies:
   - Some B2B firms with small customer portfolios visit all lost customers.
   - Most business-to-consumer (B2C) firms either sample some lost customers each interval or use a threshold criterion to determine which customers to call.
   - Ideally, the contact person is a neutral employee who does not typically interact with this customer. Salespeople who have worked previously with the lost customer should not be the contact person; they may be the cause for the transition, in which case the customer is unlikely to provide honest answers.
2 If the lost customer is not in the firm's main target segment, firms could:
   - Change their acquisition criteria, to avoid paying acquisition costs for poorly fitting customers. This issue can be especially problematic when firms reward employees to generate "new" customers.
   - Evaluate an expansion strategy to address a new subsegment of customers if it makes financial and strategic sense to appeal to these customers with a "new" offering. As described previously, Honda launched Acura largely to ensure it had an available option for satisfied Honda customers who were migrating to competitors' luxury car brands.
3 If the lost customer is in the firm's target market, firms should:
   - Fix the problem, if it involves some clear-cut product or service failure.
   - Implement retention strategies to build brand and relational loyalty if the base level of customer churn is too high (i.e., loss of customers not caused by any specific issue but a general lack of loyalty). Chapters 5–7 detail some intervention and marketing tactics about retention strategies that are likely to be most effective for each type of problem or customer group.

As a powerful diagnostic tool, lost customer analysis should be integrated into customer dynamic segmentation approaches. A choice model can benefit the lost customer analysis, and can inform analyses across all AER stages, because it predicts the likelihood of observed customer choices/responses (e.g., joining, cross-buying, leaving), using data about that customer's characteristics and past behaviors, as well as the firm's marketing interventions. Data Analytics Technique 3.2 provides an overview of a choice model analysis as a tool for understanding individual customer choices.

# Choice Model Analysis

## Description

A choice model is a mathematical model that predicts how the likelihood of an observed customer choice, or response, is influenced by a firm's marketing interventions and/or customer characteristics.

## When to Use It

- To determine a customer's most likely choice when faced with many product alternatives.
- To determine the most important factors that influence customer choice likelihood.
- To segment and target customers according to the similarities in their choice drivers.
- To simulate the potential market share for various products on the basis of customer choice.

## How It Works

In a choice model, every individual is assumed to derive an unobserved product-specific utility from several product options. The individual is assumed to pick the product option that provides the maximum utility. The dependent variable in a choice model is binary: every individual chooses (or not) a product option. Every product option's attractiveness is assumed to stem from a finite set of attributes (e.g., brand name, price). The independent variables in a choice model are the measure of the strength of attributes of each product option, e.g., product option 1 may have a low price, while product option 2 may have a higher price.

The model uses the two inputs (dependent variable, independent variables) to estimate several outputs:

1 It provides the weights (or coefficients) that each attribute would have had to cause customers to pick a certain product. This provides the most important factors that influence customer choice likelihood.
2 It is used in a predictive sense. For example, when we only observe product attributes, we can use the attributes and weights of the model to predict the choices that are likely to be made by a new set of customers. This can help a firm segment and target customers based on choice likelihood.
3 The model can be used to simulate the market share of a product category, by adding up the product choices made by all customers faced with all products. This can help managers plan their marketing efforts.

## Example

A retailer is planning to introduce a store brand of bleach (Brand C) in its bleach category, which predominantly has two national brands (Brand A and Brand B). The manager responsible for the store brand obtains transaction data from all the retail stores on the sales, price, and promotional efforts by Brand A and Brand B. With a choice model, the manager learns the weights and elasticities associated with price and promotional efforts respectively. A 1% increase in the price of Brand A decreases the sales of Brand A by 2.7%, while it increases the sales of Brand B by 1.6%. A 1% increase in the price of Brand B decreases the sales of Brand B by 3.7%, while it increases the sales of Brand A by 1.2%. A 1% increase in promotional intensity (a 10% price cut for two weeks) by Brands A and B increases their respective sales by 8% and 6%. The model fits the data very well, and hence the retail manager feels confident about the results. Also, the manager learns that frequent price promotions and lower price do help increase market share significantly.

Hence, the retail manager decides to introduce the store brand (Brand C) as a low price, generic version of bleach (price 20% below Brands A and B), with promotions held 20% more frequently than Brands A and B. The goal of the store brand introduction is to steal market share from Brands A and B, especially in a category where price seems to have a large effect on sales (as derived from the choice model).

## Customer Lifetime Value Approach

Finally, another approach for managing customer dynamics is more of a refinement than a completely separate approach, often used in conjunction with the AER dynamic segmentation method. Customer lifetime value (CLV) attempts to capture the true contribution of each customer, by determining the discounted value of the sales *and* costs associated with this customer across the expected migration paths followed throughout the relationship with the firm. In this way, CLV accounts for customer heterogeneity (MP#1), because it is calculated at the individual customer or segment level, rather than assuming all customers in the firm's portfolio have the same financial value. It also accounts for customer dynamics (MP#2), because it discounts cash flows (sales and costs) in the acquisition and expansion stages while integrating cross-selling and retention expectations for a customer or the segment's predicted migration trajectory. Determining the CLV of a customer requires good insights into probable future migration paths, based on the individual customer or segment characteristics, as well as extensive financial data at the customer or segment level. However, the payoff of CLV analysis makes the data collection efforts worthwhile.

**Example:** CLV Approach (Australia and New Zealand)

According to a survey conducted on 255 CMOs and marketing directors in Australia and New Zealand, those who responded that they "always measure the lifetime value of each customer" on average achieved a 16% increase in their annual marketing budget as compared to 0% for those who do not measure it. It also reported that 75% of the marketers are actively engaged in a CLV effort within the organization, which suggests a growing interest in the CLV approach.[31]

Using a CLV approach to manage customer dynamics thus offers several advantages, including input to make trade-offs and resource allocation decisions among different AER stages at the customer level. For example, many firms have special programs to acquire new customers, such as special finders' fees or commissions, discounts for first-time customers, and incentives to encourage employees or existing customers to promote customer acquisition. The use of such acquisition efforts often affects the retention rate and the CLV, but marketing decisions often fail to account for this linkage. For example, banking acquisition initiatives suggest that only one-third of the new customers acquired this way remain with the firm after the incentive ends. Some firms thus apply different groups, metrics, strategies, and budgets for acquisition and retention, which decouples acquisition, expansion, and retention efforts. However, optimizing acquisition and retention separately is suboptimal overall.[32]

In contrast, CLV provides all the information required for the manager to make optimal acquisition, expansion, and retention decisions. The firm knows how much effort (cost, time) that each customer is worth at any stage in its lifecycle – information that is not provided by acquisition or retention counts or rates. In turn, all the AER strategies can focus on trying to maximize CLV, which inherently accounts for the interrelations among the three stages, as well as customer heterogeneity and dynamics.

Another advantage is less readily apparent, even though it refers to the firm's overall culture. That is, a CLV approach encourages thinking about and accounting for a firm's profits as the sum of each customer's overall value, rather than thinking that a profit is the sum of product line revenue or income from different operating regions. Therefore, the customer becomes central to the firm's thinking, and marketing decisions get evaluated in light of their impact on the customer's long-term value to the firm. By starting with customers and working from there, the customer-centric perspective of the CLV helps ensure beneficial practices better than simply claiming customer centricity as a popular tagline or sentence in a mission statement. The firm is faster to detect and respond to customer and market changes. In effect, the firm is better able to manage its customer dynamics.

Consider a product-centric firm that measures its business according to product profitability, relative to a customer-centric firm that gauges its business on the basis of customer profitability. Let's imagine they both sell light bulbs. If some customers' needs and desires change, in response to growing norms for energy consciousness, the product-centric firm is unlikely to perceive any specific customer changes, because only customers more interested in green products likely make a change. All the other different types of customers might keep buying the same conventional products. Not until many customers have made the change, perhaps as a result of government incentives that encourage large segments of the population to buy the energy-conscious options, will the accumulated effects appear in the measures of product line profitability. In a customer-centric firm though, the changes appear almost instantly, because the actual profits earned from green customers are different from their expected CLV. Once detected, diagnosing the cause should be relatively straightforward, because the firm can determine which inputs to the CLV calculation have changed (e.g., acquisition costs, sales level, margin percentage, retention rates).

Several simplifications make CLV calculations even more straightforward. In Data Analytics Technique 3.3, we describe the CLV equation and provide a simple example. Assuming that the contribution margin and marketing costs do not vary over time, the CLV in dollars for the $i$th customer reduces to just five inputs:[33]

1  $M_i$ = margin for $i$th customer in $ (sales $ × margin as %)
2  $C_i$ = annual marketing cost for $i$th customer in $
3  $r_i$ = retention rate for $i$th customer as a %
4  $d$ = discount rate as a %
5  $A_i$ = acquisition cost for $i$th customer in $

Increasing margins and retention rates while decreasing acquisition and annual marketing costs and discount rates all improve the $i$th customer's lifetime value. The simplified equation also demonstrates how CLV integrates data from both acquisition ($A_i$) and retention ($r_i$) stages. Ideally, a CLV analysis takes place at the individual customer level, although firms often start by calculating the CLV for groups of similar customers or personas, then expand the number of groups as they refine the inputs to their CLV analysis. Some financial institutions track the CLV for more than 100 unique internal customer segments, which provides a fine-grained view of their customer portfolio.

**Example:** RBC (Canada)

The Royal Bank of Canada (RBC) identified, through its analyses, that medical students were high CLV customers, evaluated over long periods of time. RBC therefore implemented a program to satisfy their needs early in their careers, as well as during the progression of their careers, with products such as credit cards, help with student loans, and loans to set up new practices. In the first year, RBC's market share in this segment increased from 2% to 18%, and average sales were nearly four times higher than those to an average customer.[34] The loyalty of these customers also was very high, which reduces the risk of defection. In summary, this segment represents very high CLV customers, and the firm's targeted acquisition, onboarding, and expansion strategies allowed it to manage those valuable customers as they migrated from being students, to setting up their medical practices, to achieving professional success.

Direct marketers have been using a simplified version of the CLV for decades, targeting customers to receive expensive catalog mailings. They use three readily available customer behaviors:

1  **Recency** or time elapsed since last purchase.
2  **Frequency** of purchases in last period.
3  **Monetary** purchases in last period.

These RFM (recency, frequency, and monetary) variables put customers in rank-ordered groups, based on their value in the past year (not by modeling but by rank-order sorting). Using the profits generated from a test mailing to a few customers from each group, direct marketers then mail the catalog only to the groups with an acceptable return on investment. As expected, in head-to-head testing, CLV-based approaches consistently outperform RFM techniques. In one study, CLV even outperformed RFM based on new value generated by 45% over a 24-month period.[35]

## Description

This method quantifies the future discounted profitability of a customer. It breaks down firm- or product-level profitability to the customer level, enabling a customer-centric approach.

## When to Use It

- To identify which customers are worth acquiring and retaining.
- To determine where to target marketing programs to maximize the firm's return on marketing investments.
- To understand the "true" value of a customer to a firm, including revenues and costs.

## How It Works

Customer lifetime value is the dollar value of a customer relationship, according to its present value and the projected future cash flows from the relationship. The calculation process consists of three steps:

1  Estimating the remaining customer lifetime, or number of years over which a customer is likely to maintain a relationship with the firm, normally according to retention rates.
2  Forecasting net profits from the customer over the predicted lifetime.
3  Calculating the net present value of the future amounts. Because CLV ranks customers on the basis of profitability, it can target marketing campaigns toward the most high value customers. The simplified CLV formula is given as follows:

$$CLV_i = \frac{M_i - C_i}{1 - r_i + d} - A_i$$

where:
$CLV_i$ = customer lifetime value
$M_i$ = margin of $i$th customer in \$
$C_i$ = annual marketing cost for $i$th customer in \$
$r_i$ = retention rate for $i$th customer as a %
$d_i$ = discount rate as a %
$A_i$ = acquisition cost for $i$th customer in \$

Both current and potential customers can be segmented according to expected long-term profits or CLV. The graph below plots the CLV distribution of a firm, which consists of inactive customers (low to negative CLV), active customers (positive CLV), and highly active customers (very high CLV), and shows that the right portion of the graph highlights a firm's most active customers. Firms can use such a graph to identify and target the most profitable customers for marketing retention campaigns.

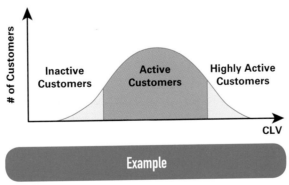

## Example

A manager of a cable company wants to determine if it is strategic to acquire the Brett family, by estimating their household-level CLV. The manager estimates that it will cost the company \$65 ($A$) to get the Bretts to switch, and the Bretts will generate \$100 profit each year ($M$), with a \$10 annual marketing cost to retain them ($C$). The estimated retention rate ($r$) is 65%, and the current discount rate is 5% ($d$). From the formula, the CLV for the Bretts is \$235, which suggests that the Bretts, on net, are profitable to the cable company.

# Framework for Managing Customer Dynamics

Figure 3.5 offers an organizing framework for managing customer dynamics, integrating the approaches and analyses described in this chapter. Three key inputs are needed to conduct a customer dynamic segmentation of the firm's existing customers and evaluate the effectiveness of prior AER strategies. Whereas MP#1 focused on the overall marketplace to narrow down which consumers or businesses a firm should target, MP#2 focuses only on existing customers, to understand how they change over time. The framework for managing customer dynamics in turn generates three outputs. Specifically, this framework identifies the firm's existing customer personas, how and why customers migrate, and how the firm should position itself relative to each persona across the different AER stages. Furthermore, it describes the AER strategies that will be most effective for each persona in each stage. These three outputs then provide inputs that inform the last two Marketing Principles. We outline a step-by-step process and conceptual example for using this framework and transforming the inputs into outputs.

## Inputs to the Customer Dynamics Framework

Of the three inputs to this framework, the first, and arguably most important, is the firm's existing customer portfolio. Ideally, a firm's customer relationship management (CRM) system provides detailed customer-level data for the dynamic segmentation analysis. Financial accounting (sales, margins), product purchase (timing, frequency, product migrations), and demographic (zip code, family size, age) data generally are readily accessible, but some of the most difficult information to capture is what customers are thinking and feeling at these different points, which entails data not found in a CRM database (e.g., surveys, focus groups).

The second input is data linking past customer responses with specific marketing programs and the programs' cost. In some cases, connecting programs (advertising, new customer promotion, price discounts, rewards program gifts) to individual customers is not feasible. But firms have alternatives. They can run small experiments, offering a marketing program or not to equal-sized, randomly split groups of customers and then tracking the performance of the customers for some period of time. This "clean test" of the effects of a program indicates how it may vary across different customer personas at various points in their lifecycle.

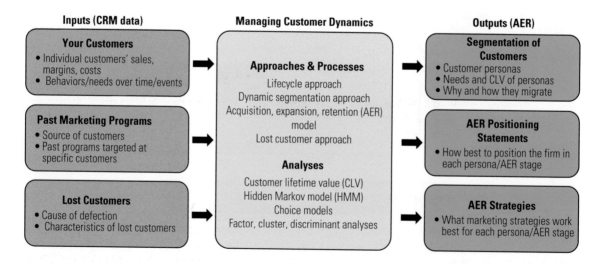

**Figure 3.5** Framework for Marketing Principle #2: All Customers Change → Managing Customer Dynamics

A third input is the qualitative and quantitative information gleaned from the lost customer analysis, which reveals the causes of customer defection, where they go, and potentially effective recovery strategies. It also can uncover ineffective AER strategies, such as when the firm acquires customers who are not in its target market, upsells or cross-sells poor fitting services, or fails to bond relationally with customers through their brands or employees. The lost customer analysis can be triangulated or compared with the insights gained from the first two inputs; much of this information likely is redundant but less susceptible to managerial bias or alternative explanations.

## Outputs of the Customer Dynamics Framework

The customer dynamics framework uses these three inputs, applies one or more of the different approaches and analyses for managing customer dynamics, and thereby generates three outputs. The first output is a description of the firm's customer personas and expected migrations to understand how they change, including:

1 Critical life event triggers.
2 The products and services customers buy at different points in their lifecycle migration.
3 When they stop buying and why.
4 How they feel at different stages in their lifecycle.
5 The CLV of customers in each persona.

The second and third outputs are closely interrelated and represent the strategic decisions that occur as part of the management of customer dynamics. Deciding how to position the firm and its offerings for each persona across AER stages are key decisions, informed by insights gained from dynamic segmentation and CLV analyses. This output appears in the form of AER positioning statements. In many ways, they parallel the decisions firms make to determine how to position themselves in the overall market to targeted customers, but with greater refinement and more focus on existing customers, by capturing differences across personas and stages. However, AER positioning statements need to be congruent with the firm's overall positioning in the marketplace to be effective.

Finally, the last outcome builds on these AER positioning statements by outlining what marketing strategies have been and may be most effective across personas and stages. Thus, AER strategies focus on the how; AER positioning statements focus on the what. As firms begin to manage customer dynamics proactively, these strategies may appear somewhat general and not based on "hard data," but over time, as firms identify gaps and collect and analyze more data, the strategies grow more robust.

## Process for Managing Customer Dynamics

To convert CRM, marketing program, and lost customer input data into dynamic segmentation and AER positioning statements and strategies, managers should follow a series of steps. The process for managing customer dynamics may appear sequential, but in reality, it often is more iterative, such that findings from one step cause the firm to go back and challenge its previous explicit or implicit constraints, requiring additional data collection and analysis. In addition, various approaches or analysis options may be available for each step, but for conciseness and ease of exposition, we outline the process that is likely to be accessible to most firms here.

### Step 1: Dynamic Segmentation

Existing customers should be divided into each AER stage based on how long they have been customers and other relevant data. Next, the cluster analysis technique outlined in Chapter 2 (Data Analytics Technique 2.1) can be applied to existing customers, using surveys and CRM data, after dividing the customer portfolio into the three AER stages. Customers in the acquisition stage have been recently acquired; for offerings with long evaluation phases, potential or prepurchase customers might be added to this analysis. Expansion stage customers have learned about the firm and its offerings (i.e., experienced users) and are interested in evaluating additional services, upgrading to higher performance products, or are beginning to identify some changing needs and desires. Finally, customers in the retention stage are showing signs of potential defection (e.g., slower repurchase rates, smaller purchase quantities, expressions of dissatisfaction), and they need to be managed with extra interventions, assuming they still fit with the firm's goals. On the first pass, the number of segments per stage should range between three and five, to make the process and subsequent execution less complex and more intuitive to managers.

## Step 2: Migration Paths and Triggers

The segments in each AER stage need to be linked together to model how customers migrate over time. In some cases, there will be little branching. A group of customers follows the same path, although perhaps at different rates, depending on their individual situations (e.g., timing of marriage, children). Otherwise, typical customers branch into different personas as they migrate over time. These links can be uncovered by observing changes in customer behaviors in the firm's CRM database (recall Figure 3.3). A specific customer's CRM data after their initial engagement with the firm might put them in segment A1 (acquisition stage, segment 1), but their CRM data today puts them in E1 (expansion stage, segment 1). Thus, this customer would have migrated from A1 to E1 over time. Customer surveys and focus groups offer alternative ways to add richness to the limited data available in a firm's CRM database. By evaluating the relative percentages and average migration times in the CRM and/or survey sample, firms can label each path with a percentage and number of years, which add insights into the frequency and timing associated with each migration path.

Qualitative data can help identify a triggering event or mechanism underpinning each migration and thereby answer questions about what causes the change. Is the migration due to a specific event (marriage, new purchasing manager), an experience or learning effect (desire for higher performance model after mastering the basic model), or a changing self-image (status seeking, performance seeking), or is the customer just bored and ready to experiment with another offering? Depending on the firm and the characteristics and size of its customer portfolio, an easy way to identify trigger events is to visit, call, or survey customers who undergo prototypical migrations to ask why their purchase behavior has changed. In turn, this understanding can provide critical information for developing AER strategies. For example, many consumer firms recognize that the birth of a first child triggers customer migration, such that consumers' needs for the firm's offering changes dramatically, so in an expansion strategy, firms can look for and launch a targeted campaign as soon as a customer has a first child.

> Qualitative data can help identify a triggering event or mechanism underpinning each migration and thereby answer questions about what causes the change. Is the migration due to a specific event (marriage, new purchasing manager), an experience or learning effect (desire for higher performance model after mastering the basic model), or a changing self-image (status seeking, performance seeking), or is the customer just bored and ready to experiment with another offering?

Firms frequently express dissatisfaction with the quality or breadth of data they have about customers. To address this issue, many firms rely on loyalty or rewards programs, which offer the substantial benefit of access to individual-level, longitudinal data. Las Vegas casinos have perfected this approach, but firms in many industries (airlines, grocery stores, coffee shops, clothing retailers, hotels) collect detailed longitudinal data about customers as they use loyalty cards. Furthermore, firms could buy additional data about their customers, then merge or fuse them with the detailed purchase or transactional data that most firms possess. If a firm can collect detailed information over multiple periods of time for a good sized sample of customers, some more powerful analysis techniques become viable, such as the HMM (Data Analytics Technique 3.1 above), which assigns customers to states/segments, links the states/segments, and determines the probability of migrating among states, according to underlying data.

**Example:** Proximus (Belgium)

One creative solution to the problem of lack of detailed customer data utilized by the Belgian telecommunications company Proximus was to gamify its loyalty program. The "Play&Gold" loyalty program engages customers by allowing them to play a game on their phone for rewards such as free minutes, discounts, and extra SMS messages. This allows Proximus to collect information about members' phone numbers, emails, dates of birth, and names, which is generally hard to come by for pre-paid mobile customers. The program has been a great success as more than 30% of pre-paid customers are monthly active users of the game.[36]

## Step 3: Customer Lifetime Value of Segments and Migrations

After a firm has mapped the dynamics of its customer portfolio, it should determine the CLV of customers in each segment and estimate the change in CLV due to each customer's migration, so that it can prioritize its AER investments. Data Analytics Technique 3.3 above outlines the analysis approaches and data elements required to calculate CLV. In an ideal case, the dynamic segmentation and CLV would take place at the customer level, but few firms have sufficient data or accounting processes sophisticated enough to track or allocate costs to this level of analysis. Instead, a first step can be to use the average or typical values for each dynamic segment (or state in HMM analyses) and migration path. When the CLV has been determined for a prototypical customer in each segment, the difference in value across two linked segments provides some indication of the effect of a specific migration.

At this point, it is often appropriate to label at least the most important segments and migration paths. The name of each label should capture the salient feature of the segment or migration, its triggering event or mechanism, and its relative importance. Once named, segments typically are referred to as personas, because they describe key features and can use visual representations to help managers understand, remember, and communicate customer dynamics to the overall organization (Figure 3.6 below contains a sample visual representation of the results of a dynamic segmentation.) Ranking personas by importance (e.g., $CLV_{typical}$ × number of customers in the segment) and migration paths by annual transition magnitude (e.g., change in $CLV_{migration\ path}$ × number of customers migrating annually) provides a commonsense way to prioritize AER strategies and subsequent marketing expenditures.

## Step 4: AER Positioning Statements

A short positioning statement for each persona should answer a few key questions, concisely:

- *Who* are the customers in this persona?
- *What* is the set of needs that the product or service fulfills for this persona?
- *Why* is this product/service the best option to satisfy the needs of this persona?
- *How* should the product/service be modified, in keeping with the needs of the customers in this persona?
- *When* do customers enter and leave this persona (trigger or migration mechanism)?

There are a few differences between such AER positioning statements and the firm's overall positioning statement:

1 AER positioning statements are internally focused on existing customers, rather than outwardly focused on all customers in the market category.
2 They are more concerned with meeting customers' needs over time than with beating competitors to earn the initial purchase.
3 AER positioning statements address "when" questions, detailing triggers and migration mechanisms, which are not included in typical positioning statements.

However, the benefits gained from both types of statements can be similar, in that a short statement provides a roadmap for various implementation decisions involved in marketing a product or service to customers – especially when the members of the firm who conduct the customer dynamic research are different from those executing specific AER programs, as is typical in most firms.

If possible, the labels for both the AER positioning statements and the AER strategies for personas with common customers who migrate together should be combined in a group description, to reduce complexity and communicate this important commonality. A common descriptive name with a tag can capture the essence of the personas as they migrate across stages, from acquisition to expansion to retention. For example, a persona focused on the environmental soundness of an offering could be labeled, respectively, a budget-minded greenie, status-minded greenie, and lapsed greenie. The AER positioning statements and strategies should be grouped together too, although when customers branch out and migrate into unique segments, the labels and AER positioning statements and strategies statements need to be unique.

## Step 5: AER Strategies

Using the AER positioning statements, insights from the dynamic segmentation, and information on the effectiveness of past campaigns (i.e., inputs to the framework), firms should develop a set of AER strategies. The AER positioning statements define the objectives; the AER strategies describe the process or how to reach these objectives. Yet the strategies still are developed and organized by stage, to match how the firm manages its marketing and acknowledge the inability of some marketing tactics (e.g., television advertising) at a specific stage to target different personas. Specifically, firms should develop acquisition strategies for all personas in this stage at the same time, while still differentiating programs that may be more effective for some specific persona, which ensures both the scalability and the customizability of the firm's offerings. Mostly applicable to expansion and retention strategies, the findings and corrective actions identified in the lost customer analysis can provide key insights to be integrated and addressed in AER strategies.

If there are many personas then some strategies may require trade-offs across personas. Therefore, the AER strategies should be developed on the basis of the ranked AER positioning statements, in recognition of the value generated from different personas and migrations. Past research provides some generic guidance into the trade-offs to consider when designing AER strategies:[37]

- A strategy that optimizes CLV maximizes neither the acquisition rate nor the retention rate.
- Investments in customer AER strategies have diminishing marginal returns.
- Underspending in AER strategies is more problematic and results in smaller CLV than does overspending.
- A poor allocation of retention investments has a larger negative effect on long-term performance than poor allocation of acquisition investments.

In Chapters 5–7, we detail the marketing tactics, programs, and strategies involved in branding, developing new offerings, and using relationship marketing to make AER strategies more effective. Finally, we note here that MP#2 cannot be resolved with a one-time, in-depth research project. Understanding and managing customer dynamics is an iterative process that must become part of the firm's ongoing marketing practice. New insights or findings often emerge "off cycle" and should be integrated into the customer dynamics framework regularly. When the results fail to reach objectives, mini-initiatives with more specialized techniques can help fix the problem. These results then can be assimilated into the overall framework. Small experiments to resolve a key question or problem often is an effective technique.

---

Understanding and managing customer dynamics is an iterative process that must become part of the firm's ongoing marketing practice. New insights or findings often emerge "off cycle" and should be integrated into the customer dynamics framework regularly.

# Managing Customer Dynamics Examples

## Dynamic Segmentation Hotel Example

To exemplify how the AER model for dynamically segmenting a firm's customer portfolio works, we apply it to the example firm in Figure 3.6. This visual summary represents ABC Hotel's dynamic segmentation and most common migration paths. Its acquisition stage customers are those it has obtained in the past six months; expansion stage customers are those whose first transaction with the firm was between six and eighteen months ago; and retention stage customers have been with the firm for more than eighteen months. From a cluster analysis of customers, using sales data and surveys of a small sample of customers in each stage, ABC Hotel uncovers two segments each in the acquisition, expansion, and retention stages.

In the acquisition stage, Learners tend to visit the hotel a few times per year, and they spend $500 annually. They value prestige and peace of mind, and they are not price sensitive. This segment consists mainly of men with high incomes, between the ages of 35 and 50 years. In contrast, One Timers tend to visit the hotel only once and spend $300 per year. They value convenience and discounts; their visits to the hotel are mainly to attend local conferences. The One Timers consist of men and women, with medium to high incomes, most of whom are 25–34 years of age.

The expansion stage includes Satisfied Customers, who visit the hotel frequently and spend $1,000 per year, while also using ancillary services provided by the hotel (i.e., dining room, spa, gym). Their preferences are similar to Learners', in that they value prestige and peace of mind and are not price sensitive. The other expansion segment, Upgraded Customers, visit the hotel twice per year, spending $750 on average, but they would return if they were offered some upgraded service during their initial visit.

Finally, in the retention stage, Loyalists visit the hotel regularly, spending $1,500 a year and using at least three ancillary services, such as the golf course, spa, salon, and gym. Bored Customers visit very infrequently, and constantly seek deep price discounts before they register.

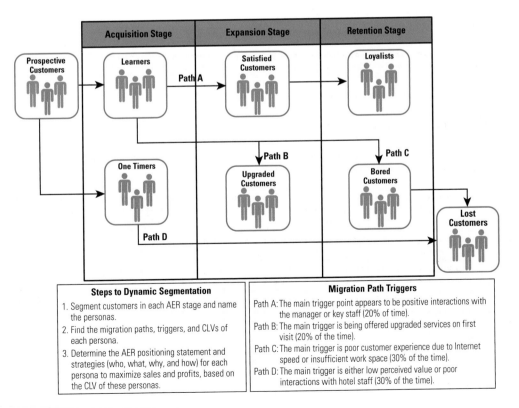

**Figure 3.6** Dynamic Segmentation: Hotel Example

By linking each AER stage, ABC Hotel also identifies the four most common migration paths and their triggers. **Path A** (accounting for 20% of the migrations) captures Learners moving into the Satisfied Customers group, and then to Loyalists. The main trigger point appears to be positive interactions with a manager or key staff on their first visit. If the staff proactively reaches out to these customers a day before and a day after each visit, customers consistently express higher satisfaction with the firm and spent more at the hotel in a calendar year. On **Path B** (20%), Learners move to Upgraded Customers; the main trigger here is an offer of upgraded services on the first visit. **Path C** (30%) involves Learners moving to Bored Customers, seemingly because of their poor customer experience with Internet speed and the amount of work space. Finally, **Path D** (30%) involves One Timers moving on to become Lost Customers, due to low perceived value or poor relational interactions with hotel staff.

Thus ABC Hotel achieves several insights:

1 In each AER stage, one of the personas offers better long-term revenue, suggesting opportunities to implement AER strategies and move customers to a better state, or at least optimize marketing investments.
2 The timing of AER strategies is key, because in some cases, ABC gets no second chance (i.e., treatment on their first visit).
3 The key triggers of positive migrations, or suppressors of negative migrations, are unique to each persona (relational interactions, upgraded services, Internet speed, work spaces).

After ABC Hotel has mapped out these dynamics of its customer portfolio, it can determine the CLV of customers in each segment and estimate the change in CLV due to each migration, which will enable it to prioritize its AER investments.

## Markstrat Simulation: Making Decisions when Dealing with Customer Dynamics

The Markstrat simulation software (see Data Analytics Technique 1.1 for an overview) provides an interactive environment to observe and react to customer dynamics, as shown in Figure 3.7.[38] In each

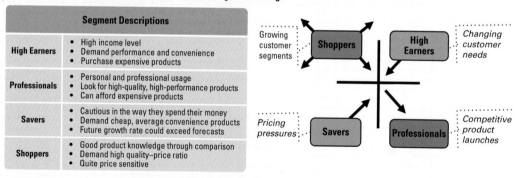

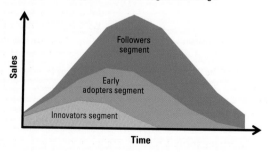

**Figure 3.7** Markstrat Simulation: Making Decisions When Dealing with Customer Dynamics

decision round, the customer segments move, representing about one year of customer migration; the size of market segments also change as customer preferences change over time, and the pace of these changes depends on firms' marketing decisions. For example, if many firms in an industry target their advertising expenditures toward a specific product or market, that segment will grow faster at the expense of other market segments, which demonstrates the impact of market mix decisions on industry and product dynamics. The simulated environment has two independent industries, a mature industry (labeled Sonites) and an emerging industry (labeled Vodites). The change of customer dynamics in the mature space is significantly slower than that in the highly dynamic emerging market, where a change in customer preferences can be very dramatic. Thus, the Markstrat environment demonstrates customer-, product-, and industry-level changes simultaneously, even as managers implement marketing decisions, and observe their effects.

# Summary

Customers are always changing; customer dynamics cannot be avoided. Marketers thus need to understand and manage changing needs to develop effective strategies. Customer dynamics arise from five sources that often operate at different levels and rates, making the problem a difficult one to manage. Individual customers may change due to *life events* (marriage, parenthood, retirement), which have immediate impacts on many aspects of their purchase decisions. Underlying these dramatic changes, customers also move relatively more slowly through a *typical lifecycle* as they age (e.g., less risk taking, more financial means). Individual changes also occur at the *product level* as consumers gain experience with and knowledge about a product category (learning effects). Moreover, learning and experience extend beyond the individual customer level to exert effects at the *society level*, where a product lifecycle is a well-recognized phenomenon, capturing prototypical changes in customers' purchase criteria as the product category or industry segment matures. Finally, each customer is situated in a changing *environmental context* (legal, demographic, culture), in which various outside entities seek to change their perceptions and behaviors (e.g., environmental sustainability). The premise that all customers change and that an effective marketing strategy must manage these ever-present customer dynamics therefore is another First Principle of marketing strategy (MP#2).

Approaches to managing customer dynamics span three categories. Each advancement aims to be faster to respond to changes and focused on smaller groups of customers – a common theme in the evolution of marketing practice over time. The first technique is a *lifecycle approach*, which identifies typical or average changes for individual customers as they mature (customer lifecycle); for product markets as the product gets launched, matures, and ultimately declines (product lifecycle); and for industries as they emerge, grow, and decline (industry lifecycle). The benefit of the lifecycle approach is that it is easy to understand and apply. But it also assumes that all people or products follow the same lifecycle curve, which is rarely the case. Some people marry early or late; some products grow and decay quickly or slowly. Thus, marketing strategies derived from average dynamics will be suboptimal. In addition, managers must account for the effects of changes in both people and products simultaneously, such that focusing on the lifecycles of only customers or only products inherently ignores another critical source of customer dynamics.

The second technique for dealing with customer dynamics is a *customer dynamics segmentation approach*, as manifested in the *AER model*. In this case, marketers apply some of the insights from MP#1 to the customer dynamics problem. Specifically, by segmenting a firm's existing customers into three stages (acquisition, expansion, and retention) during their interactions with the firm, temporally similar customers can be grouped, which also allows the marketer to identify different personas at each stage and different migration paths across stages. This approach is essentially a natural, second-order approximation of the lifecycle perspective that acknowledges that customers systematically vary across temporal stages – although it ignores differences in specific customers – by applying a segmentation solution for managing dynamics. Dividing a portfolio of customers into three discrete AER stages and then grouping them also raises concerns because customer change is often continuous, whereas this approach divides customers into segments according to specific temporal stages.

Segmentation approaches also can use *hidden Markov models* (HMM), an empirical technique that can identify customer states and determine the probability of transitioning among them, which might enhance dynamic segmentation as the temporal states and migration paths emerge from the data, rather than remaining limited to three temporal stages (AER). A *lost customer analysis* can be integrated into the customer dynamic segmentation approach too, to identify the underlying cause of the most detrimental customer change (i.e., defection) and then work backward to "fix" the problem. But this backward-looking analysis does not anticipate customer dynamics. It can only investigate them after they occur.

The third technique for dealing with customer dynamics is a *customer lifetime value (CLV) approach*, often used in conjunction with dynamic segmentation across AER segments or HMM states. CLV captures the financial value of each customer by determining the discounted value of the sales and costs associated with a customer, based on their expected purchase history and migration path over the entire lifetime with the firm. Its greatest advantage is that it provides a means to make optimal trade-off and resource allocation decisions across stages and market mix investments, in a proactive (rather than backward-looking) manner.

The organizing framework for managing customer dynamics in Figure 3.5 integrates all the approaches and analyses described in this chapter. There are three key inputs, which are required to conduct a customer dynamic segmentation of the firm's existing customers and evaluate the effectiveness of past AER strategies. Whereas MP#1 focuses on the market as a whole, to determine which consumers or businesses in the overall marketplace a firm should target, MP#2 narrows the scope to focus on just the firm's own customers and understand how existing customers change over time. The framework for managing customer dynamics also generates three outputs, used as inputs for the final two Marketing Principles. Specifically, this framework identifies existing customer personas and how and why customers migrate, as well as how the firm should position itself to appeal to each persona across different AER stages. It also describes the AER strategies that will be most effective for each persona in each stage.

## Takeaways

- The second underlying challenge that firms face when making marketing decisions is that all customers change. This principle can be either an opportunity or a threat, depending on how well the firm understands and manages it.

- Customer dynamics arise from five sources. Individual customers change due to life events and move through typical lifecycles as they age. Customer learning effects occur as customers gain knowledge about a product category. Learning and experience effects also operate at a societal level. Finally, each customer is situated in an environmental context that is constantly changing, filled with outside entities trying to change the customer's perceptions and behaviors. Each source works simultaneously and cumulatively to create customer dynamics.

- Due to rapid technological and communication developments, the speed at which customers change and their expectations about firms' response times have increased.

- There are three approaches to managing customer dynamics: lifecycle, customer dynamic segmentation, and customer lifetime value approaches.

- The lifecycle approach predicts that customers, products, and industries go through similar lifecycles that can be used to inform marketing decisions at different stages. This approach can be problematic though, because it assumes an average rate of change.

- The customer dynamic segmentation approach, with an AER model, predicts that acquisition occurs when customers are just beginning to interact with the firm (customer onboarding). Expansion is when the firm tries to cross-sell or upsell customers and increase engagement, and retention involves keeping customers who might otherwise tend to migrate to competitors.

- Hidden Markov models (HMM) can uncover states, reflecting how a large set of customer behaviors changes over time. A state is similar to a consumer segment, describing common behaviors by a group of consumers at some point in their relationship with the firm. Thus, HMM enables dynamic segmentation.

- As a powerful diagnostic tool, lost customer analysis can be integrated into a customer dynamic segmentation approach. It often features a mathematical choice model that predicts the likelihood of an observed customer choice or response (e.g., joining, cross-buying, leaving), according to data gathered from the firm's marketing interventions and customer characteristics.

- Customer lifetime value (CLV) seeks to capture the true contribution of each customer, according to the migration path this customer is predicted to follow throughout the relationship with the firm. This approach beneficially provides guidance for making trade-offs and resource allocation decisions among different AER stages. It also can change a firm's culture, such that the focus is on profits as the sum of each customer's lifetime value, rather than the sum of a product line's profits. The firm then becomes more focused on customers, enabling firms to detect and respond to market changes.

- The framework for managing customer dynamics uses three inputs: CRM, marketing programs, and lost customer data. It produces three outputs: dynamic segmentation and AER positioning statements and strategies.

## Analytics Driven Case

# Preempting and Preventing Customer Churn at TKL

### Problem Background

TKL is a leading US-based distributor of electrical component products. TKL uses a field sales force to sell to customers in three major industry segments: construction, industrial, and original equipment manufacturers (OEMs). TKL's buyers come from all continents, although US-based buyers constitute more than 75% of all sales. Even though electrical components represent a mature industry, TKL and four other market leaders jointly account for less than 40% of all industry sales. The heavy fragmentation in the industry is driven by thousands of regional competitors; regional competitors mainly compete on low prices, and serve almost every local market. Thus, TKL faces intense competition from local and small distributors in every regional market. A heavily fragmented and competitive market means perennially high customer churn rates in the industry, which results in a large number of lost/inactive customers for each major player.

However, even the traditionally dynamic industry had seen tumultuous change in the previous decade. While no radical innovations occurred at the product level, customers had evolved as the product category matured, and customers had gained experience and knowledge about a product category (like the "learning effects" described earlier in Chapter 3). For example, most buyers realized that regional competitors were the best at offering lower prices, while national competitors offered higher product quality and longer warranties. Also, as most purchases were rebuys or modified rebuys, buyers realized that they could request firms to offer more attentive sales efforts, such as faster product delivery and online purchasing. Also, with buying firms' workplaces growing younger and the lack of interest in manufacturing/construction jobs among the young generation, TKL perceived a widening gap between its products and the knowledge of the buyers' workforce. However, younger buyers were more comfortable using newer Internet-enabled technologies in their purchasing environment.

As a result, in early 2015, TKL was worried about its market position. Looking through its key performance indicators did not present a rosy picture (Table 1). TKL's average market share (across all regions) was down 8% from the 21% four years ago. Its annual sales were down from $1.1 bn to $0.9 bn, and profits were also down from $0.16 bn to $ 0.14 bn. Turning to its key customer metrics, it realized that it was facing difficulties with both customer acquisition and retention. While its new customer acquisition had been traditionally high at 9% in 2010, it was down to less than half (4%) in 2014. Moreover, TKL was also having difficulty retaining customers; churn rates had grown from 12% to 18% over the last four years.

**Table 1** Dynamics in TKL's Market Position

|  | 2010 | 2014 |
|---|---|---|
| Market share | 21% | 13% |
| Annual Sales | $1.1 bn | $0.9 bn |
| Profits | $0.16 bn | $0.14 bn |
| Customer Churn | 12% | 18% |
| Customer Acquisition | 9% | 4% |

TKL drew some solace from the fact that the industry itself was showing a poorer recovery from the Great Recession compared to other industries such as high-tech; the industry profit figures were indeed down by 15% over the last four years. But TKL did not want to rest on the notion that the entire industry was attacked, but rather wanted to approach the customer change trends in a proactive way. As a first step, it reviewed its reliability rankings on the key product attributes that buyers value, provided by third-party research firms. The ratings (Table 2) provided a first-cut insight to TKL. While TKL held steady as the most price-competitive provider in the market, it fell from #3 to #4 as a provider of warranty after purchase. However, it suffered more damage on the dimensions of delivery speed and sales support capabilities. TKL had fallen from #6 to #8 on the delivery speed attribute, and suffered a much steeper drop on sales support capabilities, where it had dropped from an already poor ranking of #8, to a sub-par #12.

**Table 2** Dynamics in Customer Perceptions of TKL

|  | Industry Rank (2010) | Industry Rank (2014) |
|---|---|---|
| Price | 1 | 1 |
| Warranty | 3 | 4 |
| Speed of Delivery | 6 | 8 |
| Sales Support | 8 | 12 |

TKL was sure that the drop in rankings on the product attributes (product is used in the general sense capturing both product and service attributes) was hurting it, but was not sure how to quantify it in economic terms. Moreover, data suggested that it had 25,000 inactive or low-performing customers in the 2010–14 period, even though it acquired 10,000 new customers every year. Given the market changes, it was not sure which customers to focus on acquiring and expanding. But TKL did believe there were large potential gains from a systematically developed acquisition strategy.

## Problem Statement

As we documented in Chapter 3, customers change; and failing to understand and address these dynamics will lead to poor business performance. A marketer therefore needs to expand the scope of static segmentation (as in the DentMax case) to embrace the notion that customers change over time, as their relationship with the firm changes. Since variation in customers' preferences over time is an inherent condition facing all marketers, an effective marketing strategy must manage these customer dynamics (MP#2). TKL's problem appears to fit the second fundamental marketing problem that all firms face while formulating marketing strategy, that is, multiple factors were working together in multifaceted ways to make all customer change in the market. So, TKL had to analyze which needs, desires, and preferences across its buyers were most important to attracting (onboarding), and growing the sales (expanding) of its buyer base, to minimize churn and inactivity. Thus, TKL launched a strategic initiative aimed at answering the following questions:

- Which product attributes are most desired by customers at the time of acquisition and expansion?
- How to effectively segment the market for buyers of electrical components, so as to decide:
  - Which customers to acquire?
  - Which customers to expand?
- Given the segmentation of customers, how should TKL modify its targeting and positioning strategy to deal with customer dynamics?

In 2015, TKL decided to employ a choice-based dynamic segmentation and targeting project to answer the questions above and to manage customer dynamics. Through segmentation, it sought to determine the key purchase attributes required to acquire customers, as well as grow them over three years.

## Data[1]

TKL focused its analytics efforts on its alternators category as a first step, with a plan to roll the analysis to all other categories if the efforts were successful. As a first step, TKL turned to its analytics team to put together a comprehensive sample database of two kinds of customers: 1,000 customers who were "recently acquired" (i.e. in late 2014), and 1,000 expansion stage customers (those acquired three years ago).

TKL sought to model the probability that a customer was acquired vs. not acquired. So, having data only on its 1,000 acquired customers would present a partial picture of its acquisition success. So, it constructed a group of customers who were in the marketing list that it used to acquire customers, but were unsuccessful in acquiring, either because the customer bought from TKL's competitors, or did not buy at all. TKL drew a stratified random sample of 1,000 non-acquired customers from the same regions where acquired customers came from. Thus, its acquisition model consisted of 2,000 customers: 1,000 in the acquired group and 1,000 in the non-acquired group. TKL also collected the following variables on the drivers of acquisition:

- *Price*: The transaction price offered to customers at the time of purchase consideration.
- *Warranty*: The days of warranty offered on the product (with 100% refund on failure), at the time of purchase consideration.
- *Delivery Time*: The days of delivery time promised to the customer, at the time of purchase consideration.
- *Sales Support*: The number of sales support staff in the regional division, at the time of purchase consideration.
- *Industry Group*: Dummy variables capturing whether the prospective customer was in the construction, industrial, or OEMs sector.
- *Firm Size*: The number of employees in the prospective customer's organization.
- *Centralized Buying Center*: A dummy variable capturing whether the buyer's organization had a centralized (1) or decentralized (0) buying center.

Next, TKL sought to model the probability that a customer who was acquired three years ago was still a customer (i.e. expanding scope of transactions) vs. whether they dropped out. So, again, having data only on its 1,000 expanding customers would present a partial picture of its marketing success.

---

[1] These analyses were performed using MEXL software as described in Data Analytics Technique 9.1 using data from the TKL Case dataset.

So, it constructed a group of customers who it was successful in acquiring, but unsuccessful in retaining. TKL drew a stratified random sample of 1,000 non-retained customers from the same regions where retained customers came from. Thus, its model consisted of 2,000 customers: 1,000 in the expanding group and 1,000 in the dropped out group. TKL also collected the following variables on the drivers of retention:

- *Price*: The average price offered to customers over the three years.
- *Warranty*: The average days of warranty offered on the product (with 100% refund on failure), to customers over the three years.
- *Delivery Time*: The days of delivery time promised to the customer, to customers over the three years.
- *Sales Support*: The number of sales support staff in the regional division, to customers over the three years.
- *Industry Group*: Dummy variables capturing whether the customer was in the construction, industrial, or OEMs sector.
- *Firm Size*: The number of employees in the customer's organization.
- *Centralized Buying Center*: A dummy variable capturing whether the buyer's organization had a centralized (1) or decentralized (0) buying center.

The variable definitions are presented in Table 3.

**Table 3** Variables in the Data

| Variable | Definition |
|---|---|
| Acquired | A dummy variable capturing if the customer was acquired (1) or not (0) |
| Expansion | A dummy variable capturing if the customer was in expansion mode (1) or not (0) |
| Price | The transaction price offered to customers at the time of purchase consideration |
| Warranty | The days of warranty offered on the product (with 100% refund on failure), at the time of purchase consideration |
| Delivery Time | The days of delivery time promised to the customer, at the time of purchase consideration |
| Sales Support | The number of sales support staff in the regional division, at the time of purchase consideration |
| Industry Group | Dummy variables capturing whether the prospective customer was in the construction, industrial, or OEMs sector |
| Firm Size | The number of employees in the prospective customer's organization |
| Centralized Buying Center | A dummy variable capturing whether the buyer's organization had a centralized (1) or decentralized (0) buying center |

## Dynamic Segmentation Exercise

The first question that TKL sought to answer through the data was: "Which product attributes are most desired by customers at the time of acquisition and expansion?"

Before we turn to the results of the acquisition and expansion choice models, we describe the intuition of a choice model briefly. In a choice model setting, every individual is assumed to derive an unobserved product-specific utility from several product options. The individual is assumed to either purchase the product or not, depending on which option gives them maximum utility. The dependent variable in a choice model is binary: every individual chooses to purchase or chooses not to purchase. In the acquisition model, the customer either decides to purchase (and thus be acquired by TKL), or not purchase. In the expansion model, the customer chooses to continue to purchase even after three years (and thus be an "expanding" customer for TKL), or stop purchasing. TKL product option's attractiveness is assumed to stem from a finite set of attributes; in this case, price, warranty, speed of delivery, and sales support. Moreover, customers in some industries, and with some firmographic characteristics, are either more or less likely to be acquired, or choose to expand. Thus, the model uses the two inputs (dependent variable, independent variables) to estimate the weights (or coefficients) that each attribute would have had to cause customers to pick a certain product. This identifies the most important factors that influence customer choice likelihood.

### Acquisition Model Results

Focusing on the results of the acquisition model in Table 4, TKL found that an increase in price had a negative impact on the probability of acquisition (relative to non-acquisition), based on the negative and statistically significant coefficient of price. Next, an increase in days of warranty offered had a positive impact on the probability of acquisition (relative to non-acquisition), based on the positive and statistically significant coefficient of warranty. Next, a decrease in days to deliver warranty offered had no statistical impact on the probability of acquisition (relative to non-acquisition). Finally, an increase in sales support offered had a positive impact on the probability of acquisition (relative to non-acquisition), based on the positive and statistically significant coefficient of sales support. Turning to industry characteristics, the probability of acquisition was higher for firms in the construction and industrial sectors relative to the OEMs sector. Also, firms that were larger (based on firm size) showed a higher probability of acquisition, while the probability of acquisition was unaffected by whether firms had a centralized buying center or decentralized buying center.

**Table 4** Results of Acquisition Choice Model

| Variables | Coefficient estimates | Standard deviation | t-statistic | P-value |
|---|---|---|---|---|
| Price (Unit: $1000) | −0.046 | 0.005 | −8.745 | 0.000 |
| Warranty | 0.046 | 0.003 | 17.892 | 0.000 |
| Delivery Time | −0.002 | 0.011 | −0.191 | 0.848 |
| Sales Support | 0.062 | 0.022 | 2.752 | 0.006 |
| Industry Group: Construction | 0.614 | 0.152 | 4.033 | 0.000 |
| Industry Group: Industry | 0.411 | 0.143 | 2.875 | 0.004 |
| Firm Size (Unit: 10) | 0.013 | 0.004 | 3.668 | 0.000 |
| Centralized Buying Center | −0.082 | 0.102 | −0.800 | 0.424 |
| Const-1 | 1.487 | 0.562 | 2.645 | 0.008 |
| Baseline | | | | |

### Expansion Model Results

Focusing on the results of the expansion model in Table 5, TKL found that an increase in price had no significant impact on the probability of expansion (relative to dropping out), based on the statistically insignificant coefficient of price. Next, an increase in days of warranty offered also had no impact on the probability of expansion (relative to dropping out), based on the statistically insignificant coefficient of warranty. However, a decrease in days to deliver offered had a positive and statistical impact on the probability of expansion (relative to dropping out). Finally, an increase in sales support offered had a positive impact on probability of expansion (relative to dropping out), based on the positive and statistically significant coefficient of sales support. Turning to industry characteristics, the probability of expansion was higher for firms in the construction and OEMs sectors, relative to the industrial sector. Also, firms that were larger (based on firm size) showed a higher probability of expansion, while the probability of expansion was higher when firms had a centralized buying center compared to a decentralized buying center.

## Targeting and Positioning for Competitive Advantage

The second major question facing TKL was: "How to effectively segment the market for buyers of electrical components, so as to decide which customers to acquire and which customers to expand?"

**Table 5** Results of Expansion Choice Model

| Variables | Coefficient estimates | Standard deviation | t-statistic | P-value |
|---|---|---|---|---|
| Price (Unit: $1000) | −0.004 | 0.005 | −0.855 | 0.393 |
| Warranty | 0.000 | 0.002 | 0.394 | 0.694 |
| Delivery Time | −0.190 | 0.014 | −13.711 | 0.000 |
| Sales Support | 0.069 | 0.022 | 3.204 | 0.000 |
| Industry Group: Construction | 0.333 | 0.104 | 3.216 | 0.001 |
| Industry Group: OEM | 0.483 | 0.177 | 2.731 | 0.006 |
| Firm Size (Unit: 10) | 0.013 | 0.003 | 4.020 | 0.000 |
| Centralized Buying Center | 0.336 | 0.097 | 3.470 | 0.000 |
| Const-1 | −0.048 | 0.461 | −0.103 | 0.918 |
| Baseline | | | | |

To answer this question, TKL tried to apply the results of the choice models it obtained from its historical data in a predictive sense. When one only observes product attributes, one can use the attributes and the weights of a choice model to predict the choices that are likely to be made by a new set of customers. This, in turn, can help a firm segment and target customers based on choice likelihood. So, TKL used the coefficients to compute the elasticities associated with product attributes, or the percentage increase/decrease in acquisition for a 1% change in the product attribute. Elasticities are useful since they are unitless quantities of the measure of influence of a product attribute, making comparability of product attributes easy.

## Segmenting on Acquisition Probability

Based on the acquisition model's results, TKL knew that the statistically significant coefficients include price, days of warranty, and sales support. It found that price and sales support appeared to be the most important drivers of acquisition, followed by days of warranty. After learning the key drivers of the high acquisition probability group, TKL sought to identify who these customers were, so that it could target its marketing offering of lowered price, high sales support and high days of warranty. Recall that in the earlier analysis, TKL had found that the probability of acquisition was higher for larger sized firms in the construction and industrial sectors relative to the OEMs sector. Thus, the high probability segment on the basis of acquisition was primarily firms located with these characteristics in TKL's marketing list.

## Segmenting on Expansion Probability

Based on the expansion model's results, TKL knew that the statistically significant coefficients included speed of delivery and sales support. It found that sales support and speed of delivery appeared to be the most important drivers of expansion. Similarly, after learning the key drivers of the high expansion probability group, TKL sought to identify who these customers were, so that it could target its marketing offering of sales support and speed of delivery. Recall that in the earlier analysis, TKL had found that the probability of expansion was higher for firms in the construction and OEMs sectors, relative to the industrial sector. Also, firms that were larger (based on firm size) showed a higher probability of expansion, while the probability of expansion was higher when firms had a centralized buying center compared to a decentralized buying center. Thus, the high probability segment on the basis of expansion was primarily firms located with these characteristics in TKL's marketing list.

## Implementing Different Acquisition and Expansion Targeting Efforts

The third major question facing TKL was: "Given the segmentation of customers, how should TKL modify its targeting and positioning strategy to deal with customer dynamics?" To see the response to this question, Table 6 summarizes the similarities and differences in the targeting strategies to acquire vs. expand TKL's customer base. First, to acquire customers, TKL should focus on price and sales warranty, while to expand the customer base, TKL should focus on emphasizing its sales support and speed of delivery. The key word here is "emphasize" – TKL should not expect that price competitiveness is not important in expanding customers, but as customers change over time, the relative importance of price (compared to speed of delivery) goes down in their minds. Thus, TKL should modify its targeting strategy as the length of its customer relationships changes.

**Table 6** Summary of Results

|  | Importance to Acquisition | Importance to Expansion |
|---|---|---|
| Price | High | Low |
| Warranty | Medium | Low |
| Delivery Time | Low | High |
| Sales Support | High | High |
| Firm Size Preferred | Large | High |
| Importance of Centralized Buying Center | Low | High |
| Construction Sector Customers | High | High |
| Industrial Sector Customers | High | Low |
| OEM Sector Customers | Low | High |

Next, while acquisition appears to be most attractive for larger sized firms in the construction and industrial sectors relative to the OEMs sector, expansion appears to be most attractive for larger firms, with centralized buying centers, located in the construction and OEMs sectors, relative to the industrial sector. This knowledge is crucial for TKL since it should mainly target acquisition or expansion efforts with firms with whom it has the likeliest chance to succeed. Thus, TKL slowly began to transform the organization with a customized segmenting and targeting strategy, to embrace the problem that its customers were ever-changing.

## Summary of Solution

The analytics exercise discussed in the case enabled TKL to obtain insights into its current standing in the marketplace, by better understanding the changes in the needs of its customers:

1 By performing separate analyses on customers that were recently acquired versus those that were in the expansions phase, TKL learnt the different product attributes which were most desired by customers at the time of acquisition and expansion.
2 It understood that it had positioned itself as very competitive on price in the market, which helped it acquire customers, but as customers changed over time, their preference for price was lowered. Thus, TKL needed to change its marketing emphasis over time to customers. It uncovered tangible ideas to further strengthen its position, using different product attributes (Table 6).
3 It learnt it could potentially target different industry segments for acquisition versus expansion efforts. For example, TKL had found that the probability of acquisition was higher for larger sized firms in the construction and industrial sectors relative to the OEMs sector, while the probability of expansion was higher for firms in the construction and OEMs sectors, relative to the industrial sector.
4 It knew that it had dropped from an already poor ranking of #8, to a sub-par #12 on sales support capabilities, so it could use model-based evidence to support its effort to grow its sales support capabilities. Thus, analytics-oriented efforts helped TKL solve the second fundamental marketing problem, that all customers change.

# Appendix: Dataset Description

## General Description of the Data

The dataset is a simulated dataset, aimed at mimicking similar datasets the authors have used in the past while working with companies. The data contain two sheets, one pertaining to acquisition analysis (nine columns and 2,000 rows), and one pertaining to expansion analysis (nine columns and 2,000 rows), each available in a separate Excel spreadsheet. In each sheet, the first column contains the names of the respondents (anonymous), and the eight other columns pertain to the data to be used to predict either acquisition probability (sheet 1), or expansion probability (sheet 2).

## Description of Variables in the Data

In both the acquisition and retention datasets, the eight-variable dataset (omitting respondent IDs) contains two types of variables. The first variable in the acquisition sheet is a dummy variable capturing if the customer was acquired (1) or not (0). The first variable in the expansion sheet is a dummy variable capturing if the customer was in the expansion model (1) or not (0). The next seven variables contain data that are used to predict the probability of acquisition and expansion respectively, and are as follows.

| Variable | Definition |
|---|---|
| Price | The transaction price offered to customers at the time of purchase consideration |
| Warranty | The days of warranty offered on the product (with 100% refund on failure), at the time of purchase consideration |
| Delivery Time | The days of delivery time promised to the customer, at the time of purchase consideration |
| Sales Support | The number of sales support staff in the regional division, at the time of purchase consideration |
| Industry Group | Dummy variables capturing whether the prospective customer was in the construction, industrial, or OEMs sector |
| Firm Size | The number of employees in the prospective customer's organization |
| Centralized Buying Center | A dummy variable capturing whether the buyer's organization had a centralized (1) or decentralized (0) buying center |

The variable description and means are also presented in Table 3 in the case. To obtain the model results, the student can directly load the data in Excel, and use the MEXL add-in pertaining to customer choice (Logit). The student should run the acquisition and expansion analysis as separate choice models, that is, they should run a choice model for the acquisition analysis and get results as shown in Table 4, and run a choice model for expansion analysis and get results as shown in Table 5.

# References

1  Duhigg, C. (2012) 'How companies learn your secrets,' *The New York Times*, 19 February.

2  BBC News (1999) 'Laura Ashley shops sold for a dollar,' *BBC News*, 29 April; Sull, D. (1999) 'Why good companies go bad,' *Harvard Business Review*, 77(4), pp. 42–52.

3  Lee, E., Mathur, A. and Moschis, G. (2003) 'Life events and brand preference changes,' *Journal of Consumer Behavior*, 3(2), pp. 129–41.

4  Lee, E., Mathur, A. and Moschis, G. (2003) 'Life events and brand preference changes,' *Journal of Consumer Behavior*, 3(2), pp. 129–41.

5  Yang, H. (2011) 'College student's apparel shopping orientation changes in relation to life events,' MS thesis, Louisiana State University.

6  Palmatier, R.W. (2006) *Relationship Marketing*. Cambridge, MA: Marketing Science Institute.

7  Leonhard, D. and Schüßler, E. (2013) 'Theorizing path dependence: A review of positive feedback mechanisms in technology markets, regional clusters, and organizations,' *Industrial & Corporate Change*, 22(3), pp. 617–47.

8  Carpenter, G.S. and Nakamoto, K. (1988) 'Market pioneering, learning, and preference,' *Advances in Consumer Research*, 15, pp. 275–9.

9  Troake, J. and McAdam, P. (2008) *Customer Relationship White Paper. Growing Customer Relationships: 90 days that make it or break it.* Xerox Global Services and BAI Research.

10  Chipotle (2009) 'Changes in customer tastes and preferences, spending patterns and demographic trends could cause sales to decline.' Available at: www.wikinvest.com/stock /Chipotle_Mexican_Grill_(CMG)/Changes_Customer_Tastes_ Preferences_Spending_Patterns_Demographic_Trends (accessed 27 January, 2016).

11  Cain, T. (2012) 'Buick brand sales figures.' Available at: www. goodcarbadcar.net/2012/10/buick-brand-sales-figures-usa- canada.html (accessed 27 January, 2016); Colias, M. (2011) 'Buick, shooting for young, affluent buyers, scores marketing deal with NCAA,' 15 March. Available at: www.autonews. com/article/2011315/RETAIL03/110319939/1259 (accessed 27 January, 2016); Libby, T. (2012) 'Buick goes against trend and attracts younger buyers.' Available at: http://blog.ihs. com/buick-goes-against-trend-and-attracts-younger-buyers (accessed 27 January, 2016).

12  Krebs, M. (2006) 'A short history of Japanese luxury cars,' *Bloomberg Businessweek*, 22 May; Chambers-Williams, G. (2008) 'Acura revs up the TL for '09,' 21 September. Available at: http://blog.sfgate.com/topdown/2008/09/21/acura-revs- up-the-tl-for-09/ (accessed 29 January 2016); Acura (n.d.) *Advance*. Available at: www.acura.com (accessed 26 January, 2016).

13  McGrath, R. (2013) 'The pace of technology adoption is speeding up.' Available at: https://hbr.org/2013/11/the-pace-of-technology- adoption-is-speeding-up/ (accessed 27 January, 2016).

14  Statista (2014) 'Method of preparation among U.S. past-day coffee drinkers by type (2014 statistic).' Available at: www. statista.com/statistics/320339/method-of-preparation-among- us-past-day-coffee-drinkers-by-type; Lerner, J. (2003) 'Keurig has some ideas brewing about consumer market,' 9 June. Available at: www.bizjournals.com/boston/stories/2003/06/09/ newscolumn1.html?page=all (accessed 29 January, 2016).

15  Kalanick, T. (2010) 'Uber's founding.' Available at https:// newsroom.uber.com/ubers-founding/ (accessed 29 January, 2016); Fleisher, L., MacMillian, D. and Schechner S. (2014) 'Uber snags $41 billion valuation,' *The Wall Street Journal*, 5 December.

16  Bauer, B. and Auer-Srnka, K.J. (2012) 'The life cycle concept in marketing research,' *Journal of Historical Research in Marketing*, 4(1), pp. 68–96; Wells, W. and Gubar, G. (1966) 'Life cycle concept in marketing research,' *Journal of Marketing Research*, 3(4), pp. 355–63; Rich, S. and Jain, S. (1968) 'Social class and life cycle as predictors of shopping behavior,' *Journal of Marketing Research*, 5(1), pp. 41–9; Ghez, G. and Becker, G. (1975) *The Allocation of Time and Goods over the Life Cycle*. Cambridge, MA: National Bureau of Economic Research; Stampfl, R. (1978) 'The consumer life cycle,' *Journal of Consumer Affairs*, 12(2), pp. 209–19; Arndt, J. (1979)

'Family life cycle as a determinant of size and composition of household expenditures,' *Advances in Consumer Research*, 6, pp. 128–32; Wagner, J. and Hanna, S. (1983) 'The effectiveness of family life cycle variables in consumer expenditure research,' *Journal of Consumer Research*, 10(3), pp. 281–91.

17  Wells, W. and Gubar, G. (1966) 'Life cycle concept in marketing research,' *Journal of Marketing Research*, 3(4), pp. 355–63; Rich, S. and Jain, S. (1968) 'Social class and life cycle as predictors of shopping behavior,' *Journal of Marketing Research*, 5(1), pp. 41–9.

18  Arndt, J. (1979) 'Toward a concept of domesticated markets,' *Journal of Marketing*, 43(4), pp. 69–75; Wagner, J. and Hanna, S. (1983) 'The effectiveness of family life cycle variables in consumer expenditure research,' *Journal of Consumer Research*, 10(3), pp. 281–91; Rouse, M. (2007) 'Customer life cycle definition.' Available at: http://searchcrm.techtarget. com/definition/customer-life-cycle (accessed 27 January, 2016).

19  Inc. (n.d.) 'Industry life cycle,' Inc.com. Available at: www. inc.com/encyclopedia/industry-life-cycle.html (accessed 27 January, 2016); Investopedia (2006) *Industry Lifecycle Definition*. www.investopedia.com/terms/i/industrylifecycle. asp (accessed 27 January, 2016).

20  California Milk Processors Board (2014) *Got Milk? News and Events*. Available at: www.gotmilk.com/#/news-events (accessed 27 January, 2016).

21  Newitz, A. (2015) 'Farewell, Radio Shack, and farewell to the twentieth century,' 3 February. Available at: http:// gizmodo.com/farewell-radio-shack-and-farewell-to-the- twentieth-ce-1683513865 (accessed 27 January, 2016).

22  FutureCast (2012) 'At last, a millennial segmentation,' April. Available at: www.millennialmarketing.com/2012/04/at-last-a- millennial-segmentation/ (accessed 29 January, 2016)

23  Accenture (2011) *Smarter Onboarding: The Key to Higher Client Retention and Cross-Sell*. Available at: www.accenture. com/us-en⌐/media/Accenture/Conversion-Assets/DotCom /Documents/Global/PDF/Industries_5/Accenture-Client- Onboarding2011.pdf

24  Che, H., Erdem, T. and Öncü, T.S. (2008) 'Consumer learning and evolution of consumer brand preferences,' *Quantitative Marketing and Economics*, 13(3), pp. 173–202; Troake, J. and McAdam, P. (2008) *Customer Relationship White Paper: Growing Customer Relationships: 90 days that make it or break it*. Xerox Global Services and BAI Research.

25  Mortimer, N. (2016) 'Asos to invest deeper in social content as half of orders now made on mobile,' 12 April. Available at: www.thedrum.com/news/2016/04/12/asos-invest-deeper- social-content-half-orders-now-made-mobile (accessed 5 August, 2016).

26  Palmatier, R.W. (2008) *Relationship Marketing*. Cambridge, MA: Marketing Science Institute; Palmatier, R.W. and Steinhoff, L. (2014) 'Understanding loyalty program effectiveness: managing target and bystander effects,' *Journal of the Academy of Marketing Science*, 44(1), pp. 88–107; Yohn, D.L. (2014) 'Great brands aim for customers' hearts, not their wallets,' *Forbes*, 8 January.

27  Weinstein, A. (2002) 'Customer retention: A usage segmentation and customer value approach,' *Journal of Targeting, Measurement and Analysis for Marketing*, 10(3), pp. 259–69.

28  Netzer, O., Lattin, J.M. and Srinivasan, V. (2008) 'A hidden Markov model of customer relationship dynamics,' *Marketing Science*, 27(2), pp. 185–204.

29  Zhang, J., Watson, G., Palmatier, R.W. and Dant, R. (2013) 'Integrating relationship marketing and lifecycle perspectives: Strategies for effective relationship migrations,' *Marketing Science Institute Working Paper Series*, 13–121, pp. 1–48; Zhang, J., Watson, G., Palmatier, R.W. and Dant, R. (2016) 'Dynamic relationship marketing,' *Journal of Marketing*, 80(5), pp. 53–75.

30  Palmatier, R.W., Gopalakrishna, S. and Houston, M.B. (2006) 'Returns on business-to-business relationship marketing investments: Strategies for leveraging profits,' *Marketing Science*, 25(5), pp. 477–93.

31  Williams, A. (2016) 'Report: Sharper customer lifetime value measurements attract bigger marketing budgets,' 5 July. Available at: www.cmo.com.au/article/602843/report-sharper-customer-lifetime-value-measurements-attract-bigger-marketing-budgets/ (accessed 5 August, 2016).

32  Gupta, S., Hanssens, D., Hardie, B., Kahn, W., Kumar, V. et al. (2006) 'Modeling customer lifetime value,' *Journal of Service Research*, 9(2), pp. 139–55.

33  Gupta, S. and Lehmann, D.R. (2005) *Managing Customers as Investments: The Strategic Value of Customers in the Long Run*. Upper Saddle River, NJ: Wharton School Publishing.

34  Dragoon, A. (2005) 'Customer segmentation done right,' 1 October. Available at: www.cio.com/article/2448413/it-organization/customer-segmentation-done-right.html (accessed 4 August, 2016).

35  Kumar, V. and Rajan, B. (2009) 'Profitable customer management: Measuring and maximizing customer lifetime value,' *Management Accounting Quarterly*, 10(3), pp. 1–18.

36  Glagowski, E. (2015) 'Proximus: From loyalty to engagement,' 1 April. Available at: www.peppersandrogersgroup.com/view.aspx?DocID=35307 (accessed 4 August, 2016).

37  Kumar, V., Thomas, J. and Reinartz, W. (2005) 'Balancing acquisition and retention resources to maximize customer profitability,' *Journal of Marketing*, 69(1), pp. 63–79.

38  Markstrat (2015) *Participant Handbook*. Available at: web.stratxsimulations.com (accessed 28 September, 2015).

## Companion website

Please visit the companion website, **www.palgravehighered.com/palmatier-ms**, to access summary videos from the authors, and full-length cases with datasets and step-by-step solution guides.

# Part 3

# ALL COMPETITORS REACT

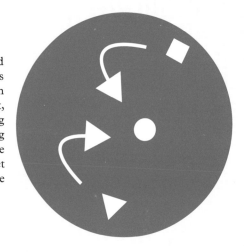

No matter how well a firm addresses customer heterogeneity and customer dynamics, competitors will constantly try to copy its success or innovate business processes and offerings to match customers' needs and desires better. Since all competitors react, through persistent efforts to copy and innovate, marketing managers must constantly work at building and maintaining barriers to competitive attacks. Managers build sustainable competitive advantages that are relevant for a specific target segment, by building high quality brands, delivering innovative offerings, and developing strong customer relationships.

Visit www.palgravehighered.com/palmatier-ms to watch the authors provide an overview of the *All Competitors React* First Principle and the relevant tools, analyses, and cases in either an executive summary or a full-length, pre-recorded video lecture format.

ALL
COMPETITORS
REACT

Chapter **4**

# Marketing Principle #3: All Competitors React → Managing Sustainable Competitive Advantage

ALL
COMPETITORS
REACT

## Learning objectives

- Explain Marketing Principle #3 and why firms require sustainable competitive advantages (SCAs).

- Define SCA.

- Identify and discuss the three conditions in a marketing strategy that produce SCA.

- Describe in detail the three sources of SCA: brands, offerings, and relationships (BOR).

- Explain the avenues that competitors have for undermining a firm's SCA.

- Understand the evolution of approaches to managing a firm's SCA.

- Critically discuss the strengths of field experiments as a means to understand the impact of BOR strategies.

- Describe a customer equity perspective.

- Outline the components and importance of acquisition, expansion, and retention (AER) and brands, offerings, and relationships (BOR) equity grids.

- Identify the three inputs and two outputs of the SCA framework.

- Detail the three-step process for managing SCA.

- Evaluate the micro–macro duality needed to develop effective marketing strategies.

# Introduction

## All Competitors React

The previous two Marketing Principles focus on a firm's potential and existing customers, in an effort to understand and manage customer heterogeneity and dynamics. In turn, the firm can develop a positioning strategy that matches its targeted customers' needs and also track these needs over time as the firm continues to engage these customers. Each firm selects target markets and positioning strategies on the basis of its own relative strengths, compared with those of competitors, but the true effectiveness of these strategies depends on how competitors react to them. No matter how well a firm addresses MP#1 and MP#2 – and perhaps especially if it addresses them effectively – competitors constantly seek to copy successful strategies or innovate their own business processes and offerings to match customers' existing and future needs and desires. These persistent efforts by all firms in the market to copy and innovate, such that *all competitors react*, constitute a third challenge that managers confront. To do so, they need to build and maintain barriers to competitive attacks, in the form of *sustainable competitive advantages* (SCAs). This is the focus of MP#3.

When managers develop their marketing strategies, they need to consider customers (heterogeneity and dynamism) but also anticipate competitors' reactions, now and in the future, to be able to build barriers that hold up against sustained competitive assaults. Anticipating and preparing for competitors by building an unassailable position for long-term success, or SCA, is critical in marketing, just as it was in Sun Tzu's famous 5th-century BC advice to military generals:[1]

> The art of war teaches us to rely not on the likelihood of the enemy not coming, but on our own readiness to receive him, not on the chance of his not attacking, but rather on the fact that we have made our position unassailable. (Sun Tzu, *Art of War*)

Because all competitors react, firms must manage their SCA to achieve and ensure long-term success. This First Principle may seem straightforward, but even so, it remains very difficult to build strong SCA that can withstand competitive assaults from multiple firms over long periods. Of the original 30 companies listed in 1928 on the Dow index, only 1 remains: General Electric (GE), which has repositioned itself in multiple company-wide initiatives. Through these transformational efforts, GE built new SCA to defend against the next wave of competitors. The changing companies on the Dow index give a good picture of the different competitive landscape as the US economy evolved. When the US was a developing economy focused on commodity production and extraction, leading firms included American Sugar, Standard Oil, and US Steel. Then in the manufacturing era, Goodyear, Boeing, and General Motors moved to the forefront. More recent developments brought the emergence of businesses based on information, finance, and service industries, including Microsoft, Visa, and Verizon.[2] To weather all these changes, GE has transformed from an industrial products company to a service-based business, and then again to a "digital industrial company" in response to the modern marketplace,[3] such that it constantly has developed significantly different and novel SCAs along the way.

These transformations are notable. Of the four Marketing Principles, managing SCA may be the most difficult to execute. Many other once-successful firms, leaders in their industry at one point, have failed to build enduring SCA.

### Example: Tesco (UK)

Consider Tesco, the UK grocery giant and the world's third largest retailer. Although it has long performed very well in the UK, when it sought to expand and adapt its strategy to compete in other markets, its SCA was not sufficient to enable it to compete. Thus, it ceded all its California-based grocery stores to a US investor and exited the US market in 2013, having left Japan in 2012. The reasons for these failures are complex, of course, but a key element was the company's lack of understanding of how to build an SCA in these markets. Tesco believed that its competitors (e.g., Walmart, Whole Foods) were not offering good enough one-stop shopping experiences for customers, so it introduced large stores with massive assortments that would enable them to fulfill all their shopping needs in one trip. But many US consumers treat shopping as a form of entertainment and prefer to visit several stores that offer smaller (but deeper) assortments; on average, Americans shop at more stores in a week than their British counterparts do.[4] Tesco also overestimated consumers' preferences for local brands, such that private labels accounted for about half of its in-store assortments, whereas competitors carried more national brands.[5] In this case, Tesco failed to ensure that the SCA that worked so well in the UK market also created barriers to competitors in other international markets.

With this recognition that SCAs are so critical and difficult to build, it may seem that firms should start by focusing on their competitors. But they cannot do so; companies must establish the strong position with a targeted customer group before they can build an SCA around that position. If they were to focus on competitors, they might beat a competitor – but only in a market segment without any more customers. Kodak and Polaroid competed for decades in the instant photography and film markets, leveraging their brands, patents, and technical innovations. But the emergence of digital photography overwhelmed both of them, and by 2012, they each had filed for bankruptcy protection, reflecting their inability to react to changes in customer desires and technologies, as well as their unwillingness to cannibalize their own film business. Kodak and Polaroid spent decades fighting each other, only to fail together as their customers' desires shifted to a new technology.[6] Focusing only on competitors often leaves firms blind to changes in their customers' needs and desires.

> Focusing only on competitors often leaves firms blind to changes in their customers' needs and desires.

On the marketing battlefield, customers are thus the very reason for the fight. They generate sales and profits, and they must be protected, both in the present and with the future in mind. There is no reason to enter the fray if customers are not the first consideration. But once the firm has chosen to join the fight, it must ensure it has sufficient battlements, in the form of a powerful SCA that enables it to reach those customer segments, faster and more effectively than its opponents. When those competitors try a new tactic, the battlefield shifts, so the firm must adapt its SCA to protect its customer segment or else give up the fight and move on to a new battleground for a different customer segment.

## Sustainable Competitive Advantage (SCA)

A strong SCA can result from several sources. Formally, a firm has a sustainable competitive advantage (SCA) when it is able to generate more customer value than competitive firms in its industry for the same set of products and service categories and when these other firms are unable to duplicate its effective strategy.[7] Thus, a good SCA meets three criteria:[8]

1 Customers care about what this SCA offers.
2 The firm does it better than competitors, which generates a relative advantage.
3 The SCA must be hard to duplicate or substitute, even with significant resources.

First, if a firm develops an SCA but customers don't want it, it has little value. Segway launched a revolutionary product innovation with its technologically advanced motorized scooter, buoyed by patent protections and significant brand awareness. But the market for these vehicles among individual consumers was minimal, so the barriers to entry that Segway built (i.e., patents, technology, brand) had little value. Uber also launched a revolutionary innovation, by matching drivers and customers in a new way that reduced wait times and fares, two factors that customers cared about a great deal. Of course, because all customers change (MP#2), a firm's existing SCA can lose value when customers stop caring about them. At one point in time, Blockbuster dominated the video rental industry, with SCA based in the brand, retail locations, and supplier relationships. But Netflix offered a different bundle of attributes that better fit customers' underlying needs (immediacy, no late fees, larger variety), which made Blockbuster's SCA mostly obsolete.[9] Because existing SCAs lose their ability to shelter a firm from its competitors when customers change and stop caring about them, we reiterate the notion that firms must first focus on customers, before building SCA, because they offer value only when a financially meaningful group of customers cares about them.

Second, performing in such a way that the firm fulfills the SCA better than competitors is particularly critical in more mature product or market segments. In rapidly growing segments, when products are in high demand and scarce, even firms that offer weaker versions can seem to do well. But as the segment matures and demand stalls, firms often fight over customers, and then those firms that are not the best in class cannot claim victory in head-to-head matchups. Their lack of relative advantage means that such firms are susceptible to competition. This process is similar to the loss of a monopoly; strong past financial performance is not always synonymous with the presence of an SCA.

**Example:** Maruti (India)

..................................................................................................................................

Maruti led India's domestic automobile market for nearly 30 years, but that was largely because of laws that limited the entry of foreign firms. With a liberalized market, new players such as Volkswagen and Ford have increased the competitive pressure on Maruti, which thus far has proven unable to reinvent itself appropriately to serve India's younger, more affluent middle class. Similarly, early entry into the dairy market enabled Iran Dairy Industries Co. (Pegah) to establish its position as the market leader. Yet, competition from new entrants like Kalleh that heavily invest in branding and new product development has since eroded Pegah's first-mover advantage and market share.

Third, being hard to duplicate is foundational to any SCA. What makes an SCA hard to copy? A new offering might fit customers' needs better than existing offerings, but if a competitor can easily copy this offering, the innovator often gets overwhelmed quickly. There are innumerable examples of first movers that failed to build an SCA and were surpassed by later entrants. Netscape Navigator enjoyed a more than 90% share of the Internet browser market in the early 1990s, with a stock price that exceeded $170. But its advantage was not particularly hard to duplicate, so as soon as Microsoft started offering a free browser (Internet Explorer) bundled with its operating systems, Netscape's days were numbered. By the late 1990s, its share price had dropped to less than 10% of its peak.[10] Friendster was the first social network, introduced years before Facebook; TiVO was the early DVR leader, but it had few barriers that could prevent cable companies from integrating the same capabilities into their existing cable boxes.

Thus, being first to market with a new idea is not sufficient to create a barrier to competitors, especially if deep-pocketed market leaders recognize the threat of an innovative new entrant and devote their resources to protecting their sales to existing customers. To make an SCA hard to copy, firms often turn to key market-based sources.

## Marketing-based Sources of Sustainable Competitive Advantage

The different sources of SCA in the marketing domain can be grouped into three main categories: brands, offerings, and relationships (Table 4.1). Using these three categories provides several advantages for marketers. In particular, each of these categories reflects a large, well-developed body of research on activities and strategies that generate customer loyalty, create meaningful barriers to competitive entry, and meet the three conditions for SCAs. In addition, firms already devote substantial resources to each of these categories and detail their investments in their financial reports as critical assets (e.g., advertising, R&D, selling expenses). Finally, firms often assign the management of these three sources of SCAs to different functional entities, so from a management standpoint, it is convenient to discuss each category separately. Ultimately, however, a firm's SCA reflects a synergistic combination of all three categories, even if each source has its own specific strengths and weaknesses, such that it might be more effective in some specific market or business environment.

**Table 4.1** Market-based Sources of Sustainable Competitive Advantage

| Source | Barriers to Duplication | Where it is Most Effective | Examples |
|---|---|---|---|
| Brands | Brand images reside in consumers' minds, which makes them difficult to duplicate, facilitates habitual buying through awareness, and provides identity benefits to customers | Large consumer markets (soft drinks, beer, fashion, automobiles) | BMW, Anheuser-Busch |
| Offerings | Cost benefits, performance advantages, access to distribution channels | Most markets, technology-based businesses (software, electronics) | Apple iPhone, Bose, Tesla |
| Relationships | Leads to trust, commitment, and interpersonal reciprocal bonds that are hard to build or duplicate | Business-to-business markets, services, complex products (test equipment, haircut, financial services) | Edward Jones, Granger |

In parallel with Table 4.1, we next provide a brief overview of the three sources of SCA. Then we describe each of them in detail in the following chapters (brands in Chapter 5, offerings in Chapter 6, and relationships in Chapter 7).

### Brands as an SCA

Using brands as an SCA is often most effective in large consumer markets (e.g., soft drinks, beer, fashion, automobiles). These firms invest in advertising, public relations (PR), and celebrity sponsorships to build brand awareness and brand images that match their positioning strategies. These brands then establish SCA through multiple mechanisms. In the simplest form, very strong awareness causes consumers to buy based simply on their recognition or habit, which reduces their cognitive effort. If brands also provide a strong and unique meaning, consumers may act according to their desire for status, to enhance their self-identity, or because of their strong positive attachment to the brand. In particular, a brand that aligns better with customers' needs than competitors' brands can provide a relative advantage, in line with the second SCA requirement. Moreover, brands can be very hard to copy. As we mentioned in Chapter 1, the CEO of Quaker Oats has even promised that: "If this business were to be split up, I would be glad to take the brands, trademarks and goodwill and you could have all the bricks and mortar – and I would fare better than you" (p. 8).[11]

Brand consultants offer evidence that it would take $81.5 billion for another company to replicate Coca-Cola's brand.[12] Pepsi and other colas may win blind taste tests, but more people still buy Coke than other soft drinks, and they enjoy that experience. Brands usually operate at subconscious levels, improving the experience beyond what is provided by objective elements, like taste.

Brand consultants offer evidence that it would take $81.5 billion for another company to replicate Coca-Cola's brand.[13] Pepsi and other colas may win blind taste tests, but more people still buy Coke than other soft drinks, and they enjoy that experience. Brands usually operate at subconscious levels, improving the experience beyond what is provided by objective elements, like taste.

As one Coca-Cola executive explains: "If Coca-Cola were to lose all of its production-related assets in a disaster, the company would survive. By contrast, if all consumers were to have a sudden lapse of memory and forget everything related to Coca-Cola, the company would go out of business."[14] Brands reside in customers' minds and are hard to copy or duplicate, such that they provide a highly valuable SCA.

## Offerings as an SCA

Using offerings (e.g., innovative products or services) as an SCA can be effective, because new and innovative products and services have the potential to disrupt virtually any market segment. Firms allocate vast budgets to research and development (R&D) so that they can introduce the newest or most innovative product, reduce costs, add supplementary services, or fundamentally alter the customer experience. If the resulting new offerings meet customers' needs better than existing offerings, and customers care about the new feature, a strong SCA emerges. For example, the home décor market has grown tremendously in India and China as the middle classes in these nations have expanded. In turn, startups such as Foyr.com and Furdo.com have combined technology and data science to provide online shoppers with three-dimensional virtual tours of homes that they can decorate virtually. Through this technology, consumers gain information about different decorating possibilities and can rapidly sort through hundreds of possibilities, at low costs. The innovative technology produces a good SCA compared with traditional rivals that provided two-dimensional renderings of blueprints.

In some cases though, the firm first must invest time and money to explain the new features and perhaps even convince customers that they "need" the new offering. New and innovative is not necessarily better, at least in customers' minds. New product failure rates are approximately 60%,[15] and the top reason reported for product failures often is the lack of need for the new offering.[16] Various techniques seek to help companies design products to fit some customer profile (conjoint analysis) or test market an offering before launching it (Chapter 6). But even the best design and marketing techniques can fail. The Edsel became synonymous with "marketing failure." Although Ford spent more than $400 million researching and developing this car, it never quite appealed to consumers and exited the market only three years later.[17] New Coke offers a more recent example. Coca-Cola tried to address consumers' asserted preferences for a sweeter formulation, but consumers absolutely revolted. As one researcher explains:

> A soda that tasted good was nice, but Coca-Cola really offered value on the basis of its strong, favorable, and unique brand associations: America, friendship, nostalgia, and the like. In changing the formula, the company walked away from all of these sources of value [in our terms, SCA], and customers reacted strongly, emotionally, and in a predictable fashion.[18]

When a firm overcomes the odds and launches a new product that meets customers' needs better than alternatives, it still may find itself susceptible to the threat of an early follower or "me-too" competitor that quickly copies its ideas. Early followers can evaluate how the first customers perceived the new offering and then introduce slight refinements that better meet their needs, whereas the first mover already has launched its product and invested in designing its existing manufacturing processes. Thus, maintaining a relative advantage over early followers is particularly difficult, because followers benefit from free-rider effects, the resolution of technological and market uncertainties, recognition of changing technologies and consumer needs, and the inertia that often constrains incumbents.[19] A survey of historical first movers reveals many now-unfamiliar firms that quickly were overtaken by their early followers: Reynolds International Pen (ballpoint pens), Bow-mar Instruments (hand-held electronic calculators), Osborne (portable computer market), and Royal Crown Cola (diet and caffeine-free colas).[20] In China, Youku Tudou and Weibo lead their respective markets, by providing alternatives to YouTube and Twitter; Xiaomi is the "Apple" of China. In Germany, Rocket Internet clearly states its dedication to copying established Internet services, to the extent that it even sells the copycat company back to the innovator in many cases.[21]

Whether an offering is hard to copy depends on the type of innovation. In some cases (e.g., pharmaceuticals like Viagra), a firm can patent its innovation and prevent competitors from copying it, so it enjoys a legally enforceable SCA. But patents are not feasible in all sectors, and in certain settings, they can be "worked around" fairly easily, such that they only delay the competition. Even in the pharmaceutical sector, patents are limited in their duration, so companies that introduce a new drug know the expiration date of their patent-based SCA. Still, being the first in a market may provide advantages, in the form of an innovative brand image, strong relational bonds, cost advantages, or other switching barriers that help the first mover retain its customers. In some cases, the use of offerings as an SCA drives a firm to develop new offerings continuously, such that the SCA reflects the firm's ability to launch a sequence of successful innovations rather than withstand competitors' assaults on any one iteration of its innovative offerings.

## Relationships as an SCA

Using relationships as an SCA is most effective in B2B, service, and complex offering settings. Strong relationships between customers and a firm's salespeople or other boundary-spanning employees can establish especially powerful barriers to customer defection, prompting customer loyalty and superior financial performance.[22] For example, B2B transactions tend to be complex, require significant two-way communication, and span long periods of time, so strong interpersonal relationships help buyers and sellers develop trust, cooperation, and flexibility. In addition, there are typically relatively fewer customers in business markets, compared with consumer markets, so advertising generally is less cost-effective. Relationships then produce SCA through higher levels of trust, commitment, and inter-personal reciprocal bonds, which enable the exchanges to adapt to changing circumstances and give buyers confidence in the fairness of future outcomes, even in the absence of explicit contractual agreements (Chapter 7).[23]

Relationships also meet the criteria for SCA. In particular, customers care about relational benefits such as enhanced trust, adaptability, and cooperation, as well the intrinsic enjoyment that might come along with their interpersonal relationships.[24] Relational sales organizations and customer service personnel often provide the best barriers to competitive entry. At Nordstrom, a US high-end retailer, the sales associates are a powerful SCA for the retailer, because the relationships between these sales associates and "their" customers often span years. In financial services settings, account managers who leave for another firm often take approximately 30% of their clients with them. These SCAs can create some confusion for the firm. The firm might assume that customers are loyal to it, but they are, in fact, bonded with the firm's salespeople. One study of loyalty among more than 300 B2B firms showed that industrial buyers would try to shift an average of 26% of their current purchases to follow a defecting salesperson, due to their relational bonds with the individual salesperson.[25]

Because relationships often take years to build, they are very hard to duplicate, which makes them an enduring SCA. Continuing our example of B2B salespeople, firms expect replacement reps to reinitiate and reinvigorate customer relationships that might have been placed at risk by the departure of a previous sales rep. But finding the right replacement is tricky, because this salesperson must find a way to meet or exceed the expectations established by the predecessor. If the products being sold are mature or commodities, customers sense little complexity or risk, so they might just lean on transactional forms of exchange, rather than devote time and effort to developing new relationships. In this sense, even strong relational bonds are not impervious to changing customer trends and preferences. In a recent industry survey, 75% of B2B customers expressed a preference for buying from a website rather than talking to a sales rep, and this rate increased to 93% when they knew what product they wanted to buy.[26] Coupled with the increasing use of the Internet, it is not surprising to find small competitors attacking large firms (with their vast sales forces) by promising easy-to-use websites and mobile apps that facilitate transactional sales. Foodpanda, one of the world's largest online food ordering marketplaces, constantly seeks to provide even better online interfaces for its customers in Southeast Asia and Europe so that they can order their food more easily while also lowering its own costs.[27]

These three sources of sustainable competitive advantage – brands, offerings, and relationships (BOR) – are additive and often work synergistically to give a firm a strong relative position in the marketplace.

---

These three sources of sustainable competitive advantage – brands, offerings, and relationships (BOR) – are additive and often work synergistically to give a firm a strong relative position in the marketplace.

---

**Example:** Starbucks (US)

Starbucks has a high-quality *brand* (valued at $5.4 billion) that customers feel emotionally attached to, which it combines with a distinctive *offering* of unique coffee-based drinks and special store environments,[28] in which customers often develop *relationships* with the employees in their local stores, who remember their drink orders or recognize them by name. Customers thus have been known to walk past an identical store to visit another outpost and buy their coffee from their favorite barista. These sources of SCAs, generated from effective BOR strategies, work together to increase customers' loyalty, and competitors find it very hard to overcome these barriers. When the three SCAs are consistent and intertwined, such as at Starbucks, the brand gets reinforced by high-caliber employees who are well trained and motivated (by healthcare and retirement benefits) to build good relationships with their customers. Rather than a franchising strategy, Starbucks maintains control over its coffee shops to ensure customers' experiences reflect its unique offering, reinforced by custom-made products that provide a unique customer relationship encounter. Furthermore, Starbucks continues to innovate its offerings (e.g., Teavana tea products) and technology-based services (e.g., mobile payment) to maintain its SCA in this category.

## Competitive Reactions: A Fundamental Assumption of Marketing Strategy

In the Starbucks example, it may seem as if its position in the market is unassailable: a high-quality, relevant brand, a strong offering, and a well-developed employee culture that promotes customer–employee relationships. But if history is any guide, no firm can count on any static bundle of SCAs and withstand the test of time without significant adaption and continued investment. Competitors displace firms by overcoming their SCA in many different ways, including:

- Technical innovations that provide competitors with a platform to launch a disruptive offering.
- Exploiting changes in customers' desires due to cultural, environmental, or other factors.
- Individual entrepreneurship that constantly seeks a better way to solve a problem.
- "Me-too" copycats that improve the efficiency or effectiveness of an existing execution.

Technical innovations represent a powerful foundation for launching a new offering that will make existing products or services obsolete. The Google Maps Navigation app offers nearly all the features of standalone GPS devices, and it can be installed on smartphones for free. Thus, following years of strong growth, TomTom lost nearly 85% and Garmin lost 70% of their stock value within the months after the navigation app was introduced.[29] In another example, Skype now accounts for more than one-third of all international long-distance calls, undermining traditional international long-distance telephone traffic carriers.

---

**Can You Name this US Firm?**

- World's biggest chain of highway restaurants
- Pioneer of restaurant franchising
- Most strongly entrenched actor and highest quality
- Most fabulous success story in restaurant chains

All quotes from various publications in 1960.

---

Second, customers' desires change with cultural, environmental, or even seemingly random factors, such that a brand becomes no longer relevant or even detrimental to the firm's performance. For example, when 1957 legislation established the US interstate highway system, the Howard Johnson restaurant chain was quick to take advantage of shifting customer behaviors to outcompete existing restaurant offerings. It purchased hundreds of parcels of land next to highway exit ramps and emerged as the "most strongly entrenched actor and highest quality" firm in the restaurant business (see above). By 1965, Howard Johnson earned more sales than McDonald's, Burger King, and Kentucky Fried Chicken by providing good, consistent food to interstate travelers.[30] But for the orange-roofed brand, this "same-ness" soon became a liability when preferences shifted, such that a new generation of out-of-town consumers came to see the offerings as "bland and dull," whereas fast food was something different, quick, and popular. Consumers' shifted to McDonald's and other fast-food restaurants; Howard Johnson's customers kept aging, which ultimately led to the chain's demise. Today, McDonald's similarly is facing a new set of changing preferences as people pursue more health-conscious consumption options. Along with these changes, the restaurant's brand reputation, long a powerful SCA for it, has suffered some damage, especially as popular media reports (e.g., the 2004 documentary film *Super Size Me*) question the health effects of offerings such as super-sized French fries – which have since been discontinued.[31]

Creative, diverse individuals also are constantly at work, trying to find a different or better way to solve a problem and offer a new product or service. These efforts sometimes replace the market leader; they even might completely redefine the marketplace. Such transformations can occur even without any specific technological innovation: Cirque du Soleil replaced large animals and top-named performers with music and theatrics to displace Ringling Bros. and Barnum & Bailey from the top spot in the circus entertainment segment. This type of innovative repositioning or repack-aging, which does not require a technological innovation, is referred to as a "blue ocean" strategy (see Chapter 6).[32]

Competitors also might copy a firm's offering and be better at executing the strategy. This "me-too" strategy has the advantage of being able to selectively offer different aspects of the offering, which may allow the firm to reduce its cost or target an emerging growth segment. Tencent is one of the largest Internet services companies in the world but its sole strategy is to copy other successful firms: "It is a company that doesn't create anything."[33]

In summary, technology, customers, and business environments constantly change, and competitors constantly try to create new ways to satisfy customers' needs and desires, all of which has great poten-tial to disrupt a firm's SCA and its market position. The more successful a firm is, the more effort competitors devote to trying to attack its position. As Steve Jobs once said: "profits attract imitators and innovators"; thus, even with an effective technology-based monopoly, Apple lowers prices over time to reduce the incentive for competitors to react.[34] But because competitors are always reacting, firms need to build and adapt their SCA to withstand the competitive assault, which represents MP#3.

> *All competitors react and an effective marketing strategy must manage the firm's sustainable competitive advantage (SCA),* which is Marketing Principle #3.

The rest of this chapter describes some approaches, analysis tools, and an overall framework for managing sustainable competitive advantage. Then, in Chapters 5–7, we focus on the three major sources of marketing-based SCAs in more detail.

# Approaches for Managing Sustainable Competitive Advantage

## Evolution of Sustainable Competitive Advantage in Marketing

The way firms build SCA for their business has evolved over time (Figure 4.1). Using strong customer relationships as a source of SCA was the norm for most of the past 3,000 years.[35] Prior to the indus-trial age, business transactions occurred in local markets, where farmers and craftspeople sold their wares directly to local customers. These "producers" were often both manufacturer and retailer, and most retailers serviced a small geographical area, which made interpersonal relationships between producers and consumers the largest barrier to competitive attacks. Similarly, relationships led to trust among merchants in the exchange of goods that were not locally produced. Thus, trade only occurred among groups with ongoing trusted relationships such as merchants along the "silk route."[36]

The Industrial Revolution changed these exchange characteristics. Manufacturers used the econo-mies of scale associated with mass production to produce a large volume of products at low cost, but

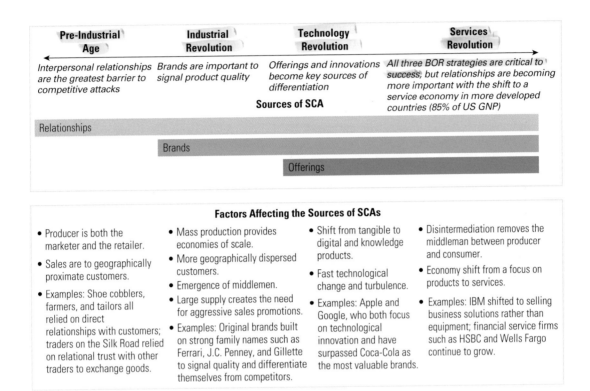

**Figure 4.1** Evolution of Approaches for Managing Sustainable Competitive Advantage in Marketing

these goods also required shipping, storage, and sales across a larger geographic area. Following the jobs, consumers relocated to cities, away from agricultural areas, which then required the transportation and storage of goods to support these emerging populous cities. Moreover, mass production generated the need for aggressive promotions to create sufficient demand for the increased volume of mass-produced goods.

Industrialization also led to the emergence of a large number of "middlemen," focused on transportation, storage, selling, and retailing.[37] As these new channels competed for business, often with diverse product quality and prices, exchanges became more transactional, which increased the importance of brands as a means to distinguish among products and provide a signal of the quality of the offerings. The increases in mass-produced products sold through middleman simultaneously undermined the effectiveness of using long-term, local relationships as a sole or primary source of SCA. Many early "brands" were family names – in effect, branding the firm's prototypical relationship by building on the store owner's history of good relationships with customers (e.g., Ferrari, Lamborghini, J.C. Penney, Ford, Adidas, Abercrombie & Fitch, Ben & Jerry's, Bentley, Campbell, Cadbury, Chanel, JP Morgan Chase, Ericsson, Gillette, Jack Daniels, Yamaha, Suzuki, Sotheby's).

The technological revolution, which began in the late 1950s with the shift from analog and mechanical technologies to digital computers and digital recordings, in turn shifted the focus to new and innovative offerings as a key source of SCA.[38] Many modern CEOs regard innovation as critical to their firms' future competiveness and an important source of SCA, required to both protect existing positions and expand into new markets. This shift, from SCAs based on *brand awareness and image* to those based on *innovative offerings*, is clearly evident in the change in rankings of the most valuable brands in 2013. After more than a decade at the top, Coca-Cola was replaced by Apple (ranked first) and Google (second). Both of these "most valuable" firms rely on technological innovations as a key source of their SCA, rather than pure brand awareness or image among a large population of consumers.[39]

Over time, the primary source of SCA has evolved: relationships in early markets, brands in the aftermath of the Industrial Revolution with the emergence of middlemen and retailers, and innovative offerings following the technology revolution and its significant disruptions to ongoing industries and firms. However, we also highlight that each new SCA adds to the last source of SCA, rather than displacing it. Apple used innovations (e.g., iPods, iPhones) to carve out its share in the markets for portable music players and phones, but it simultaneously invested in brand building to help protect its technology-based businesses, with the knowledge that competitors would be trying to copy its technological innovations. For Apple, as for most technology firms, patents are delaying tactics rather than long-term barriers to market entry, because there are many ways to achieve the same ends. But Apple also added services (e.g., music purchase and cloud storage) to its offering, to help increase the switching barriers for customers.

> Over time, the primary source of SCA has evolved: relationships in early markets, brands in the aftermath of the Industrial Revolution with the emergence of middlemen and retailers, and innovative offerings following the technology revolution and its significant disruptions to ongoing industries and firms.

Some researchers argue that developed counties are undergoing the next SCA revolution, due to the wider shift to a service economy.[40] Services, relative to products (categorized by the US government), now account for approximately 85% of the US economy.[41] They typically are produced and delivered by the same organization, such that services tend to remove the middleman (known as "disintermediation") and reinforce the bonds between producer and consumer. In addition, services are more intangible, less consistent, more perishable, and harder to evaluate than products, so customers rely more on sellers' boundary-spanning personnel, sometimes even requiring co-production.[42] These closer interactions make customer–seller relationships more critical for services, and the intangibility of the offering implies that the benefits of relationship trust are more important.[43] Thus, relationships are reemerging as more important sources of SCA in the growing services and knowledge economies, suggesting a full-circle shift in the evolution of SCA over time.

Despite the shifting emphases on the different sources of SCA, all three sources (brands, offerings, and relationships) consistently build on one another and often combine synergistically to determine a firm's SCA. To capture this additive effect and provide a framework for measuring SCA, a customer equity perspective can be useful, in that it captures the long-term benefits of the brand, offering, and relational (BOR) sources of SCA.

## Customer Equity Perspective

A customer equity perspective recommends regarding customers as financial assets, such that they can be measured, managed, and maximized, similar to any other firm asset (e.g., land, buildings, equipment, intellectual property). Customer equity for a firm refers to "the total of the discounted lifetime values of all its customers."[44] When a firm advertises to build strong brands, makes R&D investments to develop innovative products, or spends to hire and train salespeople who can enter into relationships with clients, it should increase that firm's brand, offering, and relational equities. Together, these different forms constitute the firm's customer equity and thus often represent the strongest barrier (SCA) to competitive assault.

However, accountants treat these assets very differently than other, more tangible assets that appear in a firm's financial statements. For example, marketing costs appear as an annual expense, implying (falsely) that all the benefits of this spending occur in the same year. Marketing spending also is not regarded as an investment to build an asset; instead, it appears on a firm's income statement as an expense, completely spent by the end of the year. Such treatments are clearly inaccurate, especially as research and practice confirm that brand and relationship assets persist for extended periods and can create important SCAs.

Let's consider this point with a comparison. When Intel spends $1 billion on a new manufacturing plant to make its next generation microprocessors, the firm depreciates the cost over 30 years, such that only a portion of the cost comes out of any single year's profit. The remaining amount stays on the firm's balance sheet as an asset. But when Intel spent $1 billion on its "Intel Inside" marketing campaign, the full cost was subtracted from that year's profit, ignoring the long-term benefits of the SCA that resulted from the branding campaign. Nor are any of these benefits captured on Intel's balance sheet. To address this obvious inaccuracy, some firms started using brand equity measures to capture the benefits of marketing expenditures. By tracking their brand equity over time, they gain a sense of the relative size of the SCA generated by their strong brands. Such an equity perspective, generated through marketing expenditures, thus captures a firm's SCA from BOR investments, as underlies a customer equity perspective.

To take this perspective, Figure 4.2 offers the example of a consumer who wants a beer. If an unknown bartender pours the beer in an unlabeled glass and asks the consumer to put a price on it, the noted price would represent offering equity – that is, the price for performance or the product-only value. Then, if the bartender identifies the brand of beer while pouring it into the glass, the difference in the price that the consumer would pay, versus the price of the unlabeled beer, represents the brand equity. Finally, if the consumer's favorite bartender served the branded beer while chatting about topics of interest to both of them, learned over their long and friendly relationship, the difference in the accepted price reflects relationship equity. Figure 4.2 displays how these three equities combine in an additive *customer/BOR equity stack*. When summed across all the firm's customers, it represents the firm's overall customer equity.

In support of this sort of investment perspective on marketing, rather than an accounting perspective, a meta-analysis of nearly 100 empirical studies published between the 1960s and the 2010s revealed that investments in personal selling produce *positive, incremental financial benefits* to firms.[45] These benefits are especially pronounced if the firm sells products in the early stage of their lifecycles and in Europe compared with the US, but across the board, investments in a current period lead to benefits for several periods in the future. Thus, investments in relationship assets offer multi-period payoffs.

At the individual customer level, customer equity is analogous to the customer's lifetime value (CLV). Then, when each customer's equity is added together, it generates the firm's overall customer equity. In this sense, the customer equity perspective is well suited to using a CLV analysis approach (Chapter 3), because each market-based equity can be assessed as an addition to the customer's discounted cash flow over time. Tiffany & Co.'s strong brand equity is the main reason that consumers willingly pay higher prices for its jewelry, and this additional profit increases each customer's lifetime

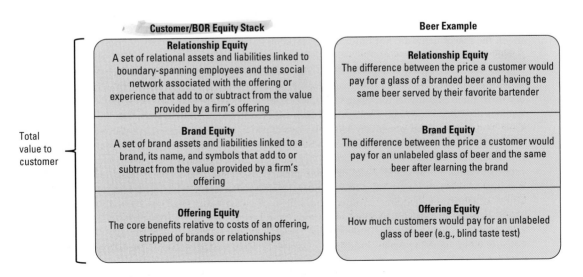

**Figure 4.2** Customer Equity Perspective: Brand, Offering, Relationship Equity Stack

value. However, if Tiffany stopped investing in its brand and cut its marketing expenditures, its brand equity would depreciate – just as the equity of an abandoned manufacturing plant diminishes with neglect.

Thus, BOR equities are similar to tangible assets. They generate a return on assets, can be built through investments, and depreciate over time if not maintained. Many firms have in-house metrics, or else use industry metrics, to assess their firm's brand equity. These measures provide helpful, intermediate metrics for determining the effectiveness of their efforts to build brand equity. Once a firm devises a way to measure customer equity, it can use a variety of analysis techniques to understand which marketing investments and strategies generate the greatest equities (e.g., multivariate regression; Chapter 7) and how to optimize its investments (e.g., response modeling; Chapter 8).

> BOR equities are similar to tangible assets. They generate a return on assets, can be built through investments, and depreciate over time if not maintained.

Another simple but powerful approach to understanding the financial impact of different BOR investments does not require intermediate metrics but instead applies experimental analysis techniques. Experiments provide strong tests of causality, by randomly assigning customers to multiple groups (i.e., treatment and control). For example, a randomly selected treatment group might see a new marketing program, while the control group does not. The sales to each group then reflect the differential effects of these programs across the different conditions. Data Analytics Technique 4.1 provides an overview of experiments and a detailed example. Because experiments are relatively inexpensive, marketers can test multiple programs before launching them. Many firms test advertising campaigns, new product launches, and changes to the sales organizations in a few diverse markets to understand if they will produce the desired business objectives prior to full-scale rollouts.

Although they are weaker tests of causality, another effective technique relies on natural experiments that purposefully (rather than randomly) apply a marketing treatment to one group, then compares the effects of different marketing strategies. Imagine, for example, that a competitor has entered three geographic markets. A firm might designate the sales team in one region to match the competitor's prices, tell another team to promise free shipping, and leave a third team unchanged in its policies. Any variation in the effects on sales across regions helps reveal which strategy is most effective. However, if the territories differ substantively (e.g., size, brand strength, types of products sold), the firm needs to account for such variables, to "control" for the differences due to these factors and isolate the effects of the marketing strategies. That is, in a true experiment, customers are randomly assigned, and the other factors are randomly distributed across the groups, but in a natural experiment, the assignments are not random, so marketers need to use mathematical controls to account for pertinent differences.

This customer equity perspective involves building and maintaining a parallel "customer-centric accounting process," outside the firm's normal financial accounting process. But is it worth it? There are three main arguments for using customer equity accounting and a BOR equity stack. First, BOR equities are often the *primary* source of a firm's SCA. As the executives from Quaker Oats and Coca-Cola whom we quoted previously know, brands are key profit generators, not the tangible assets that tend to be tracked in more detail. So, the better question might be: Does it make sense to have hundreds of accountants close the books each month, filing quarterly earnings statements and annual reports to track a firm's land, buildings, and inventories when these elements are not the critical determinants of a firm's long-term performance? These typical accounting measures can capture brand equity if a business acquires another firm whose price is higher than the "book value" of tangible assets, because in these transactions, customer equity enters the balance sheet as an asset and is depreciated as "goodwill." Regular financial statements do not capture customer equity though, largely because its intangibility makes it difficult to measure. Risk-averse (and cost-averse) firms prefer to not measure customer equity, rather than measure it and open themselves up to the vagaries or controversies of such measures.

Second, to make optimal decisions, a firm needs a framework that measures, tracks, and reports customer equities. Many of their decisions involve trade-offs: between BOR strategies and non-marketing investments (manufacturing plants), across the three BOR categories, across different marketing programs within each equity category (e.g., football sponsorship and jersey advertising versus online banner advertising), and over time (now versus next year). To understand these trade-off decisions, managers need a system that tracks the effects of each investment. Some executives remain hesitant to invest in marketing campaigns, for which they cannot "see" the payoff. To justify the return on investment in accounting systems, they capture all the costs in the present year but need to estimate the results across many years in the future, making it difficult to link specific marketing efforts to changes in sales and profits. Without systematic ways to demonstrate these linkages, firms often under-invest in difficult-to-measure categories.

Third, effective customer equity systems represent an SCA in their own right. Picture yourself as a brand manager, working for a consumer packaged goods (CPG) firm that competes with Unilever. Your firm does not take a customer equity perspective on BOR investments, as Unilever does. Your annual bonus is based on sales growth and profits earned by your brand; you also plan to leave your job in the next few years. Your experience suggests that if you cut advertising for your brands, sales do not decrease much immediately, because the strong brand equity keeps customers coming back. But the cuts show up as significant cost savings in your reports. The savings from cutting advertising get added to your brand's profits for that year, giving you an excellent profit measure. You take your huge bonus, then move on to your next job. In the long term and across many product brands, however, Unilever will outperform your firm, because Unilever's brand managers receive incentives based on brand equity too, such that they make more effective BOR investment decisions. This logic has been the key motivator leading CPG firms to build brand equity metrics and set performance targets using both financial and brand equity metrics.

Suboptimal marketing decisions happen in firms every day, at many different management levels, and especially during economic downturns. Of course, it is unreasonable to expect firms to be able to measure advertising responses accurately across multiple advertising vehicle combinations, then set media budgets and allocations optimally for each period. But evidence consistently shows that firms do not even stay abreast of new marketing avenues for their BOR strategies. According to practitioner reports, most firms remain unsure about whether to adopt Internet advertising and how to alter their advertising strategy to include the Internet.[46] During recessions, when consumer demand shrinks, BOR strategies offer a real opportunity (rather than a threat, as is more commonly perceived) for a firm to demonstrate why it is the best choice. Instead, firms consistently underspend on their BOR strategies during recessions, such that they leave money on the table.[47]

Consider how firms set advertising expenditures in reality. One CPG firm might base its expenditures on industry averages, which violates MP#1 by assuming that advertising pays off equally across all customer groups and forgetting that all customers differ. Another firm sets advertising expenditures as a percentage of sales, which violates MP#2 by assuming that advertising pays off equally today and in the future, ignoring that all customers change (advertising often pays off more in a product's initial launch). But Unilever uses a customer equity perspective and allocates its advertising budget across product brands and time, according to the effect on brand equity metrics it creates, giving it insight into which marketing programs have the greatest effect on brand equity, when the effects of advertising investments start to decline, and which of its brands are most responsive to its advertising investments. Advertising is a vast investment for most CPG firms, and brand equity is a key barrier to competitors, so Unilever's customer equity approach represents a significant SCA, especially relative to a competitor using an industry average or percentage of sales approach.

Many firms' primary SCAs result from their BOR investments and strategies, but other sources of SCA are available too, including deep and low-cost financial resources, human resource strategies, and operational processes. These aspects fall outside the scope of a marketing strategy, so the framework we present in the next section focuses instead on implementing a customer equity perspective using a BOR equity stack.

### Description

Marketing experiments test how customers might respond to marketing decisions, while ruling out confounds that otherwise would be present when comparing a treatment to a control group.

### When to Use It

- To determine if there is a direct causal relationship between a specific BOR (brand/offering/relational) investment and customer or firm outcomes.
- To choose among a set of BOR investment strategies and tactics, according to their financial impacts (e.g., lift in sales).

### How It Works

An experiment seeks to establish a causal relationship between an independent variable (e.g., BOR investment) and an outcome. Causality implies:

1 the independent variable and outcome variable co-vary (e.g., 10% off the price on a website and greater online sales)
2 the independent variable precedes the outcome variable in time (e.g., online sales are measured after the price promotion begins)
3 alternative explanations for the measured effect can be ruled out.

To ensure causality, the marketing experiment needs to be designed well:

1 A good treatment group needs to be in place. A treatment reflects the precise statement of the causal BOR relationship to be tested (e.g., how much an increase in the commission paid to a salesperson increases sales by this salesperson); a treatment group is the group of subjects (i.e., salespeople) who receive this treatment.
2 We need a comparison or control group, in which the causal factor stays constant (e.g., commissions to another group of salespeople stay the same).
3 The treatment and control groups absolutely must be similar in all other respects (e.g., size, demographic makeup, selling motivation, experience). To achieve this criterion, most experiments use random assignments to the treatment and control conditions. With a random assignment, in a probabilistic sense, the chances of subjects receiving the treatment are equal across the different groups.

Then, in the following equation,

$$Y_i = \beta_1 I_j + \beta_2 X_i + \varepsilon_i$$

$Y_i$ is the dependent variable of interest for customer i, the indicator variable $I_j$ is coded 1 if subject I is assigned to the treatment group and 0 otherwise, the coefficient $\beta_1$ is the treatment effect, and the vector coefficient $\beta_2$ captures any characteristics of the subject or environment that need to be statistically controlled for to establish the causal treatment effect, other than the random assignment of the treatment. Finally, $\varepsilon_i$ captures random statistical error.

After conducting the experiment, if $\beta_1$ is statistically significant, the treatment effect is legitimate. Depending on the goal of the analysis, experiments can feature an "after-only" design, such that they measure the effect of a marketing action on customer behavior *after* customers have been exposed to marketing action, or a "before-and-after" design and measure the effect of the marketing action both before and after customers have been exposed to it.

DFG, a floral delivery company, was having its quarterly marketing budget meeting. Noting that the company spent $250,000 in annual advertising, one manager questioned whether it was warranted, or if DFG was overspending. In the ensuing discussion, some managers insisted that local television advertising was crucial to creating brand equity and generating revenues, while others believed the company was heavily overspending.

To resolve the predicament, DFG decided to use a controlled experiment. First, to ensure causality, it defined the treatment as a 10% increase in local television spots in the next quarter in 50 selected regional markets (treatment territories). As a control group, it used 50 territories in which the amount of local television spending remained the same. In addition, DFG gathered brand awareness, brand recall, and sales figures in the quarter preceding (T0) and the quarter during (T1) the treatment, then calculated the differences between T0 and T1, across the treatment and control territories (i.e., before-and-after design). To ensure validity, DFG statistically controlled for the demographic (income, education, age, race, and gender distribution) and economic (buying power, retail penetration, Internet penetration) makeup of both the control and treatment territories. For the brand awareness measure, its equation was:

$$Change\ (brand\ awareness_i) = \beta_1 I_j + \beta_2 X_i + \varepsilon_i$$

where *Change (brand awareness$_i$)* is the change in T1 (over T0) in brand awareness in territory i, the indicator variable $I_j$ is coded as 1 if the territory I is assigned to the treatment group and 0 otherwise, the coefficient $\beta_1$ is the treatment effect, the vector coefficient $\beta_2$ captures any characteristics of the territory that need to be statistically controlled for to establish the causal treatment effect, and $\varepsilon_i$ captures random statistical error.

The company estimated three regression equations to obtain the coefficient $\beta_1$ from three different models, capturing the statistical changes in brand awareness, brand recall, and sales, respectively, due to increases in local television advertising relative to the control condition. The treatment effect was significant in each regression; the growth of brand awareness, brand recall, and sales in the treatment territories were 1.5%, 3.2%, and 3%, respectively, when DFG increased its local television advertising (cf. the control group).

DFG earns $25,000,000 in sales annually, so the experiment gave the decision makers in the company confidence that the growth in sales due to local television advertising would pay off. Thus, an experiment helped resolve an internal conflict within DFG.

# Framework for Managing Sustainable Competitive Advantage

The organizing framework for managing sustainable competitive advantages (SCAs) integrates the preceding approaches and analyses (Figure 4.3). There are three key inputs, two of which are outputs of the frameworks for MP#1 and MP#2. The third captures long-term trends that might disrupt a firm's existing and future SCA. Specifically, MP#1 focuses on what consumers or businesses in the marketplace want, as well as how the firm should position itself in this space, and MP#2 focuses on the firm's customers to understand what AER (acquisition, expansion, retention) strategies are most effective when these customers change. A natural next step is to build and maintain strong barriers around customers to withstand competitive attacks, now and in the future, which is the essence of MP#3. The framework for managing SCA also generates two outputs: descriptions of the firm's SCA now and in the future and BOR strategies to build and maintain these SCAs.

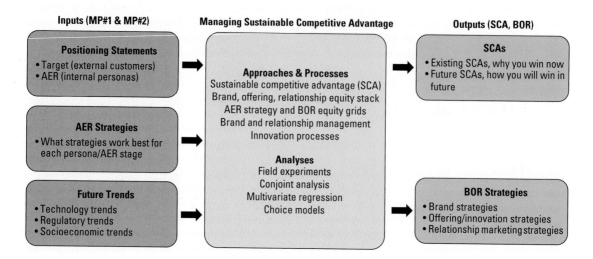

**Figure 4.3** Marketing Principle #3: All Competitors React → Managing Sustainable Competitive Advantage

## Inputs to the Sustainable Competitive Advantage Framework

Of the three inputs to this framework, the first, and arguably most important, is *positioning statements* from the first two marketing principles. That is, the MP#1 positioning statement answers three key questions:

1 *who* customers are
2 *what* set of needs the product or service fulfills
3 *why* this product/service is the best option to satisfy customer needs (relative to competition).

It captures the conclusion of the STP (segmentation, targeting, positioning) process. After evaluating customers' needs and preferences, the manager selects target segment(s) to address and identifies certain product features or aspects to use to appeal to this target segment (status, price, performance) better than competitors can. This final step in the positioning process is the critical link to MP#3; it identifies which aspects of the offering can surpass the competition. It also provides clear guidance on where the firm should invest to build and maintain its SCA. If the product is differentiated by exclusivity and high status (Tiffany jewelry, Ferrari cars), the firm needs to invest in its brand, avoid discount pricing or promotions, and display the products in high-end retail environments.

The AER positioning statements, an output of MP#2, focus in detail on the firm's existing customers by answering who, what, why, and when questions for each persona in the firm's customer portfolio. In addition to their distinct focus – AER positioning statements are internally focused on existing customers rather than outwardly focused on all the customers in the market category – we note two pertinent differences:

1 AER positioning statements involve meeting customers' needs over time rather than beating competitors to the initial purchase.
2 AER positioning statements address the "when" question, detailing triggers and migration mechanisms that drive customer dynamics.

Therefore, when added together, the two positioning statements provide insights into what aspects of a BOR equity stack are key to *winning* customers in the overall marketplace and then *keeping* these customers as they change over time.

The second input for the SCA framework is the *AER strategies* from MP#2. Positioning statements define the objectives; AER strategies describe the process for reaching those objectives. Organized by stage and personas, the AER strategies provide key guidance into how a firm should invest to acquire and keep customers. Thus, they provide a granular summary of how to win/acquire and then keep/

retain customers. However, the strategies must be aggregated and reorganized by brand, offering, and relationship categories to match the foundations for SCA, that is, the firm's BOR equity stack.

A third input to the managing SCA framework is *long-term technology, regulatory, and socioeconomic trends*, which clearly can disrupt any organization's SCAs. For example, the growth of mobile phones has disrupted multiple elements of the marketing strategies of most firms, including how they increase engagement among customers and the channels in which their products are available. With this last input, the framework avoids the threat of focusing solely on existing customers and competitors and thus failing to recognize long-term trends or discontinuous changes in the external environment.[48]

**Example:** Brussels Airlines (Belgium)

Simon Lamkin, CIO of Brussels Airlines, Belgium's national carrier, has emphasized the importance of adapting its marketing model with the changing technological trends. With regards to the digital imperative for airlines to change with new technologies, Lamkin said: "We have all got to digitally transform to provide the tools to our guests that can help them get through the whole air travel experience. We need to allow them to book online and do everything they need to do from their mobile devices."[49]

## Outputs of the Sustainable Competitive Advantage Framework

With these three inputs and the application of one or more of the different approaches for managing SCA, the framework generates two outputs (which we discuss in even more detail in Chapters 5–7). The first output is a description of the firm's SCA now and in the future. The descriptions need to clearly address the three conditions for SCA: customers care about it; the firm does it better than competitors; and it is hard to duplicate or substitute. This output, a description of SCA, offers a high-level statement of how the organization will win in the competitive marketplace over time. It aggregates all individual target segments and personas to ensure compatibility, and it requires the firm to recognize the core foundation for its long-term success. By clearly identifying the roots of a firm's sustainable, long-term competitive advantages, senior leaders can invest and manage the necessary resources more appropriately. Investments in and management of the firm's overall SCA is part of the top management team's responsibilities. The marketing strategy is a critical element of the SCA but is not all the SCA consists of.[50] That is, the relative advantages generated from brands, offerings, and relationships constitute the input of the marketing strategy to the firm's overall SCA.

The second output of the SCA framework is detailed BOR strategies that aggregate and reorganize each targeted customer segment and persona according to its needs (accounting for customer heterogeneity) and the most effective strategies across time (accounting for customer dynamics) in the brand, offering, and relationship categories. For example, by integrating insights into the needs of multiple personas across different AER stages, the firm can identify the most effective overall brand strategy, which is important for several reasons. First, a firm cannot institute a different brand strategy for every customer persona or across its acquisition and retention stages, especially because brand strategies often are mutually exclusive (e.g., everyday low cost vs. exclusive status). Marketing programs often spill over to multiple personas and stages, so a high-level strategy is needed to ensure a consistent brand strategy, effective for multiple customer groups. Second, it is inefficient to develop different BOR initiatives for each persona in each stage, from cost, employee expertise, and implementation perspectives.

Both these outputs (SCA and BOR strategies) represent aggregations of insights gained from more fine-grained analyses, combined and reorganized to support effective macro-level decision making. This micro–macro duality is critical to a successful marketing strategy. True comprehension of customers occurs at micro levels (avoiding aggregation bias), but strategic and resource decisions occur at macro levels (e.g., advertising, R&D, and sales force strategies).

## Process for Managing Sustainable Competitive Advantage

Converting positioning statements, AER strategies, and future trends into SCA and BOR strategies is not a straightforward process. It requires aggregating detailed insights across different personas at different relationship stages to identify the most effective brand, offering, and relationship strategies to

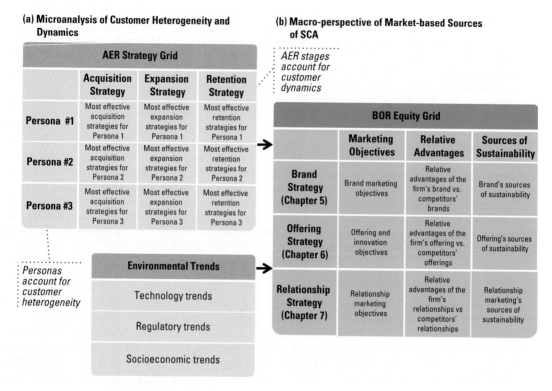

**Figure 4.4** AER Strategy and BOR Equity Grids

build and maintain firms' SCA. The process also needs to account for trends to ensure that firms build SCAs that will be relevant now and in the future. A simplified step-by-step version of the process is summarized in Figure 4.4.

Converting positioning statements, AER strategies, and future trends into SCA and BOR strategies is not a straightforward process. It requires aggregating detailed insights across different personas at different relationship stages to identify the most effective brand, offering, and relationship strategies to build and maintain firms' SCA.

### Step 1: Acquisition, Expansion, and Retention (AER) Strategy Grid

The output of MP#2 is a microanalysis of customer heterogeneity and dynamics in the firm's customer portfolio; it captures the most effective AER strategies for each relevant persona. The insights from MP#2 then can be inserted into the *AER strategy grid* to reveal high-impact BOR strategies, as in Figure 4.4(a). Each box in this grid describes the most effective strategy for a unique persona at a single point in time. For example, the most effective acquisition strategy for Persona #1 could be word of mouth from existing customers; Persona #2 customers may come from direct mail to people who recently relocated near one of the retailer's locations.

### Step 2: Key Trends

In addition to AER strategies, managers should account for key environmental trends (e.g., long-term technology or regulatory changes) so that investments in BOR strategies lead to SCA, now and later. Ignoring long-term environmental changes may lead to resource expenditures to build a brand image or innovative new product offering, even though those factors no longer represent an SCA. The shift to online digital media was a pervasive technology and consumer trend; traditional bookstores that ignored this trend when developing their BOR and SCA strategies likely are no longer in business. As another example, some US states chose not to tax online sales, which led many Internet firms to move their headquarters to these very states.

### Step 3: Brand, Offering, and Relationship (BOR) Equity Grid

Using the inputs from the AER strategy grid and key environmental trends, the *BOR equity grid* can be completed to describe three key pieces of information for the BOR strategies, as shown in Figure 4.4(b). The first piece of information is the marketing objectives, obtained from the positioning statements and AER strategies that are most relevant to the specific marketing strategy. This information captures top-level goals that are pertinent to the marketing domain (i.e., brand, offering, relationship). It requires identifying common, important aspects across the different personas and AER strategies that resonate with each BOR marketing domain. For example, which brand objectives (awareness, image, meaning) best support the selected AER strategies and overall positioning strategy? (This step would be repeated for the firm's offering and relationship strategies.)

The next two data elements in the BOR equity grid focus on key aspects that are critical for building SCA (relative advantages over competition) and maintaining the SCA over time (sources of sustainability). This BOR equity grid thus offers a high-level summary of what the firm is trying to achieve with each BOR strategy in its effort to meet its own positioning objectives while withstanding competitive attacks, now and in the future.

The conversion from microanalyses of customer heterogeneity and dynamics into a macroperspective of market-based drivers of SCA is presented simply in Figure 4.4, but, in reality, it is a complex iterative process, typically shifting and evolving over time. It also requires top managers to make multiple strategic trade-offs.

There is, however, a natural order for making BOR strategic decisions and building a customer equity stack:

1 A firm should make brand decisions, which are influenced by the firm's overall positioning objectives from MP#1 and MP#2 and largely determine how the firm will be positioned in the overall marketplace and in existing customers' minds.
2 The firm can focus on its offering decisions; product and service innovation and R&D efforts need to support both brand strategies and the firm's positioning objectives.
3 Relationship strategies normally are determined last, because they involve the delivery and experiential aspect of offerings.

This ordering is especially evident when the offering has a large service component, because in this case, boundary spanners are critical to the customer experience and the firm's overall value proposition. The detailed discussion of brands, offerings, and relationships in the subsequent chapters thus follows this sequence.

## Summary

No matter how well a firm addresses the previous two Marketing Principles, competitors will always try to copy successful firms' strategies or innovate their offerings to match customers' existing and future needs and desires better. That is, *all competitors react*, which is the third "problem" that marketing managers must address by building and maintaining barriers (MP#3). Managers must simultaneously focus on customers' needs and competitors' actions, while also anticipating future competitors' actions, so that they can build barriers that withstand competitive assaults. These barriers are *sustainable competitive advantages* and must meet three conditions: customers must care about whatever the SCA offers; the firm must do it better than competitors; and it must be hard to duplicate.

Market-based sources of SCAs can be grouped into three main categories: brands, offerings, and relationships (BORs). Over time, the key source of marketing-based SCA has evolved from relationships, to brands during the Industrial Revolution, to innovative offerings during the technology revolution. Developed countries are seeing the next revolution in SCA, in response to the shift to a service economy. Services are more intangible, less consistent, more perishable, and harder to evaluate than products, so customer relationships with sellers' boundary-spanning personnel become more important.

With a *customer equity perspective*, customers are assets, and each customer provides a sort of profit center that should be tracked and managed to improve firm performance. A firm's advertising to build strong brands, R&D investments to develop innovative products, and spending on salespeople who enter into enduring customer relationships lead to brand, offering, and relational equities, which together represent the firm's customer equity. This combined equity often is the firm's strongest barrier to competitive assaults. Yet, marketing spending rarely is treated as an asset on a firm's balance sheet; it often is considered an expense, despite research that shows that BOR assets last for extended periods and represent important SCAs.

The managing SCA framework features three inputs: two from MP#1 and MP#2, and a third that captures long-term environmental trends that can disrupt the firm's SCA. That is, MP#1 provides insight into what customers want and how the firm should position itself to satisfy them; MP#2 provides insights into the most effective AER strategies when customers change. Furthermore, the framework generates descriptions of the firm's SCA now and in the future and the BOR strategies it should use to build and maintain these SCAs as outputs. Both outputs aggregate insights gained from more fine-grained analyses, in an effort to support more effective macro decision making. This *micro–macro duality* is critical to a successful marketing strategy, because the true understanding of customers occurs at micro levels, but strategic and resource decisions occur at macro levels.

Managing SCA in turn involves three key steps. The insights from MP#2 should be described in an *AER strategy grid*, which should inform the design of high-impact BOR strategies. Each box in the grid describes the most effective strategy for a unique persona at a specific point in time. Then managers should account for key environmental trends to ensure that investments in BOR strategies lead to SCA now and in the future. Finally, using the inputs from MP#1, the AER strategy grid, and key environmental trends, the *BOR equity grid* can be completed to describe key information for each BOR strategy: key objectives from positioning statements and AER strategies, relative advantages versus competition, and sources of sustainability. This BOR equity grid ultimately provides a high-level summary of what the firm is trying to achieve through its BOR strategy to meet its positioning objectives and withstand its competition over time.

The natural ordering of BOR strategic decisions begins with brand decisions, which depend on the firm's overall positioning objectives (MP#1 and MP#2). Thereafter, the firm can focus on its offering decisions, because its product and service innovation and R&D efforts should support not only its positioning objectives but also its branding strategies. Finally, relationship strategies come last, to determine the appropriate delivery and experiential aspects of the offerings.

## Takeaways

- All competitors react. Firms must address competitive attacks by building and maintaining sustainable competitive advantages (SCAs).

- Customers generate sales and profits; firms must protect them from constant attacks by competitors. Although SCAs are critical, firms must first establish their differentiated position with a targeted customer group before building SCA around this position.

- Every SCA must meet three conditions: customers must care about what it offers; the firm must do it better than competitors; and it must be hard to duplicate.

- In marketing domains, the primary sources of SCA are brands, offerings (innovative products or services), and relationships (BOR). The strongest SCAs use all three strategies in combination to reinforce the differentiated and targeted appeal of a firm to customers.

- Experiments can reveal the causality of BOR investments, by randomly assigning customers to multiple groups with different BOR investment levels/designs, including both treatment and control groups, to minimize potential confounds.

- Competitors have many ways to undermine a firm's SCA, including technical innovations, exploiting customers' changed desires, finding better solutions to a problem, and introducing "me-too" offerings with greater efficiency.

- A customer equity perspective implies that customers should be considered as assets, managed and tracked that way, to improve firm performance. Investments in brands, offerings, and relationships represent important sources of customer equity.

- There are three inputs to the SCA framework: the output of MP#1 about what customers want and how the firm should position itself, the output of MP#2 about the most effective AER strategies as customers change, and long-term environmental trends.

- The two outputs of the SCA framework are a description of a firm's SCA now and in the future, and a description of the BOR strategies needed to achieve it.

- The three-step process for managing SCA includes an AER strategy grid, an analysis of key environmental trends, and a BOR equity grid.

- Technology, regulatory, and socioeconomic trends constantly change; a firm's competitors constantly try to find new ways to satisfy customers' needs and desires. These changes all have the potential to disrupt any firm's market position.

## Analytics Driven Case

# Fighting Competitive Attack at Exteriors Inc.

## Problem Background

Founded in 1921 in Virginia, Exteriors Incorporated (EINC) is the leading manufacturer of roofing shingles in the US. It is a company of over 5,000 employees, providing roofing solutions to home builders and intermediate contractors. EINC had always positioned itself as the elite player in the market, known for the highest quality products without compromise, even if it was the highest priced player in the market. EINC pioneered several product innovations in the roofing industry. For example, it was the first firm to increase the weight/thickness of its shingles to 220 pounds per square, when the industry norm was at 180 pounds per square. The thickness of its shingles provided customers (both homeowners and home builders deciding to go with them) with better longevity and resistance to environmental stress. Market research in 2013 showed that its shingles proved to be the longest lasting products in the US market, and this fact had remained unchanged for nearly three decades. EINC's product variety in terms of colors, textures, and aesthetics was also unmatched; its own internal reports showed that its variety was almost three times that of its nearest competitor. Consequently, it was also the most widely sought after manufacturer in the market, with nearly 98% of its customers rating them highly on customer satisfaction and overall customer experience. It was the most widely distributed product on the market, being one of the few brand names that customers could relate to in an unaided brand recall exercise. Consequently, it also had the brand with the highest brand equity, as reported by third-party market research firms.

The roofing industry was seeing major changes, however; none more pronounced than in the 2000–14 period:

1  With massive growth in construction in Brazil, China, and India, market demand for roofing products had shot up in the last two decades. Consequently, a number of new players had entered the market, positioning themselves competitively on product strength and durability, variety, ease of installation, and price.
2  These foreign players had entered the US market, and after quickly inferring that EINC was the top player when it came to product quality, they had focused their attention on offering products with lower prices that were easier to install than EINC products. With lower prices, they had gradually begun to erode EINC's impressive 76% market share in 2000, and brought it down to 58% by 2014.
3  These players were relentless with price cuts, and appeared to be playing a loss leader strategy in the US, just to gain US market share.
4  The recession had placed a massive damper on new home construction in the 2009–12 period, and the lower priced players benefited rapidly, since their strength was lower price, which was highly desired by home builders in the US who enjoyed the price reduction, since it supported the pricing pressure they were seeing from new homeowners.
5  While the market started to recover in 2013, and home construction figures inched up to 2004 levels, the foreign players were realizing that low price alone would not work to gain even more market share.

Foreign competitors reduced their warranty length from 10 years to 8 years, and capitalized on the idea that new homeowners would trade off lower price in the present against future costs eight years down the road. As the foreign players predicted, the combination of lower price and lower warranty length maintained their market advantage against EINC, and this competitive attack was slowly but surely beginning to have a negative impact on EINC's unrivaled market leadership.

In 2014, EINC called for a strategic marketing meeting with the sales director, R&D director, and marketing research director. The goal of the meeting was to address the competitive threat. In particular, EINC planned to establish a new roofing product in 2016, to serve the competitive market needs and protect its differential competitive advantage. The new roofing product was to be directed at installers using its traditional roofing product, and erode the attacks that foreign players were placing on the market, by being superior on product attributes that mattered to customers.

However, the sales, R&D, and market research teams had different opinions of what constituted the best new product. The sales director was emphatic about a 10% price reduction. According to the sales director, EINC had lost touch with its customers; and the recession had greatly increased price sensitivity to the point where even the best of brands had to reduce price to compete. Moreover, the sales teams believed that they were constantly in touch with their customers as boundary spanners, and the voice of the customer suggested that EINC's prices were too high. This was exactly in opposition with the view of the R&D director. According to the R&D director, EINC's differential competitive advantage was its premium quality product, albeit offered at a premium price. The R&D team were confident that the new product they had developed, which was much superior on aesthetics and life expectancy, was at least one standard deviation better than most competitors, and the best bet for EINC going forward. The market research director disagreed with the sales director and the R&D director. The market research team believed that there was no change needed to price, and no heavy investments in technical product attributes were needed. Rather, they said, the key attribute was the usage experience of their contractors. The market research team felt that most of their contractors faced a rebuy rather than a first buy decision with EINC, given EINC's market presence and leadership standing in the market. The key to rebuy, according to the market research team, was the roof installation process. The foreign players had greatly improved their installation experience for contractors, reducing the time required for installation down from a market average of two weeks to about one week.

Thus, EINC was faced with the dilemma of numerous product attribute combinations to contend with while designing the new product. Moreover, all suggestions seemed rife with uncertainty. A price reduction would directly affect EINC's market share positively, but erode long-term perceptions about EINC, and signal that EINC was diluting its brand presence. Investing millions of dollars in improving the aesthetics and life expectancy of its product would certainly improve the product's quality, but would it be preferred by customers? Finally, improving installer satisfaction by reducing the speed of installation also would come with a cost of operating with lower margins. So, EINC was indeed facing a troublesome marketing dilemma, induced by competition.

## Problem Statement

Competitors always react; and failing to understand and address these competitive retaliations will lead to poor business performance. Thus, firms must address competitive attacks by building and maintaining sustainable competitive advantage (SCA). As we documented in this chapter, market-based sources of SCAs can be grouped into three main categories: brands, offerings, and relationships (BORs).

EINC knew the importance of its brand equity, which had helped it charge a high price premium, improve sales, reduce costs, and made it more difficult for competitors to encroach on its business. Changing the price of the new product from its typical high price point would signal to the market that EINC was altering how its brand should be perceived in the market.

EINC was also keenly aware of its offering equity. Offering equity refers to the core value that the performance of the product or service offers the customer, absent any brand or relationship equity effects. When a firm produces a product or service that is no different from competitors' offerings (i.e., me-too offerings), it generates little offering equity or SCA. So, most firms attempt to develop innovative offerings, differentiated from competitors' products, to generate at least some relative advantage. EINC had always been at the forefront, with respect to offering equity, constantly trying to develop new and innovative offerings to say ahead of its foreign competitors. By developing a new product with longer life expectancy and better aesthetics, it would attempt to increase its offering equity.

Finally, EINC would also want to grow relationship equity with its new product. Relationship marketing efforts seek to improve relationship characteristics (e.g., experiences) with exchange partners and build relationship equity, in the hope of ultimately improved financial performance. Reducing the speed of installation would help EINC increase installer satisfaction and, in turn, their future purchase behaviors, and thereby improve EINC's financial outcomes. Therefore, EINC knew that building an SCA involved finding the right mix of brand, offering, and relationship equity in the new product. To build SCA, EINC decided to apply a scientific and customer-oriented approach to design a new product, using market feedback from customers to help launch the product and thus protect competitive position. EINC launched a strategic initiative aimed at answering the following questions:

- What is the relative importance of brand (price), offering (life expectancy, aesthetics), and relationship (speed of installation) building attributes in EINC's desired new product?
- What is the customer's willingness to pay for life expectancy, aesthetics, and speed of installation?

## Data[1]

### Survey

EINC focused its analytics efforts on validating the critical BOR drivers as a first step, with a plan to conduct more rigorous analyses to determine the relative importance of the attributes in a second step, before beginning new product development. Thus, as a first step, EINC turned to its market research team to survey a sample of 20 customers about the importance of the four key attributes under consideration: price, life expectancy, aesthetics, and speed of installation.

Table 1 presents the survey results. All 20 customers were asked to rate the importance of each of the four attributes on a scale of 1 to 7, where 1 represents least important, and 7 represents most important. As we can see, price was rated as the most important (mean = 6.8), followed by speed of installation (mean = 6.6), life expectancy (mean = 6.5), and aesthetics (mean = 6.1). This represented both good news and bad news for EINC. The high survey scores demonstrated that all four attributes

---

[1] These analyses were performed using MEXL software as described in Data Analytics Technique 9.1 using data from the EINC Case dataset.

**Table 1** Attribute Survey Results

| Product Attribute | Mean Importance Rating from Survey |
|---|---|
| Price | 6.8 |
| Speed of Installation | 6.6 |
| Life Expectancy | 6.5 |
| Aesthetics | 6.1 |

were considered important by customers. However, since all the importance scores were high, there was low discriminability among the attributes.

## Conjoint Model

As a second step, EINC turned to conjoint analysis, since it was proven to be a better approach to understanding the importance of the trade-offs among the attributes. The basic assumption of conjoint measurement is that customers cannot reliably express how they weight separate features of a product in forming their preferences. However, we can infer the relative weights by asking for their evaluations (or choices) of alternate product concepts through a structured process. Conjoint analysis argues that a product consists of multiple attributes that together provide benefits to a customer. For example, a roofing customer might think about brand (price), offering (life expectancy, aesthetics), and relationship (speed of installation) building attributes. When EINC decides to develop a new roofing product, it cannot just ask customers about what features they care about; most customers would say they wanted the best version of all the features. Instead, the firm can simulate a trade-off. Would you rather have better aesthetics or more life expectancy? The trade-offs reflect how customers actually make decisions, because few of them can afford the best options for all attributes in every product. Thus, during a conjoint exercise, rather than directly asking customers about the significance of product attributes, the analyst uses a more realistic setting and asks customers to evaluate alternative scenarios or product profiles, each with multiple product attributes. Then it is possible to infer the significance of each product attribute from the ratings that customers provide for each scenario, reflecting their overall product preference.

EINC then moved to specifying the different attribute combinations it wished to test. It chose three combinations of life expectancy (low resistance, medium resistance, and high resistance), two combinations of aesthetics (no perceptive imperfections, or minimal imperfections), three combinations of speed of installation (1 week, 1.2 weeks or 1.5 weeks from date of order), and three levels of price (a price index of $8, $9, and $10).[2] Next, EINC worked towards specifying a set of nine product bundles, with varying levels of each of the four product attributes, for which it wished to obtain customers' overall evaluations, in such a way that those evaluations could then be decomposed into the part-worth value that each customer attaches to each level of each attribute. In the actual conjoint task, each customer was asked to rate each of the twelve product bundles on a 100-point scale, where 100 represented the most desired product bundle. The implicit idea is that customers could provide rating scores for products (which induce trade-offs about product attributes) as a whole, but could not directly assess product attributes. Table 2 shows the product attribute mix, while Table 3 shows the nine product bundles.

**Table 2** Attribute Design Matrix

| Attributes | Level 1 | Level 2 | Level 3 |
|---|---|---|---|
| Life Expectancy | Low Resistance | Medium Resistance | High Resistance |
| Speed of Installation | 1 week | 1.2 weeks | 1.5 weeks |
| Shingle Aesthetics | No Imperfections | Minimal Imperfections | |
| Price | 8 | 9 | 10 |

---

[2] The actual prices are masked with price indices for confidentiality purposes.

**Table 3** Product Bundles

| Attributes | Bundle 1 | Bundle 2 | Bundle 3 | Bundle 4 | Bundle 5 | Bundle 6 | Bundle 7 | Bundle 8 | Bundle 9 |
|---|---|---|---|---|---|---|---|---|---|
| Life Expectancy | Low Resistance | Low Resistance | Low Resistance | Medium Resistance | Medium Resistance | Medium Resistance | High Resistance | High Resistance | High Resistance |
| Speed of Installation | 1 week | 1.2 weeks | 1.5 weeks | 1 week | 1.2 weeks | 1.5 weeks | 1 week | 1.2 weeks | 1.5 weeks |
| Shingle Aesthetics | No Imperfections | No Imperfections | Minimal Imperfections | Minimal Imperfections | No Imperfections | No Imperfections | No Imperfections | Minimal Imperfections | No Imperfections |
| Price | 10 | 9 | 8 | 9 | 8 | 10 | 8 | 10 | 9 |

## Part-worth Results

EINC collected data from such a conjoint task from 20 key respondents (who were in charge of product decisions), so as to estimate the underlying value of each product attribute, or its part-worth utility. The estimated part-worth utilities from a conjoint analysis could provide the answers to many of its questions, such as which product configurations are optimal.

Table 4 provides the mean values of the part-worths for each product attribute-level combination, estimated by the conjoint analysis. Focusing on life expectancy, relative to the lowest level (low resistance) that received a base score of 0, medium-resistance products received a part-worth score of 11.95 and high-resistance products received a mean score of 35.85. Thus, high-resistance products were preferred the most, but, more interestingly, much more heavily than medium-resistance products were preferred to low-resistance products. Next, looking at speed of installation, relative to the slowest level (1.5 weeks) that received a base score of 0, medium speed of installation products received a part-worth score of 15.2, and high speed of installation products received a mean score of 37.65. Again, high speed of installation products were preferred the most, and much more heavily than medium speed of installation products were preferred to low speed of installation products. Third, looking at aesthetics, relative to the minimal imperfections that received a base score of 1.35, products with no imperfections received a part-worth score of 7.55, suggesting that they were not much more useful than products with no imperfections. Finally, focusing on price, relative to the highest price product that received a base score of 0, medium-priced products received a part-worth score of 5.25, and low-priced products received a mean score of 17.45.

**Table 4** Part-worth Means across Respondents

| Life Expectancy | Life Expectancy | Life Expectancy | Speed of Installation | Speed of Installation | Speed of Installation | Shingle Aesthetics | Shingle Aesthetics | Price | Price | Price |
|---|---|---|---|---|---|---|---|---|---|---|
| Low Resistance | Medium Resistance | High Resistance | 1 week | 1.2 weeks | 1.5 weeks | No Imperfections | Minimal Imperfections | 8 | 9 | 10 |
| 35.85 | 11.95 | 0 | 37.65 | 15.2 | 0.2 | 7.55 | 1.35 | 17.45 | 5.25 | 0 |

## Willingness to Pay Results

With the rating scores from the customers, EINC estimated the part-worth utilities associated with each product attribute. With the part-worths estimated for each product, EINC could now estimate the willingness to pay for non-price attributes in the product bundle. The intuition is as follows. EINC knows that customers prefer a low-priced product (part-worth = 17.45) over a high-priced product (part-worth = 0). Note that the low-priced product had a price index of 8, while the high-priced product had a price index of 10. Thus, the part-worth difference between the product with price index of 8 and 10 was 17.45, which implies that one price index unit is equal to 8.725 part-worth units (10 − 8 = 2 = 17.45 units, or a price index of 1 is = 8.725 units). This means that:

- The part-worth difference between a low life expectancy product (part-worth = 0) and high life expectancy product (part-worth = 35.85) was 35.85 units. EINC estimates that customers are willing to pay a quantity of 35.85/8.725 = 4.1 price units more for a product with high life expectancy.
- The part-worth difference between a low-quality aesthetics product (part-worth = 1.35) and high-quality aesthetics product (part-worth = 7.55) was 6.2 units. EINC estimates that customers are willing to pay a quantity of 6.2/8.725 = 0.71 price units more for a product with high-quality aesthetics.
- The part-worth difference between a low speed of installation (part-worth = 0) and high speed of installation (part-worth = 37.65) was 37.65 units. EINC estimates that customers are willing to pay a quantity of 37.65/8.725 = 4.31 price units more for a product with high speed of installation.

Table 5 summarizes the results, which highlight the importance of life expectancy and installation speed, while also quantifying the benefits of each of the attributes in the product bundles.

**Table 5** Willingness to Pay for New Product

| Attribute | Difference in Price Units Between "Low" and "High" Version |
|---|---|
| Price | 2 |
| Life Expectancy | 4.1 |
| Aesthetics | 0.71 |
| Speed of Installation | 4.31 |

## Modifying BOR Strategies to Thwart Competitive Attack

Taken together, when EINC reviewed the attributes in unison, it realized that products with the highest life expectancy (high resistance), that were delivered within a week, were rated the best. Interestingly, aesthetics did not matter as much as EINC thought they would. Also, the price part-worths were not as large as the life expectancy and speed of installation attributes, suggesting that its consumers were not as sensitive to price as they were to other product attributes.

How did the findings alter EINC's BOR strategy? Recall that EINC was grappling with the right mix of brand, offering, and relationship attributes. EINC knew the importance of its brand equity, which had helped it charge a high price premium, improve sales, reduce costs, and made it more difficult for competitors to encroach on its business. Based on the results, lowering the price of the new product from its typical high price point would not be required as consumers were not as sensitive to price as it had feared. Thus, it could retain its high price point, high-quality positioning in the marketplace. Next, EINC was also keenly aware of its offering equity. EINC had always been at the forefront, with respect to offering equity, constantly trying to develop new and innovative offerings to say ahead of its foreign competitors. By developing a new product with longer life expectancy and better aesthetics, it would attempt to increase its offering equity. However, based on the results, it learnt that a change in life expectancy was much more desirable than aesthetics, a point it conveyed to the R&D director. Finally, EINC would also want to grow relationship equity (installation experience) with its new product. The results indicated that reducing the speed of installation would help EINC increase customer satisfaction and, in turn, their future behaviors.

Therefore, EINC's SCA, stemming from the right mix of brand, offering, and relationship equity, would involve retaining higher price, improving life expectancy, and reducing the speed of installation. It could also use the willingness to pay estimates of life expectancy to develop new pricing policies that could charge premium prices to customers who truly desired higher speed installations.

## Summary of Solution

The analytics exercise discussed in the case enabled EINC to obtain a better grip of its current standing in the marketplace, by better understanding the changes in the needs of its customers, when competitors attack:

1 It was able to balance the passion of the management team, stemming from marketing, R&D and sales force viewpoints, with the business rationale stemming from analytics, to developing its new product. While each management team viewed their respective contributions to the team as driving the success of products, EINC was able to use a customer-centric approach to design the new product.
2 Related to the earlier points, it was able to use feedback from customers before the launch of the product to develop a product configuration with brand, offering, and relationship attributes that should combine to determine the success of the product. Note that from the results, it is not clear that any one strategy alone works to combat competitive threat; EINC needed to tweak all three BOR strategies, and using an analytical approach helps determine the right BOR mix.
3 Using conjoint analysis, it was able to identify segments for which a given offering generates sufficient incremental value. For example, even within its offering equity generating process, it learnt that customers preferred products with more life expectancy more than they preferred products with elegant aesthetics. This is difficult a priori, and also difficult to argue without objective evidence. Having performed its analysis, it could now use the willingness to pay estimates of life expectancy to develop new pricing policies that could identify the segments of customers to whom it could charge premium prices for higher life expectancy and faster speed of installation. Thus, analytics-oriented efforts helped EINC solve the third fundamental marketing problem, that all competitors react.

## Appendix: Dataset Description

### General Description of the Data

The dataset is a simulated dataset, aimed at mimicking similar datasets that the authors have used in the past while working with companies. The data contain one Excel sheet, which has one data table on the conjoint study design, one data table on the nine different bundles shown to respondents, and one data table on how the 20 respondents ranked each of the nine bundles on a score of 1–100.

### Description of Variables in the Data

The conjoint study contains three parts. The first part is called the study design, which is the descriptor of the attributes and the levels of the products being considered. EINC considered four key attributes: price, life expectancy, aesthetics, and speed of installation. Except for aesthetics (two design levels), each of the attributes had three levels. The attributes and design levels are given below in the Excel sheet.

| Attributes/Levels | Level 1 | Level 2 | Level 3 |
|---|---|---|---|
| Life Expectancy | Low Resistance | Medium Resistance | High Resistance |
| Speed of Installation | 1 week | 1.2 weeks | 1.5 weeks |
| Shingle Aesthetics | No Imperfections | Minimal Imperfections | |
| Price | $8 | $9 | $10 |

Based on the attribute-level combos, the 20 respondents in the survey were shown nine different products, each of which is a combination of different attributes. This is the second sheet in the data.

| Attributes/ Bundles | Bundle 1 | Bundle 2 | Bundle 3 | Bundle 4 | Bundle 5 | Bundle 6 | Bundle 7 | Bundle 8 | Bundle 9 |
|---|---|---|---|---|---|---|---|---|---|
| Life Expectancy | Low Resistance | Low Resistance | Low Resistance | Medium Resistance | Medium Resistance | Medium Resistance | High Resistance | High Resistance | High Resistance |
| Speed of Installation | 1 week | 1.2 weeks | 1.5 weeks | 1 week | 1.2 weeks | 1.5 weeks | 1 week | 1.2 weeks | 1.5 weeks |
| Shingle Aesthetics | No Imperfections | No Imperfections | Minimal Imperfections | Minimal Imperfections | No Imperfections | No Imperfections | No Imperfections | Minimal Imperfections | No Imperfections |
| Price | $10 | $9 | $8 | $9 | $8 | $10 | $8 | $10 | $9 |

Finally, each of the 20 respondents gave a score of 1–100 to each of the nine bundles, shown in the last table in the dataset.

To obtain the model results, the student can directly load the data in Excel, and use the MEXL add-in pertaining to Conjoint analysis (estimate preference part-worths), and obtain results as shown in Table 4.

# References

1 Tzu, S. (5th century BC) *The Art of War*. Translated by Griffith, S.B., 1963. Oxford: Clarendon Press.

2 CNBC (2014) *The History of the Dow 30*. Available at: www.cnbc.com/2014/07/02/history-of-dow-30.html (accessed 23 July, 2014).

3 Maddox, K. (2015) 'GE's new CMO: How to market a digital industrial company,' *Advertising Age*, 7 October.

4 Neill, J. (2013) 'Tesco's foray, and failure, in the U.S.,' *Advertising Age*, 4 October.

5 Silverthorn, S. (2010) 'Tesco's stumble into the U.S. market,' *Harvard Business School Working Knowledge*, 25 October.

6 Chopra, A. (2013) 'How Kodak and Polaroid fell victim to the dark side of innovation.' Available at: http://betanews.com/2013/12/12/how-kodak-and-polaroid-fell-victim-to-the-dark-side-of-innovation/ (accessed 23 July, 2015).

7 Barney, J.B. and Clark, D.N. (2007) *Resource-Based Theory: Creating and Sustaining Competitive Advantage*. Oxford: Oxford University Press.

8 Peteraf, M.A. and Barney, J.B. (2003) 'Unraveling the resource-based tangle,' *Managerial & Decision Economics*, 24(4), pp. 309–23.; Barney, J.B. and Hesterly, W.S. (2012) *Strategic Management and Competitive Advantage: Concepts and Cases*, 3rd edn. Englewood Cliffs, NJ: Prentice Hall.

9 Satell, G. (2014) 'A look back at why Blockbuster really failed and why it didn't have to,' 5 September. Available at: www.forbes.com/sites/gregsatell/2014/09/05/a-look-back-at-why-blockbuster-really-failed-and-why-it-didnt-have-to/ (accessed July 23, 2015).

10 Dunn, K. (2014) 'The first great internet browser war.' Available at: http://internet-browser-review.toptenreviews.com/the-first-great-internet-browser-war.html, (accessed 23 July, 2015); Andrews, P. and Flores, M.F. (1997) 'Internet wars – Microsoft vs. Netscape: Goliath takes on David – Navigator still ahead – but losing ground,' *Seattle Times*, 11 March; Beattie, A. (2009) 'What were the "browser wars"?' Available at: www.investopedia.com/ask/answers/09/browser-wars-netscape-internet-explorer.asp (accessed 23 July, 2015).

11 Rivkin, S. and Sutherland, F. (2004) *The Making of a Name: The Inside Story of the Brands We Buy*. Oxford: Oxford University Press.

12 Interbrand (2016) *Best Global Brands* Available at: http://interbrand.com/best-brands/best-global-brands/2015/ranking/ (accessed 23 February, 2016).

13 Interbrand (2016) *Best Global Brands* Available at: http://interbrand.com/best-brands/best-global-brands/2015/ranking/ (accessed 23 February, 2016).

14 DiFrisco, M.G. (n.d.) *How-to-Branding*. Available at: www.how-to-branding.com/Branding-Examples.html (accessed 23 July 2015); Design Council (n.d.) *The Power of Branding*. Available at: www.designcouncil.org.uk/news-opinion/power-branding (accessed 23 July, 2015).

15 Landry, E.C., Meer, D. and Sharma, S. (2015) 'Creating what consumers want,' 26 January. Available at: www.forbes.com/sites/strategyand/2015/01/26/creating-what-consumers-want/ (accessed 23 July, 2015).

16 Griffine, E. (2014) 'Why startups fail, according to their founders,' *Fortune*, 25 September.

17 Groth, A. (2014) '22 of the most epic product fails in history,' *Business Insider*, 31 July.

18 Turner, D. (2011) 'Marketing failure: New Coke,' *Foster School of Business Blog*, 11 April.

19 Lieberman, M.B. and Montgomery, D.B. (1988) 'First mover advantages,' *Strategic Management Journal*, 9, pp. 41–58

20 Robinson, W.T., Kalyanaram, G. and Urban, G.L. (1994) 'First-mover advantages from pioneering new markets: A survey of

empirical evidence,' *Review of Industrial Organization*, 9(1), pp. 1–23.

21  Cowan, M. (2012) 'Inside the clone factory: The story of Germany's Samwer brothers,' *Wired*, April.

22  Palmatier, R.W., Dant, R.P., Grewal, D. and Evans, K.R. (2006) 'Factors influencing the effectiveness of relationship marketing: A meta-analysis,' *Journal of Marketing*, 70(4), pp. 136–53.

23  Samaha, S.A., Palmatier, R.W. and Dant, R.P. (2011) 'Poisoning relationships: Perceived unfairness in channels of distribution,' *Journal of Marketing*, 75(3), pp. 99–117.

24  Palmatier, R.W., Scheer, L.K., Evans, K.R. and Arnold, T. (2008) 'Achieving relationship marketing effectiveness in business-to-business exchanges,' *Journal of the Academy of Marketing Science*, 36(2), pp. 174–90.

25  Palmatier, R.W., Scheer, L.K. and Steenkamp, J.B.E.M. (2007) 'Customer loyalty to whom? Managing the benefits and risks of salesperson-owned loyalty,' *Journal of Marketing Research*, 44(2), pp. 185–99.

26  Demery, P. (2015) 'A million B2B sales reps will lose their jobs to e-commerce by 2020.' Available at: www.internetretailer.com/2015/04/13/million-sales-reps-will-lose-their-jobs-e-commerce-2020 (accessed 15 January, 2016).

27  Mishra, A. (2015) 'Foodpanda fires over 500 employees, will stop own delivery in six cities,' 30 December. Available at: www.livemint.com/Companies/44bsSS8LYs7TY8wppoSbFO/Foodpanda-fires-more-than-500-employees-will-stop-own-deliv.html (accessed 17 January, 2016).

28  Interbrand (2016) *Best Global Brands* Available at: http://interbrand.com/best-brands/best-global-brands/2015/ranking/ (accessed 23 February, 2016).

29  Downes, L. and Nunes, P. (2013) 'Big-bang disruption,' *Harvard Business Review*, 91(3), pp. 44–56.

30  Wells, G. (n.d.) 'Howard Johnson's.' Available at: www.roadsidefans.com/features/howard-johnsons (accessed 23 July, 2015).

31  Lyle, R. (n.d.) 'Why McDonald's must promote healthier options to arrest steep falls in sales.' Available at: http://globalceo.com/why-mcdonalds-must-promote-healthier-options-to-arrest-steep-falls-in-sales/ (cached) (accessed 23 July, 2015).

32  Kim, W.C. and Mauborgne, R. (2005) *Blue Ocean Strategy: How to Create Uncontested Market Space and Make the Competition Irrelevant*. Boston, MA: Harvard Business School Press.

33  Einhorn, B. and Stone, B. (2011) 'Tencent: March of the Penguins,' *Business Week*, 8 August.

34  Will, G.F. (2015) 'How income inequality benefits everybody,' *Washington Post*, 25 March.

35  Palmatier, R.W. (2006) *Relationship Marketing*. Cambridge: Marketing Science Institute.

36  Parvatiyar, A. and Sheth, J.N. (1995) *Handbook of Relationship Marketing*. Thousand Oaks, CA: Sage.

37  Shaw, E.H. and Tamilia, R.D. (1962) 'Robert Bartels and the history of marketing thought,' *Journal of Macromarketing*, 21(2), pp. 156–63.

38  Schoenherr, S.E. (2008) 'The digital revolution.' Available at: http://web.archive.org/web/20081007132355/http://history.sandiego.edu/gen/recording/digital.html (accessed 23 July, 2015); Hudson, P. (2013) 'Why the tech revolution is the industrial revolution of our time,' *Elite Daily*, 29 March.

39  DiFrisco, M.G. (n.d.) *How-to-Branding* Available at: www.how-to-branding.com/Branding-Examples.html (accessed 23 July, 2015); Design Council (n.d.) *The Power of Branding*. Available at: www.designcouncil.org.uk/news-opinion/power-branding (accessed 23 July, 2015).

40  Vargo, S.L. and Lusch, R.F. (2004) 'Evolving to a new service dominant logic for marketing,' *Journal of Marketing*, 68(1), pp. 1–17.

41  Fang, E., Palmatier, R.W. and Steenkamp, J.B.E.M. (2008) 'Effect of service transition strategies on firm value,' *Journal of Marketing* 72(5), pp. 1–14.

42  Palmatier, R.W. (2006) *Relationship Marketing*. Cambridge: Marketing Science Institute.

43  Palmatier, R.W., Dant, R.P., Grewal, D. and Evans, K.R. (2006) 'Factors influencing the effectiveness of relationship marketing: A meta-analysis,' *Journal of Marketing*, 70(4), pp. 136–53.

44  Rust, R.T., Zeithaml, V.A. and Lemon, K.N. (2000) *Driving Customer Equity: How Customer Lifetime Value is Shaping Corporate Strategy*. New York: The Free Press.

45  Albers, S., Mantrala, M.K. and Sridhar, S. (2010) 'Personal selling elasticities: A meta-analysis,' *Journal of Marketing Research*, 47(5), pp. 840–53.

46  Moorman, C. (2013) *The CMO Survey*. Available at http://cmosurvey.org/results/survey-results-august-2013/ (accessed 17 January, 2016).

47  Srinivasan, R., Lilien, G.L. and Sridhar, S. (2011) 'Should firms spend more on R&D and advertising during recessions?,' *Journal of Marketing* 75(3), pp. 49–65.

48  Christensen, C. (2011) *The Innovator's Dilemma*. New York: First Collins Business Essentials.

49  Flinders, K. (2016) 'Never lose track of customer journey, says Brussels Airlines CIO,' 28 July. Available from: www.computerweekly.com/news/450300924/Never-lose-track-of-customer-journey-says-Brussels-Airlines-CIO (accessed 8 August, 2016)

50  Hamel, G. and Prahalad, C.K. (1996) *Competing for the Future*. Cambridge, MA: Harvard Business Review Press.

## Companion website

Please visit the companion website, **www.palgravehighered.com/palmatier-ms**, to access summary videos from the authors, and full-length cases with datasets and step-by-step solution guides.

ALL
COMPETITORS
REACT

Chapter **5**

# Marketing Principle #3: Managing Brand–based Sustainable Competitive Advantage

ALL
COMPETITORS
REACT

## Learning objectives

- Define and describe five benefits of brand equity.
- Explain why a strong brand enhances sales and profits and how it provides a competitive edge.
- Describe the associative network memory model of brand equity and how it works.
- Critically discuss the key branding elements of a brand strategy.
- Explain the trade-offs involved in designing a firm's brand architecture.
- Outline in detail the method to create a brand strategy using brand positioning, brand architecture, and brand extensions.
- Understand and describe the three-step process for building brand equity.
- Outline the commonly used marketing communication formats and discuss the pros and cons of each.
- Define qualitative and quantitative analyses and identify when each is most effective for understanding and measuring brand equity.

# Introduction

## Brand Basics

The American Marketing Association defines **brands** as a "name, term, design, symbol, or any other feature that identifies one seller's good or service as distinct from those of other sellers."[1] Usually, managers characterize a brand by describing all the **brand elements** used to identify it, including its name (e.g., Apple), symbol (e.g., silhouette of an apple with a bite removed), package design (e.g., sleek white box), and any other features that serve to differentiate that brand's offering from competitors'. Some firms, like IKEA and Siemens, use a stylized version of the firm's name as the brand; other firms give unique names to each product they offer, such as Unilever's Dove, Lipton, and Knorr product brands.

A firm's brand equity often represents a substantial portion of its overall value. Interbrand's list of the top 10 global brands in 2014 valued Apple's brand at the top of the list at $118.2 billion, followed by Google ($107.4 billion), and Coca-Cola ($81.6 billion). Samsung ($45.5 billion), Toyota ($42.4 billion), and Mercedes-Benz ($34.3 billion) were the only three non-US firms to make the global list (Figure 5.1).[2]

## Brands as SCA

The third Marketing Principle focuses on the importance of building and maintaining barriers to competitive attacks, or sustainable competitive advantages (SCAs), because competitors are continually reacting to any firm's success. Without these barriers or SCAs, competitors ultimately undermine the firm's business, taking its customers and damaging its financial performance. Investments to build brand awareness and brand images among customers can produce a strong competitive barrier. Such brand-related benefits often are the initial market-based SCA for a firm, because they stem directly from the firm's strategic positioning and the overall marketing for all the company's offerings. That is, the positioning statements generated in relation to MP#1 and MP#2 provide key information that help the firm design its brand message to make target customers aware of the brand and how it continues to meet their needs over time.

Customers' awareness of, knowledge about, and behaviors in response to a brand generate the firm's brand equity, one of the three major components of the customer equity stack, along with offering and relationship equities. **Brand equity** is the set of assets and liabilities linked to a brand, its name, and

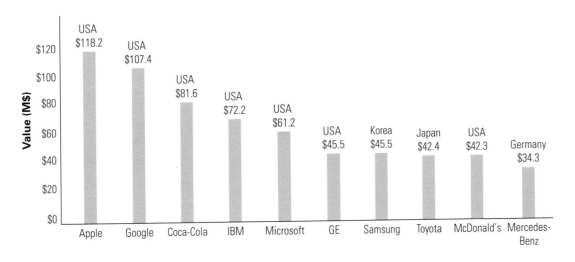

**Figure 5.1** Ranking of the 10 Most Valuable Global Brands
*Source:* Data from Interbrand (2014) *Best Global Brands.*

its symbol, which add to or subtract from the value provided by the firm's offering and relationships.[3] For a firm, brand equity equals the sum of all the customer lifetime value (CLV) associated with all future and existing customers that can be attributed to the firm's brand. Brands can influence consumers' behavior, and brand equity captures the value of those behaviors to the firm.

Thus, brand equity "lies in the mind of the customer," which means that it is difficult for competitors to copy it, adding to the sustainability of brand-based barriers.[4] But this status also makes it hard for firms to adapt or change their brand identity. Apple could not rapidly gain a reputation as a low-price provider of basic computers, for example, because the strength of its identity as a higher priced, innovative brand is firmly entrenched. If the power of brands as SCA thus depends on the minds of customers, then an important question emerges: How does an individual consumer's mind process brand information? Understanding the brand-building process, as it takes place among consumers, can provide insights into many different brand-building strategies that firms might adopt, including which ones are most effective and why each strategy works best in any particular situation.

> Brand equity "lies in the mind of the customer," which means that it is difficult for competitors to copy it, adding to the sustainability of brand-based barriers.

## Associative Network Memory Model of Brand Equity

A leading psychological model describes how brands work. The *associative network memory model* argues that the human mind is a network of nodes and connecting links. The key characteristics of a brand, which influence its brand equity, are captured as nodes and linkages.[5] Specifically, **brand awareness** or **familiarity**, which reflects the customer's ability to identify a brand, is indicated by the size or strength of the node for that memory, as shown in Figure 5.2. It is often measured using aided

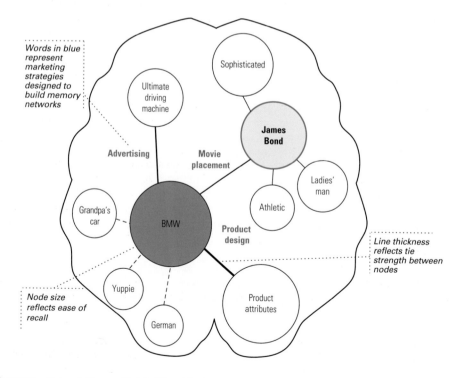

**Figure 5.2**  Associative Network Memory Model of Brand Equity

and unaided recall tasks.[6] **Brand image**, or customers' perceptions and associations with the brand, is represented by the links of the brand name node to other informational nodes in the model. Unique linkages to a brand name capture the brand's identity and differential (dis)advantage, relative to its competitors. The thickness of a line between two nodes represents the strength of the association between these two memories in a consumer's mind.

A firm has many ways to strengthen or build positive linkages to a brand node, to ensure that the brand identity matches the ideal positioning in a target market. For example, Figure 5.2 represents an associative network memory model for a potential customer of BMW automobiles; the size of the BMW node represents a particular customer's awareness of BMW. The more often a customer is exposed to BMW advertisements, riding in a friend's BMW, or just seeing models on the road, the stronger BMW's brand node becomes (i.e., it grows in size). Firms can measure the awareness of their brands by asking targeted customers to name 3 to 5 cars (unaided recall), or they can offer a list of 20 cars and ask customers to select the 3–5 they are most familiar with (aided recall). Brand awareness is the frequency with which BMW is named.

If BMW's marketing department wants to build more linkages with this node, it could pay to have James Bond drive a BMW in a movie, establishing a link between BMW and the James Bond node, as well as Bond's existing linkages (e.g., sophisticated, ladies' man, athletic), as shown in Figure 5.2. A movie placement can be very effective, because this single marketing move can link a constellation of characteristics to the central brand node, which would be more difficult to achieve through traditional television or print advertisements. In addition, movie placements often make these links more subtly, so they can avoid the reactance and skepticism that customers often feel toward obvious paid advertising.[7] But as Figure 5.2 shows, other product design features and tag lines (e.g., "Ultimate Driving Machine") can be linked to the brand node using more traditional marketing strategies.

In the network memory model, brand strategy involves first building awareness to provide an anchor point, then building linkages to positive, unique memory nodes to establish an identity that matches target customers' needs in a cost-efficient manner.[8] When a customer sees (hears, touches) the brand name, it activates that brand node, leading to the cascading activation of other connected nodes – as long as strong linkages exist – which create the customer's brand experience. Prior research has shown that these linkages can activate a wide range of cognitive and emotional responses.[9]

## Benefits from Brand Equity

There are many benefits of building brand equity; together, these benefits ultimately can improve a firm's sales, reduce its costs, and make it more difficult for competitors to encroach on the firm's business.[10] Brands change how people think, although often at a level below their conscious awareness, which makes it very difficult for customers to ignore brand effects. For example, one classic experiment shows that the taste of beer differs when the customer knows the brand of the beer they are drinking.[11] Customers are not just repeating the brand messaging; the beer actually tastes different when linked to a brand name. Because brand identification activates a brand node associated with that beer, it spreads across other strongly linked nodes in the drinker's memory network. Thus, the part of the brain that processes taste receives input from both the customer's taste buds and the brand's memory network. These two inputs then merge to establish the customer's taste perceptions. A key benefit is that *brands can change customers' actual experiences*. They can change the taste of food or drink, the excitement of driving a car, the comfort felt in a coffee shop, and the visual appeal of diamond jewelry.[12]

> A key benefit is that *brands can change customers' actual experiences*. They can change the taste of food or drink, the excitement of driving a car, the comfort felt in a coffee shop, and the visual appeal of diamond jewelry.

Most benefits from strong brands are associated with three general areas: sales growth, profit enhancement, and loyalty effects. First, sales benefit from strong brands, because brands make it easier to acquire new customers, who perceive less risk, higher quality, and better performance of a brand with strong equity.[13] Similarly, it is easier for firms to launch new products, product extensions, and brand extensions, because their strong brand name provides protection, in the form of various attributes linked to the new introductions, even before the firm spends any of its marketing budget on the product launch. When Siemens launches a new electronic product, its brand identity (i.e., well-designed, highly reliable, German-engineered products) immediately attaches to the new offering. Furthermore, existing customers tend to speak positively about and recommend (i.e., word of mouth [WOM]) firms and products with high brand equity.[14]

Second, the benefits that drive sales growth also can enhance a firm's profitability by reducing costs (e.g., WOM provides free customer acquisition, relatively less marketing is needed to retain brand loyal customers) or allowing the firm to charge higher prices for its products. Higher prices often are inherently tied to brand positioning in a market. Chanel, Ferrari, and Gucci all charge significant premiums for their products, mostly due to customers' perception of their exclusive brand image. These products help confer high status onto customers who use them, and that status is a key part of their brand equity. In addition, firms with strong brand equity can gain easier access to various sales channels (retailers, distributors, specialty catalogs, web platforms) than competitors with less or no brand equity.[15] In one study, Kellogg's brand value emerged as more than 25% higher than that of General Mills, based on customers' perceptions of each brand.[16]

Third, a strong brand makes customers more loyal, which often provides the largest barrier to competitive entry. This significant source of SCA arises because strong brands generate more favorable attitudes (attitudinal loyalty), which skew customers' perceptions and subsequent behaviors. If Apple suffers supply chain problems that lead to late product deliveries, many loyal customers would attribute the problems immediately to the company's offshore suppliers. Apple's strong brand protects it from the repercussions of such service failures, but if a similar problem were to plague Gateway or Acer, their customers likely would blame these weaker brands for the problems and perhaps even switch to a competitor to make their future purchases.

**Example:**  SAB (South Africa)

South African Breweries (SAB), named the "Most Admired Company in South Africa" by Ask Afrika, a South African market research company, is a prime example of using brand loyalty to prevent competitive entry. While many international brewers have attempted to gain a slice of SAB's over 90% market share, SAB's brand strength is a very difficult barrier to overcome.

Strong brands also generate repeat purchase behaviors (behavioral loyalty), in the form of habitual purchase behavior, which can be reinforced by high brand awareness and the connection between the customer's self-identity and the brand identity of the firm or product. When both attitudinal and behavioral loyalty are high, it creates **true loyalty**, manifested in consumers' positive feelings and actions (see Figure 5.3).[17] If they buy but have ambivalent or negative feelings (termed **spurious loyalty**), then at the first convenient opportunity, they will switch. For example, an employee might use a particular software package at work, because it is all that the employing firm supports, but if given a choice (e.g., on a personal computer), they gladly switch to a different system. Such customers are not truly loyal. On the flip side, customers might express positive attitudes but fail to actually buy a firm's products, which constitutes **latent loyalty**. This form of loyalty often arises due to a lack of local purchase access or prices beyond their means.

Overall, however, high brand equity enhances a firm's sales and profits, allowing it to continue to market its products, conduct R&D, and fight competitors in a multitude of ways. A strong "war chest" earned from superior sales and profits gives the firm the resources and time it needs to respond to innovative product entries or low-cost competitors; in some cases, it even might use these resources to acquire a firm that provides an existential threat to its survival. Because strong brands increase customers' attitudinal and behavioral loyalty, switching behavior diminishes. Very loyal customers avoid even evaluating competitive offerings, to prevent themselves from feeling tempted or disrupting their sense of supportive brand attachment.

**Behavioral Loyalty (repeat purchases)**

|  | **High** | **Low** |
|---|---|---|
| **High** | **True Loyalty** *High levels of attitudinal and behavioral loyalty* | **Latent Loyalty** *Positive attitudes but does not buy the firm's products* |
| **Low** | **Spurious Loyalty** *Buys products but has ambivalent or negative feelings* | **No Loyalty** *No positive feelings and no purchases* |

*Attitudinal Loyalty (strong positive feelings)*

**Figure 5.3** True Loyalty Matrix

# Brand Strategies

## Brand Positioning

Brand positioning reflects how and where the firm hopes to appear in customers' mind. In a way, it reflects the firm's ideal associative network memory model, the one it hopes that customers hold in mind. It captures the aspirational level of awareness, key associations, and overall product or company image the firm seeks in the marketplace. The *BOR equity grid* from Chapter 4 provides a starting point for this discussion, because it describes the marketing objectives associated with the brand strategy, the relative advantage(s) that the brand can offer over relevant competitors, and the source of the sustainability of this advantage. That is, it captures many of the elements that brand managers need to develop their brand strategies. The firm's positioning statements are also important, although they can be more abstract or high level, rather than specific to the brand strategy. Furthermore, the AER strategies across personas, as outlined in the *AER strategy grid*, might be helpful, but they are unique to each persona and AER stage, whereas the brand usually needs to be consistent across all personas and stages. Generally, it is not possible to offer differentiated brand strategies at this level of granularity.

Thus, the *BOR equity grid* provides the objectives, relative advantages (over competitors), and sources of sustainability (how it wins over time) that are required to use brands as SCA. But other elements also are required to develop a brand strategy, including:

- **Brand objectives**: describe what the brand needs to accomplish as a performance outcome, such as driving customer acquisition or generating a price premium by establishing a perception of status.
- **Brand awareness**: describes the firm's desired level of recognition, as demonstrated by target customers' ability to recall the firm's brand name. Most firms prefer a high level of awareness, but achieving it requires substantial time and marketing expenditures, so it is important to specify a threshold level of awareness that the firm is willing to pay for, among a particular set of customers.
- **Brand relative advantage**: captures the brand's **points of difference**, or the key ways it differs from its competition. In addition, the **points of parity** are those aspects of the brand that may not be unique but still are required by customers in the target market.

- **Brand sustainability**: how the brand is going to maintain its relative advantage over time, whether by generating an exceptionally high level of awareness among difficult-to-reach decision makers or maintaining a tough-to-achieve but strong image that matches targeted customers' self-identity.
- **Brand image**: describes the high-level, abstract perspective of the brand network, according to what comes to customers' minds when they think of the brand. Brand associations instead describe the specific words, colors, logo, fonts, emotions, features, music, smells, people, animals, or symbols that are linked to a brand.
- **Brand identity**: pulls it all together and describes who the brand is. If it were a person, what would they be like? A brand's identity is often subsumed by customers who use the product, because the customer seeks to connect the brand's identity to their own self-identity.[18]

If brand managers can describe all these brand elements, they gain a clear picture of what they want the brand to do, know the key methods they are going to use to achieve their goals, and recognize many of the building blocks needed to develop a brand strategy. Two other strategic decisions also describe how these brand elements will apply to a firm's various offerings over time: brand architecture and brand extensions.

## Brand Architecture

Brand architecture defines both the rationale and the structure among the firm, its products, and its brand/product extensions – in essence, how the brand is used at different levels in the organization. As Figure 5.4 shows, at one extreme is a house of brand architecture, such that the firm focuses on branding each major product with its own unique set of brand elements (e.g., P&G, Inditex, Reckitt Benckiser). At the other end is a branded house architecture, where a firm uses a single set of brand elements for all its products (e.g., GE, Mitsubishi, Virgin Group, Reliance Group). Thus, P&G applies different brand elements to each of its major soap products (Tide, Cheer, All, Ariel, Purex) but devotes little effort or money to promoting the P&G parent brand. General Electric (GE) uses one set of brand elements for all its products, across such diverse categories as aircraft engines, refrigerators, and real estate financing.

Why do firms select such different brand architectures when designing their brand strategies? Overall, firms should shift toward a house of brands approach if they need a separate brand for each entity (divisions, categories, products) to avoid a problematic association or channel conflict across entities.

**Example:** Honda (Japan)

When Honda launched its Acura line to target the luxury automotive market, it needed to give the cars a new, distinct brand identity to match customers' desires for status and exclusivity, rather than the economy and reliability linked to the Honda brand. P&G does not want the same brand associations for its Pampers diaper brand and its Crest toothpaste brand, so these two products have totally different brand identities. Furthermore, P&G maintains a full set of brand identities for Tide, All, and Cheer laundry detergents so that it can target various customers with relatively similar products, but different brand identities, on the same retail shelf. Most customers are unaware that the same firm makes all of them; in some grocery stores, P&G laundry detergents take up more than half of the shelf space for this category. Such dominance would not be possible if all the products were branded with the P&G name. However, these benefits also come at a cost (literally). Every time P&G launches a new product category (e.g., Swiffer floor mops), it must spend tens if not hundreds of millions of dollars to build the brand from scratch. It cannot leverage the substantial equity it has already built into its other brands. Thus, a house of brands approach requires spending more marketing dollars every year to maintain the various brands, with few spillover benefits, even within the same portfolio.

At the other end of the spectrum is a branded house architecture, used when a master brand can contribute to the offering by adding associations to all the various entities that will enhance their value. Of course, the association between the entities also needs to be credible.

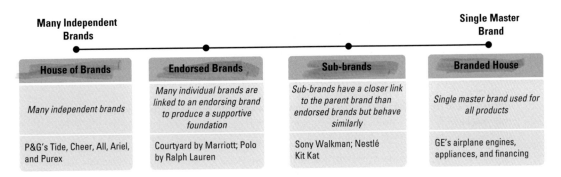

**Figure 5.4** Brand Architecture Spectrum

**Example:** General Electric (US)

A branded house approach provides communication efficiencies; when GE launches a new product, like a stand-alone backup electrical generator for home use, it immediately enjoys the positive associations of the GE master brand, which are highly relevant for such a product. Not only do the product launch and brand-building costs decrease, but these benefits also accelerate product diffusion throughout the marketplace. Each new GE product starts with high overall brand awareness and meaningful linkages to the high-quality manufacturer of electrical products, which lowers consumers' perceptions of product adoption risk. However, these linkages must be credible. If GE were to launch a new line of perfume, many of its brand linkages would be inconsistent with the desired attributes for this new product, thus undermining the perfume's own brand image.

Despite this presentation of brand architecture as two extremes on a spectrum, in reality, firms often use intermediate or hybrid brand structures to gain the benefits of both approaches. Two types of hybrid brand architectures are endorsed brands and sub-branding. Marriott hotels uses an **endorsed brand strategy** for the Courtyard Marriott chain. It suggests the approval and imprimatur of the Marriott brand but also makes it clear to customers that Courtyard hotels stand on their own and offer something different from typical Marriott hotels. Sony instead uses a **sub-branding strategy** when it assigns some major product categories, such as PCs, the Viao brand name. Branding a laptop as a Sony Viao means that it enjoys spillover benefits from Sony (awareness and linkages) but also differentiates the Viao name so that it can establish linkages unique to PCs. Similarly, Maruti Udyog has long held the majority market share in the Indian passenger car market, due in part to its successful, synergistic sub-branding collaboration with Suzuki, the Japanese car manufacturer. The sub-brand name Maruti Suzuki signals that the local Indian company, whose brand identity involves local connections, also has integrated the benefits of the Japanese firm's expertise in building and selling efficient compact cars.

## Brand Extensions

**Brand extensions** pertain to the approach the firm uses to launch new offerings by leveraging an existing brand, whether through line or category extensions. In **brand line extensions** (often simply called "line extensions"), the new offering is in the same product category but targets a different segment of customers, usually with a slightly different set of attributes. Thus, Crest toothpaste has launched at least 12 different types of toothpaste, for children, people with dentures, and those who want whiter teeth. In **brand category extensions**, the new offering instead moves to a completely different product category, such as when Crest introduced dental floss, mouthwash, and whitening strips.

About 80% of all product extensions are line extensions, which are less risky and enable the firm to address multiple customer segments with just slight variants to their focal product. Of the many benefits that brand extensions offer a firm, the following are key:[19]

- Accelerates new product acceptance by reducing customers' perceived risk.
- Lowers the cost of new product launches by building on the established brand.
- Reduces the time needed to build the new product's brand by leveraging existing brand characteristics.
- Increases the probability of gaining channel access by reducing perceived risk.
- Helps enhance the image of the parent brand by linking it to newer and/or emerging product features.
- Expands the size of the market that the firm can access, by serving additional subsegments with new offerings.

About 80% of all product extensions are line extensions, which are less risky and enable the firm to address multiple customer segments with just slight variants to their focal product.

However, not all brand extensions achieve all these benefits. The many examples of unsuccessful brand extensions (e.g., Kleenex diapers, Ben-Gay aspirin, Smucker's ketchup) highlight the limits on a firm's ability to stretch its brand into new segments and categories. Over time, researchers have developed some guidelines for improving the chances of success for brand extensions.[20] First, there must be perceived fit between the parent brand's image and the extension on a dimension that is relevant to the customer. Customers might evaluate fit according to a technical, manufacturing, or usage context, and it is not always easy to identify the most relevant dimensions.

### Example: McDonald's (US)

McPizza (an extension under the McDonald's brand name) never made the profitable run it was expected to achieve, due to the lack of credibility McDonald's had for making pizza, compared with established rivals like Domino's or Pizza Hut. In contrast, McCafe, McDonald's attempt to brand its coffee and compete with Starbucks, led customers to perceive a credible brand extension. In this case, they had experience buying coffee from McDonald's, so expanding their purchases to include flavored and espresso coffee options resonated with them. In another example, although Kleenex and diapers are both paper products that focus on absorption, the usage context of tissues seemed incongruent with imagining diapers on a baby's bottom. Thus, Kleenex diapers failed to capture any market share.

Second, brand extensions can be stretched farther if done incrementally. For example, Oreo first began expanding simply by adding more filling to the middle or covering its traditional cookies with chocolate. As consumers grew accustomed to the idea of variations on their favorite treat, the brand's owner gradually introduced more distant variations, reflecting customer demand. Oreo pie crusts were a natural extension, because many bakers already crushed up the cookies to line their homemade pies. Ice cream sandwiches were a slightly more risky extension, because they appear in a completely different section of the grocery store and require consumers to associate the Oreo brand with a frozen treat. Yet, the sandwich concept helped make this incremental extension resonate with consumers.

Third, higher quality brands generally can be extended further. So, Porsche can sell branded clothing, gloves, sunglasses, luggage, paper clips (in the shape of a Porsche), and baby products. But Hyundai is unlikely to succeed if it were to seek to sell similar product extensions under its brand name.

**Vertical extensions** of brands to lower priced markets often undermine the image of the parent brands. But brand extensions can move upmarket, as well as down, to access new customers. When moving upmarket, the extension needs to be realistic, so customers recognize and accept the brand fit. In addition, the new upmarket product should be differentiated in some way. When moving a brand extension down market, the firm instead needs to elevate and differentiate the parent brand, to decrease any potential (negative) brand overlap and make the brand extension distinguishable in a clear way.

# Managing Brand-based SCA

## Three Steps to Building Brand Equity

The three key steps to building brand equity to increase a firm's SCA start with *building a high level of brand awareness* among the firm's targeted customers, which then provides an anchor point for linking the easily recallable brand name to the elements that define its meaning and image (Figure 5.5). Building awareness involves making the brand easy to recall (brand depth) across a wide range of potential purchase and usage situations (brand breadth). Awareness should be high for the complete constellation of brand name elements: its name, logo, jingle, package shape, and other elements that the firm uses to identify its offering.[21]

The second step *links the brand name to the brand's points of parity and difference,* which helps define the brand's relative advantage. This step defines how the brand will be positioned against its competition. Some linkages might get transferred from the parent brand, depending on the firm's brand architecture. For example, when Ericsson or Nokia launches a new product under their strong parent brands, the new product's sub-brands immediately take on some meaning from those parents. To establish what the brand means to customers, brand managers typically start with points of parity related to how the brand meets some basic level of performance, then add key points of difference that reflect how or why this brand will perform "better" than competitive options. Because points of difference are a key relative advantage of a brand when it first launches, significant financial resources and promotional efforts are applied to make these differentiation points memorable and link them strongly to the brand name.

The third step involves *building a deep emotional connection or "relationship" between the brand and targeted customers.* Moving beyond functional differentiation implies a true, emotional connection – the essence of building a powerful, long-lasting brand image. A strong brand image often is what gives a firm a long-term sustainable advantage, because it connects with consumers at a deep level and is hard for competitors to replicate. If a brand can connect to an individual consumer's self-identity or who they want to be, that customer often exhibits high levels of both attitudinal and behavioral loyalty (true loyalty). It also can drive positive WOM, transforming customers into strong brand advocates.[22]

All three steps are evident in Coca-Cola's "Share a Coke" campaign. Launched in 2014, the marketing campaign featured personalized bottles, in which the traditional Coke logo was replaced with 250 of the most common names among US millennials. By adding names to bottles, Coca-Cola created a powerful connection between an individual consumer and the brand; it also offered near endless storytelling potential. The campaign was a massive success, generating more than 125,000 posts on social media, over 353,000 shares of virtual bottles through the campaign website, and a 96% positive or neutral sentiment toward the campaign.[23]

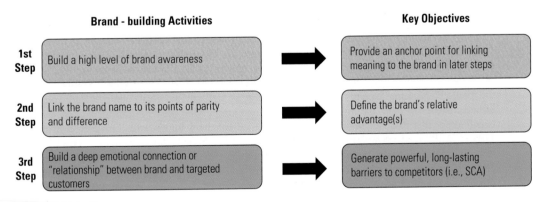

**Figure 5.5** Three Steps to Building Brand Equity

## Integrated Marketing Communications

Integrated marketing communications (IMC) refers to the process of designing and delivering marketing messages to customers while ensuring that they are relevant and consistent over time and channels.[24] To execute the three brand-building steps and effectively implement the firm's brand strategy, a firm typically uses multiple marketing communication formats, each of which has different strengths and weaknesses that define when each will be most effective, as well as the optimal combination of different formats. Some of the most commonly used marketing communication formats, and their key strengths, are as follows:

- **Advertising**: a form of communication that businesses use to persuade customers to act, think, or recognize in ways favorable to their firm. Its implementation may involve print, audio, or visual media; these formats have evolved to fit customers' appetite for different channels of communication. Advertising offers an important means to increase customer awareness and perceptions of a firm, gain access to new customers, and improve the company's standing.[25] The benefits of a successful ad campaign also can detract from the standing of rival firms, which improves the relative position of the advertiser, both within its targeted market and beyond. Advertising is very effective in consumer markets, especially when the firm's target market includes large numbers of customers. Icons created during the golden age of advertising include the Golden Arches, the Nokia jingle, and the seven rings of the Olympic Games.
- **Sales promotion**: refers to any action a firm takes to promote sales, usage, or recognition of its products or services. The focal methods might include add-on benefits, deals, or other pitches that incentivize both old and new customers to become more engaged with the promoting firm. Its main strength is its ability to increase tangible consumption of the firm's offering. In addition, sales promotions with retailers and resellers can encourage those supply chain partners to buy up stock or inventory in exchange for a bonus. Examples include buy-one-get-one-free deals, mail-in rebates, coupons, prizes, and tradeshow sales pushes, all of which require an immediate purchase that will boost sales, at least in the short term.[26]
- **Public relations (PR)**: according to the Public Relations Society of America, PR is "a strategic communication process that builds mutually beneficial relationships between organizations and their publics."[27] It requires managing dynamic interactions between firms and customers to manage the brand's image for the outside world in the best possible light by anticipating, planning, and evaluating customers' reactions to important company decisions. The strength of a firm's PR team can often determine the public opinion of key company decisions, which should signal courses of action and choices to be made at all levels of management to further the cause of a company. Whether in the form of customer service, community building, or press releases, PR has the capability to affect the image and goals of the company in the public sphere. SeaWorld faced a PR nightmare following the release of a documentary that accused it of animal abuse – a relationship-damaging event so impactful that it continues to influence choices by vacationers. The PR undertaken by smaller, more niche companies such as Razer instead results from community managers' attempts to build tight-knit communities of online gamers, such that the relationship between the firm and the customer grows stronger.[28]
- **Events and experiential marketing**: creating positive experiences for customers through events that support face-to-face contacts between companies and customers. By engaging customers in a voluntary, participatory way, the practice offers the most effectiveness when the focal event grabs attention and provides further value to the customer, such as through a free sample, discount, or other bonus. A successful event and experience marketing program ties the positive interaction by a customer and an event to the company that is putting on the show, creating a long-lasting relationship that is based on the combination of a good impression of the company and a sense of involvement or togetherness with the brand.[29] Nothing screams "experience" quite as well as Red Bull's sponsorship and extensive online coverage of Felix Baumgartner's stratosphere jump, tying the rush and thrill of the event to the brand image that Red Bull seeks to promote as an energy drink for extreme, energetic consumers.
- **Direct and interactive marketing**: two distinct but closely related strategies. Direct marketing funnels information about goods and services straight to customers, without a middleman, using channels such as mail, television, and telemarketing. It is the most simple and direct way of reaching out to and establishing personal relationships with potential customers, with the convenience of being available directly in customers' homes. Interactive marketing then attempts to overcome the one-sided limitations of direct marketing by incorporating feedback from and decisions by a customer into

what is being advertised. For example, Amazon markets directly to customers with its recommendations, but these suggestions also are personalized for each user, on the basis of algorithms that account for what the user has looked at in the past. This interactive form of marketing is thus more focused and more likely to suggest the goods and services desired by unique customers, which should increase the possibility of a sale. It also enables the firm to appeal to as many market niches as possible.[30]

- **Word of mouth (WOM)** advertising: the dissemination of information by individual customers to build a firm's or product's reputation and generate sales. This form of marketing relies on satisfied customers, using their own reputation to vouch for the reliability, quality, and appeal of the product or service in question. In this sense, WOM marketing is very effective, because customers' friends or family vouch for the efficacy of a product or service. Although it is difficult to manage, the rise of social media has moved WOM into the digital realm, in the form of "shares," "likes," and "favorites." This digital WOM also has redefined "buzz" by tying it to certain keywords. Therefore, the popularity of an ad campaign focused on WOM is easier to track.[31] One recent study revealed that consumers were willing to pay more for a product with an "excellent" rating (5) than for one with a "good" rating (4); the premiums reached an astounding 99% for legal services, with 38% for hotels and 20% for real estate agents.[32]
- **Personal selling**: occurs when members of the firm or agents engage with customers to advance the firm's interests. They play various roles in the overall process of finding, securing, and closing a sale. For example, sales force personnel are often essential representations of the firm; they create a human point of contact for customers. A well-trained, motivated sales force often is especially critical in B2B settings, because of the relatively few customers in a B2B firm's target market and the more complex nature of their offerings and selling processes. Both IBM and Siemens expend most of their marketing budgets on maintaining a direct sales organization that carries their marketing message to their B2B customers, while also building relationship equity (see Chapter 7), in addition to brand equity.

Using brands as an SCA is often most effective in large consumer markets, such as those for soft drinks, beer, fashion, or automobiles. Firms invest heavily in advertising, PR, and celebrity sponsors to build brand awareness and brand images in customers' minds and ensure that these images match the firm's positioning strategy.

> Using brands as an SCA is often most effective in large consumer markets, such as those for soft drinks, beer, fashion, or automobiles.

**Example:** Turkish Airlines (Turkey)

Turkish Airlines has been investing in sponsorship agreements and advertisements in order to expand its brand visibility among the target audience while emphasizing its global reach. Its advertisement titled "Kobe vs. Messi: The Selfie Shootout" has been viewed more than 100 million times on YouTube, and was named the advertisement of the decade in 2013.

Personal selling is more effective in B2B markets, with fewer customers, a longer and more complex sales process, and business customers who need a customized and solutions-oriented approach. Yet, at the same time, traditional distinctions about which marketing communication format is most effective for consumer versus business markets also are blurring. In the early 1990s, for example, computer microprocessors were a relatively unknown component of PCs: unseen by the consumer, not understood in their function or design, and ignored by most end-customers. After failing to trademark its naming conventions for its microprocessors, Intel decided to launch a new marketing program with its business customers and original equipment manufacturers (OEMs) such as Dell, Hewlett-Packard, and Sony, in an effort to create brand awareness among end-customers. As the OEMs began placing "Intel Inside" logos in their advertising and marketing materials:

> The name "Intel Inside" became one of the first trademarks in the electrical component industry. This campaign focused the entire organization around the brand and created a highly effective advertising campaign. The Intel Inside campaign aimed to "educate both the retail sales associates and the customers about the value of Intel microprocessors, and to explain to them the differences between the microprocessors" – without the technical jargon.[33]

Within just a few years, Intel had successfully created a sense that any computer sold without the "Intel Inside" logo was inferior in quality.

When making allocation decisions across different marketing communication formats, in the pursuit of key brand-building objectives, it also can be helpful to understand how customers process information and are persuaded to change their behavior. Across the many and varied models of communication and information processing, most of them can be broken down into six steps that customers must pass through to be persuaded by the different communication formats:

1 The customer must be **exposed** to the communication message, whether that means hearing or seeing it.
2 The message needs to capture customers' **attention**, so that they receive it.
3 The customer must **understand** the desired marketing message.
4 The customer needs to develop favorable **attitudes** toward the message.
5 The customer must generate **intentions** to act, in accordance with the information in the communication message.
6 The person then must actually **behave** in the desired way.

This six-step process sometimes is simplified as the "think → feel → act" model, which aligns well with the process for building brand equity.

The intuition behind integrated marketing communications (IMC) is that super-additive benefits accrue across communication vehicles. Consumers view multiple media in bits and pieces, but they also frequently see advertising from the same firm across multiple media channels. Seeing an advertisement from the same firm in a new medium can induce memory reinforcement effects, such that the consumer remembers the previous advertisement because they have seen the second advertisement. The purchase of the firm's product then is due to the joint persuasiveness of both advertisements. The first advertising medium's effectiveness increases, due to the presence of the second medium (and vice versa), which means the integrated message is more powerful than both messages working individually.

Thus, a key characteristic of effective IMC is the *consistency* of the message across formats and time. That is, each marketing communication format has its own specific strengths, but a deep and broad awareness of the brand and links from the customer to the brand require congruency and a lack of conflict. Otherwise, marketing expenditures will cancel each other out and leave customers unsure of the brand's actual positioning. For example, noting research that suggested its customers wanted a high-end burger, McDonald's launched the "Arch Deluxe" – a burger "with the grown-up taste." It sought to convey a brand image of sophistication and refinement – images that conflicted with McDonald's existing, and powerful, brand, which was built on convenience. The complexity associated with imagining a new line of "sophisticated" products confused customers who understood the simplicity of the McDonald's brand. After spending more than $100 million on advertising, McDonald's quietly pulled the Arch Deluxe.[34]

---

Consumers view multiple media in bits and pieces, but they also frequently see advertising from the same firm across multiple media channels. Seeing an advertisement from the same firm in a new medium can induce memory reinforcement effects, such that the consumer remembers the previous advertisement because they have seen the second advertisement. The purchase of the firm's product then is due to the joint persuasiveness of both advertisements.

---

## Research Approaches to Understanding and Measuring Brand Equity

To track the effectiveness or returns on marketing expenditures that seek to build brand equity over time, as well as understand the state of the brand following changes in strategy or competitive disruptions in the marketplace, a firm needs to measure its brand equity. However, collecting and analyzing the brand metrics of multiple brands across many different customer groups and geographies can be time-consuming and expensive. Different approaches, methods, and metrics for measuring a brand's health are available, depending on the manager's objectives.

A **brand audit** evaluates the brand's health to understand its strengths and weaknesses, such that it provides a foundation for designing and implementing a new brand strategy. Because the brand's meaning resides in customers' minds, an audit attempts to understand levels of awareness, meaning, and image across different customer groups and geographies. It often starts broadly, using more qualitative techniques in an exploratory investigation, then narrows the focus to measure specific brand attributes quantitatively. This approach can be very effective for other marketing problems or questions too, across all four Marketing Principles.

With an exploratory qualitative analysis, the less structured method can use smaller samples. It is best used early in a research process but also is more open to researchers' biases. Still, a qualitative analysis can help the firm refine its ideas, even when it doesn't know exactly what it is looking for, such that analysts can discover some unknown factors. A focus group of potential customers often identifies surprising brand associations that managers had not considered and that would not arise in more structured brand surveys. Some other common qualitative methods include:

1 **Case studies**: evaluate a single business situation and tell in-depth stories, although they are not very generalizable to other situations.
2 **Interviews**: flexible and time effective and thus can support larger sample sizes.
3 **Focus groups**: when well moderated, can generate deep insights from small groups of customers who discuss different aspects of the brand among themselves.
4 **Observation**: which operates in real time and is undirected, can also uncover some highly pertinent and unexpected insights.

Researchers typically begin qualitative analyses with open-ended questions, then gradually move to more specific questions about the brand while following up on interesting or unexpected responses. Some common topics explored in this qualitative stage might prompt questions such as the following: What does the brand mean to you? What positive and negative images come to mind when you think of this brand? How is this brand similar to or different from its competitors? Why would you buy, or not, this product brand?

The counterpoint, a quantitative analysis, is more deductive, designed to test theories and ideas, using data and specific analysis techniques. It requires larger sample sizes and is best used later in the brand audit process, to test and measure the discoveries from the qualitative stage, or else empirically test different ideas. A sampling of the vast range of quantitative techniques has been described throughout this book, often in detail in the Data Analytics Techniques. But the wealth of techniques can be grouped into three major categories:

1 Approaches focused on *data reduction* seek to condense many customers or attributes to a smaller set, defined by their similarity (e.g., factor analysis, cluster analysis). For example, 30–50 brand attributes might be collapsed into 3–4 major brand factors that capture the essence of the different linkages, but in a more simplified way.
2 Empirical approaches also work to *link variables to outcomes* or identify the causes or drivers of desired outcomes (e.g., experiments, multivariate regression analysis, choice models). Linking the 3–4 key attributes from the data reduction to customers' purchase decisions can help reveal which brand attributes are most critical for driving customer behavior.
3 Other empirical models attempt to *understand trade-offs among variables to optimize their mix* and maximize some specific outcome (e.g., conjoint analysis, response models). For example, a manager might want to understand the optimal way to allocate a marketing budget to different communication formats (e.g., advertising, personal selling, direct mail) to build the most brand equity.

For qualitative and quantitative analyses, the *data sources* and *samples* are critical factors. In most situations, the firm wants to focus on customers in its target market, so that the responses gathered are relevant to the firm's potential customers. But respondent selection also needs to be random and without any systematic bias, so that the results can be generalized to the population of customers from which it is drawn. In some situations, it makes sense to qualify respondents, to ensure they are knowledgeable and unbiased. Data also can be captured from multiple sources: surveys, mall intercepts, the firm's own database, or secondary sources. One common approach for brand studies relies on some form of customer survey, because with online, mailed, or intercept surveys, the company can obtain the responses of potential customers to multiple survey questions, thereby generating a sufficiently large sample for empirical analysis. In addition, because brands reside in customers' minds, databases and other secondary sources often cannot provide relevant insights into customers' brand perceptions. Data Analytics Technique 5.1 provides an overview of the survey process and a typical brand audit survey.

## Description

Surveys are used to gather customer feedback about a firm, experience, or brand, by asking customers to respond to a series of questions.

## When to Use It

- To understand how customers think or feel about an entity or topic (e.g., brand, new product).
- Best to use when such feelings or thoughts are not observable in other types of data.

## Designing a Survey

Experiments can establish the causal impact of marketing actions (e.g., new ad campaign), but they often cannot answer "why" or "how" questions: Why did customers respond so positively to that ad campaign? What makes them love a brand so much that they pay more just to buy it? How do customers make up their minds about whether to buy a certain brand? In such cases, surveys offer a clear advantage. They directly elicit responses from customers (or potential customers), and thus they provide deep, qualitative and quantitative feedback to the brand about its standing in the marketplace. To conduct a good survey, the firm must take into account four crucial factors:

1  The objectives for conducting the survey must be clear. A firm should have a specific, written statement of how the survey findings will relate back to the firm's marketing program. Some objectives might include gauging responsiveness to a firm's advertising efforts (to help it tweak its advertising copy), obtaining feedback on service staff (to improve service quality), or comparing the preferences of customers who use or don't use the firm's products (to understand the target population).
2  The firm must be careful to sample customers appropriately for any survey. Appropriateness involves obtaining a credible quantity (i.e., number of responses) but also credible quality, such that the firm receives relevant feedback according to the criteria used to separate those who are included in the survey from those who are not. If a firm is conducting a survey to obtain feedback about its service staff, for example, it needs to make the survey available to customers who recently used its service, because they are the ones most likely to recall the service experience accurately.
3  Surveys should contain penetrating, precise questions. Designing questionnaires is one of the most important parts of the survey design. All questions must measure the property they are supposed to measure, and they must mean the same thing to everyone. Furthermore, survey designers need to avoid the pitfall of asking loaded questions, which will cause a response bias. Thus, writing survey questions is an iterative process.
4  The firm should conduct the survey and store the data in a structured format, following a consistent process for organizing and analyzing survey data. The process should be defined well before it ever receives the first responses. Then the survey responses should be analyzed qualitatively (open-ended questions) or quantitatively (scale-type questions), often with the assistance of analytical software.

## Brand Audit Example

Brand A is one of 16 luxury cars available in India. To understand how it is perceived by customers, and improve its brand appeal, the owners of the brand conducted a nationwide, online survey of customers. An excerpt from the survey is presented below.

### Survey

You are cordially invited to provide your valued opinion in a short survey about luxury cars. We will ask you a few questions about various brands of luxury cars, and this survey should take you about eight minutes to complete. Thank you very much for your time and support.

## Brand Image

Think of Brand A, and please answer these questions. For each question, a score of 1 is regarded as "strongly disagree" and 5 is regarded as "strongly agree."

### Brand Mystery

- Brand A awakens good memories for me.
- Brand A is part of my life.
- Brand A captures the times.

### Brand Sensuality

- Brand A's design is really well done.
- Brand A sells incredible cars.
- Brand A's products are designed to please.

### Brand Intimacy

- I feel happy when I use Brand A's products.
- I feel satisfied with Brand A.
- I will stay with Brand A.

## Results

The survey was answered by 1,000 customers. The results reflect the brand's image (comprised of mystery, sensuality, and intimacy). According to the questionnaire responses, Brand A scored very well on brand mystery and brand intimacy, with mean scores in the range of 4.2 to 4.9 on the 5-point scale. But customers did not like the brand's design (M = 3.8) and did not believe that the brand sold incredible products (M = 3.3). Thus, the brand sensuality measures were significantly lower. Using these survey results, the firm launched an immediate redesign of its car to address this brand weakness and planned a new advertising campaign to launch the new product.

| Brand Mystery | Mean (out of 5) | Std Deviation |
|---|---|---|
| Brand A awakens good memories for me. | 4.8 | 1.1 |
| Brand A is part of my life. | 4.4 | 0.6 |
| Brand A captures the times. | 4.9 | 1.5 |
| **Brand Sensuality** | | |
| Brand A's design is really well done. | 4.0 | 0.5 |
| Brand A sells incredible cars. | 3.3 | 0.9 |
| Brand A's cars are designed to please. | 3.8 | 1.1 |
| **Brand Intimacy** | | |
| I feel happy when I use Brand A's products. | 4.2 | 1.3 |
| I feel satisfied with Brand A | 4.8 | 0.7 |
| I will stay with Brand A. | 4.9 | 0.7 |

The **brand metrics** proposed by various consulting firms (e.g., Interbrand, Young & Rubicam) and consumer packaged goods firms (e.g., P&G, Unilever) provide a more nuanced way to measure brand characteristics. Their main advantage stems from their accumulated evidence. These firms have built massive databases of brand metrics, so each brand can be compared to many other world-class brands across multiple dimensions. Multi-firm studies in specific industries also provide a clear comparison that is strongly relevant to the firm's market. For example, Young & Rubicam, a brand and communication agency, uses a BrandAsset® Valuator to capture customer survey responses across four dimensions: knowledge (awareness and understanding), relevance (connection to targeted customers), differentiation (relative advantage versus competition), and esteem (brand respect).[35] In contrast, Interbrand, the brand strategy agency, uses empirical models to isolate the effect of brands (i.e., brand equity), relative to other tangible assets, on the firm's financial performance. Using these models, firms can gain ideas for how best to build and manage their brands to optimize impacts on long-term financial performance.[36]

## Summary

Marketing Principle #3 focuses on building and maintaining barriers, or sustainable competitive advantages (SCAs), to withstand competitive attacks, based on the premise that competitors continually react to a firm's success. Investments in building a firm's brand awareness and image in customers' minds can erect strong barriers. It is often the initial market-based SCA a firm builds, as a direct reflection of the firm's positioning in the overall marketing for the company's offerings. Customers' awareness of, knowledge about, and behaviors due to the presence of the brand generate *brand equity*, or the set of brand assets and liabilities linked to the brand, its name, and its symbols that add to or subtract from the value provided by the firm's basic offering and relationships.

A leading psychology model describes how brands work. This *associative network memory model* argues that the mind is a network of nodes and connecting links, so key characteristics of a brand that influence brand equity can be captured as nodes and linkages. For example, *brand awareness* or *familiarity*, which reflects a customer's ability to identify a brand, is indicated by the size or strength of the node for that memory, often measured with aided or unaided recall tasks. In this network memory model, a brand strategy involves first building awareness, to provide an anchor point, and then building linkages to positive, unique memory nodes to achieve an identity that matches target customers' needs, all in a cost-efficient manner.

Most benefits of strong brands can be grouped into three main areas: sales growth, profit enhancement, and loyalty effects. Enhanced sales growth results because strong brands can acquire customers more easily, due to their perceptions of lower risk, higher quality, and better performance. These benefits, in turn, can enhance the firm's profitability, by reducing acquisition costs or allowing the firm to charge higher prices for its products. Strong brands also lead to more loyal customers, which often provide the largest barrier to competitive entry as a significant source of SCA.

The *brand architecture* defines the rationale and structure among the firm, its products, and its brand/product extensions – in essence, how the brand gets used at different levels within the organization. At one extreme is a *house of brand architecture*, where the firm focuses on branding each major product with its own unique set of brand elements. At the other end is a *branded house architecture*, where firms use a single set of brand elements to refer to the firm and all its products. In general, a house of brands strategy is appropriate if the firm needs a separate brand for each entity to avoid negative associations or channel conflict. Although this discussion suggests that brand architecture involves two extremes, in reality firms use intermediate and hybrid brand structures to gain benefits from both approaches, such as sub-branding and endorsed brands.

With *brand extensions*, firm seek to launch new offerings by leveraging an existing brand name. Brand extensions consist of either line or category extensions. In *brand line extensions*, the new offering is in the same product category but targets a different segment of customers, usually with a slightly different set of attributes. In *brand category extensions*, the new offering is in a completely different product category. *Vertical extensions* can move up market or down market, to access new customers.

Increasing brand equity to strengthen a firm's SCA involves three steps: *building a high level of brand awareness* among targeted customers, which provides an anchor for the elements that define the easily recalled brand's meaning and image; *linking the brand name to the brand's points of parity and difference*, to define the brand's relative advantage; and *building a deep emotional connection or "relationship" between the brand and targeted customers*.

In the integrated marketing communications (IMC) process, the design and delivery of marketing messages to customers makes sure that they are relevant and consistent over time, such that the messages have an overarching, synergistic theme. To execute brand building, a firm typically uses multiple marketing communication formats: advertising, sales promotions, public relations, events and experiential marketing, direct and interactive marketing, word of mouth, and personal selling. Each format has specific strengths. In addition, it is critical that any links developed with the brand are congruent and not in conflict across all these formats.

To track the effectiveness of marketing expenditures and measure the brand's equity over time, the firm can conduct a *brand audit*, an evaluation of the brand's health, to understand its strengths and weaknesses. A *qualitative analysis* is more exploratory and less structured, such that it uses smaller samples and works best early in the research process. A *quantitative analysis* is more deductive, can test theories and ideas, relies on data and analysis, and requires larger sample sizes. The *brand metrics* developed by different brand consultants offer the advantage of large databases, such that each firm can compare its brands against world-class or benchmark brands across multiple dimensions.

## Takeaways

- Investments in building a firm's brand awareness and image in customers' minds represent a strong barrier to competitive attacks and often provide the initial market-based SCA for a firm.
- The associative network memory model argues that the mind is a network of nodes and connecting links. The key characteristics of a brand that influence brand equity can be captured as nodes and linkages.
- Brands change how people think, often below a conscious level. Perceptions of brands even can change customers' actual experiences (e.g., making beer taste better).
- Benefits from strong brand equity include sales, profit enhancement, and loyalty effects.
- Key branding elements include the brand objective, brand awareness, brand relative advantage, brand sustainability, brand image, and brand identity.
- Brand architecture defines the rationale and structure that link the firm, its products, and its product and/or brand extensions. It defines how the brand is used at different levels across the organization. Noting the range of brand architecture structures available, firms must make strategic decisions, based on their branding strategy.
- Brand extensions can leverage existing brands as line or category extensions.
- The three steps to building brand equity are: building a high level of brand awareness; linking the brand name to the brand's points of parity and difference; and building a deep emotional connection or "relationship" between the brand and targeted customers.
- Integrated marketing communication (IMC) is a process for sharing relevant, consistent marketing messages with consumers, across a variety of formats, including advertising, sales promotion, public relations, events and experiential marketing, direct and interactive marketing, word of mouth, and personal selling.
- To understand and measure brand equity, firms use qualitative and quantitative assessments of their brand's health, which helps them identify areas for improvement.

# References

1 American Marketing Association (n.d.) *Dictionary: B.* Available at: www.ama.org/resources/Pages/Dictionary. aspx?dLetter=B (accessed 8 September, 2015).

2 Interbrand (2014) *Best Global Brands.* Available at: www. bestglobalbrands.com/2014/ranking/ (accessed 14 September, 2015).

3 Aaker, D.A. (1991) *Managing Brand Equity.* New York: The Free Press.

4 Keller, K.L. (2000) 'The brand report card,' *Harvard Business Review*, 78(1), pp. 147–58.

5 Anderson, J.R. (1983) *The Architecture of Cognition.* Cambridge, MA: Harvard University Press; John, D.R., Loken, B., Kim, K. and Alokparna, B.M. (2006) 'Brand concept maps: A methodology for identifying brand association networks,' *Journal of Marketing Research*, 43(4), pp. 549–63; Keller, K.L. (1993) 'Conceptualizing, measuring, and managing customer-based brand equity,' *Journal of Marketing Research*, 57(1), pp. 1–22.

6 Schöntag, K. and Teichert, T.A. (2010) 'Exploring consumer knowledge structures using associative network analysis,' *Psychology & Marketing*, 27(4), pp. 369–98; Pitta, D.A. and Prevel Katsanis, L. (1995) 'Understanding brand equity for successful brand extension,' *Journal of Consumer Marketing*, 12(4), pp. 51–64.

7 Balasubramanian, S.K. (1994) 'Beyond advertising and publicity: Hybrid messages and public policy issues,' *Journal of Advertising*, 23(4), pp. 29–46.

8 Baker, W.E. (2003) 'Does brand name imprinting in memory increase brand information retention?,' *Psychology & Marketing*, 20(12), pp. 1119–35.

9 Dimofte, C.V. and Yalch, R.F. (2011) 'The mere association effect and brand evaluations,' *Journal of Consumer Psychology*, 21(1), pp. 24–37.

10 The Hartford (2015) 'Advantages of strong brand equity.' Available at: www.thehartford.com/business-playbook/ in-depth/advantages-strong-brand-equity (accessed 31 August, 2015); Keller, K.L. (2013) *Strategic Brand Management: Building, Measuring, and Managing Brand Equity*, 4th edn. Upper Saddle River, NJ: Pearson/Prentice Hall; Mizik, N. (2014) 'Assessing the total financial performance impact of brand equity with limited time-series data,' *Journal of Marketing Research*, 51(6), pp. 691–706.

11 Allison, R.I. and Uhl, K.P. (1964) 'Influence of beer brand identification on taste perception,' *Journal of Marketing Research*, 1(3), pp. 36–9.

12 Lowrey, T.M. and Shrum, L.J. (2007) 'Phonetic symbolism and brand name preference,' *Journal of Consumer Research*, 34(3), pp. 406–14; Rao, A.R. and Monroe, K.B. (1989) 'The effect of price, brand name, and store name on buyers' perceptions of product quality: An integrative review,' *Journal of Marketing Research* 26(3), pp. 351–7; Yorkston, E. and Menon, G. (2004) 'A sound idea: Phonetic effects of brand names on consumer judgments,' *Journal of Consumer Research*, 31(1), pp. 43–51; Wänke, M., Herrmann, A. and Schaffner, D. (2007) 'Brand name influence on brand perception,' *Psychology & Marketing*, 24(1), pp. 1–24.

13 Stahl, F., Heitmann, M., Lehmann, D.R. and Neslin, S.A. (2012) 'The impact of brand equity on customer acquisition, retention, and profit margin,' *Journal of Marketing*, 76(4), pp. 44–63; Keller, K.L. (2013) *Strategic Brand Management: Building, Measuring, and Managing Brand Equity.* Upper Saddle River, NJ: Pearson/Prentice Hall.

14 Keller, K.L. (2001) *Building customer-based Brand Equity: A Blueprint for Creating Strong Brands.* Marketing Science Institute Working Paper Series, 1–107, pp. 3–38.

15 Palmatier, R.W., Stern, L. and El-Ansary, A. (2014) *Marketing Channel Strategy*, 8th edn. Upper Saddle River, NJ: Prentice Hall.

16 Goldfarb, A., Lu, Q. and Moorthy, S. (2009) 'Measuring brand value in an equilibrium framework,' *Marketing Science*, 28(1), pp. 69–86.

17 Watson, G., Beck, J., Henderson, C. and Palmatier, R.W. (2015) 'Unpacking loyalty: How conceptual differences shape the effectiveness of customer loyalty,' *Journal of the Academy of Marketing Science*, 43(6), pp. 790–825.

18 Aaker, J.L. (1997) 'Dimensions of brand personality', *Journal of Marketing Research*, 34(3), pp. 347–56; Escalas, J.E. and Bettman, J.R. (2005) 'Self construal, reference groups, and brand meaning,' *Journal of Consumer Research*, 32(3), pp. 378–89.

19 Keller, K.L. (2012) *Strategic Brand Management*, 4th edn. Upper Saddle River, NJ: Pearson/Prentice Hall.

20 Keller, K.L. (2012) *Strategic Brand Management*, 4th edn. Upper Saddle River, NJ: Pearson/Prentice Hall.

21 Keller, K.L. (1987), 'Memory factors in advertising: The effect of advertising retrieval cues on brand evaluations,' *Journal of Consumer Research*, 14(3), pp. 316–33.

22 Kim, S.S., Morris, J.G. and Ray, S. (2014) 'The central role of engagement in online communities,' *Information Systems Research*, 25(3), pp. 528–46.

23 Minguez, K. (2014) 'Case Study: 3 Famous Coca-Cola Marketing Campaigns'. Available at: www.webpagefx.com/ blog/marketing/case-study-coca-cola-marketing/ (accessed 14 September, 2015); Tadena, N. (2014) 'Coke's Personalized Marketing Campaign Gains Online Buzz,' *The Wall Street Journal*, 15 July.

24 American Marketing Association (n.d.) *Dictionary: I.* Available at: www.ama.org/resources/Pages/Dictionary.aspx?dLetter=I (accessed 8 September, 2015).

25 Edell, J.A. and Burke, M.C. (1987) 'The power of feelings in understanding advertising effects,' *Journal of Consumer Research*, 14(3), pp. 421–33; Zhao, H. (2000) 'Raising awareness and signaling quality to uninformed consumers: A price-advertising model,' *Marketing Science*, 19(4), pp. 390–6.

26 Huang, J. and Yin, X. (2014) 'Effects of price discounts and bonus packs on online impulse buying,' *Social Behavior and Personality*, 42(8), pp. 1293–1302.

27 Public Relations Society of America (n.d.) *What is Public Relations?* Available at: www.prsa.org/aboutprsa/ publicrelationsdefined/ (accessed 8 September, 2015).

28 Wynne, R. (2013) 'What does a public relations agency do?' Available at: www.forbes.com/sites/robertwynne/2013/04/10/what-does-a-public-relations-agency-do/ (accessed 14 September, 2015).

29 Harmeling, C.M., Palmatier, R.W., Houston, M.B., Arnold, M.J. and Samaha, S.A. (2015) 'Transformational relationship events,' *Journal of Marketing*, 79(5), pp. 39–62.

30 Ansari, A. and Mela, C.F. (2003), 'E-customization', *Journal of Marketing Research*, 40(2), pp. 131–45; Zhang, J. and Krishnamurthi, L. (2004) 'Customizing promotions in online stores,' *Marketing Science*, 23(4), pp. 561–78.

31 Whitler, K. (2014) 'Why word of mouth marketing is the most important social media.' Available at: www.forbes.com/sites/kimberlywhitler/2014/07/17/why-word-of-mouth-marketing-is-the-most-important-social-media/ (accessed 14 September, 2015).

32 Comscore (2007) 'Online consumer-generated reviews have significant impact on offline purchase behavior.' Available at: www.comscore.com/Press_Events/Press_Releases/2007/11/Online_Consumer_Reviews_Impact_Offline_Purchasing_Behavior (accessed 25 January, 2016).

33 Whitwell, S. (2005) 'Ingredient branding case study: Intel.' Available at: www.intangiblebusiness.com/news/marketing/2005/11/ingredient-branding-case-study-intel (accessed 14 September, 2015).

34 Naylor, T.J. (2014) 'McDonald's arch deluxe and its fall from grace.' Available at: www.benzinga.com/general/topics/14/08/4769457/mcdonalds-arch-deluxe-and-its-fall-from-grace (accessed 14 September, 2015); Haig, M. (2012) 'Brand failures.' Available at: www.slideshare.net/Goodbuzz/brand-failures-11856435 (accessed 14 September, 2015).

35 Young & Rubicam (2010) 'Brand Asset Valuator: Consumer awareness is the key to brand value.' Available at: www.valuebasedmanagement.net/methods_brand_asset_valuator.html (accessed 14 September, 2015).

36 Interbrand (2014) *Best Global Brands* and *Creating and Managing Brand Value*. Available at: http://interbrand.com/best-brands/best-global-brands/methodology/ (accessed 14 September, 2015).

## Companion website

Please visit the companion website, **www.palgravehighered.com/palmatier-ms**, to access summary videos from the authors, and full-length cases with datasets and step-by-step solution guides.

ALL
COMPETITORS
REACT

Chapter **6**

# Marketing Principle #3: Managing Offering–based Sustainable Competitive Advantage

ALL
COMPETITORS
REACT

## Learning objectives

- Describe offerings and innovations and explain how they lead to sustainable competitive advantages (SCAs).
- Outline the innovation radar framework, including the four key questions that help define the innovation space.
- Critically discuss the mechanisms by which innovative offerings increase firm value.
- Understand marketing's role in new offering and innovation strategies.
- Identify and describe disruptive repositioning and disruptive technology strategies for developing innovative offerings.
- Explain the differences between red and blue ocean markets.
- Describe why firms' new products often fail to "cross the chasm" and outline strategies to avoid the key pitfalls.
- Discuss why disruptive technologies often enter the market at the low end or in completely new markets.
- Describe a stage-gate development process and how this process increases the speed of project development and likelihood of success, while also reducing costs.
- Outline the people-based and product-based factors that influence innovation diffusion during product launch.
- List the three key steps to building offering equity.
- Describe the usefulness of conjoint analysis for developing and launching new offerings.
- Explain the benefits and limitations of using a Bass diffusion model to forecast future product sales.

# Introduction

## Offering and Innovation Basics

Offering is a purposely broad term that captures both tangible products and intangible services provided by firms. Although "product" often serves as a sort of shorthand label to describe a firm's offering, this terminology diminishes the importance of the service component of any firm's business. But a firm's offering spans the entirety of the core component of the customer value proposition that adds value by providing more functionality at the same or lower costs, or an innovative solution to a previously unaddressed customer need. Brands and relationships might add other benefits and affect the user experience, but they cannot function without the foundation of a suitable core offering. Accordingly, firms spend most of their R&D budgets to improve their offerings or create new ones that can generate differential advantages over competitors' offerings. For example, we described in Chapter 5 how Intel devoted substantial resources to building its brand and ensuring that consumers wanted "Intel Inside" their computers. It thus enjoys a significant market share lead over its rival AMD. And yet Intel still spends nearly $3 billion each quarter on R&D, dedicated to efforts to maintain its leading performance in the semiconductor industry.[1] Although $3 billion quarterly sounds like a lot, it is just a drop in the bucket of the total US national spent on R&D: an estimated $1.6 trillion in 2014.[2] Various factors (e.g., firm size, business diversity, industry competition) affect how much each firm spends on R&D, but as a general rule, most firms willingly tap both their internal accruals and external financing options to ensure they can spend enough to develop new offerings.[3]

> Brands and relationships might add other benefits and affect the user experience, but they cannot function without the foundation of a suitable core offering.

The process of innovation – the "creation of substantial new value for customers and the firm by creatively changing one or more dimensions of the business"[4] – is what enables firms to identify and develop valuable new offerings that establish and ensure their sustainable competitive advantage (SCA). To drive its growth, General Electric pursues 100 "imagination breakthrough" projects each year. A recent survey of executives identifies innovation as a top strategic priority for 74% of companies – cited as more critical than cost reduction for defining their long-term success.[5] As the process for generating SCA through novel or improved offerings, innovation enables the firm to devise new, distinct solutions that separate it from its competitors. Using offerings as an SCA thus strongly reflects the underlying innovation process, in theory and in practice.

Innovation, its definition, and its process are thus expansive notions, extending in scope well beyond just product or technology innovation. For example, Starbucks' successful business innovation was not based primarily on technology; it revolved around designing a unique customer experience or "third place," other than home and work, where customers could relax and spend time. Certainly, Starbucks also pursues product innovations, such as new espresso drinks, and technological innovations, such as its mobile ordering app. But in blind taste tests, McDonald's coffee often beats Starbucks' brews, and still millions of customers visit Starbucks, and spend more per cup, on a daily basis.[6] In addition to its initial offering-based SCA, Starbucks takes an innovative strategic approach, focused on building a strong, authentic brand and avoiding a franchising model to expand. Therefore, it employs relatively well-compensated, motivated employees who are willing to build strong customer relationships.

**Example:** Dell (US)

Dell clearly operates in a technology space, but perhaps its most compelling innovation has been the ordering and logistics processes that it introduced in the market. They may seem more commonplace today, but the notion of building to order "semi-custom" computer products and selling them directly to consumers online was radical when it first appeared. Thus, Dell's SCA did not depend on its design or manufacturing competencies; Dell even outsourced the manufacturing. Rather, the SCA came from an offering in which it built computers to order, sold them online, and significantly cut costs by avoiding the expenditures associated with maintaining storefronts and inventory or suffering obsolescence costs. The innovation emerged from the company's business processes and go-to-market strategy.

## Offerings and Innovation as SCA

Innovative new offerings help firms build and maintain SCA and barriers to the competitive attacks that arise because competitors continually react to a firm's success (MP#3). However, most offerings must be augmented by and linked to brands and relationships to protect the firm's SCA, because it generally is relatively easy for competitors to copy offerings, given enough time and money (unless the offering is protected by patents or trade secrets). Still, new innovations establish the foundation for the value that can be added by brands and relationships. Thus, innovation is critical to develop offerings that can serve as sources of SCA. What are some of the different ways a firm can innovate? An innovation radar summarizes some key means.

### Innovation Radar

The framework in Figure 6.1 does a good job of capturing some of the many different ways a firm can innovate; it helps define the innovation space according to what, who, how, and where aspects.[7] First, the most obvious method is to *change what the firm offers*, in line with a traditional view of new product or service innovation. This change might entail offering, platform, or solution innovations. Second, *changing who the customer is* represents another route that involves innovations related to customers, experiences, and value capture. For example, when Home Depot grouped multiple categories of products and targeted them at DIY (do-it-yourself) customers, rather than contractors, it radically and innovatively changed the identity of the customer for these products and services. Third, *changing how you sell to customers* pertains to the processes, organizations, and supply chains that a firm uses. When Progressive Insurance started sending employees to meet with customers at the site of their car accidents or soon after the accident, and paying claims on the spot rather than requiring customers file detailed claims, it generated novel advantages for the customer and the firm. Fourth, *changing where to sell to customers* comprises presence, networking, and brand innovations. For example, Enterprise Rent-A-Car was the first to locate its rental facilities in neighborhoods and commuter-heavy suburbs, rather than airports. Its first-mover advantages in these locations enabled it to block out competitors like Avis and Hertz, at least for a while.

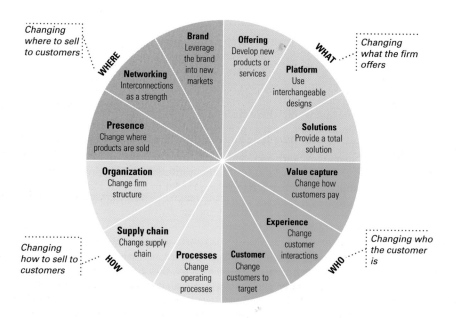

**Figure 6.1** Innovation Radar: A Multidimensional Approach to Innovation

*Source:* Adapted from Sawhney, M., Wolcott, R.C. and Arroniz, I. (2006) "The 12 different ways for companies to innovate," *MIT Sloan Management Review*, 47(3), p. 75.

However, as Enterprise learned, first movers with an innovative offering often cannot maintain their market share leadership once me-too competitors start mimicking their innovation. One historical study, spanning 65 years of market entries and their related first-mover advantage, reveals a 47% failure among technology pioneers; within a decade of their innovation, only 11% of these pioneers remained leaders in their offering categories.[8] A first-mover advantage is nearly always trumped by early followers who are not just quick but also better. The lesson? *Best beats first.* Firms cannot rest on their innovation laurels but instead must build additional SCA (e.g., brands, relationships) around new offerings if they hope to maintain a leadership position. According to a study of 264 industrial product markets, market pioneers generally enjoy higher survival rates than later entrants, but they face the same uncertainty when it comes to pioneering really new products.[9] Thus, moving first, whether in B2C or B2B markets, is not a guarantee of success.

> A first-mover advantage is nearly always trumped by early followers who are not just quick but also better. The lesson? *Best beats first.*

## Benefits from Offering Equity

By building offering equity, an innovative firm can make it more difficult for competitors to encroach on its business. **Offering equity** refers to the core value that the performance of the product or service offers the customer, absent any brand or relationship equity effects. When a firm produces a product or service that is no different from competitors' offerings (i.e., me-too offerings), it generates little offering equity or SCA. So, most firms attempt to develop innovative offerings, differentiated from competitors' products, to generate at least some relative advantage. As we know, competitors will quickly copy successful offerings, so each firm must constantly try to develop new and innovative offerings to stay ahead of its me-too competitors and maintain its offering equity as a source of SCA. For example, Alibaba, now the world's most popular online shopping marketplace, started off as an online website that helped exporters sell products directly to consumers. But it also has continually innovated, including a recent move into the financial services domain to enable consumers to use the virtual currency available in its Alipay service to invest in the stock market.

### Example: BlueScope (Australia)

BlueScope is an international supplier of steel products based in Australia. It has patented its groundbreaking Castrip process that produces 70% less greenhouse gas emissions and requires 10% of the floor space of conventional steel mills. To protect its offering equity from foreign competitors, the innovation is patented. The protected innovation is highly anticipated to enhance BlueScope's positioning as a leading global supplier of steel products and solutions.[10]

Research conducted with thousands of firms shows that simply announcing a new product can increase a firm's stock price by 0.5% on that same day.[11] Another research project, including more than 20,000 different innovations, shows that launching new offerings also has long-term positive effects on firm value, and this effect is even greater for radically innovative offerings that really change the game, compared with incremental, minor innovations.[12] Thus, new, truly innovative offerings can enhance firm value in the short and long term. How exactly do they do so?

In many cases, a new offering provides more value to customers, in the form of enhanced performance. For instance, due to limited access to credit cards as well as prevalence of collect on delivery as the payment method, online shopping is more difficult in the Middle East. In order to address the challenges, Maktoob introduced CashU, a payment platform enabling online buyers to effectively shop online. Firms typically charge higher prices for a superior offering, which can enhance their profitability, even if the new offerings tend to be more expensive to produce. In markets like the US pharmaceutical sector, government agencies even reward meaningful innovations with patent protections, such that drug companies enjoy a virtual monopoly market. They have the exclusive right to sell their innovative compound, so the prices are high, enabling the firms to not only recoup their R&D expenditures but also support ongoing R&D efforts that are needed to achieve future innovations. The estimated cost of developing a new drug is more than $1 billion, so a key source of funding for new drugs is ongoing revenue from existing products that the pharmaceutical company owns.[13]

In addition, new offerings often motivate customers to switch from competitors to the innovative firm, to gain access to the new product. Such switching behavior might signal that the customer really believes the new offering performs better than existing alternatives, or it might arise because the customer just wants to have the newest offering (these buyers are often labeled innovators or early adopters). In any market, there are some early adopters who always want the newest offering, whether or not the new features or attributes add any material value for them (e.g., newest cell phone, dinner at the latest restaurant).[14]

New offerings also can help the firm acquire new customers or enter new markets when they offer similar performance but at a lower price. Customers often rebuy the same brand, out of habit or because it is convenient, with little thought. But if a firm offers a new innovation that can lower the prices they pay, it often provides a clear path to customer acquisition and sales expansion among existing customers.

Whether the innovation is radically new or represents an incrementally new offering, its arrival in the market sparks benefits for other divisions and departments in the firm too. For example, sales-people have a good reason to make sales calls to new and existing customers, with a new sales pitch about an exciting new opportunity, rather than just repeating the same sales line about older products that customers already know about. Similarly, advertising effectiveness increases when the firm has new products to offer.[15] The effect can carry over to human resource departments too, such that firms with new and innovative offerings are better able to recruit and keep the best talent, which, in turn, can create additional barriers to competitive attacks.[16] Thus, customer, employee, and market expansion all emerge as key potential benefits of offering innovative products.

Furthermore, offering new and innovative products tends to enhance the firm's brand, even if customers don't buy the new offering. Bose, Apple, BMW, and Samsung base their strong reputations largely on their innovativeness and strong offering performance. Such benefits influence customers' purchase decisions, even if they only buy an entry-level product that includes few of the truly innovative features that made the firm's reputation. These brands often seek to introduce new offerings with some minimal frequency to maintain a leading image.

Yet, we must constantly remember that SCAs based solely on new products tend to be short-lived. Before competitors can react (as they always do; MP#3) and copy or even leapfrog an innovation, the firm should build other, more lasting SCAs. Always having the newest and best offering is virtually impossible, so firms try to add brand-based or relational SCA to their offering, to enhance its equity, before direct competitors emerge. At its founding in 1995, for example, eBay was among the first firms to launch an online auction platform. Then, through its relational (high WOM), branding and other marketing strategies, the eBay name became synonymous with online auctions, creating a strong SCA that other online auction sites have largely been unable to overcome.

**Example:** TomTom (the Netherlands)

Netherlands-based electronics company TomTom launched its first navigation product in 2002 when there were relatively few firms focusing on this area. Through quick innovation and responding to customers' needs, TomTom was able to stay ahead of its competitors and build itself into a world-recognized brand that, by 2007, had more than 50% of the market share in Europe for navigational devices.[17] However, GPS-enabled smartphones have now disrupted TomTom's once strong position in this application.

Overall, greater offering equity, generated from the firm's new and innovative products and services, provides more value (better performance, lower costs) to customers, which leads to SCA and superior sales and profits. Innovative new offerings help firms expand their customer bases and increase the effectiveness of their advertising, direct selling, and employee recruitment and retention efforts. Even though the barriers to competitive copycat options typically are short in their duration (with the exception of patent-protected products), they still provide a powerful platform for firms to build synergistic, longer lasting SCA using brands and relationships (see Chapters 5 and 7).

# Offering and Innovation Strategies

Marketing contributes to and defines offering and innovation strategies in two main ways. First, it helps the firm develop innovative offerings by collecting customer input and forecasting customer and market trends, so that the firm can understand the trade-offs among potential product attributes (e.g., conjoint analysis). Second, marketing is responsible for launching the new offering to customers to generate sales with acceptable profit levels. Many good products, however, fail to achieve their set financial objectives due to poor product launches. Thus, extensive efforts go into test marketing and understanding the factors that will influence whether customers adopt a new offering and increase the likelihood of a successful launch.

## Developing Innovative Offerings

### The Stage-gate Approach

Most firms rely on a **stage-gate development process** to increase the speed of their offering development and enhance their likelihood of success, while also reducing development costs.[18] As Figure 6.2 shows, a stage-gate model divides the development process into a series of steps or stages. Each project is evaluated, on multiple dimensions, by independent evaluators in each stage. This method helps ensure effective development approaches through several elements. First, in each stage, the feasibility of the new development project is evaluated from multiple perspectives: customer, technology, financial, and operations, for example. The depth and focus of these analyses across such dimensions also shifts as the project advances; the focus might be on technology early in the project, then emphasize the operation perspective more in later stages. However, no project receives continued funding unless it meets preset standards across these dimensions at each stage-gate evaluation.

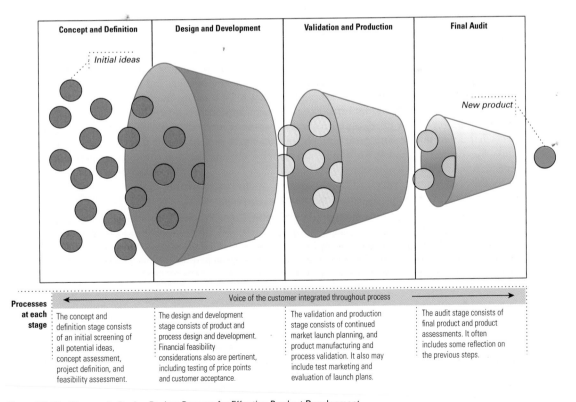

**Figure 6.2** The Stage-gate Design Review Process for Effective Product Development

Second, in each review stage, the evaluators who determine if the project will receive continued support must be external to the project team. This requirement provides some degree of independence to the process. Members of a project team almost invariably become vested in the new offering, so their evaluations understandably tend to be biased. This bias, or the designers' curse, often means that once developers or designers accept some new feature, they perceive its great value – far more than would be assigned the feature by non-users. Some studies even suggest that innovators or managers involved in a project provide ratings of the innovative features of the new offering that are up to nine times better than the ratings provided by general consumers.[19] In line with the Nobel Prize-winning research by Kahneman and colleagues, people naturally evaluate alternatives according to the value they perceive, which is relative to some reference point – typically, the product or service they currently own or use.[20] Therefore, evaluations of new offerings that are relative to this reference point are presented as either gains or losses (i.e., better or worse than the current offering). In turn, because people are loss averse, they seek to avoid losses more than they work to achieve gains. Therefore, the designers' bias, if not addressed, is likely to lead to new offering launches that fail to meet the designers' or managers' expectations. Similarly, a reference point that already has been revised, to include a new feature, leads people to overestimate the value of that feature, were they to lose it, which represents an *endowment effect*. In one classic experiment with students in a classroom, half of the class receives a coffee mug in the opening moments. At the end of class, the students who received the mug are asked how much they would sell it for; those who did not receive a mug indicate how much they would pay to buy the mug. Even after just this short period of time, the endowment effect rears up, such that the sellers would demand more than twice as much as the buyers indicated they would pay to obtain the new mug.[21]

Third, the stage-gate method gives firms plenty of opportunity to cancel projects at early stages. With this rapid decision, the resources (human, time, financial) that had been devoted to the new offering can be redeployed to other projects. Thus, poor projects cannot jam up the development pipeline, and good projects are less likely to be slowed down or starved of resources, simply because too many projects are in that pipeline. Furthermore, key resources constantly get reallocated, according to the new information available at each stage, to lead to better resource trade-off decisions (see Chapter 8; managing resource trade-offs, MP#4).

Even with the many refinements to this popular process, such as overlapping stages to shorten development time or increasing the customer input component at each stage to account better for customer dynamics during the development process (MP#2), it continues to prove very effective. Yet, it also has one notable downside. Incremental innovations often pass each stage-gate review more easily, because they involve less risk and are easier to evaluate. Radical and potentially valuable innovations instead might struggle to pass through the stages, especially if their novelty is difficult to understand. In response, some firms establish alternative approaches for highly innovative projects. For example, some product development teams are assigned dedicated time and resources to spend on projects that do not need to pass through the stage-gate process; other firms rely on "skunk works" and offer dedicated funding to radical innovations, outside the more traditional process for incremental projects.[22]

In their efforts to foster radical innovation, many Indian firms employ a *jugaad* practice, in conjunction with traditional stage-gate processes. *Jugaad* is a Hindi word referring to an innovative fix or simple work-around, so these innovation practices seek creative, quick, unconventional, and frugal solutions to problems.[23] The basic intuition is that agile innovation practices can vary with each problem stage and product, rather requiring the same stage-gate process for all innovative ideas. Without a set process, the main goals for this form of innovation are to reach unattainable outcomes and to push innovators beyond their existing mental boundaries.

**Example:** Tata Motors (India)

Tata Motors innovated the Nano, the cheapest car in the world, launched in 2009 at a sale price of just $2,000. Most car manufacturers use a sedan chassis to begin building new models; Tata challenged the conventional wisdom and started with a blueprint featuring a scooter's backbone. The ultimate product cost less to build and thus was affordable in the Indian market, but perhaps even more important, it turned out to be better suited to busy Indian traffic patterns, which require quick and frequent maneuvering.

## Repositioning Strategies

An innovative offering can result from dramatically repositioning an existing offering, such as removing some features or adding others, so that the total offering appeals to a different customer segment with a "new" value proposition. The advantage of this strategy is that it generally does not require a new technology or invention, and thus marketers can take the lead in these efforts.

> An innovative offering can result from dramatically repositioning an existing offering, such as removing some features or adding others, so that the total offering appeals to a different customer segment with a "new" value proposition.

According to the red ocean versus blue ocean framework (see Table 6.1), firms can use more or less disruptive methods to build new markets and create new demand or else fight over existing demand.[24] "Red ocean" markets – thus named to reflect the metaphor of blood in the water – are very competitive and populated by "sharks" fighting over the same customers. Many of these firms try to claim differentiation based on the same or similar attributes; they launch new product or service extensions that represent just incremental innovations. These relatively minor extensions make up the large majority of all new offerings and incremental sales, but they also represent significantly less profit. The competition keeps pricing power low. Traditional segmentation, targeting, and positioning (STP; see Chapter 2) and stage-gate design processes are very effective in red ocean markets, however, because the customers are well known, and although their needs change (MP#2), those changes can be better anticipated over time.

**Table 6.1** Comparison of Red and Blue Ocean Strategies

| Red Ocean Strategies | Blue Ocean Strategies |
| --- | --- |
| New offerings are brand and line extensions, representing incremental innovations (uses STP processes) | Less numerous but more radical and repositioned offerings, focused on creating new markets |
| Account for the majority of sales but earn lower relative profit levels | Success generates higher profit levels |
| High competitive rivalry in existing markets | Creates a new market with less competitive rivalry |
| Must beat existing competition | Often transforms the image of competitors' brand features, such that they become a negative attribute in the new market |
| Attempts to capture a portion of existing market demand | Attempts to create new market demand |

*Source:* Inspired by Chan, K.W. and Mauborgne, R. (2005) *Blue Ocean Strategy: How to Create Uncontested Market Space and Make the Competition Irrelevant.* Boston, MA: Harvard Business School Press.

To pursue more disruptive repositioning strategies, firms instead can seek out "blue ocean" markets, a metaphor reflecting the blue hue of the deep ocean waters that are far from land. These markets are less competitive, marked by few firms in the uncharted waters, but the distance from land also creates a significant risk of failure. Blue ocean strategies redefine the market space, introduce unexpected features, and fundamentally change the entire value proposition. When successful, they create entirely new market segments that customers might never have asked for or even knew they wanted, such that many traditional market research methods are ineffective.

**Example:** Cirque du Soleil (Canada)

Consider a notable example of a successful blue ocean repositioning strategy. Cirque du Soleil removed two familiar features associated with traditional circuses like Ringling Bros. and Barnum & Bailey: large animals (e.g., elephants, lions) and big name stars (e.g., The Flying Wallendas, Antoinette Concello). Then it added theater-like productions, each with a different theme and original music. It raised prices while redefining the target market. Rather than children and families, it sought to appeal to adults, couples on dates, and business clientele. That is, Cirque du Soleil removed substantial cost drivers from the innovative offering, added new and unexpected features that had not even been requested by circus customers, developed a new targeted market, and applied an outsider's view to the market. With this transformation, the factors that previously had been market benefits became weaknesses. The Barnum brand is so closely linked to large circus animals and clowns that it could not gain a reputation as a theatrical event that would be valuable for someone trying to impress a date or a business client.[25]

But one-time market leaders are unlikely to take the disruption lying down. They respond to the innovation by shifting their offering to match the emerging competitor. For example, on recognizing the exponential rise in Internet-based shopping and mobile commerce, Best Buy, the US electronics retailer, moved relatively quickly to close or downsize many of its stores and thus reduce its costs, while also strengthening its online channels and building more seamless multichannel shopping experiences.[26] Because, as we have learned, these barriers and SCAs are inherently short-lived, especially when a market grows and expands to include new competitors, brands often constitute the most effective tools. Consumers are likely to recognize and appreciate the Best Buy brand, especially if it can revise its offerings to match those provided by disruptive, innovative competitors.

## New Technology-based Innovation Strategies

A technological innovation can undermine a firm's leadership position in a market, even if that firm is doing everything else well. Technological disruptions often come as big surprises to managers. For example, Digital Equipment Corp. (DEC) was happily selling $14 billion worth of minicomputer equipment worldwide when its founder and CEO Ken Olsen famously noted that he saw "no reason for any individual to have a computer in his home."[27] By failing to anticipate or adapt when small PCs disrupted its minicomputer market, DEC made a disastrous miscalculation.[28]

> A technological innovation can undermine a firm's leadership position in a market, even if that firm is doing everything else well.

To describe the process and ultimate outcomes of innovative technologies, Clayton Christensen has offered the framework, shown in Figure 6.3, which highlights two main categories of these technologies.[29] Sustaining technologies are well understood and typically exploited by market leaders, and produce continuous, incremental improvements over time. Market leaders rely on sustaining technologies to improve the performance of established products along familiar dimensions valued by mainstream customers; ultimately, however, the product likely overshoots these customers' needs. For example, major telecoms companies kept offering new features to their product and service offerings, such as voicemail, caller ID, and better clarity. The sustaining technology options (e.g., digital services, fiber connections) helped them improve their offerings, mostly for demanding business customers at first but then for everyday consumers too. As a result, consumers wound up with a sophisticated bundle of home phone services, offering high degrees of reliability, fidelity, and innovative service options, many of which exceeded their needs. If market-leading firms also depend too heavily on a stage-gate development process, which furthers incremental product improvements devoted to well-understood customers and technologies, the market might become stagnant and ripe for the introduction of a radically new technology.

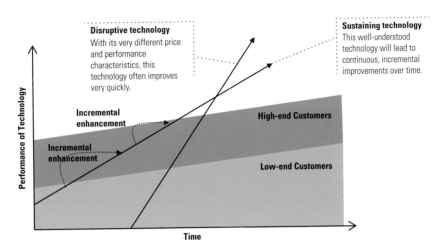

**Figure 6.3** Sustaining vs. Disruptive Technical Innovations

*Source:* Inspired by Christensen, C.M. (1997) *The Innovator's Dilemma: When New Technologies Cause Great Firms to Fail.* Boston, MA: Harvard Business School Press.

**Disruptive technologies** present highly different price and performance characteristics or value propositions. When they first emerge, they might produce "worse" performance than a well-refined, sustaining technology. That is, a disruptive technology usually underperforms established products for mainstream customers, at least initially. Then, the market leaders, with their investments in existing offerings and staff of engineers who focus on available technologies, tend to assume the new technology is not suitable for their customers. They remain focused on promoting solutions using sustaining technologies, assume that all their customers need and want are a broad bundle of features, and generally ignore the disruptive technology. For example, when VoIP (voice over Internet protocol) technology first appeared, most major telecoms companies noted its poor reliability and fidelity and assumed it would not be a threat. But the disruptive pricing strategy offered by VoIP – including free options that allowed even students studying abroad to stay in regular touch with their families at home, without incurring huge phone bills – created a strong appeal that helped alter the telecoms market.

Most disruptive technologies enter the low end of existing markets, with worse performance (according to the performance measures defined by the traditional market) and substantially lower prices. Students calling home to their families abroad were willing to accept the occasional dropped call or weak connection, for example, because they could always call back for free. Others create completely new markets, because the unique value proposition of the new technology means that it addresses customers' needs in different ways that an existing technology cannot achieve. This entrance route often makes it even more difficult for existing providers to sense the competitive threat of the disruptive technology. Even as MapQuest and Yahoo! introduced customized navigational guidance offerings, firms such as Garmin, the market leader in the portable GPS-based navigation market, seemed unconcerned. But these technologies grew and expanded to become free navigational apps that Google and Apple added to smartphones. The combination of clear navigational guidance provided by the same smartphone that customers were using for most of their day-to-day tasks proved irresistible, such that the market for separate, portable GPS navigation devices largely disappeared.

Another key aspect of disruptive technologies that many existing firms fail to recognize is their remarkably steep *performance trajectory*, much steeper than the one for sustaining technologies.[30] Even VoIP technology took only a few years to achieve sufficient reliability, clarity, and service options that it could compete head to head with existing telecoms lines. Thus, Skype already had gained approximately 300 million monthly users by 2015.

With perfect hindsight, the importance of a new disruptive technologies seems obvious. But that perception and assumption is inaccurate. History provides a wealth of examples of strong firms that could not predict the future (DEC and PCs; Kodak and digital photography). Various factors cause market leaders to fail to anticipate the threats or opportunities of emerging, potentially disruptive technologies. For example:

- Especially when they first emerge, disruptive technologies often appear to appeal only to small, niche, or relatively unappealing customer segments.
- The potential markets for disruptive innovations are hard to evaluate, because, by definition, they are unknown, which makes them more risky.
- Executives and engineers might be locked into an existing technology they already know well, causing them to exhibit a *status quo bias*.
- In their efforts to compete, firms might offer more than customers really need and assume that those customers want all the available features, such that they believe incorrectly that disruptive technologies that offer less on some dimensions will be insufficiently viable.
- Firms fail to appreciate the steep performance trajectory that new technologies often follow.

## Launching and Diffusing Innovative Offerings

An estimated 40% of new offerings launched on the market fail to meet business objectives.[31] These failures might result from *poor designs*, such as when a new product fails to offer any relative advantage over existing solutions that is worth a price premium, or from *poor launches*, such that the new offering diffuses too slowly throughout the potential customer base because it is inappropriately targeted, positioned, or not competitive. Because the success of a new offering launch is determined by how fast and extensively it diffuses throughout a target population, we focus on the factors that drive new product diffusion.

> An estimated 40% of new offerings launched on the market fail to meet business objectives.

Consider the Segway. The product certainly was interesting and novel, but its initial launch targeted automobiles, seeking to replace people's cars with another option priced at $5,000. As a type of motorized scooter, it may have been more successful to start if it had targeted a narrow segment of consumers who valued its unique features. Instead, the company sold 24,000 units in the five years after the launch – radically less than the forecasted 10,000 per week.[32]

**Example:** Kellogg's (US)

When it launched Breakfast Mates – a single serving of breakfast cereal, a spoon, and a serving of pasteurized milk that did not require refrigeration – Kellogg's positioned the innovation as a solution for harried parents who wanted to give their children breakfast in the morning but were often rushing out the door to make it to school on time. The positioning was ineffective, however, because Kellogg's failed to realize that parents hated the idea of giving their children a product that would enable them to spill milk all over the back seat of the car.[33]

To support more rapid diffusion, such that the innovative firm can generate sales, acquire new customers, recoup development costs, build customer awareness and loyalty, gain market share, and establish strong SCA, various factors are pertinent and can determine the most effective launch strategy. They fall into two main categories: people-based and product-based factors.

### People-based Factors that Influence Innovation Diffusion

To explain new offerings' diffusion rates, it can be informative to classify consumers into groups, according to their propensity to adopt new products and which persuasive arguments will prompt them to adopt. Then an effective launch strategy seeks to appeal to each group in turn with convincing arguments that get them to embrace the innovation.

According to Geoffrey Moore, the adoption lifecycle of an innovative offering suggests five groups of potential users:[34]

- **Innovators** are the first to adopt, often before the new offering even is officially launched. They actively seek new technologies in a specific domain, because being the first to have each new introduction is part of how they define their personas. Although sales to this group tend to be relatively small, these adopters prove that the technology works and endorse it for other consumers.
- **Early adopters** see the benefits of the new technology and are willing to adopt it after just a few references. Along with providing some initial sales, this group represents the main source of WOM testimonials and references.
- The **early majority** consists of much more pragmatic consumers, who need to be convinced that the new product really works. They find little value in having anything new just for the sake of being new, or in playing with cool technology. They demand evidence and a full range of supporting materials, unlike the previous two groups.
- The **late majority** and **laggards**, the last two groups, also want more evidence, but they are especially hard to persuade. Typically, they become convinced of the value of a new offering only after most of their peers are productively using the new innovation and it has become virtually unavoidable.

Moore's adoption lifecycle also contains the important concept of crossing the chasm, such that many new offerings fail to survive the jump from the early adopter to the early majority groups. Therefore, managers need to develop launch strategies that purposefully seek to cross the chasm.[35] Instead, when firms spread their R&D and marketing resources too thin, trying to reach a wide variety of market segments, they might be able to convince only innovators and early adopters in each of these segments to try their innovative offering. For example, a company selling a new type of business machine might seek to sell to industrial customers, schools, and government agencies. But when more risk-taking early adopters in all three of these sectors already have purchased all that they can, the firm has not done enough to refine its offering to match the unique needs of any of the specific market segment. Nor has it gathered feedback and testimonials that will satisfy buyers in the early majority with the segment-specific evidence they demand. This firm would have fallen into the chasm.

> Moore's adoption lifecycle also contains the important concept of crossing the chasm, such that many new offerings fail to survive the jump from the early adopter to the early majority groups.

A better approach may be to pick a few vertical segments (i.e., specific segment applications) and concentrate on them, to ensure that the newly developed offering satisfies these segments very well. With this approach, the marketing department can focus on dedicated advertising to raise awareness and develop supporting materials that will appeal to the customers in these few segments. With this information, the firm is better able to meet the particular needs of early majority customers in the targeted segments. For example, the Australian innovator Xero started off with the simple, focused goal to improve invoicing and accounting workflow tasks for accountants who typically relied on Microsoft Excel. Ultimately, the revised and innovative software product it produced spread to firms of various types around the world and led to Xero being valued at more than $2 billion.[36]

The adoption lifecycle approach clearly and systematically integrates aspects of MP#1 and MP#2. That is, it accounts for customer heterogeneity, by dividing customers into groups according to adoption tendencies and specific needs. It also accounts for customer dynamics, in that early customers provide the information required to convince later customers to adopt. The metaphor of "crossing the chasm" also helps explain the innovation adoption process in an intuitive way. Yet, this approach also suffers from the threat of an aggregation bias. It assumes that customers in each group behave similarly, and it ignores other potential sources of variation, such as the characteristics of the offering, even though different offerings have very different adoption rates.

### Product-based Factors that Influence Innovation Diffusion

Another long stream of research, starting with Everett Rogers, shows that specific product characteristics can capture 40–80% of the variation in the speed with which offerings diffuse.[37] Note that Rogers used the term "product" in the broad way we have described previously, so we retain that usage here, even though the five factors he described can refer to services too. Changing each of the following five factors can alter the rate of product diffusion, all else being equal:

1 **Relative advantage**: If a customer perceives a higher relative advantage of a product, such that it appears better than an existing offering, it speeds up that product's diffusion. This relative advantage factor captures multiple dimensions, including technical performance, cost savings, and status. Although this relative advantage is a necessary condition for product adoption, it is not a sufficient one. That is, if the other four factors fail to support product diffusion, even a significant relative advantage can lead to slow adoption rates. For example, a new keyboard layout for English language typists is significantly more efficient than the traditional QWERTY keyboard, but it has attracted few users because of its lack of compatibility.

2 **Compatibility**: Customers gauge new products according to how consistent they are with their existing values, uses, and experiences. Greater compatibility with existing product usages speeds product adoption. If, instead, a new offering requires consumers to break a habit or violate their traditional beliefs, adoption slows down considerably. Plastic wine stoppers work better than traditional corks, but consumers perceive the plastic versions as lower in status, so their adoption has been slow.

3 **Complexity**: A more complex product, which is more difficult to understand or use, generally suffers from slow diffusion; education instead can speed up acceptance. Google's very simple search screen helped expand its spread, in contrast with options that demanded users enter multiple search criteria or other information. The nearly blank page and straightforward search options lowered the complexity of its use, even though the offering itself was highly sophisticated, which helped Google capture vast market share relatively quickly.

4 **Trialability**: More opportunities to try an offering easily speed up its diffusion. Providing customers with free samples and demo versions or encouraging test drives are tactics that marketers use to enhance trialability. This factor is especially critical for high-cost offerings, products that take time to learn, or offerings that are risky in some other way, to help consumers overcome these barriers to adoption.

5 **Observability**: Finally, when an offering's benefits are highly visible to others, it speeds up new product diffusion, because others readily see the benefits, without the firm needing to expend marketing resources to communicate about them. This factor is especially salient for status or prestige products. However, observability can have a negative effect if there is some social stigma involved with usage, which is why sellers promote some sensitive or embarrassing personal products by promising to ship them in unidentifiable packaging, with no distinguishing labels visible.

Marketers launching new offerings need to evaluate their innovations on these five factors, then develop plans for leveraging these factors to encourage adoption. For example, if a product is particularly complex, the firm likely needs to expend extra effort to increase its trialability and observability to help ensure its spread and enhance acceptance. If the firm can optimize the people-based and product-based factors associated with its new offering, it will greatly increase the likelihood of its launch success, as well as its offering equity.

---

If the firm can optimize the people-based and product-based factors associated with its new offering, it will greatly increase the likelihood of its launch success, as well as its offering equity.

---

# Managing Offering-based Sustainable Competitive Advantage

## Steps to Building Offering Equity

Building offering equity involves three main steps. First, the firm must *develop an offering or offering portfolio that provides customers with the largest relative advantage among all competitors in the market.* The lack of a meaningful relative advantage, from a customer's perspective, is perhaps the greatest cause of new product failure, whereas a significant advantage speeds diffusion and raises higher barriers to competition. Because so many firms use stage-gate development processes to speed their development and reduce costs, leading to incremental innovations, a competitive option can be to maintain a parallel strategy (e.g., *jugaad* innovation) to develop truly disruptive, radical innovations. Just like a balanced investment portfolio can help protect investors, firms might seek to mix their radical and incremental innovation efforts, instead of devoting all their energy to either big blockbuster innovations or continuous streams of minor product extensions. This recommendation reflects the importance of considering the entire offering portfolio that a firm develops; for example, pharmaceutical firms generally have drugs in various stages of development (e.g., discover, test, launch), some of which seek to address conventional health problems better, while others shoot for the proverbial moon by seeking to cure cancer or find other ways to radically improve people's lives. Tracking the entire offering portfolio reveals a firm's existing advantages but also its potential for future revenue and success.[38] In their attempts to balance their innovation processes and offering portfolios to maintain strong performance, both now and in the future, firms can turn to techniques such as conjoint analysis to design optimal offerings, understand trade-offs across product attributes, and meet customers' dynamic needs (Data Analytics Technique 6.1).

Second, in line with MP#1, offering equity requires a firm to *segment, target, and position that new offering in a way that accounts for both people- and product-based diffusion factors*. The segmentation and targeting strategies should focus on those segments with the greatest relative advantage and in which the new offering is most compatible with existing technologies. They should avoid segments in which the new offering would remove features, to avoid a negative endowment effect among consumers. If they are introducing disruptive innovations, managers might want to focus proactively on the low end of the market or new market segments, to avoid head-to-head competition with established offerings that perform better on certain factors. Marketing campaigns also should offer various ways for targeted users to experiment with the new offering, then make these early adopters highly visible to non-users. Free samples, warranties, and trial periods are effective methods to reduce perceived risk; the free samples that pharmaceutical manufacturers provide to physicians have clear benefits in terms of finding the right patients for the latest drug options.[39] Similarly, positioning strategies should focus on the relative advantage, compatibility, and simplicity of the new offering. Because failed launches are expensive and damaging, many firms engage in test marketing to determine the most effective targeting, positioning, and marketing mix strategies for new consumer offerings.[40]

Third, and associated with MP#2, firms need to *manage the customer migrations from innovators and early adopters to early majority stages*. To accelerate product acceptance across groups and ensure greater launch success, firms can devote most of their R&D and marketing resources to a few segments and persuade their gatekeepers, who then provide the references and testimonials needed to persuade more pragmatic customers in subsequent stages. This method to get across the chasm helps ensure sufficient sales achieved through the initial target markets. Once the product has been accepted widely in these segments, the launch can be expanded to other segments, using testimonials and the lessons from the early successes.

## Research Approaches for Designing and Launching New Offerings

As we discussed in Chapter 5, qualitative techniques such as observation, focus groups, and customer interviews are effective early in the development process; they can reveal some important needs that may be just emerging or that are unknown to the firm. With observational techniques, P&G was able to recognize that consumers did not like leaning over or touching a mop, so it leveraged this latent need in developing the Swiffer mop innovation and related cleaning products.[41]

Then, to avoid the risks associated with the high failure rate of new offerings, firms can use different techniques, such as **conjoint analysis**, to improve their decision making and avoid unsuccessful launches (see Data Analytics Technique 6.1). This powerful technique to evaluate the value of different attributes and design an optimal new offering for a targeted customer segment is especially helpful when those attributes involve inherent trade-offs, such as demanding a longer battery life but a smaller size and lighter weight.[42] These characteristics are related – a longer battery life generally requires a bigger, heavier battery – so to determine the optimal trade-off of attributes, conjoint analysis collects input from multiple customers to identify the level of each feature that maximizes their purchase likelihood.

Prior to national launches, many firms conduct sophisticated test marketing and experimentation (see Data Analytics Technique 4.1) to try out different launch scenarios. Test markets often span diverse locations; empirical models then can provide forecasts of national or global sales. This critical step ensures that the marketing and production investments match the expected demand. Without accurate forecasts, the firm's capacity might not match customer demand; if the supply is insufficient, customers might just buy competitors' products, even if they are suboptimal, because they are available.

With a conjoint analysis, marketers can design and develop new products by thinking of products as bundles of attributes, then determining which combination of attributes is best suited to meet the preferences of customers.

- To identify product attribute trade-offs that customers are willing to make for a new product.
- To predict the market share and impact of a proposed new product (i.e., bundle of attributes).
- To determine the amount that customers are willing to pay for a new product

Conjoint analysis assumes that a product consists of multiple attributes that together provide benefits to a customer. For example, a smartphone customer might think about call quality, operating system, screen size, and camera quality benefits. If a firm decides to design a new smartphone, it cannot just ask customers about what features they care about; most customers would say they wanted the best version of all the features. Instead, the firm can simulate a trade-off: Would you rather have better camera quality or a smaller (or bigger) screen size? The trade-offs reflect how customers actually make decisions, because few of them can afford the best options for all attributes in every product.

Another basic assumption underlying conjoint measurement is that customers cannot reliably express how they weight the separate product features when forming their preferences. Instead, marketers need to infer these relative weights by asking for evaluations (or choices) of alternate product concepts, using a structured process. Thus, during a conjoint exercise, rather than directly asking customers about the significance of product attributes, the analyst uses a more realistic setting and asks customers to evaluate alternative scenarios or product profiles, each with multiple product attributes. Then it is possible to infer the significance of each product attribute from the ratings that customers provide for each scenario, reflecting their overall product preference. The conjoint formula is:

$$R(P) = \sum_{j=1}^{k_j} \sum_{i=1}^{m} \beta_{ij} x_{ij}$$

where P is the product bundle, comprising certain attributes; $R(P)$ is the rating associated with product P; $\beta_{ij}$ is the part-worth utility associated with the $j$th level ($j = 1, 2, 3, ..., k_j$) of the $i$th attribute; $k_j$ is the number of levels of attribute I; $m$ is the number of attributes; and $x_{ij}$ equals 1 if the $j$th level of the $i$th attribute is present in product P, and 0 otherwise.

With the data collected from such a conjoint experiment, we can estimate the underlying value of each product attribute, or its part-worth utility ($\beta_{ij}$). The estimated part-worth utilities from a conjoint analysis can provide the answers to many marketing questions, such as which product configurations are optimal and how much market share an offering is likely to capture.

## Example

A smartphone manufacturer wants to design a new phone for its target demographic. The main product attributes the manufacturer wants to focus on are camera resolution quality, screen size, and price. The manufacturer also wants to understand customers' willingness to pay for the new smartphone. Thus, it designs a conjoint study for 250 customers to provide a product rating score (0 = least preferred, 100 = most preferred) for eight alternative smartphones, according to their price, camera resolution, and screen size. The question for one of the eight products is provided here for illustration.

| How likely are you to buy this smartphone? Use a scale from 0 to 100, where 0 ="definitely will not purchase" and 100 = "definitely will purchase". | |
| --- | --- |
| Price | $500 |
| Camera Resolution | 5 MP |
| Screen size | 2.5 inches |
| Your Rating (0 to 100, where 100 is most likely to buy): | |

With the rating scores from the 250 customers, the manufacturer can apply the conjoint formula and estimate the part-worth utilities associated with each product attribute. Let's say that our hypothetical customers, reasonably, prefer the $500 smartphone more (part-worth = 25) than the $600 option (part-worth = 0). They also want an 8 MP smartphone (part-worth = 10) rather than a 6 MP one (part-worth = 0) and a 6.5-inch screen (part-worth = 20) more than a 5.5-inch one (part-worth = 0).

The part-worth difference between the 5.5- and 6-inch phone options $(20 - 0 = 20)$ is twice as great as the difference between the 8 and 6 MP versions $(10 - 0 = 10)$, so screen size appears twice as important as camera resolution quality. The part-worth difference between the $500 and $600 smartphones was 25 $(25 - 0 = 25)$, which implies that each part-worth unit is worth $4 ($100 = 25 units, or 1 unit = $4). Noting that the part-worth difference between the 5.5- and 6-inch phone options was 20 units, the manufacturer can estimate that customers are willing to pay $80 ($4 × 20 units = $80) more for a 6-inch screen than for a 5.5-inch version.

Thus, this manufacturer should produce a phone with 6 MP camera quality, a 6-inch screen size, and a price that is $80 more than the base price of $500.

Another model also seeks to predict diffusion. The **Bass model** captures many of the people- and product-based factors we discussed previously, but it also integrates pricing and advertising levels to predict adoption rates.[43] The Bass model, developed by academic Frank Bass, combines the *coefficient of innovation (p)*, which reflects a person's propensity to adopt a product independent of the number of previous adopters; the *coefficient of imitation (q)*, or the propensity to adopt as a function of the number of existing adopters; and the size of the market. Historical data are available for the $p$ and $q$ values for thousands of existing offerings, so a firm can take information about a similar offering to model its own offering's diffusion. Of course, this model makes some important assumptions. It refers to first-time purchases, without accounting for multiple purchases of a product. It features only a binary diffusion process (innovators versus imitators) and does not distinguish prior adopters and potential adopters. Nor does it include other marketing mix variables, and it imposes the restriction that each innovation is independent, without any competitive effects. Yet, even with these limitations, the Bass model captures diffusion effectively and parsimoniously. For example, DirecTV used a Bass model, based on adoption rates for cable television services, to generate its five-year forecast and justify its investments in multiple satellites to extend its coverage. The forecast, derived three years before the service ever launched, ultimately fell within 6–26% of actual customer purchase over time.[44] Furthermore, the Bass model has been modified many times over and is universally lauded for its practical appeal.

## Summary

*Offerings* are the core components of a value proposition; they add value by providing functionality at a lower cost or with an innovative solution. Businesses devote a lot of effort and resources to innovate their offerings, and through this process of *innovation*, they can identify and develop new valuable offerings that create their SCA. Four key areas of change can define the innovation space: changing what the firm offers, changing who the customer is, changing how the firm sells to customers, and changing where it sells to customers.

By building *offering equity*, the firm gains benefits that make it more difficult for competitors to encroach on its business, and it achieves better financial performance. Offering equity is manifest in the price customers are willing to pay for the performance of the offering, reflecting its core value, separate from any brand or relationship equity. A new offering provides more value if it leads to enhanced performance or similar performance with lower costs. Furthermore, new offerings can help firms acquire new customers and enter new markets. Still, these sorts of SCAs due to new offerings tend to be short-lived. Before competitors react, copy, or surpass an innovation, the firm needs to build other, synergistic, long-lasting SCAs.

To develop offerings and innovation strategies, marketing should gather customer input, forecast customer and market trends, and conduct market research to help clarify the trade-offs among new offering attributes. Then, marketing is responsible for launching the new offering and quickly generating sales and profits. Most firms rely on *stage-gate development* processes, which evaluate each innovation on multiple dimensions in stages. In emerging markets, the potentially expensive stage-gate processes are often substituted by *jugaad* innovation processes, or frugal processes that are defined by a lack of structure and that focus on creative solutions at low costs. Another strategy for developing innovative offerings is to dramatically reposition an existing product, removing some features and adding others so that the total offering appeals to a different customer segment according to a new value proposition. These moves help build SCA, such that displaced market leaders struggle to match the emerging competitor. Many firms also use branding efforts to build additional barriers to competition after a disruptive repositioning effort.

A new enabling technology or invention also might change the underlying premise of an offering. *Sustaining technologies* are well understood and typically exploited by market leaders that seek continuous, incremental improvements. *Disruptive technologies* instead introduce very different price and performance characteristics, such that the new technology typically offers "worse" performance than some well-refined, sustaining technology. However, the performance trajectories of such technologies generally are steep. Market leaders that fail to recognize that also cannot anticipate the threats, or opportunities, of emerging and potentially disruptive technologies.

A new offering's success largely depends on how fast and how far it diffuses. The various approaches used to define an innovation's *diffusion rate* can mainly be categorized as focused on either *people-based* or *product-based factors*. People-based factors attempt to explain the variation in a new offering's diffusion rate according to the differences among people, who can be classified as *innovators, early adopters, early majority, late majority*, or *laggards*. Product-based factors instead suggest that changing the relative advantage, compatibility, complexity, trialability, and observability of an offering affects the rate of its diffusion.

To build offering equity, firms thus need to develop offering portfolios that provide customers with the best relative advantage. They should develop a segmentation, targeting, and positioning strategy for the new offering that accounts for people- and product-based factors, and then manage the migrations from innovators and early adopters to early majority customer groups. However, new offerings struggle with high failure rates, so various techniques offer promise for improving decision making and reducing the chances of an unsuccessful launch. *Conjoint analysis* helps managers evaluate the potential value of various attributes and design optimal products for targeted customer segments. A *Bass model* uses characteristics to capture many of the people- and product-based factors, as well as pricing and advertising levels, to predict product adoption rates.

## Takeaways

- Most firms rank innovation as a top strategic priority. Innovation involves more than new technologies or products; it can reflect changes in business processes or go-to-market strategies.
- Firms can innovate in four primary ways: changing their offering, changing who the customer is, changing how they sell to customers, or changing where they sell.
- Offering equity captures the core value that the customer obtains from a new offering, absent any brand or relationship equity.
- A first-mover advantage is often short-lived, so firms must continually develop new offerings to build their SCA, in terms of offering equity.
- New and innovative offerings increase firm value by providing more value to customers (through enhanced performance or better performance for the price), motivating customers to switch, expanding customers and markets, and establishing a brand image as a leading, innovative company.
- A stage-gate development process improves the speed of product development, the success likelihood, and the development costs.
- Two strategies for developing an innovative offering are repositioning strategies (i.e., blue ocean) and technology-based strategies.
- People-based factors influence innovation diffusion, according to the adoption lifecycle, which describes differences in people's propensity to adopt new products (innovators, early adopters, early majority, late majority, and laggards). Firms must bridge the chasm between early adopters and the early majority to succeed.
- Product-based factors influence innovation diffusion. Marketers need to evaluate the relative advantage, compatibility, complexity, trialability, and observability of new offerings, then develop ways to leverage them to encourage adoption.
- Three key steps to building offering equity are developing an offering portfolio that provides customers with the best relative advantage among competitors; segmenting, targeting, and positioning the new offering to account for people- and product-based factors to speed up diffusion; and managing customer migration from innovators and early adopters to early majority stages.
- Conjoint analysis can facilitate the design and launch of new offerings by helping managers define the optimal product, according to the value assigned to various product attributes by consumers. Bass models also are helpful, because they use historical data related to the coefficients of innovation and imitation to predict adoption rates.

# References

1 Kampmen, J. (2015) 'Report: AMD R&D spending to near-10-year low,' 27 March. Available at: http://techreport.com/news/28033/report-amd-r-d-spending-falls-to-near-10-year-low (accessed 9 August, 2016).

2 Battelle and *R&D Magazine* (2013) '2014 global R&D funding forecast,' *R&D Magazine*, 55(6), pp. 33–4.

3 Erickson, G. and Jacobson, R. (1992) 'Gaining comparative advantage through discretionary expenditures: The returns to R&D and advertising,' *Management Science*, 38(3), pp. 1264–79.

4 Sawhney, M., Wolcott, R.C. and Arroniz, I. (2006) 'The 12 different ways for companies to innovate,' *MIT Sloan Management Review*, 47(3), p. 75.

5 Rigby, D. and Bilodeau, B. (2015) 'Management tools & trends 2015,' 10 June. Available at: www.bain.com/publications/articles/management-tools-and-trends-2015.aspx (accessed 9 August, 2016).

6 *Seattle Times* (2007) 'A bitter shot for Starbucks: McDonald's wins taste test,' *The Seattle Times*, 3 February.

7 Sawhney, M., Wolcott, R.C. and Arroniz, I. (2006) 'The 12 different ways for companies to innovate,' *MIT Sloan Management Review*, 47(3), p. 75.

8 Golder, P. and Tellis, G. (1993) 'Pioneer advantage: Marketing logic or marketing legend?,' *Journal of Marketing Research*, 30(2), pp. 158–70.

9 Robinson, W.T. and Min, S. (2002) 'Is the first to market the first to fail? Empirical evidence for industrial goods businesses,' *Journal of Marketing Research*, 39(1), pp. 120–8.

10 Australian Government, Department of Education and Training (2015) 'Giving Australia a competitive advantage in global steel markets,' 11 December. Available at: www.education.gov.au/giving-australia-competitive-advantage-global-steel-markets (accessed 9 August, 2016).

11 Chaney, K.W., Devinney, T.M. and Winer, R.S. (1991) 'The impact of new product introductions on the market values of firms,' *Journal of Business*, 64(4), pp. 573–610; Lee, H., Smith, K.G., Grimm, C.M. and Schomburg, A. (2000) 'Timing, order, and durability of new product advantages with imitation,' *Strategic Management Journal*, 21(1), pp. 23–30; Sood, A. and Tellis, G.J. (2009) 'Demystifying disruption: A new model for understanding and predicting disruptive technologies,' *Marketing Science*, 30(2), pp. 339–54.

12 Sorescu, A.B. and Spanjol, J. (2008) 'Innovation's effect on firm value and risk: Insights from consumer packaged goods,' *Journal of Marketing*, 72(2), pp. 114–32; Pauwels, K., Silva-Risso, J., Srinivasan, S. and Hanssens, D.M. (2004) 'New products, sales promotions and firm value, with application to the automobile industry,' *Journal of Marketing*, 68(4), pp. 142–56.

13 Wizeman, T.M., Robinson, S., Giffin, R.B. and Institute of Medicine (2009) *Breakthrough Business Models: Drug Development for Rare and Neglected Diseases and Individualized Therapies: Workshop Summary*. Washington, DC: National Academies Press.

14 Meyer, R.J., Zhao, S. and Han, J.K. (2008) 'Biases in valuation vs. usage of innovative product features,' *Marketing Science*, 27(6), pp. 1038–96.

15 Bruce, N.I., Foutz, N.Z. and Kolsarici, C. (2012) 'Dynamic effectiveness of advertising and word of mouth in sequential distribution of new products,' *Journal of Marketing Research*, 49(4), pp. 469–86; Bruce, N.I. (2008) 'Pooling and dynamic forgetting effects in multitheme advertising: Tracking the advertising sales relationship with particle filters,' *Marketing Science*, 27(4), pp. 659–78.

16 Pitta, D.A., Wood, V.R. and Franzak, F.J. (2008) 'Nurturing an effective creative culture within a marketing organization,' *Journal of Consumer Marketing*, 25(3), pp. 137–48; Mast, K. (2011) 'How to create a culture of innovation that attracts & retains top talent,' InnovationManagement.se, 17 February.

17 Turpin, D. (2011) 'Case study: Why TomTom is a map for mastering international markets,' 16 March. Available at: www.theaustralian.com.au/business/business-spectator/case-study-why-tomtom-is-a-map-for-mastering-international-markets/news-story/05df438723cfd82115842357683af79e (accessed on 5 August, 2016).

18 Cooper, R.G. (2008) 'Perspective: The Stage-Gate® idea-to-launch process – update, what's new, and NexGen system,' *Journal of Product Innovation Management*, 25(3), pp. 213–32; Cooper, R.G. (1990) 'Stage-Gate systems: A new tool for managing new products,' *Business Horizons*, 33(3), pp. 44–54.

19 Gourville, J.T. (2006) 'Eager sellers and stony buyers: Understanding the psychology of new-product adoption,' *Harvard Business Review*, 84(6), pp. 98–106.

20 Kahneman, D. (2003) 'Maps of bounded rationality: Psychology for behavioral economics,' *American Economic Review*, 93(5), pp. 1449–75; Kahneman, D. and Tversky, A. (1979) 'Prospect theory: An analysis of decision under risk,' *Econometrica: Journal of the Econometric Society*, 47(2), pp. 263–91.

21 Kahneman, D., Knetsch, J.L. and Thaler, R.H. (1991) 'Anomalies: The endowment effect, loss aversion, and status quo bias,' *Journal of Economic Perspectives*, 5(1), pp. 193–206.

22 Bommer, M., DeLaPorte, R. and Higgins, J. (2002) 'Skunkworks approach to project management,' *Journal of Management in Engineering*, 18(1), pp. 21–9; Leavitt, H.J. and Lipman-Blumen, J. (1995) 'Hot groups,' *Harvard Business Review*, 73(4), p. 109.

23 Radjou, N., Prabhu, J. and Ahuja, S. (2010) *Jugaad Innovation: Think Frugal, be Flexible, Generate Breakthrough Growth*. San Francisco, CA: John Wiley & Sons.

24 Chan, K.W. and Mauborgne, R. (2005) *Blue Ocean Strategy: How to Create Uncontested Market Space and Make the Competition Irrelevant*. Boston, MA: Harvard Business School Press.

25 Chan, K.W., Mauborgne, R., Bensaou, B. and Williamson, M. (2009) 'The evolution of the circus industry (part A),' 1 June. Available from: www.blueoceanstrategy.com/teaching-materials/cirque-du-soleil/ (accessed 25 August, 2016).

26 ICTPulse (2012) 'Size no longer matters: 4 takeaways from the Best Buy downsize,' 4 April. Available from: www.ict-pulse.

com/2012/04/size-no-longer-matters-4-takeaways-from-the-best-buy-downsize/ (accessed 25 August, 2016).

27  Kahn, E. (2007) *Innovate or Perish: Managing the Enduring Technology Company in the Global Market.* Hoboken, NJ: Wiley & Sons.

28  Mangelsdorf, M. (2011) 'Lessons from Ken Olsen and Digital Equipment Corp.,' 17 February. Available at: http://sloanreview.mit.edu/article/lessons-from-ken-olsen-and-digital-equipment-corp/ (accessed 25 August, 2016).

29  Christensen, C.M. (1997) *The Innovator's Dilemma: When New Technologies Cause Great Firms to Fail.* Boston, MA: Harvard Business School Press.

30  Christensen, C.M. (1997) *The Innovator's Dilemma: When New Technologies Cause Great Firms to Fail.* Boston, MA: Harvard Business School Press.

31  Castellion, G. and Markham, S.K. (2012) 'Perspective: New product failure rates: Influence of argumentum ad populum and self-interest,' *Journal of Product Innovation Management,* 30(5), pp. 976–9.

32  Schneider, J. and Hall, J. (2011) 'Why most product launches fail: Getting attention for a new offering is a big challenge. Five causes of flops – and how to avoid them (Idea Watch),' *Harvard Business Review,* 89(4), pp. 21–4.

33  Cashberry (2006) 'Brand idea failures: Kellogg's Cereal Mates,' 12 November. Available from: http://brandfailures.blogspot.com/2006/11/idea-failures-kelloggs-cereal-mates.html (accessed 25 August, 2016).

34  Moore, G.A. (2006) *Crossing the Chasm: Marketing and Selling Disruptive Products to Mainstream Customers,* rev. edn. New York: Collins Business Essentials.

35  Moore, G.A. (2006) *Crossing the Chasm: Marketing and Selling Disruptive Products to Mainstream Customers,* rev. edn. New York: Collins Business Essentials.

36  Pullar-Strecker, T. and Read, E. (2014) 'Xero has now lost over half its value,' 10 October. Available at: www.stuff.co.nz/business/industries/10602525/Xero-has-now-lost-over-half-its-value (accessed 25 August, 2016).

37  Rogers, E.M. (1995) *Diffusion of Innovations,* 4th edn. New York: Free Press.

38  Grewal, R., Chakravarty, A., Ding, M. and Liechty, J. (2008) 'Counting chickens before the eggs hatch: On the valuation of new product development portfolios in the pharmaceutical sector,' *International Journal of Research in Marketing,* 25(4), pp. 261–72.

39  Joseph, K. and Mantrala, M. (2009) 'A model of the role of free drug samples in physicians' prescription decisions,' *Marketing Letters,* 20(1), pp. 15–29.

40  Ladik, F., Kent, L. and Nahl, P.C. (1960) 'Test marketing of new consumer products,' *Journal of Marketing,* 24(4), pp. 29–34.

41  Brown, B. and Scott, A. (2011) 'How P&G tripled its innovation success rate,' *Harvard Business Review,* 89(6), pp. 64–72.

42  Green, P.E. and Srinivasan, V. (1990) 'Conjoint analysis in marketing: New developments with implications for research and practice,' *Journal of Marketing,* 54(4), pp. 3–19; Vriens, M. (1994) 'Solving marketing problems with conjoint analysis,' *Journal of Marketing Management,* 10(1/3), pp. 37–55.

43  Bass, F.M. (1969) 'A new product growth for modeling consumer durables,' *Management Science,* 15(5), pp. 215–27; Lilien, G.L., Rangaswamy, A. and De Bruyn, A. (2013) *Principles of Marketing Engineering,* 2nd edn. State College, PA: DecisionPro Inc.

44  Bass, F.M., Gordon, K., Ferguson, T.L. and Githens, M.L. (2001) 'DIRECTV: Forecasting diffusion of a new technology prior to product launch,' *Interfaces,* 31(3), pp. S82–93.

## Companion website

Please visit the companion website, **www.palgravehighered.com/palmatier-ms**, to access summary videos from the authors, and full-length cases with datasets and step-by-step solution guides.

ALL
COMPETITORS
REACT

Chapter **7**

# Marketing Principle #3: Managing Relationship-based Sustainable Competitive Advantage

## Learning objectives

- Define relationship marketing and explain how it can lead to a sustainable competitive advantage.
- Explain the influences of commitment, trust, and gratitude on customer decision making and how these influences can be leveraged in relationship marketing programs.
- Compare and contrast the four mechanisms linking relationships with financial performance.
- Describe factors that exert positive and negative influences on relationship formation.
- Critically analyze the elements that determine a customer's relationship orientation.
- Outline the targets for which customer relationship marketing will be most effective.
- Describe the lifecycle of relationships and identify effective relationship marketing strategies for each stage.
- Explain the two-step process for building relationship equity.
- Outline the benefits of using multivariate regression analysis to understand the drivers of relationship equity.
- Describe the value of linking relationship marketing programs to customer lifetime value as a means to understand relationship marketing effectiveness.

# Introduction

## Relationship Marketing Basics

From the earliest days of written history, interpersonal relationships have been critical to trade and business.[1] Firms spend billions of dollars every year to implement customer relationship management systems to help build and maintain strong customer relationships.[2] This **relationship marketing (RM)** process – namely, identifying, developing, maintaining, and terminating relational exchanges to improve performance – can produce relationship equity. This form of equity, in combination with brands and offerings, in turn can lead to a sustainable competitive advantage (SCA). The American Marketing Association's 2004 definition of marketing highlighted the key role of relationships: "an organizational function and a set of processes for creating, communicating, and delivering value to customers and for *managing customer relationships* in ways that benefit the organization and its stake-holders"[3] (emphasis added). That is, managing relationships is a key focus for marketing, beyond traditional marketing mix factors (e.g., promotion, product, price).

Relationship marketing and branding strategies that focus on building equity (see Chapter 5) often overlap. As you will recall, brand equity is mainly a product-oriented notion,[4] in the sense that it arises when customers respond differently (usually, more favorably) to a service or product because they are able to identify its brand. Rather than dealing with products, and describing how the brands of those products extend to the firm, RM addresses relationships. However, both processes seek to build an intangible form of customer equity to increase loyalty, purchases, or financial outcomes among customers. Therefore, especially as customers' attitudes about the firm expand and encompass every-thing associated with that firm – including its brands, products, and relationships – the distinction between branding and RM and the distinct impacts of brands or relationships are difficult to isolate. Furthermore, overall customer equity consists of the combination of relationship equity, as we discuss in this chapter, with brand equity (Chapter 5) and value equity (Chapter 6). That is, it is important to distinguish brand equity from relationship equity, even though, in practice, they often appear to overlap.

The relative importance of building relationships versus other strategies also depends on the specific exchange context. For example, strong relationships tend to be more effective for improving perfor-mance among *services* than among product offerings, in *business-to-business* (B2B) versus business-to-consumer (B2C) markets, and for *channel partners* rather than direct customers.[5] Recent research suggests that customer relationship value has exceeded brand value as a percentage of the total enter-prise value, based on the prices that firms pay when acquiring firms.[6]

Semantically, RM and customer relationship management (CRM) also often overlap, such that the terms are used interchangeably. But, more accurately, CRM combines relationship marketing with information technology in an attempt to integrate processes, people, operations, and marketing.[7] Thus, **customer relationship management (CRM)** is the managerially relevant, organization-wide, customer-focused application of RM, using IT to achieve performance objectives. Many firms have implemented CRM systems to integrate and synthesize customer data based on the belief that enhanced customer insights will improve financial performance. Standard Bank, a leading South African banking group, deployed eFinance, a Siebel Systems' CRM suite. Prior to this change, Standard Bank's retail banking services were fragmented across product lines, but using its new inte-grated view of customers it saw a 78% increase in their conversion rate and a significant increase in cross-selling and upselling services.[8]

> Recent research suggests that customer relationship value has exceeded brand value as a percentage of the total enterprise value, based on the prices that firms pay when acquiring firms.

## Relationships as SCA

Marketing Principle #3 focuses on building and maintaining barriers, or sustainable competitive advantages (SCAs), to competitive attacks, based on the premise that competitors react continually to a firm's success. Investments in building a firm's relationship equity by developing B2B and B2C relationships can represent a strong barrier to competitors. **Relationship equity** refers to the aggregation of relational assets and liabilities, associated with the firm's boundary-spanning employees and social networks linked to the offering or experience, that add to or subtract from the value provided by the firm's offering. Efforts to build relationship equity often come after generating brand and value equities, because relational interactions are part of the product and service delivery or experience, which occurs after the product is designed and launched and brands have been promoted to the targeted customer segment. Yet, relationships powerfully affect behavior; relational-based decision making is ingrained in people's psyches. For example, nearly one-third of human brain activity focuses on relational interactions, because they support cooperation and evolutionary advances.[9] The varied psychological processes and emotions associated with relational or seemingly relational interactions (e.g., gift–gratitude, anger–punishment, guilt–reciprocation, love–hate) help explain customers' responses to marketers' actions and thus the effectiveness of RM.[10]

Such effects have prompted more researchers and managers to focus on RM, especially in light of the relatively recent transition toward service-based economies.[11] Services now represent approximately 85% of the US economy. Compared with products, they are more intangible, less consistent, more perishable, and harder to evaluate, so customers and boundary-spanning personnel participate more closely in the production and consumption of services. The close resulting interactions also make the customer–seller relationships more critical; the intangibility of the service offering means trust is more important. As economies undergo this transition, customer–seller relationships expand (i.e., fewer middlemen, higher interaction levels) and grow more important to customers (i.e., reduced risk and need for cooperation).

Other trends affecting this focus on RM include technology advances (e.g., communication, logistics, computing), global competition, and rapid product commoditization. For example, improvements to communications and logistics abilities allow producers and consumers separated by great distances to transact, such that traits and norms from local markets are duplicated at a global level. Consumers want trust and confidence in the global marketplace, and to find it, they often seek relational-based exchanges.

## Relationship Marketing Theory

Researchers from various disciplines study the impacts of relationships on human behavior, creating a rich theoretical foundation for understanding relationship marketing in particular. For example, *social exchange theory* has established that commitment and trust are central to strong business relationships, with **commitment** defined as an enduring desire to maintain a valued relationship and **trust** as confidence in a relationship partner's reliability and integrity.[12] Committed relationship partners thus devote extra effort and work to maintain and strengthen relational bonds, which enhances cooperation, financial performance, and other positive outcomes.

**Example:** Corning (US)

Corning is a committed partner to Apple, manufacturing all the touchscreens for the iPhone since the inception of the iPhone in 2007. As new manufacturers step into the market with tougher, lighter, and glossy touchscreens, Corning is forced to innovate to maintain its relationship, as a top supplier, with Apple. In turn, Apple also devotes attention to Corning's R&D effort by informing Corning about the desired properties of the new touchscreens (e.g., size, toughness, texture). These efforts on the part of Apple and Corning support and strengthen the relationship bond between these partners.[13]

The influence of RM on decision making also is supported by *gratitude*, which prompts a need for *reciprocation*. This process generates feelings of pleasure, whereas failing to reciprocate generates feelings of guilt. According to evolutionary psychologists, reciprocity and gratitude are genetically and socially hardwired feelings, so they innately contribute to the effectiveness of RM strategies.[14] Customers satisfy obligations to salespeople by purchasing. Gratitude also catalyzes prosocial behavior for as long as the emotion lasts. It can lead to longer-term effects when this feeling prompts norms of reciprocity and solidifies a relationship. Noting the importance of gratitude in consumer decision-making processes, Cadbury India launched a series of televised advertisements stressing the importance of happy moments worth being grateful for: graduating from school, victory by a favorite sports team, success of a loved one. Each moment then was associated with the consumption of Cadbury's Dairy Milk chocolate. The well-received advertising campaign thus helped link consumption of the treats to a sense of gratitude in consumers' minds, while also increasing Cadbury's market share. Gratitude and reciprocity, together with trust and commitment, largely capture the effects of interpersonal relationship marketing and explain the strong empirical support for the impact of interpersonal relationships on customer decision making. In the conceptual model in Figure 7.1, interpersonal RM thus encompasses gratitude, reciprocity, trust, and commitment, which offer a combined indicator of relationship equity.

> Gratitude and reciprocity, together with trust and commitment, largely capture the effects of interpersonal relationship marketing and explain the strong empirical support for the impact of interpersonal relationships on customer decision making.

Beyond these theoretical foundations, *relationship theory* also needs to encompass the elements of interfirm relationships, which involve groups of employees on both sides of the business exchange. For example, in firm-to-firm relationships, multiple interactions involve many people – in effect, networks of relationships. Sociology research offers *network theory* to describe the effects of the structure of an interaction among multiple entities (e.g., individuals, firms) in a network.[15] Applied to interfirm relationships, this perspective suggests three determinants of exchange performance: relationship quality (composite of trust, commitment, gratitude, and reciprocity norms), relationship breadth (number of relationships), and relationship composition (diversity/attractiveness of contacts).[16] The seller's RM activities influence all three of these core and distinct dimensions of interfirm relationships that define the relationship equity of an interfirm exchange. In particular:

- **Relationship quality**: Similar to the notion of tie strength (i.e., relational bonds between actors) from network theory, the quality of relational bonds with an exchange partner refers to diverse interaction characteristics, such as commitment, trust, gratitude, reciprocity norms, and exchange efficiency. Each of these characteristics is interrelated but still captures unique aspects of relational bonds, such that they can affect specific exchange outcomes differently.[17]
- **Relationship breadth**: As a measure of the number of relational bonds with an exchange partner, this dimension suggests that when relationships feature many interpersonal ties, they can provide information, profit opportunities, and protections against severed ties (e.g., due to reorganizations, turnover). With greater breadth, the departure of a particular contact person from one firm should have a less long-lasting impact on the interfirm relationship.[18] Because of these benefits, a seller and customer that share broader interpersonal ties should achieve better exchange performance.

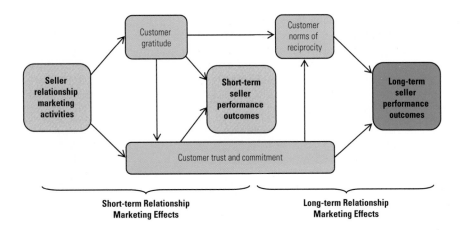

**Figure 7.1** Model of Interpersonal Relationships

- **Relationship composition**: A diverse, authoritative contact portfolio increases a seller's ability to effect change in its customers' organizations. With diverse contacts, the seller can confirm information across different perspectives and gain access to critical decision makers. Imagine a new product approval process, which might include the customer's engineering, manufacturing, quality, and purchasing departments. A strong relationship with a quality control manager has little impact on the purchasing department's cost-based calculations. That is, even high-quality relationships with multiple contacts (breadth) are ineffective if they do not feature key decision makers or include only similar positions. Different areas within a customer firm make key decisions, not just the people with the most authority or "key" decision makers, so an effective seller must develop a relationship portfolio composed of diverse contacts.

Figure 7.2 depicts the impacts of these three determinants on performance.

## Benefits from Relationship Equity

Relationship marketing efforts seek to improve relationship characteristics (e.g., quality, breadth) with an exchange partner and build relationship equity, in the hope of ultimately improved financial performance. That is, RM activities do not affect financial performance directly. Instead, they help build relationship equity, which influences customer behaviors, which improves the seller's financial outcomes. This chain of effects operates through four mechanisms.

The first mechanism is cooperative behaviors, or coordinated, complementary actions between partners to achieve a mutual goal. As a means to create value beyond what each individual firm could do on its own, cooperation increases customers' flexibility and adaptiveness to sellers' requests for changes, information, or reciprocation. But if the customer obtains its portion of that created value before the seller (or vice versa), then the seller must wait for the reciprocal benefits. Such delayed responses, especially if waiting is difficult or uncomfortable, indicate the need for trusting relationships. In parallel, commitment encourages the parties to remain in their valued relationships and bonds, even if the reciprocity is delayed or non-equivalent.[19] If relationships lack trust or commitment though, the parties generally cooperate only to the extent that the benefits they earn are equivalent and simultaneous. On the crowdsourcing platform My Starbucks Idea, consumers of the coffee shop freely post their ideas related to how Starbucks could improve its value proposition, including new products, better service, or the removal of some existing ideas. The forum attracts thousands of committed visitors every day, even though consumers know full well that the chances that Starbucks might implement their ideas are very slim. But in this case, the extent of the relationship remains under the consumer's control; each person can devote just as much effort to the cooperation as they find appropriate, without being required to enter into a fully committed bond.

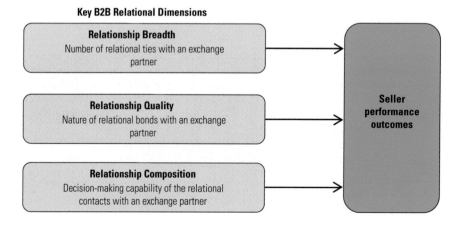

**Figure 7.2**  Model of Interfirm (B2B) Relationships

The second mechanism is relational loyalty, defined as the likelihood that the customer provides the seller benefits in the exchange process due to their relational attitudes and ties. For example, customers might engage in only limited searches for alternatives, rebuy without soliciting competitive bids, or disclose competitive quotes to give the favored seller a chance to win the business. Relationships positively influence this loyalty, because customers perceive less risk dealing with trusted partners, act on relationally generated belonging, and minimize costs by buying from valued sellers.[20] Loyalty, in turn, becomes a crucial determinant of firm success in competitive marketplaces.

**Example:** E-Commerce (China)

E-commerce is a fiercely competitive and growing market in China, with annual consumer spending of $540 billion and hundreds of notable players, and yet 61% of consumers are loyal mainly to just three firms: Taobao, JD, and Tmall. A recent report indicates that many of these loyal consumers remain open to receiving promotions from these e-commerce brands via email or mobile messaging. They also are 19% more likely to visit their preferred brands' websites, where they not only spend more but also are more forthcoming when it comes to sharing private information about their brand preferences.[21]

The third mechanism is *referrals*, commonly referred to as word of mouth (WOM), reflecting the likelihood that a customer comments positively about a seller to others. Relational bonds, feelings of gratitude, and positive attitudes drive the motivation and willingness to provide requested or unrequested referrals.[22] Because it is not affected by switching costs or lack of time or motivation, WOM provides an effective indicator of customer loyalty; only customers with strong, trusting relationships are likely to risk their reputations by advocating a seller to another friend or colleague.[23] However, referrals and WOM differ from loyalty-favored behaviors, because they represent different performance-enhancing pathways. Loyalty affects financial outcomes by altering the exchange process *with the loyal customer*; referrals affect them by *generating business with new customers*. Among these new customers, strong WOM can be extremely valuable, especially considering evidence that shows that consumers are willing to pay more for a product with an "excellent" rating (a form of WOM by other consumers) than for one with a "good" rating, promising premiums that range from 20% for real estate agents to 99% for legal services.[24]

The fourth and last mechanism is empathic behaviors, or a greater likelihood of being influenced by perceptions of the seller's position. Customers in a strong relationship may attribute service failures to external causes that the seller cannot control, which would reduce the impact of those failures on their purchase behaviors. Their sensitivity to and empathy for the seller's difficult position (e.g., offshore competition, reduced sales and profits) also may prevent them from imposing the price reduction pressures that are common responses to service failures.

## Relationship Marketing Strategy

### Building and Maintaining Relationships

To use relationship equity as a competitive advantage, managers first must find ways to build and maintain strong relationships. Relationship marketing strategies comprise various activities, rewards, and loyalty programs that seek to encourage strong customer–seller relational bonds. Most firms focus their relational investments on dedicated RM programs, for good reason. Marketing departments tend to treat RM as another form of promotion and leverage the processes they have developed for traditional advertising or direct marketing campaigns. By implementing specific RM programs, the firm can budget for its efforts more clearly and better evaluate the programs' effectiveness. Moving beyond this sort of implementation, such as by changing the firm's culture, training boundary-spanning personnel, or developing new marketing channels, is harder and more risky to achieve.

### Building Relationships

As Table 7.1 summarizes, several RM factors affect relationships and relational equity.[25] *Unfairness* and conflict have the greatest impacts; they hurt all aspects of relationship quality. The recognition

**Table 7.1** Highest Impact Relationship Marketing Activities

| Relationship Activity | Definitions | Correlation Coefficient between Activity and Relationship Quality |
|---|---|---|
| Conflict | Overall level of disagreement between exchange partners | −0.67 |
| Seller expertise | Knowledge, experience, and overall competency of seller | 0.62 |
| Communication | Amount, frequency, and quality of information shared between exchange partners | 0.54 |
| Relationship investments | Seller's investment of time, effort, spending, and resources focused on building a stronger relationship | 0.46 |
| Similarity | Commonality in appearance, lifestyle, and status between individual boundary spanners or similar cultures, values, and goals between buying and selling organizations | 0.44 |
| Relationship benefits | Benefits received, including time saving, convenience, companionship, and improved decision making | 0.42 |
| Dependence on seller | Customer's evaluation of the value of seller-provided resources, for which few alternatives are available from other sellers | 0.26 |
| Interaction frequency | Number of interactions or number of interactions per unit time between exchange partners | 0.16 |
| Relationship duration | Length of time the relationship between the exchange partners has existed | 0.13 |

*Note:* The results in this table are from a meta-analysis performed by Palmatier et al. (2006), which only evaluated relationship activities studied in previous research.

*Source:* Palmatier, R.W., Dant, R.P., Grewal, D. and Evans, K.R. (2006) 'Factors influencing the effectiveness of relationship marketing: A meta-analysis,' *Journal of Marketing*, 70(4), pp. 136–53.

that the strongest effect is a negative one is insightful, in that people pay more attention to the bad than the good, and even strong relationships can suffer lasting damage. Partners must resolve problems and disagreements to prevent their potentially corrosive, relationship-damaging effects.

Among the positive influences, when a customer perceives that a seller is knowledgeable or credible – such that it possesses **seller expertise** – information from this seller seems reliable, valuable, and persuasive. The more valuable information, provided by the competent seller, makes the exchange relationship more important to the customer, who in turn seeks to help strengthen and maintain it. Accordingly, firms must train their boundary-spanning employees well. Inexperienced or unskilled employees can have seriously detrimental impacts.

Another positive effect results from **communication**, or the amount, frequency, and quality of information shared by exchange partners.[26] Bilateral communication builds relationships, helps resolve disputes, aligns goals and expectations, and uncovers new value opportunities. With clear, informative communication, both parties gain confidence in promises; the identification of new value-creating opportunities also increases commitment. Thus, communication indicates a significant positive effect on all relationship aspects.

**Relationship investments** represent the time, resource, and effort investments – such as preferential treatment, gifts, or loyalty programs – that improve relationships. The relationships then are marked by efficiency, convenience, companionship, and good decision making. When relationship investments are irrecoverable, they also create psychological bonds and reciprocity expectations.[27] In turn, the benefits of these investments lead customers to perceive more relationship value, welcome relationship-building efforts, and invest their own resources in the strong relationship.

..............................................................................................................

When John Lewis, a department store chain in the UK, noticed that 75% of the company's online traffic came from mobile devices, the company invested heavily in mobile marketing (e.g., Click and Collect system). The increased customer engagement through this channel generated significant increases in profits and customer interactions.[28]

When the parties share common cultures, values, and goals, their similarity tends to indicate that they will work toward mutual goal achievement, which should strengthen the exchange relationship. Uncertainty also declines when similar partners share common perspectives. The resulting confidence, at both interpersonal and interorganizational levels, enhances relationship equity.[29] For example, in a sales context, domain knowledge similarity between the customer and sales reps helps improve sales outcomes by smoothing the relationship development process. Knowledge transfer and exchange is easier among similar individuals or organizations due to the common background language that they share.

Finally, three antecedents – dependence on seller, interaction frequency, and relationship duration – have smaller effects. Common strategies, such as those designed to lock in customers, increase switching costs, or increase customer dependence, appear less effective. In some cases, they even might disrupt customer relationships. Still, dependence has a positive effect on commitment, because customers work to maintain relationships with sellers on which they depend. Relationship duration, the length of the relationship between exchange partners, and interaction frequency, the number of interactions per of unit of time between exchange partners, offer weaker strategies, in that they only work through familiarity, habit, and convenience.

The different RM strategies thus demonstrate widely varying effectiveness. Overall, however, the most effective strategies minimize conflict; improve seller expertise, bilateral communication, and relationship investments and benefits; and match the boundary spanner's and organization's characteristics to targeted customers. Although generating customer relationship benefits and investing in customer relationships strengthen most aspects, increasing customer dependence and interaction frequency or just maintaining the relationship over time are only minimally effective RM strategies.

## Maintaining Relationships

A negative event can overwhelm an accumulation of positive activities. Long-term RM success thus often depends more on preventing the bad than on promoting the good. Negative activities generally have approximately twice as strong an effect as positive activities, but not all negative events are the same. Perceived *unfairness* or *betrayal* is probably the most potent relationship poison,[30] with direct and powerful negative effects, such as undermining customer cooperation, flexibility, and performance. It also aggravates the negative effects of more conventional activities, such as daily conflict, disagreements, or opportunism. A party that invests heavily in the relationship, only to have the partner free-ride or cheat, seeks to punish this failure to reciprocate. Perceptions of unfairness thus lead directly to emotional, punitive, and retaliatory behaviors. For example, customers often leave only after some perceived unfairness pushes them to expend the substantial effort and cost required to switch to another brand.

Unfortunately, companies seemingly welcome the toxic poisons, by engaging in actions that generate and even encourage perceptions of unfairness. When customers believe that their ratio of benefits to costs is worse than others', they feel compelled to restore the balance, often by punishing the company. Yet, loyalty programs seek to create just such imbalanced ratios. Bystanders – the customers not targeted by the program – despise the unfair treatment they receive. In an airline study, for example, bystanders' perceptions of unfairness when they watched other customers receive priority boarding were so high that they harmed their loyalty and annual sales intentions ten times as much as these tactics improved customers targeted for these programs.[31] Arguably, that outcome might be fine from a financial perspective, especially if loyalty programs truly target the firm's most valuable customers, namely, the ones who account for the majority of its sales. Yet, unfair treatment during initial interactions likely prevents any relationship from developing, even if the prospective customer might turn out to be highly valuable.

When managers recognize unfairness as a relationship poison, they should find the antidote by revising their RM and loyalty programs to make the benefits for targeted customers invisible to bystanders. If that is impossible, they need to issue clear, constant, and comprehensive explanations for why certain customers receive different treatment. They also need to seem legitimate to customers. For example, contracts between sellers and customers might be legally viable but still unfair, so firms that cite contracts likely suffer retaliation from customers who find any chance to "get even." It is difficult, if not impossible, to build a strong customer relationship solely on the foundation of a contract, as many cell phone and cable providers have come to learn.

> It is difficult, if not impossible, to build a strong customer relationship solely on the foundation of a contract, as many cell phone and cable providers have come to learn.

**Example:**  United Airlines (US)

United Airlines learned the lesson too. It cited its contractual policies when it refused to spend $1,200 to repair a passenger's guitar that its baggage handlers had carelessly broken. That is, the passenger received word that he was ineligible for compensation because he failed to make the claim within United's stipulated 24-hour timeframe. The passenger vented his frustration by creating a song entitled "United Breaks Guitars" and uploaded it on YouTube. As of 2014, it garnered almost 14 million views and is estimated to have cost United Airlines $180 million.[32]

In addition, constant communications about preferable treatment could have the unfortunate effect of suppressing gratitude among target customers, by eliminating the pleasurable element of surprise. A study designed to evaluate airline rewards (e.g., priority boarding, priority check-in, reduced baggage fees) found that among targets, gratitude accounts for about 60% of the incremental lift in annual sales, but for bystanders, unfairness accounts for about 70% of the incremental *sales drop*. Bad is stronger than good, so firms need to think about building positive sentiment through RM programs but also mitigating any negative sentiment from RM programs that cause perceptions of unfair treatment.

Ultimately, preemptive approaches might be the best antidote. Through training initiatives, firms might help boundary spanners identify situations likely to generate unfairness perceptions and learn strategies to address the perceptions immediately. Overall, maintaining relationships requires preventing bad events (e.g., unfairness, unresolved conflict) while also persisting at least at a base level of positive RM efforts (e.g., communication, investing in the relationship).

## Targeting and Adapting Relationship Marketing Strategies

Various causal drivers thus are responsible for RM effectiveness and building relationship equity; however, their effects also depend on environmental or contextual factors. For example, seller expertise might be a strong positive antecedent to relational equity in general, but its influence also depends on whether customers are rebuying a commodity product (e.g., gasoline), in which case they have little interest in expertise, or investing in a highly technical, unfamiliar product (e.g., HDTV), in which case they likely find this RM activity very valuable. Understanding these contingencies can help managers target customers with specific, appropriate, adapted activities and strategies that optimize the returns on their RM investments.

### Factors that Affect Customers' Desire for Relationships

Relationship marketing is not effective for all customers. Some customers simply seek to avoid relationships. In line with MP#1, customers differ, so sellers must address this heterogeneity to determine how to allocate RM resources across customer portfolios. Relationship marketing should succeed best among customers that require a relational governance structure to address their uncertainty or dependence, that cannot predict or address their challenges in advance, or that lack other governance or institutional protections.[33] When contextual factors increase a customer's **relationship orientation**, or desire to engage in a strong relationship, they also increase its receptivity to relationship building, prompting more effective RM.

In contrast, RM with customers without a strong relationship orientation imposes costs without parallel benefits. The customer incurs costs, such as the opportunity costs associated with communicating with the seller and participating in the RM programs. Imagine a customer who contacts a seller's call center to obtain a product sample but then must endure an extended follow-up visit from a salesperson full of queries, small talk, and relationship-building entreaties. Furthermore, RM demands some inter-personal reciprocity, which may make the customer feel personally indebted and uncomfortable.

Optimal RM effectiveness means that the level of RM activities matches the customer's relationship orientation.[34] Some determinants of a customer's relationship orientation include:

- **Relationship proneness**: the basic tendency of an individual to engage in relationships. This stable, individual difference variable implies that a relationally prone customer experiences a higher relationship orientation toward sellers.
- **Exchange and product uncertainty**: captures volatility, monitoring difficulty, and the speed of technological changes. Greater uncertainty increases the need for adaptability, as is likely for exchange partners with strong relationships.
- **Product category involvement/dependence**: reflects the importance of and customer need for a particular product category, due to personal-, firm-, or role-related needs, values, and interests, which increase an entity's relationship orientation.
- **Relational norms**: vary across exchange contexts but broadly reflect the value placed on customer–seller relationships in an industry or shopping context. Each context has some "bandwidth of working relationships" that "reflects the explicit or implicit relationship strategies."[35] Strong relationship norms enhance an individual's or firm's relationship orientation.
- **Relationship-centric reward systems**: encourage strong customer–seller relationships through evaluation systems, compensation programs, and policies. If a business buyer's rewards depend mostly on price reductions, multiple sourcing, or the number of transactions, the buyer embraces a transaction orientation. If a buyer receives relationship-focused incentives, it should exhibit a higher relational orientation.
- **Services**: are less tangible and consistent but more perishable than products, such that they demand more customer and boundary spanner involvement. Stronger relationships between customers and sellers appear more critical for services than for products. Because evaluations of service offerings tend to be ambiguous, service intangibility also may make the benefits of relational trust more critical.
- **Business-to-business markets**: feature greater complexity, such that they require adaption and strong relational governance structures. Thus, RM is more effective in B2B than in B2C markets. One sales force management text estimates that B2B firms spend close to $800 billion annually on sales forces, and yet: "Usually working alone and unsupervised, salespeople are entrusted with a company's most important asset: its relationship with its customers. Often salespeople have considerable control over this relationship; to some customers, the salesperson is the company" (p. 521).[36]
- **Emerging markets**: with their fewer institutional protections to business exchange make RM more effective than in developed markets. Customer relationships exert a 55% greater effect on performance in the BRIC countries (Brazil, Russia, India, and China) than in the US, for example.[37]

## Aligning Relationship Marketing Strategies with Customers' Relationship Orientation

Costly RM efforts can undermine performance. However, aligning RM efforts with the customer's relationship orientation helps balance the flexibility, monitoring, and safeguarding benefits against the added costs that the customer incurs to build and maintain those relationships. For customers with a higher relationship orientation, RM leads them to perceive the exchange as efficient, which improves relational equity and thus seller performance. But according to one study, customers with a low relationship orientation would shift 21% of their business to another supplier that offered completely automated transactions (i.e., no salesperson).[38] Thus, understanding each customer's relationship orientation is particularly critical in response to cost-reducing and productivity-enhancing efforts that minimize the time business customers have available to meet with sellers, even as sellers increase their relationship-building efforts.

> According to one study, customers with a low relationship orientation would shift 21% of their business to another supplier that offered completely automated transactions (i.e., no salesperson).

Organizational policies and procedures that promote relationship building, such as compensation systems that incentivize salespeople to engage indiscriminately in intensive relationship building, will likely alienate customers, especially those with a low relationship orientation. A portfolio of customers distributed across a relationship orientation spectrum demands targeted approaches. A unilateral emphasis on RM will create unnecessary expenses and misalignments with the relational governance preferences of many customers.

### Factors that Leverage Relationship Marketing Delivery Effectiveness

The effects of RM programs also depend on their delivery, which largely determines the inferences that customers make about the seller. For example, if customers believe the seller has more or less free will in offering RM benefits, or does so sincerely or opportunistically, they likely develop different feelings of gratitude. These feelings, in turn, affect their short-term customer behavior in response to RM activities. For example, if the seller offers the RM benefit of its own accord, it is exhibiting **free will** rather than contractual or mandated behavior, such as by giving an unexpected gift or performing a random act of kindness. An RM investment likely takes on new meaning if it is not part of a formal RM program. Thus, higher levels of gratitude result from RM investments when the customer perceives the investments as acts of free will rather than contractual fulfillments or duties.[39]

People also consider other parties' **motives**, defined as the desire or need that incites their action. Customer inferences about motives play key roles in their perceptions of sellers' actions, such that they experience gratitude when the favor implies benevolent intentions rather than an ulterior, marketing motive. Because relationships often begin with some investment (e.g., time, effort), in a noncontractual context, the person who initiates the investment generally suffers some **risk**, due to the subjective possibility that the investment fails to prompt reciprocated behavior. Higher perceived risk generally induces higher levels of gratitude though. Most people appreciate a gift, especially if it has value; value and appreciation also increase if the gift is necessary. That is, **need** is a condition in which a person requires or desires something, so if a need exists, the relevant situation invokes higher value. When a recipient obtains a needed item, or one that creates more risk for the partner, the recipient's gratitude should increase.[40]

## Relationship Dynamics and Lifecycle Stages

Relationships operate according to a lifecycle process, during which they develop, shift, and ultimately dissolve, according to the path-dependent stages in Figure 7.3.[41] Most relationships begin with an **exploratory or early stage**, featuring limited confidence in the partner's ability and trustworthiness but also a willingness to explore the relationship to determine if the potential benefits exceed those

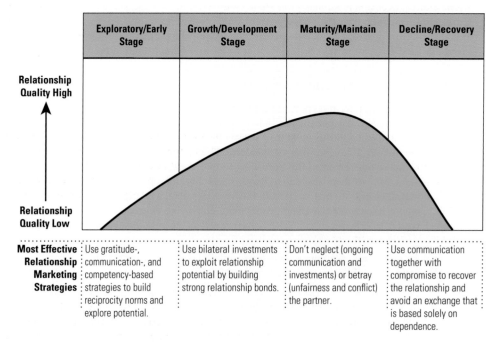

**Figure 7.3** Customer Relationship Lifecycle

available from alternative options. During early communications, the parties realize synergistic norms and goals through reciprocated transactions. If the initial experiences are positive and produce the desired outcomes, as well as evidence of trustworthiness, relationships move into the **growth or developing stage**. The escalation of reciprocated transactions and increased affective attachment produce trust, commitment, and satisfaction.

If the relationship continues, the partners continue to obtain benefits and greater interdependence, such that they reach the **maturity or maintaining stage**. Their calculative trust gets replaced by knowledge- and affective-based trust, communication, and other relational norms that reinforce their common goals. Both firms view their partner's behaviors as predictable, and mutual investments occur. In combination, these factors increase the partners' willingness to make long-term commitments to and investments in the relationship. They expect continued interactions. However, even successful relationships can enter a **decline or recovery stage** in response to specific events (conflict, unfairness, betrayal) or passive neglect (failure to communicate, ending investments)

Across the different relationship stages detailed in Figure 7.3, RM strategies should be adapted as follows:

- **Early**: Use gratitude-, communication-, and competency-based strategies to build reciprocity norms and explore potential.
- **Growth**: Use bilateral investments to exploit relationship potential, although the window for investments is small. For example, Cricket Australia and the Channel Nine broadcasting system regularly team up for mutual gains: Cricket Australia assigns Channel Nine exclusive TV rights to its national and international cricket tournaments, and Channel Nine agrees to invest in the latest digital technology to provide more engaging and incisive cricket telecasts for fans.
- **Maintain**: Don't neglect (ongoing communication and investments) or betray (unfairness and conflict) customers. Flipkart, India's fastest growing online retail startup, invests significantly in technology to ensure that every customer who returns a product is issued a full refund within 30 days, knowing the importance of being perceived as a fair retailer among consumers.
- **Recovery**: Use communication together with compromise to rebuild relationships and avoid exchanges based solely on dependence. As important venues for firms to receive feedback, review websites allow consumers to express their opinions and provide product ratings, but their reviews often highlight product failure experiences. This negative feedback can damage firms' reputations and adversely affect their performance; therefore, many hotels (e.g., The Ritz London) respond publicly and immediately to consumers' online complaints on Tripadvisor.com to avoid any damage to their image, especially among prospective consumers who use the websites to obtain prepurchase information.

## Managing Relationship-based Sustainable Competitive Advantage

### Building Relationship Equity

The process of building relationship equity consists of two main steps. First, a firm needs to develop a strong foundation that supports relationship building and maintenance. Primarily, it must organize, hire, train, and build systems for employees that support positive relational interfaces with customers. In addition, the firm needs to establish and institute fundamental processes conducive to positive relational exchanges. Second, with this foundation, the firm can begin to implement relationship marketing and loyalty programs targeted at specific customer groups, designed to generate specific relational outcomes across the firm's customer portfolio. Some academic research detailing best practices in this effort is summarized in Table 7.2.

#### Step 1: Developing a Strong Relationship Foundation

Unfairness and unresolved conflict can undo years and fortunes spent on relationship building. In many cases, it is counterproductive to increase RM budgets without a well-designed process for dealing with customer problems, service failures, or trust violations. Sellers must design customer conflict resolution within the framework of their overall RM activities, such as creating a culture that emphasizes the importance of resolving problems, supported by formal systems for correcting

**Table 7.2** Relationship Marketing Best Practices

| How to Build and Maintain Strong Customer Relationships |
|---|
| • Assign customers a dedicated contact person, even if customers interface through multiple channels (e.g., call center, online) |
| • Conduct RM audits to verify that the seller's organizational elements (RM strategy, leadership, culture, structures, and control) and business processes are aligned with RM objectives |
| • Do not let conflict go unresolved, because it will overwhelm other relationship-building efforts |
| • Focus the largest portion of RM investments on selecting, training, and motivating boundary-spanning employees, who represent the most effective means to build and maintain relationships |
| • Institute RM programs focused on increasing the amount, frequency, and quality of communication with customers, especially early in the relationship lifecycle, because communication is a strong driver of relationship quality and future relationship growth |
| • Minimize the proactive use of financial RM programs (e.g., price rebates, points programs) for relationship building; rather consider these programs as price/volume discounts or competitive responses |
| • Measure multiple aspects of relational assets (relationship quality, breadth, composition, and growth/velocity) on an ongoing basis |
| • Allocate RM investments dedicated to specific programs primarily to social and structural programs |
| **How to Target and Adapt Relationship Marketing** |
| • Give customers an opportunity to reciprocate soon after receiving an RM benefit (not quid pro quo), which takes advantage of high levels of gratitude, prevents guilt rationalization, and leads to a relationship marked by reciprocity |
| • Leverage RM investments by providing the benefit when the customer's need is the highest and the benefit provides the most value |
| • Leverage RM investments by designing programs to increase customers' perceptions of seller's free will, benevolence, risk, and cost in providing the RM benefit (leave some random or discretionary element to programs) |
| • The effectiveness of RM can be enhanced by actively targeting investments toward customers with high relationship orientation (need and desire for a relationship) |

*Source:* Adapted from Palmatier, R.W. (2008) *Relationship Marketing.* Cambridge, MA: Marketing Science Institute.

customer issues. That is, the culture of the selling firm is important, and all elements, from hiring and training salespeople to compensation and support systems, must encourage the seller's representatives to pursue and maintain good relationships with customers.

Unfairness and unresolved conflict can undo years and fortunes spent on relationship building. In many cases, it is counterproductive to increase RM budgets without a well-designed process for dealing with customer problems, service failures, or trust violations.

These individual, boundary-spanning personnel with whom customers interact usually are the most critical means to create and maintain strong customer relationships, so firms also should empower boundary spanners to resolve issues immediately. At Ritz-Carlton hotels, for example, employees may spend up to $1,000 solving customer issues on their own, without any approval. The interpersonal relationships of customers with boundary spanners affect customer behaviors more than their relationships with the selling firm.[42] To take advantage of this strong impact of interpersonal relationships, sellers should assign a dedicated contact person to customers, especially in B2C settings; if the customer calls and the dedicated contact person is not available, other employees can acknowledge that they are filling in and give the customer the option to wait until the contact person is available, leave a message, or agree to let the substitute handle a critical issue. Similar tactics even might be implemented in call centers.

Inbound calls rarely get handled by a specific rep, but Vanguard, a mutual fund company, assigns all "flagship customers" a dedicated representative and phone number. Outgoing calls, direct mail, and upselling or cross-selling efforts always should come from the contact person. Even web-based interfaces can reference this dedicated staffer (e.g., with a picture) or offer an option to email the contact person.

Because so many drivers of customer relationships revolve around boundary spanners, sellers need to dedicate their RM investments to selecting, training, and motivating boundary-spanning employees. Expensive advertising and rebate programs likely will be wasted if the customers' interactions with contact employees are poor – especially if the firms sell exclusive, luxury, technical, or complex products and services. Whether the seller is Flipkart or the Ritz, strong RM firms expend significant effort to ensure the effectiveness of their boundary-spanning personnel.

Increasing the amount, frequency, and quality of communication with customers also can be effective, especially when the communication comes through parallel channels. Early in the relationship lifecycle, communication drives relationship quality and growth, with multiple dividends. In addition to this immediate impact, communication can improve relationship quality over time, such as by unveiling new cooperative value creation ideas or preventing ugly conflict or service failures.

However, regardless of the extensiveness of such external communication, a poor alignment of internal, organizational elements (e.g., corporate leadership, strategy, culture, control) with RM can undermine any effort to build customer relationships. If internal control systems discourage salespeople or boundary spanners from developing relationships with customers, for example, they can have far-reaching and detrimental effects. Sellers thus should conduct internal RM audits and design flexible RM policies and programs, such that their appropriately motivated boundary spanners recognize their ability to adapt their RM activities to their customers' specific relationship orientations.

### Step 2: Implementing Targeted Relationship Marketing and Loyalty Programs

Different RM programs build different forms of relational ties that generate varying returns from different types of customers.[43] Relationship marketing investments in specific programs should be allocated primarily to social and structural, rather than financial, programs.

**Social RM programs** use social engagements like meals and sporting events to convey the customer's special status.

**Example:** Telstra (Australia)

Telstra, Australia's telecoms giant, launched a loyalty program called "Thanks" that rewards its customers with movie tickets and access to live music and sporting events. Mark Buckman, the chief marketing officer of Telstra, indicated that: "We want our customers to turn into advocates for our business. They stay longer with you, they spend more money with you and they recommend you to friends and family." The program was launched to recognize the relationship Telstra has with its customers, while enhancing the commitment to the brand.[44]

The difficult-to-duplicate bonds that result from such special treatment often prompt customers to reciprocate, with repeat sales, recommendations, or ignoring competitive offers. The financial returns of social RM investments have direct, significant impacts on profit – greater than those of other RM investment types and reaching return on investment (ROI) values of approximately 180%.[45] Yet, social programs also lead customers to build relationships with the salesperson rather than the selling firm, so they could defect if the salesperson turns over or leaves the firm. This cautionary note suggests that multiple members of the firm should maintain at least some communications with customers. Still, perhaps because of the interpersonal nature of their delivery (i.e., salespeople allocate their available resources in real time at their own discretion), a social program's effects appear largely immune to contextual factors.

**Structural RM programs** provide investments that customers might not make themselves, such as in electronic order processing interfaces or customized packaging. They generally increase the customer's efficiency, convenience, or productivity, creating a hard-to-quantify but substantial customer benefit. With their considerable setup costs and benefits, the existence of these programs binds customers and sellers closely. The competitive advantages resulting from these structural bonds occur because customers increase their business with the seller to take full advantage of their value-enhancing offerings. With regard to profit, the influence of structural RM investments depends on interaction frequency. If customers show an average interaction frequency (a few times per week), short-term returns break even. If they engage in frequent interactions, the ROI for structural RM is about 120%.[46] To leverage structural relationship investments, sellers should focus on customers who can get the most value from customized structural solutions and who participate in relatively more frequent interactions. Many firms are partnering to expand the benefits their customers receive from their loyalty and rewards programs. These structural changes to loyalty programs can generate long-term benefits for customers from both firms.

**Example:** Your World Rewards (UAE & US)

Emirates Airline and Starwood Hotels & Resorts Worldwide, Inc. formed a partnership, Your World Rewards, to provide reciprocal benefits to Emirates Skywards and Starwood Preferred Guest (SPG) customers. The combined program allows Skywards and SPG elite members to gain points and rewards when they fly with Emirates or stay with Starwood. Platinum members of both programs can receive the highest level of rewards or exclusive benefits such as elite check-in, complimentary in-room Internet access, and priority check-in. Thierry Antinori, executive vice president and chief commercial officer of Emirates Airline, reports that: "The combination of Emirates' growing global network, Starwood's innovative take on hospitality and our top-rated loyalty programs allow us to recognize our most valuable customers with a heightened level of service and greater rewards wherever they travel – be it to one of our more than 140 destinations or at any of Starwood's 1,200 hotels."[47]

**Financial RM programs** provide economic benefits, in the form of special discounts, giveaways, free shipping, or extended payment terms that ultimately tend to offer little relative advantage, because competitors can easily match them. Customers attracted by incentives also tend to seek out deals and are less profitable to serve. This is not to discount the benefits and returns that financial programs can provide in some situations. Rather, they cannot be the only type of program used to build relationships. Instead, tactics such as price reductions or rebates should represent price or volume discounts or responses to competitors' moves.[48] It is extremely easy to misallocate financial RM programs too; a customer service employee can simply hand out a financial incentive (e.g., free sample, special discount).

Overall, targeting RM programs toward customers with high relationship orientations will make them more effective. For customers who do not desire strong relationships or who perceive RM activities as a waste of time, unwanted hassle, or extra cost, improper targeting could lead them to shift to transaction-oriented sellers. For example, many firms understandably allocate their RM resources to their biggest customers or those with the most potential, but this criterion ignores the customer's viewpoint.

Instead, sellers need to leverage their RM investments by designing and delivering programs that increase their customers' perceptions of the seller's free will, benevolence, risk, and cost. Those percep-tions should invoke gratitude for the RM benefit received. In contrast, RM benefits that everyone receives, that come in response to a request, that match a competitor's offer, or that constitute part of the overall product or service offering generate less gratitude and thus little need to reciprocate. Ideally, all programs would retain some random or discretionary elements, rather than devolving into totally structured, quid pro quo programs that do little to promote relationships (e.g., airline loyalty points programs). Sellers instead can generate higher returns by carefully structuring and designing the delivery of their programs.

The next step, beyond inducing gratitude, is getting customers to act on these feelings in ways that produce the most benefits. For example, sellers should create opportunities for customers to recipro-cate but avoid any sense of demanding quid pro quo. These opportunities not only allow the seller to leverage the customer's gratitude but also prevent guilt rationalization and encourage more reciprocity norms. A feeling of gratefulness toward a seller can, in the worst-case scenario, generate feelings of guilt, which customers try to relieve by rationalizing their failure to reciprocate (e.g., assigning a nega-tive motive to the seller). Gratefulness also decays over time. Therefore, an airline might be better off if it contacts frequent fliers with offers for discounts on upgrades if they book a certain number of flights within the next six months, for example. This offer grants each flier a ready opportunity to act on feel-ings of gratitude and should create reciprocity norms in their relationship. This recommendation is especially notable in the context of research that shows that people often reciprocate far in excess of the value received and even then continue to feel grateful.

Finally, RM investments should be targeted and adapted according to the relationship stage. They can concentrate on early growth stages, when customers are more receptive to relationship building and competitive rivalry may be lower. Later on, as the relationship matures, existing structures, links, and communication processes should represent competitive barriers and support SCA. In the maintenance stage, RM investments can be reduced, to match customers' needs. Sellers also might explore opportunities to expand the relationship, with new products or services, to shift the customer back onto a growth trajectory.

## Measuring Relationship Equity

A central measure of the effectiveness of RM efforts is relationship equity, which should be assessed on an ongoing basis to support learning and refinement over time (similar to brand equity). Relevant measures would acknowledge the multidimensional aspect of customer relationships. In interfirm relationships, sellers need to capture the breadth (number of contacts) and composition (authority and diversity) of their customer contact portfolio and focus on any weaknesses. If a customer satisfaction survey only includes one informant who reports on relationship quality, the results likely will be misleading, because this single measure cannot reveal the varied, different relational ties that might bind the two firms, or whether existing contacts influence key decisions by the customer firm. Lifecycle stage measures, together with measures of the direction and rate of growth of the relationship (i.e., relational velocity), might provide a better leading indicator of the relationship's future, because customers in stagnant or mature relationships probably require new RM tactics. If a customer no longer requires a relationship, the seller should move it to a more transactional interface or else find a way to reinvigorate the exchange with new offerings. Some fundamental characteristics of business relationships, which also reflect the measures required to capture relationship equity, are summarized in Table 7.3.

**Table 7.3** Key Relationship Dimensions and Example Measures

| Constructs | Definitions | Representative Measurement Items |
|---|---|---|
| **Relationship Quality** | | |
| Commitment | An enduring desire to maintain a valued relationship | I am [My firm is] willing "to go the extra mile" to work with this salesperson [selling firm]. I feel [My firm feels] committed to the relationship with this salesperson [selling firm]. I [My firm] would work hard to maintain my [our] relationship with this salesperson [selling firm]. |
| Trust | Confidence in an exchange partner's reliability and integrity | This salesperson [selling firm] gives me a feeling [us feelings] of trust. This salesperson [selling firm] is always honest. This salesperson [selling firm] is trustworthy. |
| Gratitude | Feelings of gratefulness, thankfulness, or appreciation toward an exchange partner for benefits received | I feel [My firm feels] grateful to this salesperson [selling firm]. I feel [My firm feels] thankful to this salesperson [selling firm]. I feel [My firm feels] obligated to this salesperson [selling firm]. |
| Reciprocity norms | Internalized patterns of behaviors and feelings that regulate the balance of obligations between two exchange partners | I [My firm] would help this salesperson [selling firm] if there was a need or problem in the future. In the long term the benefits this salesperson [selling firm] and I [my firm] receive from each other will balance out. Buying from this salesperson [selling firm] makes me [us] feel good. I [My firm] would expect this salesperson [selling firm] to help me [us] in the future. |

*(Continued)*

**Table 7.3** (*Continued*)

| Constructs | Definitions | Representative Measurement Items |
|---|---|---|
| **Interfirm Relationships** | | |
| Relationship breadth | Number of relational ties with an exchange partner | How many different relationship ties are there among employees at [selling firm] and your firm? (number) |
| Relationship composition | Decision-making capability of the relational contacts at an exchange partner | [Selling firm] knows the key decision makers at our firm. [Selling firm] has relationships with the important gatekeepers at our firm. [Selling firm] deals with the important decision makers in our company. [Selling firm] has contacts with what percent of the key decision makers at your firm? (percentage) [Selling firm] has contacts in how many different functional departments in your firm? (number) |
| **Other Measures** | | |
| Relationship orientation | Customers' desire to engage in a strong relationship with a partner to conduct an exchange | This business transaction requires a close relationship between me and [selling firm] to ensure its success. A close relationship with [selling firm] is important to my success. A strong relationship with [selling firm] would be very helpful in buying this product. I **don't** need a close relationship with [selling firm] to successfully buy this product. (Reverse) I believe that a strong relationship with [selling firm] is needed to successfully buy this product. |
| Lifecycle stage | Qualitative path-dependent phases through which a relationship transitions. Relationships typically expand during the exploration and buildup stages, peak and remain relatively flat during the maturity stage, and weaken during the decline stage | *Exploration:* You both are in the very early stage of discovering and evaluating compatibility, integrity, and performance of the other party. *Buildup:* You both are receiving increasing benefits from the relationship, and the level of trust and satisfaction is growing in such a way that you are increasingly willing to commit to a long-term relationship. *Maturity:* You both have an ongoing, long-term relationship in which both parties receive acceptable levels of satisfaction and benefits from the relationship. *Decline:* One or both of you have begun to experience dissatisfaction and are evaluating alternatives, contemplating relationship termination, or beginning to end the relationship. |

*Source:* Adapted from Palmatier, R.W. (2008) *Relationship Marketing*. Cambridge, MA: Marketing Science Institute.

A central measure of the effectiveness of RM efforts is relational equity, which should be assessed on an ongoing basis to support learning and refinement over time (similar to brand equity).

An effective measure of relational equity requires a clear definition of the target of that measure. A request that the customer report on the quality of their relationship with the seller must specify, for example, whether the relationship target is the selling firm, an aggregate entity, the primary sales contact, or a sales team. Leaving the target ambiguous will cause each measure to vary, depending on the degree to which it represents the individual- or firm-level relationship. Individual-level relationships are less stable over time (e.g., due to job changes) but typically have greater impacts on customer behavior and financial outcomes.

If RM efforts inherently result in longer relationships, then it may seem that duration should be a good proxy for relationship strength or equity. However, this measure is not very effective. In research into the impact of relationship duration on customer profitability, long-term customers reasonably constitute most of the firm's profits, but short-term customers are important too; they capture nearly 30% of the firm's profits.[49] A different study indicates that long-term customers (more than six years) offer higher sales growth, inventory turnover, and returns on invested capital, but they also account for lower gross margins.[50] In most cases, relationship duration, especially after the first year, fails to increase customer profits or prices, so it is a poor proxy for relationship equity.

Another approach links RM programs and relationship equity measures to customer lifetime value (recall the CLV Data Analytics Technique 3.2), to isolate what portion of the CLV results from relationship equity or specific RM programs.[51] Data Analytics Technique 7.1 describes how multivariate regression can facilitate this approach, because it can link many different variables or drivers (i.e., independent variables) to an outcome variable of interest (i.e., dependent variables, or CLV in this example) and then discover which independent variables significantly affect the outcome and by how much.

Although this CLV approach is helpful, in that it integrates multiple financial outcomes into one measure and captures future financial benefits, it cannot capture some of the potential benefits of a strong relational bond, such as positive WOM that leads to new customer acquisition. Strong customer relationships also accrue knowledge-based benefits and insights, helping sellers identify new product opportunities, test and refine new product concepts, and accelerate the adoption of new product launches. Therefore, strong relationships likely influence sellers' financial performance in ways that financial metrics cannot reveal. Such effects are especially difficult to capture because they occur in a time and location that differs greatly from the site at which the customer's relational behaviors take place. For example, the seller might use critical information that a relational customer provides it to develop a proprietary new product. The profitable sales that the seller generates with different customers in different markets due to this product likely would accrue only many years in the future.

## Summary

*Relationship equity* reflects the relational assets and liabilities linked to boundary-spanning employees and social networks associated with an offering or experience that add to or subtract from the value provided by a firm's offering. Investments to build a firm's relationship equity by developing relationships with customers in turn represent strong barriers to competitors. The process of identifying, developing, maintaining, and terminating relational exchanges to enhance performance is *relationship marketing* (RM), and effective RM leads to relationship equity. Although RM and branding activities both seek to build intangible customer equity and enhance customer loyalty, purchase behaviors, or financial performance while reducing marketing costs, they differ. Branding focuses on product(s), with extensions to the firm; RM primarily focuses on relationship(s) and their extensions to the firm.

The impact of relationships on human behavior is a frequent topic for research in various domains, granting marketing a rich theoretical landscape to draw from in understanding RM. For example, *social exchange theory* shows that commitment and trust are central to any relationship, and the psychological theory related to the emotion of gratitude, which leads to reciprocity desires, affirms the impact of RM. *Network theory* from sociology also provides insights into the impact of structural interaction characteristics in a network. A *network perspective* applied to interfirm relationships suggests that relationship quality, relationship breadth, and relationship composition influence exchange performance.

Furthermore, RM activities affect financial performance, although not directly. The link of relationships to financial performance operates through four mechanisms: increased cooperation, loyalty, referrals or word of mouth, and empathic behaviors.

The range of activities, rewards, and loyalty programs that make up RM strategies are all designed to build and maintain strong customer–seller relational bonds. In general, the most effective strategies minimize conflict; improve seller expertise, bilateral communication, relationship investments, and relationship benefits; and match boundary spanners and organizational characteristics with targeted customers. They need to do more than simply increase customer dependence and interaction

## Description

Multivariate regression is a statistical approach used to quantify the sign and magnitude of the relationship between a focal dependent variable (marketing outcome in our context) and several independent variables (e.g., marketing efforts).

## When to Use It

- To determine how one of multiple marketing interventions incrementally affects observed marketing outcomes.
- To compare the effects of multiple marketing interventions on marketing outcomes.
- To predict the likely market outcomes due to various combinations of marketing interventions.

## How It Works

The purpose of multivariate regression is to capture the statistical association between a focal marketing outcome of interest (e.g., sales, loyalty, CLV, profitability) and several marketing interventions that simultaneously may affect the focal outcome (e.g., RM efforts, marketing mix). Performing a multivariate regression enables five important discoveries:

1 We can discern whether a particular marketing intervention truly influences a marketing outcome. That is, multivariate regression can provide statistical validation of the significance of the impact of a certain marketing intervention.
2 We learn the sign of the relationship between a marketing intervention and a marketing outcome. In some cases, the sign is well known a priori (e.g., as the price increases, sales decrease), but in others, it remains unclear. For example, a firm may not know whether a financially oriented RM program offering free shipping ultimately increases CLV. The regression can help the firm verify the sign of the relationship.
3 Multivariate regression helps researchers compare the relative strength of multiple marketing interventions. For example, a firm may need to know which of its social, structural, or financial RM efforts are most and least influential, and this determination is enabled by a regression analysis.
4 With multivariate regression, we can control for confounds while gauging the relationship between marketing interventions and marketing outcomes. For example, while trying to understand the relationship between financial RM efforts by a supplier firm devoted to a buyer firm and marketing outcomes earned from this buyer firm, we might control for the buyer firm's size, because larger firms typically buy more, regardless of whether they receive marketing interventions.
5 Multivariate regression enables predictions of the marketing outcomes following from various scenarios of marketing interventions, which is useful in scenario analysis. If the marketing outcome is given by Y, and we have three marketing interventions (X1, X2, and X3), and two confounds (Z1 and Z2), the formula is given by

$$Y = \beta_1 x_1 + \beta_2 x_2 + \beta_3 x_3 + \beta_4 z_1 + \beta_5 z_2 + \varepsilon$$

where $\beta_1$ to $\beta_5$ are the coefficients (or weights) that capture the sign and strength of the relationship between the marketing interventions and the marketing outcome, and $\varepsilon$ is a random error term. In most cases, we would have data about past outcomes and marketing inventions/confounds, then rely on software such as SAS or SPSS to provide the sign, strength, and statistical significance of the coefficients.

A B2B supplier of electrical equipment is going through a redesign of its RM efforts directed at buyers, and it seeks to ensure that it is investing in RM efforts that boost the CLV of each of its buyers. Currently, the supplier is investing in three kinds of RM efforts: social (e.g., meals, sporting events), structural (e.g., customized packaging), and financial (e.g., free giveaways of small electrical parts that are part of the electrical installation service it provides).

To perform this exercise, the supplier created a database of the CLV of its 3,500 buyers, as well as its investments in social RM, structural RM, and financial RM for each of these buyers. It also collected data on the buyers' locations (east or west coast), the number of employees in the buyer firm, and the firm industry type (corporate or government). The results are given in the table.

| Variable | Coefficient Capturing Weight of Intervention | p-Value for Statistical Significance |
|---|---|---|
| Social RM Efforts | 1.26 | 0.03 |
| Structural RM Efforts | 0.20 | 0.89 |
| Financial RM Efforts | 2.50 | 0.01 |
| Buyer Firm Location (East Coast) | 0.80 | 0.02 |
| Buyer Firm Number of Employees | 1.10 | 0.03 |
| Buyer Firm Industry (Corporate) | 0.08 | 0.41 |

1 Social RM and financial RM efforts paid off, whereas structural RM efforts did not exert any statistically significant impact on buyer CLV (coefficient = 0.20, $p > .05$).
2 Financial RM and social RM efforts significantly increased CLV; financial RM efforts were twice as effective as social RM efforts, because the coefficient associated with financial RM (coefficient = 2.50, $p < .05$) was approximately twice as large as the coefficient associated with social RM (coefficient = 1.26, $p < .05$).
3 Firms on the East Coast were much more likely to buy compared with firms on the west coast (coefficient = 0.80, $p < .05$). Similarly, larger firms generally had a higher CLV than smaller firms (coefficient = 1.10, $p < .05$). Whether the buyer was a corporate or government buyer did not matter (coefficient = 0.08, $p > .05$).
4 The supplier used the coefficients obtained from this regression to predict the increase in the CLV when it instituted various financial and social RM combinations.

Based on the analysis, the supplier also launched another study, to understand why its structural RM efforts were not successful.

frequency or maintain the relationship over time. To be able to maintain relationships, sellers also need to prevent negative influences, such as those stemming from unfairness or unresolved conflict. These negative effects are powerful and can destroy all aspects of relationship quality.

The effectiveness with which RM can build relationship equity also varies with the context. A customer's relationship orientation increases its receptivity to relationship building efforts, leading to more effective RM. To optimize this RM effectiveness, sellers should match their RM activities to the level of the customer's relationship orientation.

Relationship equity builds through two main steps. First, develop a strong foundation that supports relationship building and maintenance across the firm by increasing the amount, frequency, and quality of communication with customers, especially early in the relationship lifecycle. Second, once the foundation exists, implement specific RM and loyalty programs targeted at specific customer groups. *Social RM programs* use social events to personalize the customer relationship and convey a buyer's special status. *Structural RM programs* facilitate investments that customers likely would not make themselves but that increase customer efficiency and productivity. *Financial RM programs* provide economic benefits, such as special discounts or free shipping, in exchange for customer loyalty. Regardless of their type, all RM programs ideally retain some surprise or discretionary elements, because structured quid pro quo programs get integrated into the overall value proposition and lose their ability to encourage relationships.

To understand the effectiveness of RM efforts, firms need to measure their relational equity on an ongoing basis. Effective measures first need to define the target, because failing to do so can cause each measure to vary, depending on the degree to which it represents an individual- or a firm-level relationship. Probably the most effective approach for understanding the key drivers to relationship equity is to link RM programs and relationship equity measures to customer lifetime value (CLV).

## Takeaways

- Relationship marketing's (RM) influence on decision making is supported by the underlying psychological emotion of gratitude, which leads to a desire to repay.

- The linkages between relationships and financial performance operate through four mechanisms, including increased cooperation, loyalty, word of mouth, and empathetic behaviors.

- The most effective RM strategies emphasize positive factors such as seller expertise, communication, relationship investment, and similarity, while minimizing negative factors such as unfairness and conflict.

- The effect of negative activities on relationships is twice as strong as positive activities; it is important to prevent negative events while continuing positive RM.

- Bystanders of loyalty programs often perceive their treatment as unfair; this is why loyalty program preferential treatment should be invisible to bystanders.

- To optimize RM effectiveness, sellers must match the level of RM activities to the customer's relationship orientation. Some of the factors that determine a customer's relationship orientation are relationship proneness, exchange and product uncertainty, product category involvement or dependence, relational norms, relation-centric reward systems, services, B2B markets, and emerging markets.

- Because RM is not effective for all customers, sellers must determine where to allocate RM resources across their customer portfolios.

- Factors that help leverage the effectiveness of RM delivery include free will, motive, risk, and value.

- Relationships operate through a typical lifecycle with four phases: exploration, growth, maturity, and decline/recovery. Each phase requires different RM strategies.

- There are two steps to building relationship equity: developing a strong relationship foundation and implementing targeted RM and loyalty programs.
- To understand the effectiveness of RM efforts, firms should measure their relational equity on an ongoing basis and link it to customer lifetime value.

# References

1 Sheth, J.N. and Parvatiyar, A. (1995) 'The evolution of relationship marketing' *International Business Review*, 4(4), pp. 397–418.

2 Columbus, L. (2013) 'Gartner predicts CRM will be a $36B market by 2017,' 18 June. Available at: www.forbes.com/sites/louiscolumbus/2013/06/18/gartner-predicts-crm-will-be-a-36b-market-by-2017/#617f75b0c1ec (accessed 8 October, 2015).

3 Palmatier, R.W. (2008) *Relationship Marketing*. Cambridge, MA: Marketing Science Institute (p. 3).

4 Rust, R.T., Lemon, K.N. and Zeithaml, V.A. (2004) 'Return on marketing: Using customer equity to focus marketing strategy,' *Journal of Marketing*, 68(1), pp. 109–27.

5 Palmatier, R.W., Dant, R.P., Grewal, D. and Evans, K.R. (2006) 'Factors influencing the effectiveness of relationship marketing: A meta-analysis,' *Journal of Marketing*, 70(4), pp. 136–53.

6 Brinder, C. and Hanssens, D.M. (2015) 'Why strong customer relationships trump powerful brands', 14 April. Available at: https://hbr.org/2015/04/why-strong-customer-relationships-trump-powerful-brands (accessed 9 August, 2016).

7 Frow, P. and Payne, A. (2005) 'A strategic framework for customer relationship management,' *Journal of Marketing*, 69(4), pp. 167–76.

8 Marlin, S. (2011) 'South African Bank installs CRM solution,' 16 November. Available at: www.banktech.com/data-and-analytics/south-african-bank-installs-crm-solution/d/d-id/1288616 (accessed 9 August, 2016).

9 Becker, H.S. (1986) *Doing Things Together: Selected Papers*. Evanston, IL: Northwestern University Press; Trivers, R.L. (1971) 'The evolution of reciprocal altruism,' *Quarterly Review of Biology*, 46(1), pp. 35–57; Trivers, R.L. (1985) *Social Evolution*. Menlo Park, CA: Benjamin/Cummings.

10 Cialdini, R.B. and Rhoads, K.V. (2001) 'Human behavior and the marketplace,' *Marketing Research*, 13(3), pp. 8–13; Dahl, D.W., Honea, H. and Manchanda, R.V. (2003) 'The nature of self-reported guilt in consumption contexts,' *Marketing Letters*, 14(3), pp. 159–71; Dahl, D.W., Honea, H. and Manchanda, R.V. (2005) 'Three Rs of interpersonal consumer guilt: Relationship, reciprocity, reparation,' *Journal of Consumer Psychology*, 15(4), pp. 307–15; Palmatier, R.W., Jarvis, C., Bechkoff, J. and Kardes, F.R. (2009) 'The role of customer gratitude in relationship marketing,' *Journal of Marketing*, 73(5), pp. 1–18; Palmatier, R.W., Scheer, L.K., Houston, M.B., Evans, K.R. and Gopalakrishna, S. (2007) 'Use of relationship marketing programs in building customer–salesperson and customer–firm relationships: Differential influences on financial outcomes,' *International Journal of Research in Marketing*, 24(3), pp. 210–23.

11 Palmatier, R.W., Stern, L.W. and El-Ansary, A.I. (2014) *Marketing Channel Strategy*, 8th edn. Upper Saddle River, NJ: Pearson Prentice Hall.

12 Morgan, R.M. and Hunt, S.D. (1994) 'The commitment-trust theory of relationship marketing,' *Journal of Marketing*, 58(3), pp. 20–38; Moorman, C., Zaltman, G. and Deshpande, R. (1992) 'Relationships between providers and users of market research: The dynamics of trust,' *Journal of Marketing Research*, 29(3), pp. 314–28.

13 Dormehl, L. (2014) 'How Corning won Apple back and built the strongest Gorilla Glass yet,' 26 November. Available from: www.cultofmac.com/304120/corning-gorilla-glass-4/ (accessed 25 August, 2016).

14 Emmons, R.A. and McCullough, M.E. (2004) *The Psychology of Gratitude*. Oxford: Oxford University Press; Gouldner, A.W. (1960) 'The norm of reciprocity: A preliminary statement,' *American Sociological Review*, 25(2), pp. 161–78; Ostrom, E. and Walker, J. (2003) 'Trust and reciprocity: Interdisciplinary lessons for experimental research,' *Contemporary Sociology*, 33(4), pp. 493–4.

15 Borgatti, S.P. and Foster, P.C. (2003) 'The network paradigm in organizational research: A review and typology,' *Journal of Supply Chain Management*, 45(2), pp. 5–22; Van den Bulte, C. and Wuyts, S.H.K. (2007) *Social Networks and Marketing*. Cambridge, MA: Marketing Science Institute.

16 Palmatier, R.W. (2008) 'Interfirm relational drivers of customer value,' *Journal of Marketing*, 72(4), pp. 76–89; Palmatier, R.W. (2008) *Relationship Marketing*. Cambridge, MA: Marketing Science Institute.

17 Crosby, L.A., Evans, K.R. and Cowles, D. (1990) 'Relationship quality in services selling: An interpersonal influence perspective,' *Journal of Marketing*, 48(1), pp. 68–81; Kumar, N., Scheer, L.K. and Steenkamp, J.B.E.M. (1995) 'Interdependence, punitive capability, and the reciprocation of punitive actions in channel relationships,' *Journal of Marketing Research*, 35(2), pp. 225–36.

18 Bendapudi, N. and Leone, R.P. (2002) 'Managing business-to-business customer relationships following key contact employee turnover in a vendor firm,' *Journal of Marketing*, 66(2), pp. 83–101.

19 Anderson, J.C. and Narus, J.A. (1990) 'A model of distributor firm and manufacturer firm working partnerships,' *Journal of Marketing*, 54(1), pp. 42–58; Palmatier, R.W., Dant, R.P., Grewal, D. and Evans, K.R. (2006) 'Factors influencing the

effectiveness of relationship marketing: A meta-analysis,' *Journal of Marketing*, 70(4), pp. 136–53.

20  Doney, P.M. and Cannon, J.P. (1997) 'An examination of the nature of trust in buyer-seller relationships,' *Journal of Marketing*, 61(2), pp. 35–51; Garbarino, E. and Johnson, M.S. (1999) 'The different roles of satisfaction, trust, and commitment in customer relationships,' *Journal of Marketing*, 63(2), pp. 70–87; Hewett, K., Money, R.B. and Sharma, S. (2002) 'An exploration of the moderating role of buyer corporate culture in industrial buyer-seller relationships,' *Journal of the Academy of Marketing Science*, 30(3), pp. 229–39; Macintosh, G. and Lockshin, L.S. (1997) 'Retail relationships and store loyalty: A multi-level perspective,' *International Journal of Research in Marketing*, 14(5), pp. 487–97.

21  Eplison (2016) 'Epsilon's loyalty report highlights emerging Chinese consumer behaviors across sectors.' Available at: http://pressroom.epsilon.com/epsilon-study-finds-chinese-consumers-most-loyal-to-e-commerce-players/ (accessed 22 February, 2016).

22  Barksdale, H.C., Johnson, J.T. and Suh, M. (1997) 'A relationship maintenance model: A comparison between managed health care and traditional fee-for-service,' *Journal of Business Research*, 40(3), pp. 237–47; Hennig-Thurau, T., Gwinner, K.P. and Gremler, D.D. (2002) 'Understanding relationship marketing outcomes: An integration of relational benefits and relationship quality,' *Journal of Service Research*, 4(3), pp. 230–47.

23  Verhoef, P.C., Franses, P.H. and Hoekstra, J.C. (2002) 'The effect of relational constructs on customer referrals and number of services purchased from a multiservice provider: Does age of relationship matter?,' *Journal of the Academy of Marketing Science*, 30(3), pp. 202–16.

24  comScore (2007) 'Online consumer-generated reviews have significant impact on offline purchase behavior.' Available at: www.comscore.com/Press_Events/Press_Releases/2007/11/Online_Consumer_Reviews_Impact_Offline_Purchasing_Behavior (accessed 18 February, 2016).

25  Palmatier, R.W., Dant, R.P., Grewal, D. and Evans, K.R. (2006) 'Factors influencing the effectiveness of relationship marketing: A meta-analysis,' *Journal of Marketing*, 70(4), pp. 136–53.

26  Mohr, J.J., Fisher, R.J. and Nevin, J.R. (1996) 'Collaborative communication in interfirm relationships: Moderating effects of integration and control,' *Journal of Marketing*, 60(3), pp. 103–15.

27  Wulf, K.D., Odekerken-Schröder, G. and Iacobucci, D. (2001) 'Investments in consumer relationships: A cross-country and cross-industry exploration,' *Journal of Marketing*, 65(4), pp. 33–50; Smith, J.B. and Barclay, D.W. (1997) 'The effects of organizational differences and trust on the effectiveness of selling partner relationships,' *Journal of Marketing*, 61(1), pp. 3–21.

28  Digital Marketing Institute (2016) 'Digital case study: John Lewis' secret to digital success.' Available at: https://digital marketinginstitute.com/blog/digital-case-study-john-lewis-secret-to-digital-marketing-success (accessed 9 August, 2016).

29  Boles, J.S., Johnson, J.T. and Barksdale, H.C. (2000) 'How salespeople build quality relationships: A replication and extension,' *Journal of Business Research*, 48(1), pp. 75–81; Doney, P.M. and Cannon, J.P. (1997) 'An examination of the nature of trust in buyer-seller relationships,' *Journal of Marketing*, 61(2), pp. 35–51; Nicholson, C.Y., Compeau, L.D. and Sethi, R. (2001) 'The role of interpersonal liking in building trust in long-term channel relationships,' *Journal of the Academy of Marketing Science*, 29(1), pp. 3–15.

30  Samaha, S.A., Palmatier, R.W. and Dant, R.P. (2011) 'Poisoning relationships: Perceived unfairness in channels of distribution,' *Journal of Marketing*, 75(3), pp. 99–117.

31  Steinhoff, L. and Palmatier, R.W. (2016) 'Understanding the effectiveness of loyalty programs: Managing target and bystander effects,' *Journal of the Academy of Marketing Science*, 44(1), pp. 88–107.

32  Ayres, C. (2009) 'Revenge is best served cold – on Youtube,' *The Times*, 22 July.

33  Heide, J.B. (1994) 'Interorganizational governance in marketing channels,' *Journal of Marketing*, 58(1), pp. 71–85; Williamson, O.E. (1988) 'Technology and transaction cost economics: A reply,' *Journal of Economic Behavior & Organization*, 10(3), pp. 355–63.

34  Palmatier, R.W., Scheer, L.K., Evans, K.R. and Arnold, T.J. (2008) 'Achieving relationship marketing effectiveness in business-to-business exchanges,' *Journal of the Academy of Marketing Science*, 36(2), pp. 174–90.

35  Anderson, J.C. and Narus, J.A. (1991) 'Partnering as a focused market strategy,' *California Management Review*, 33(3), p. 95.

36  Zoltners, A.A., Sinha, P.K. and Lorimer, S.E. (2012) 'Building a winning sales management team: A managerial perspective,' in Lilien, G.L. and Grewal, R. (eds) *Handbook of Business-to-Business Marketing*. Cheltenham: Edward Elgar Publishing, pp. 521–38.

37  Samaha, S.A., Beck, J.T. and Palmatier, R.W. (2014) 'The role of culture in international relationship marketing,' *Journal of Marketing*, 78(5), pp. 78–98.

38  Palmatier, R.W., Scheer, L.K., Evans, K.R. and Arnold, T.J. (2008) 'Achieving relationship marketing effectiveness in business-to-business exchanges,' *Journal of the Academy of Marketing Science*, 36(2), pp. 174–90.

39  Emmons, R.A. and McCullough, M.E. (2004) *The Psychology of Gratitude*. Oxford: Oxford University Press; Gouldner, A.W. (1960) 'The norm of reciprocity: A preliminary statement,' *American Sociological Review*, 25(4), pp. 161–78; Palmatier, R.W., Jarvis C., Bechkoff, J. and Kardes, F.R. (2009) 'The role of customer gratitude in relationship marketing,' *Journal of Marketing*, 73(5), pp. 1–18.

40  Tesser, A., Gatewood, R. and Driver, M. (1968) 'Some determinants of gratitude,' *Journal of Personality and Social Psychology*, 9(3), pp. 233–6; Tsang, J.A. (2006) 'The effects of helper intention on gratitude and indebtedness,' *Motivation and Emotion*, 30(3), pp. 198–204.

41  Frazier, G.L. (1983) 'Interorganizational exchange behavior in marketing channels: A broadened perspective,' *Journal of Marketing*, 47(4), pp. 68–78; Wilson, D.T. (1995) 'An integrated model of buyer-seller relationships,' *Journal of the Academy of Marketing Science*, 23(4), pp. 335–45; Dwyer, F.R., Schurr, P.H. and Oh, S. (1987) 'Developing buyer-seller relationships,' *Journal of Marketing*, 51(2), pp. 11–27; Palmatier, R.W., Houston, M.B., Dant, R.P. and Grewal, D. (2013) 'Relationship velocity: Toward a theory of relationship dynamics,' *Journal of Marketing*, 77(1), pp.13–30.

42  Palmatier, R.W., Scheer, L.K. and Steenkamp, J.B.E.M. (2007) 'Customer loyalty to whom? Managing the benefits and risks of salesperson-owned loyalty,' *Journal of Marketing Research*, 44(2), pp. 185–99.

43  Berry, L.L. (1995) 'Relationship marketing of services: Growing interest, emerging perspectives,' *Journal of the Academy of Marketing Science*, 23(4), pp. 236–45; Bolton, R.N., Smith, A.K. and Wagner, J. (2003) 'Striking the right balance designing service to enhance business-to-business relationships,' *Journal of Service Research*, 5(4), pp. 271–91; Cannon, J.P., Achrol, R.S. and Gundlach, G.T. (2000) 'Contracts, norms, and plural form governance,' *Journal of the Academy of Marketing Science*, 28(2), pp. 180–94; Palmatier, R.W., Gopalakrishna, S. and Houston, M.B. (2006) 'Returns on business-to-business relationship marketing investments: Strategies for leveraging profits,' *Marketing Science*, 25(5), pp. 477–93.

44  Ad News (2013) 'Telstra launches 'Thanks' loyalty program,' 25 February. Available at: www.adnews.com.au/adnews/telstra-launches-rewards-scheme-with-walk-on-ewan-mcgregor-movie-part (accessed 9 August, 2016).

45  Palmatier, R.W., Gopalakrishna, S. and Houston, M.B. (2006) 'Returns on business-to-business relationship marketing investments: Strategies for leveraging profits,' *Marketing Science*, 25(5), pp. 477–93.

46  Palmatier, R.W., Gopalakrishna, S. and Houston, M.B. (2006) 'Returns on business-to-business relationship marketing investments: Strategies for leveraging profits,' *Marketing Science*, 25(5), pp. 477–93.

47  ETurboNews.com (2014) 'Starwood Hotels & Resorts and Emirates Airline announce new partnership,' 10 November. Available at: www.eturbonews.com/52410/starwood-hotels-resorts-and-emirates-airline-announce-new-partne (accessed 9 August, 2016).

48  Cao, Y. and Gruca, T.S. (2005) 'Reducing adverse selection through customer relationship management,' *Journal of Marketing*, 69(4), pp. 219–29; Bolton, R.N., Kannan, P.K. and Bramlett, M.D. (2000) 'Implications of loyalty program membership and service experiences for customer retention and value,' *Journal of the Academy of Marketing Science*, 28(1), pp. 95–108.

49  Reinartz, W.J. and Kumar, V. (2000) 'On the profitability of long-life customers in a noncontractual setting: An empirical investigation and implications for marketing,' *Journal of Marketing*, 64(4), pp. 17–35.

50  Kalwani, M.U. and Narayandas, N. (1995) 'Long-term manufacturer-supplier relationships: Do they pay off for supplier firms?,' *Journal of Marketing*, 59(1), pp. 1–16.

51  Venkatesan, R. and Kumar, V. (2004) 'A customer lifetime value framework for customer selection and resource allocation strategy,' *Journal of Marketing*, 68(4), pp. 106–25.

## Companion website

Please visit the companion website, **www.palgravehighered.com/palmatier-ms**, to access summary videos from the authors, and full-length cases with datasets and step-by-step solution guides.

# Part 4

# ALL RESOURCES ARE LIMITED

Most marketing decisions require trade-offs across multiple objectives, because the resources available to address these needs often are interdependent and limited. When marketing strategies allocate spending to brand advertising, or innovative new products, or expand the sales organization to build stronger relationships, they often rely on the same fixed resource pool. A firm only has so many resources so important trade-offs are unavoidable. Managing resources optimally is critical; marketing resources provide the levers to implement what the firm learns from the first three marketing principles.

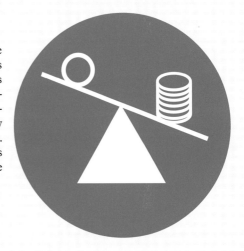

Visit www.palgravehighered.com/palmatier-ms to watch the authors provide an overview of the *All Resources are Limited* First Principle and the relevant tools, analyses, and cases in either an executive summary or a full-length, pre-recorded video lecture format.

ALL
RESOURCES
ARE LIMITED

Chapter **8**

# Marketing Principle #4: All Resources Are Limited → Managing Resource Trade-offs

## Learning objectives

- Critically discuss why all resources are limited.
- Detail the importance of managing resource trade-offs.
- Identify and discuss the five sources or factors that make ongoing resource trade-offs critical to an effective marketing strategy.
- Describe in detail the evolution of approaches to resource allocation.
- Explain the differences between anchoring and adjustment heuristics and attribution approaches for resource allocation.
- Describe why the attribution approach has advantages over other methods when making resource trade-off decisions.
- Define and explain the key inputs and outputs for the framework for managing resource trade-offs.
- Critically assess the two types of metrics and the pros and cons of each.
- Understand and explain the five-step process for managing resource trade-offs.

# Introduction

## All Resources Are Limited

The final, perennial issue facing managers as they make strategic marketing decisions is that *all resources are limited*. A firm's marketing decisions require trade-offs across multiple objectives, so scarce resources are allocated to meet different needs, according to decisions that are highly interdependent. The marketing manager of just a single retail store must trade off scarce resources and efforts every month, across advertising dollars, sales staff hours, retail shelf space, and merchandise inventories for hundreds of categories – never mind the complexity involved in making such decisions for an entire chain of stores. We combine all these marketing mix allocation decisions under the single descriptive term **resource trade-offs**.[1] Getting any of these trade-off decisions wrong can have cascading effects, influencing every other outcome that follows from a particular decision. For example, spending mostly on advertising without ensuring the necessary inventory could lead to stockout situations when consumers visit stores. Similarly, misallocating retail shelf space to products targeting customers that rarely visit the store would lead to massive losses due to obsolescence and unnecessary inventory costs.

Managing resources optimally is critical, because marketing resources provide the primary action levers that firms can use to implement what they have learned from the previous three Marketing Principles. First, to effectively *manage customer heterogeneity* (MP#1), managers conduct segmentation and targeting. Yet, they also need to allocate their fixed resources across these identified target segments effectively.

Second, to effectively *manage customer dynamics* (MP#2), managers develop acquisition, expansion, and retention (AER) strategies that they use to serve customers effectively as they move as across life-cycle stages. But to carry out these carefully specified strategies, managers need adequate marketing dollars, in support of all three stages, and those costs can rapidly become non-trivial. Imagine a simplified example. If the marketing manager of a firm is ordered to reduce marketing budgets by 5%, they could cut both acquisition and retention budgets by 5% each or cut acquisition budgets by 25% and leave retention budgets unchanged. But which option leads to better performance over time?

Finally, to *build sustainable competitive advantages* (MP#3), managers introduce new products, enter new markets, build strong brands, and spend on relationship marketing (BOR strategies). For example, Amazon expanded into bricks-and-mortar retail in 2014, partly buoyed by the idea that it could use physical sites as distribution centers. Similarly, P&G manages 22 brands that earn more than $1 billion in annual US sales, but it is constantly introducing new products to stay competitive.[2] Determining which sustainable competitive advantages (SCAs) are most appropriate and which resources to devote to each element of these competitive barriers remains a constant challenge, especially as competitors keep testing existing sources of advantage. Some firms try to avoid dealing head on with resource trade-offs by relying on the same allocation strategies across time.

**Example:** Microsoft (US)

Microsoft released several lower-end smartphones between 2010 and 2015, but the US technology giant was late to recognize the burgeoning consumer smartphone segment and therefore underinvested in growing its business and building sufficient SCA in this area.[3] Even after buying Nokia's device business in 2014, the Windows operating system achieved only a 3% global market share among mobile devices, trailing Apple and Google by substantial amounts.[4]

Firms are not just reluctant to adopt new technologies; others seemingly refuse to embrace new marketing channels and communication formats. One recent academic survey reveals that firms have a long way to go before they can claim to have integrated social media into their strategies.[5] On a seven-point scale (where 1 = "not integrated at all" and 7 = "very integrated"), 22.3% of the marketers surveyed chose a value of 1 to describe their social media efforts. Even if the trade-off does not involve some innovation along these lines, companies still make mistakes. In its ongoing battle with Walmart and Amazon, for example, Best Buy decided to aggressively boost its marketing expenditures, extend store hours, and open new stores in certain locations. But the market regarded these strategies as "more of the same," such that the company's stock price and profits have struggled in recent years.

As illustrated by these examples, trade-offs among multiple marketing options are never easy, especially when multiple factors influence firm performance. If firms fail to develop reasonable methods to manage these complex trade-offs, they risk losing segments of customers or product market share to competitors, as well as suffering lower returns on their marketing investments. We note several important insights when it comes to resource trade-off decisions:

1  Resource trade-off decisions are tough. They change over time, depend on many different factors, and require difficult-to-obtain information if they are to be optimal.
2  Trade-off decisions occur across all four Marketing Principles, on a real-time basis, so it is not as if a trade-off can be made once and then be considered resolved forever. Nor can firms make trade-off decisions in some easy sequence or in isolation.
3  Resources (money, time, messaging) are inherently limited; no one has unlimited funds or time to execute marketing strategies. Therefore, finding the right way to allocate each limited resource across various demands is critical to success.

## Sources of Resource Trade-offs

If every firm operated in a stable industry and had access to unlimited resources, while selling to customers with the same needs that never changed over time, such that competitors did not change their strategies, then resource allocation decisions and trade-offs would be easy. Firms could learn what worked best, then maintain their resource allocations decisions over time and for all their customers. Of course, as we know from the other three Marketing Principles, this description is far from the reality. Instead, firms must make resource trade-off decisions continually, for five key reasons that we summarize in Table 8.1.

The first and perhaps most fundamental reason for resource trade-offs is the recognition that a *firm's resources are inherently limited*. Because of this limitation, we even have a term to describe a firm's resource surplus available for discretionary activities. **Resource slack** refers to the "potentially utilizable resources a firm possesses that it could divert or redeploy to achieve organizational goals."[6] Resource slack provides a firm with actual or potential resources that enable it to initiate changes in its marketing strategy. Firms differ substantially in how much they choose to emphasize marketing, but across the board, their amount of resource slack generally depends heavily on the economy. Recurring events in world economies, including recessions, have widespread effects. These organic downturns significantly contract demand for goods and services, which lowers most firms' sales and profits, such that firms wind up with much less resource slack. If they believe they need to conserve those limited slack resources, many firms choose to cut marketing-related, franchise-building investments, which means that marketers are forced to work with smaller budgets.[7] According to a 2009 *Bloomberg Businessweek* poll asking how firms were being affected by the economic downturn, 93% of respondents mentioned cost cutting, and almost 37% reporting drastic budget cuts of greater than 20%.[8] Such moves resonate globally; big Indian IT vendors such as Infosys, Satyam, TCS, and Wipro bore much of the brunt of cost-cutting measures by US and European companies affected by the recession, because those firms slashed their spending on technology and innovation. Consumers are similarly more calculative with their spending during tough economic times, leading them to postpone their purchases or negotiate harder.

A second reason explaining the need for resource trade-offs stems from the *changes in customers' needs*. From Chapter 2, we know that market segmentation methods provide descriptions of industry segments, including, for each named segment, salient purchase preferences, demographic variables, and segment potential. These detailed descriptions of target segments are critical and necessary, but, over time, the size and attractiveness of each industry segment can change, as might the number of targeted segments, along with the appropriate level of a firm's commitment to the various segments. For example, industry research reveals four classic segments in the hospitality industry: backpackers, couples, families, and business travelers.[9] Backpackers and solo travelers like exploring the city rather than staying at the hotel, and they require more inexpensive room options. Couples instead place a premium on room interiors and hotel conditions. Families seek child-friendly and inexpensive

**Table 8.1** Sources of Resource Trade-offs

| Source | Idea | Examples |
|---|---|---|
| Limited resources and resource slack | Firms have some given level of usable resources that can be diverted or redeployed to achieve organizational goals. However, this slack must be shared and allocated across many different marketing needs. Resource allocation processes need to find ways to optimize the return on marketing investments. | Organic downturns like recessions significantly contract demand for goods and services, lowering a firm's sales and profits, and the firm's subsequent resource slack. Resource allocations must adapt to these changing conditions and the varying amounts of resource slack. |
| Changes in customers' needs | Market segmentation provides a description of the industry segments. A firm then moves from the overall market landscape to the specific segment(s) of interest to the firm. Yet, over time, the size and attractiveness of each of the industry segments changes, which means that the number of targeted segments may change, and a firm's commitment to segments will change. | In 2005, the hotel industry mostly concentrated on luring business travelers; today, it spends much more on marketing to young couples. Young couples are the fastest growing demographic, and they seek innovative and inexpensive hospitality solutions. |
| Changes in the lifecycle stage of a firm's products | Firms try to balance their product portfolios to have products in all lifecycle stages, to help offset resource needs. Introductory stage products require larger resource allocations to their launch, testing, and advertising to create awareness. They require different allocations as they enter the growth, maturity, and decline stages. Changes in technology and the success or failure of new products also alter any firm's product portfolio constantly. | Xero software is in the process of disrupting traditional bookkeeping and accounting online offerings owned by large Australian firms. The large banks have had to reshuffle and introduce products that will enable them to maintain a healthy product portfolio mix. |
| Changes in the product market landscape, due to the entry and exit of competitors | When the firm moves into a reasonably advantageous market position, competitors quickly make a countermove. Such counterattacks have the potential to negate the impact of the incumbent's advantage, and often create jostling for secondary demand – firms stealing market share from one another rather than creating primary demand. Firms have to constantly change their resource trade-off decisions during competitive counterattacks. In some cases, resource trade-offs have to be made in anticipation of new entrants. | Tylenol's prices were slashed, its advertising and sales force budgets increased, thus attacking its competitor drug Datril, damaging Datril's entry strategy and helping Tylenol's long-term performance. |
| Changes in the effectiveness of marketing activities | Even if a firm is operating during a stable economic window, with fixed consumer segments, homogeneous preferences for products across different lifecycle stages, and no major competitive entry, the effectiveness of marketing activities change over time, such that the aggregated market becomes less or more responsive to marketing efforts. For example, sales cycles have lengthened due to more relationship selling, product complexity, and informed and demanding customers. | Mass media advertising effectiveness has declined since the 1990s in the US, Europe, and Asia. |

restaurants, on-site play areas, entertainment, and discounts for additional rooms in which their children can stay. Business travelers have a high willingness to pay. Therefore, hotels likely make very different pricing, promotion, amenity, and loyalty program decisions, depending on which segments they target. They have to make allocation decisions; the luxury Marriott hotel chain caters less to backpackers than it does to the other segments. However, the size, needs, and financial payoffs across these segments are not fixed but instead change often. After a firm conducts an STP (segmentation, targeting, positioning) analysis, its revised marketing strategy likely requires significant changes to its resource allocations, especially if it chooses to exit or enter new segments.

The third reason for ongoing resource trade-offs is the *changes in the lifecycle stage of a firm's products.* Firms try to balance their product portfolio to have products across all lifecycle stages and thereby help offset resource needs. For example, products in the introduction stage require investments to launch the offering, time for sales to accrue, consumer tests to refine the product, and advertising to increase awareness. Once those products reach the growth stage, the firm enjoys stronger sales, but it also needs to shift its resource allocations and invest to meet growing demand. Still later, the firm needs to devise appropriate differentiation strategies for products in the maturity and decline stages, because these markets have become saturated, consumers' needs mostly are being met, and the company likely seeks to reduce its marketing costs to maintain its margins. Beyond this natural progression, as technology changes or new products enter the competitive sphere, the firm's product portfolio shifts as well, often in unexpected ways, which means that the marketing manager has to reallocate spending across the overall product lifecycle.

**Example:**  Smith's Snackfood Company (UK/Australia)

Smith's Snackfood Company, a British-Australian company producing snack foods (e.g., corn chips), records all the inputs and outputs throughout a product's lifecycle from pre-farm preparations, on-farm processes to post-farm transportations. The data show that one of the significant trade-offs during the packaging and processing stage for corn chips is between resource usage and emission of greenhouse gases. This assessment enables Smith's Snackfood to make more informed decisions on its resource allocations across the product lifecycle stage.[10]

A fourth reason that firms constantly adjust their resource trade-offs stems from *changes in the product market landscape, due to entries and exits by competitors.* Recall that any time a firm gains a reasonably advantageous market position, competitors quickly counter with efforts of their own. Such counterattacks have the potential to negate the impact of the incumbent's advantage and often create jostling for secondary demand, such that they aim to steal market share from one another rather than creating more primary demand. This phenomenon is perennial. In the 1970s, McNeil Consumer Healthcare, owner of Tylenol (a US brand of pain-relieving drugs), slashed the price of Tylenol, increased advertising, and expanded its sales force to attack its competitor drug Datril (owned by Bristol-Myers), which hindered the entry strategy for Datril and helped Tylenol maintain and increase its market share. In other cases, resource trade-offs occur in anticipation of new entrants. In the US, branded prescription drugs usually hold a patent for a fixed time, a period in which their owners enjoy monopoly rights in the market they created through their innovative R&D efforts. Once these patents expire, generic copycat rivals often flood the market, with less expensive drug alternatives that steal market share from the branded first movers. Each pharmaceutical firm therefore must decide whether and when to start investing in marketing efforts to encourage consumers to continue buying the branded versions of their drugs, which extends their product lifecycles and revenues beyond the patent-protected periods.

The final factor that makes ongoing resource trade-offs necessary is *changes in the effectiveness of marketing activities.* Even during stable economic times, marked by relatively stable consumer segments, homogeneous product preferences, and no major competitive entry, marketing activities can lose or gain effectiveness over time, depending on customers' responsiveness to ongoing marketing efforts. After a number of widespread organizational changes and poor financial performance, HSBC, the UK-based multinational banking and financial services company, revitalized its marketing activities to reconnect with its customers. HSBC tackled difficult topics, such as energy savings, aging work-force, and developing markets, in its traditional adverts and increased its use of social media platforms to engage customers.[11] In business settings, some sales cycles have lengthened as more firms engage in personal selling and introduce products with increased complexity, to deal with their better informed, more demanding customers. As a result, personal selling effectiveness has consistently gone down over the past four decades, in the US as well as in Europe.[12] Similarly, mass media advertising has lost some effectiveness in the past two decades, especially in the US, Europe, and Asia.[13] Trading off resources when the effectiveness of different marketing channels keeps changing can be challenging, and firms must constantly vary their allocations across different planning horizons, even completely reversing their stable allocation rules in some cases.

These five sources and drivers of resource trade-offs highlight the ongoing nature of this decision. Firms must address it at many different levels to ensure that they develop effective marketing strategies. Most marketing strategies require significant investments, so understanding how to best allocate the available resources is key to success.

> Most marketing strategies require significant investments, so understanding how to best allocate the available resources is key to success.

## All Resources Are Limited: A Fundamental Assumption of Marketing Strategy

As summarized previously, firms have limited resources. Combined with the many other underlying factors that are changing, this means that firms must constantly make resource trade-offs to optimize their marketing strategy. That is, the very fact that all resources are limited is a fundamental problem that all firms must address to develop an effective marketing strategy. Therefore, the recognition that all resources are limited and that an effective marketing strategy must manage ever-present resource trade-offs is the fourth and final Marketing Principle (MP#4).

> *All resources are limited,* and an *effective marketing strategy must manage the ever-present resource trade-offs* is Marketing Principle #4.

The approaches for dealing with the three previous Marketing Principles in many ways help create MP#4. Each of the earlier MPs require resources and trade-off decisions since no firm has unlimited budget, time, or trained employees to do everything. For example, it is not viable for a firm to sell to every customer segment, offer all possible products, or have a brand image that satisfies all customers, so a firm must make resource trade-offs. The insights from MPs#1–3 provide the objectives or roadmap, while MP#4 provides the tools for effective resource allocation. Thus, MP#4 is critical to effectively implementing a marketing strategy based on insights gained from the other three MPs.

In particular, MP#1 requires segmenting the market and using a GE matrix to select *target segment(s)* with varying levels of market attractiveness to match different firm competencies. A natural next step in this process is to allocate resources across target segments to achieve the firm's desired positioning strategy, as captured in its positioning statements. That is, implementing MP#1 requires the firm to allocate fixed resources across segments, which is the essence of MP#4. Resource trade-offs also refer to more than just financial resources; they involve managers' time, mutually exclusive marketing messages, and so on. For example, it is difficult for a firm to be all things to all people, such as by positioning itself to target both high-end, status-minded consumers and price-conscious discount shoppers. These two brand positioning strategies typically are mutually exclusive, so each firm must trade off its efforts to leverage each of them. Similarly, MP#2 recommends managing customer migration across the AER stages, using the AER positioning statements and strategies based on the customer lifetime value that can be generated across personas and stages. Again, implementing MP#2 requires the firm to allocate fixed resources across personas and AER stages, as in MP#4. The output from MP#3 is a statement that defines how a firm can go about building and maintaining an SCA, now and into the future, using brands, offerings, and relationships (BOR strategies). Implementing BOR strategies often requires vast investments in advertising, R&D, and sales personnel – typically among the largest expenditures for executing a marketing strategy. For this reason, researchers already have developed powerful models to improve resource allocations across the BOR strategies (e.g., advertising and sales force response models).

In some situations, it may seem like marketers could ignore resource trade-offs. The newspaper industry in the 1980s and 1990s enjoyed virtually a monopoly market, with massive profit margins.

The speed at which the print newspaper industry has declined since came as a surprise to just about everyone – especially those marketing managers who had grown accustomed to spending their resources freely. Various newspaper companies have suffered insurmountable losses. Gatehouse's stock went from $22 per share to approximately $0, leading to its delisting. In 2008 alone, McClatchy stock fell 94%, Lee fell 97%, and the stock for the *New York Times* company fell 60%. After selling for $1.2 billion in 1999, the *Minneapolis Star Tribune* declared bankruptcy in 2009. Even *The Wall Street Journal*, which Rupert Murdoch purchased in 2008 for $5.5 billion, recently had to write down $8.4 billion in assets, about 40% of it attributed to the purchase.[14] Can we explain this industry disintegration? Although many factors come into play, the newspaper industry clearly failed to react with an optimal allocation of its resources when faced with evidence that it was not serving customers' needs well enough. It did not segment either readers or advertisers into manageable or distinct categories for targeting with specific marketing actions. In the face of economic downturns, increased competition, and technological advances that threatened it, the newspaper industry also sought to cut costs, rather than allocate resources to developing stronger segmentation strategies or differentiating its offerings. Many of these cuts took place in the newsrooms, such that between 1992 and 2002, the number of journalists working for newspapers decreased by around 6,000 people or 5%.[15] But newspaper professionals and academics warned that this allocation of resources was far from optimal, because cutting these ongoing investments to increase profits wound up destroying the quality and integrity of the product,[16] in that the personnel reductions led to a loss of quality and diversity in content and thus direct hits to circulation rates.[17]

As this example shows, cutting costs redirects resources to other plausible areas, such as profit to shareholders. However, cutting costs to maintain profit margins earned during a monopoly market does not create any SCA, and fails to address MP#3. At the same time, not allocating resources to encourage emerging segments or protect existing segments represented a poor resource allocation and a failure in relation to MP#4.

All resources are constrained; even if a firm's existing resource allocation policies appear effective, rapid and often unexpected changes in the legal, economic, technological, or innovation landscape demand constant vigilance. As conditions change, resource allocations will become unbalanced. Thus firms need ways to identify misallocations and adjust spending levels quickly, in response to each new situation. A firm's marketing strategy must account for resource trade-offs, or else its ability to execute MPs#1–3, and thus its overall marketing strategy, will suffer. The rest of this chapter focuses on some approaches, processes, and analysis tools for managing resource trade-offs.

# Approaches for Managing Resource Trade-offs

## Evolution of Approaches for Managing Resource Trade-offs

The evolution of approaches for managing resource allocation suggests two main and overlapping eras: the heuristics era and the data era. Figure 8.1 depicts the evolution of approaches for dealing with resource allocation over these two eras.

### Heuristics Era

Firms constantly decide how to allocate resources across different customer segments, different customer stages, different offerings, different regions, and different marketing communication formats. In the absence of hard data about the attractiveness of each resource option, managers solve the resource allocation problem using simple rules of thumb, driven by intuition and judgment. These solutions are also called heuristics, thus the **heuristics era**. Heuristics are simple to understand and easy to use, which makes them appealing when managers confront complex resource allocations with stringent time pressures. For example, a manager might simply make advertising investments always 4% of total sales, without any further analysis or thought.

A more advanced technique would approach the resource allocation problem in a way similar to the method for selecting target segments using the GE matrix. Recall from Chapter 2 that the GE matrix

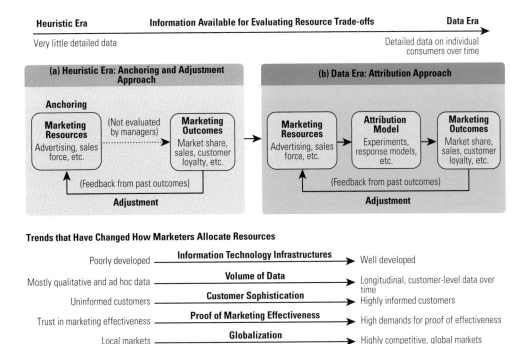

**Figure 8.1** Evolution of Approaches for Managing Resource Trade-offs

analysis tool helps managers visualize and select target segments. The y-axis indicates the attractiveness of a certain resource option; the x-axis indicates the competitive benefits a firm could obtain from investing resources in that option. Then, the size of the resulting "bubble" in the matrix indicates the extent of the resource opportunity. Large bubbles in the upper-right corner of the graph are the best; smaller bubbles in the lower-left represent the worst resource allocation opportunities for a firm.

Even as performance data and detailed analyses of marketing investments became more widely available, due to the introduction of scanner panels and improved information technology, many managers continued to rely on rule-of-thumb heuristics – they just updated them with data-derived numbers. Thus, for example, they might assign a certain portion of the budget to each resource option, according to metrics that reflect how many sales in the previous year were generated by each resource option. Thousands of sales organizations use such past year sales heuristics to assign their sales forces across different selling territories. A 2014 survey of 1,000 advertising and promotion managers revealed that 72% of them allocate resources across products, regions, and marketing instruments by relying on some form of heuristics.[18] Thus, the heuristics era persists – largely because firms tend to be risk averse and prefer transparent resource trade-offs, so they adopt simple, even if suboptimal, approaches to managing their resources.

A 2014 survey of 1,000 advertising and promotion managers revealed that 72% of them allocate resources across products, regions, and marketing instruments by relying on some form of heuristics.

## Data Era

In the **data era,** firms started using historical data that revealed the link between their past resource trade-off decisions and outcomes, such that they could determine the actual effects of certain resources on specific outcomes. The scientific approaches, based on data and empirical models, reveal whether each firm should continue its level of resource commitments or adjust them. Heineken, the Netherlands-based brewing company, partnered with Shopperception, the Buenos Aires startup, to gather an immense amount of data related to customers' shopping behaviors. By installing three-dimensional sensors at various retail establishments, the brewing company was able to find the optimal location and shelf position for moving its products.[19]

**Example:** Optimal Strategy for Advertisements (China)

To discern whether and when to target consumers with mobile advertising, a large Chinese mobile phone provider conducted a large-scale study in which it sent 4,400 mobile users a promotional text between 8 a.m. and 8 p.m. The consumers responded directly to the offer, paying using their phones. With the resulting information about when and how consumers responded to the advertisements, the firm was able to determine its optimal strategy, which was to target customers between 10 a.m. and 12 p.m., and then again between 2 p.m. and 4 p.m. By doing so, it could prompt average purchase rates that were twice what the firm had been achieving.[20]

The data era is transforming the very notion of resource allocations, from an inherently heuristic-driven approach to a more scientific modeling approach that links a specific resource commitment to performance outcomes. Three trends over the past several decades have contributed to the emergence of this era:

1 Resource allocation decisions have become considerably more complex, involving new products, segments, and markets that can be communicated about and to through various new marketing channels, such as online display, paid search, mobile and social media, along with traditional marketing channels.

2 Data-driven resource allocation has become a *cost of doing business*. In particular:

> Rapid technological and environmental changes have transformed the structure and content of marketing managers' jobs. These changes include (1) pervasive, networked, high-powered information technology (IT) infrastructures, (2) exploding volumes of data, (3) more sophisticated customers, (4) an increase in management's demands for the demonstration of positive returns on marketing investments, and (5) a global, hypercompetitive business environment. (p. 114)[21]

3 Marketing function has come under more scrutiny, with increasing demands for accountability. To defend their increased marketing spending, marketing managers must constantly justify their budgets to senior executives. Thus, showing that marketing investments pay off and are invested optimally, using clear and incontrovertible evidence, is almost tantamount to gaining more funding for the marketing department.

Through this natural evolution of marketing, reflecting advances in technology, data-driven approaches are slowly replacing heuristics-driven approaches. But in the next few sections, we provide descriptions of some of the most persistent and popular approaches to resource allocations, both heuristics- and data-based.

## Anchoring and Adjustment Heuristics Approach

As the heuristic approach for managing resources in Figure 8.1(a) indicates, the marketing outcomes box might include outcomes such as market share, sales, brand loyalty, customer satisfaction, and stock price. Each outcome potentially is influenced by managers' past decisions about various resource trade-offs (i.e., the marketing resources box). The link between these boxes (dotted line) is not evident. For example, imagine four firms. One firm chooses to increase all its advertising by 25%. Another firm decides to invest 50% more in marketing in one of it regions but cut marketing by 50% in another region. A third firm prefers to reduce its efforts toward one of its customer segments and devote more attention to several other segments. The fourth firm always sets its advertising at 1% of its sales, regardless of region, product, or competitive actions. Each of these decisions represents an "anchor," or the base decision rule that managers use to make their marketing resource allocation decisions. But, the effects of these anchors are not immediately, or sometimes even ever, evident. Still, managers can adjust their decisions in each period, such as after they observe the response to their efforts in the previous period. For example, the manager that chooses to spend 1% of sales on advertising observes sales every period. If those sales stay relatively constant, the firm could keep its expenditures the same ("business as usual"), increase the amount of advertising as a percentage of sales upward to see if that increases sales, or lower the amount of advertising to test the potential for damage. The adjustment generally reflects what managers believe represents the best decision; it could be based on some scientific evidence or data. Therefore, the solid line going back from the outcomes box on the right to the resources box on the left represents the adjustments that managers make to their heuristics as they gain information about the results of their existing resource allocations. Such **anchoring and adjustment heuristics** are widely used, although the exact anchoring rules vary in practice.[22]

- In the **percentage of sales method**, marketing resources reflect the sales revenue earned from the focal product. The firm determines the amount to spend by choosing a fixed percentage of sales revenue that should go toward marketing. This method certainly is simple to implement, and it prevents the firm from ever overspending, because it can only allocate a certain percentage of what it earns through sales. If competitors also allocate their resources using the same method, then strong industry standards develop about how much to spend on marketing.
- With the **percentage of profits method**, the resources dedicated to marketing instead vary with the profits earned by the product in previous periods. This method works better than the percentage of sales method in more volatile industries, where political, social, demographic, or economic factors likely have stronger, more immediate impacts.
- Managers who adopt the **historical method** simply set their present resource allocations to a level very close to the previous year's spending. This heuristic assumes that there are virtually no changes in the market, so there is little reason to change resource allocation levels. It is mostly useful in industries in which political, social, demographic, and economic factors are not volatile or powerful.
- Finally, the **competitive parity method** implies that managers set resource allocation levels to match those of their competitors. This method is most widely used in markets where competition is intense, and marketing allocations might be regarded as the cost of competing. In this case, individual firms might not know what the best resource levels are, but the collective wisdom of the crowd can offer some insights. However, this method can never reflect precisely what the firm needs to spend on marketing, because it depends solely on benchmarking and ignores differences in firms and their customers.

Taken at face value, most heuristic approaches fail to account for Marketing Principles #1–3. For example, using the percentage of past sales to set advertising across all segments violates MP#1, because it assumes that advertising will pay off equally across all customer groups, ignoring that all customers differ. If the firm sets its advertising expenditures at historical levels, it violates MP#2 by anticipating that advertising will pay off the same way today that it did in the past, which ignores that all customers change. However, in stable markets, these methods are popular, largely because of their simplicity, and they can provide some benefits. For example, in an experimental simulation study, conducted over a five-year planning horizon, a percentage of sales rule (total budget allocated proportional to the previous year's sales) outperformed a naive allocation (equal distribution across all products and activities, ignoring heterogeneity in customer or product portfolios),[23] especially in more volatile scenarios in which market demand is not known with certainty.

> Taken at face value, most heuristic approaches fail to account for Marketing Principles #1–3.

But scientific approaches are available that could direct marketing resource allocation decisions even more effectively. So why do these heuristics continue to hang on? One reason is simply organizational inertia. Even when firms encounter new technologies, they are reluctant to use them, because they already feel comfortable with their existing, simple (inefficient, suboptimal) practices. Scientific analyses, by their very nature, are more complicated and require more time, patience, and risk taking by the firm. But, resource allocation decisions are crucial to organizational functioning, so firms prefer to stay with tried-and-tested methods. They also recognize that any allocation decision represents a trade-off; one segment/product/marketing vehicle/region gets more resources, so another gets less. In their desire to establish a transparent explanation for why some entities get less than others, they might prefer the straightforward and clear anchoring and adjustment heuristics approach.

## Attribution Approach

To understand the problem with anchoring and adjustment approaches, refer back to Figure 8.1(a). Recall that each marketing outcome in the box on the right is influenced by the previous resource trade-offs listed in the box on the left, even though these links are not necessarily evident to managers (dotted line). However, once managers observe the outcomes achieved at the end of a period, they can *react* to poor resource allocation decisions. If profits drop by 10% after a 25% advertising decrease, that manager had better readjust the advertising allocation quickly.

Even in such a seemingly direct case, managers still cannot know for certain why profits decreased by 10%: because they should have increased advertising by 25% instead of a 25% decrease (i.e., they spent too little and did not reach maximum sales), or because they should have decreased it by 50% (i.e., they spent too much and reduced profits). Such questions are perennial for marketers.

P&G spent more than $6 billion on advertising in 2012 and IBM spent around $1 billion that same year;[24] yet even with these massive investments, these firms remain uncertain about how to allocate their vast advertising resources across different communication channels and formats. To understand the link between marketing resources and marketing outcomes better, they can add another box and create the attribution model in Figure 8.1(b). These mathematical models help systematically answer the question: How does a specific increase in a particular resource option, while keeping all else equal, affect a certain outcome of interest?

Using Figure 8.1(b), assume that a manager is trying to maximize a marketing outcome, like market share. They review prior decisions and trade-offs related to a particular variable from the marketing resources box, say, advertising. With an attribution model, this manager relies on past decisions and outcomes to derive a mathematical assessment of how much impact each resource trade-off truly had on each outcome. This historical evaluation reveals which marketing decisions worked and, just as important, which marketing decisions did not. Yet, it also entails model-based "what-if" scenarios that can inform optimal resource trade-off decisions.

So, let's say that a firm realized its advertising was increasing its market share, so it decided to increase advertising spending by another 50%. But in the following period, market share actually only increased by 2%, signaling that the firm has probably overspent on advertising. This provides the firm key information on the ideal allocation. Specifying an attribution model, such that the firm learns the exact dollar impact that a small resource increase will exert, also can provide answers to two more important questions:

1 What is the relative dollar value impact of a marketing investment?
2 What is the profit-maximizing level of investment?

By using an attribution model, managers can allocate resources to optimize their desired outcome, as well as avoid waste or reliance on arbitrary heuristics. In turn, rather than *reactive* resource allocation strategies, managers can implement *proactive* ones. These attribution models come in two main categories, namely, experimental and response model attributions, as we discuss below.

### Experimental-based Attribution

Firms operate in environments in which various factors operate simultaneously. For example, in the intensely competitive, dynamic online retail sector in China, managers of Alibaba would find it hard to prove (or disprove) that their marketing resources pay off in specific marketing outcomes. Yet, managers still must make constant, rapid decisions about whether to commit resources and how much to commit. Suppose that Macy's (a US upmarket department store) wants to understand whether it should really be investing in search advertising. On the one hand, most people start their product search online using a search engine such as Google, so advertising Macy's offerings by investing in organic search keywords is reasonable and could boost sales. On the other hand, Macy's already is a well-known brand, and its loyal shoppers are going to visit its website anyway, so search advertising might just be wasteful spending.

How can Macy's determine which argument is accurate? Table 8.2 provides a summary of the experimental attribution approach, which involves an intervention, outcome, design of the experimental condition, and the control condition. That is, with a controlled field experiment, Macy's might first select an **intervention** of interest, such as the level of search advertising to pursue. The experiment would involve adjusting this level in a limited fashion, such as increasing search advertising expenditures by 10% in the Midwestern region. Then, Macy's needs to identify the **outcome** of interest, such as offline sales, online sales, or online visits to its website in the Midwestern region (where it increased search advertising expenditures) relative to all other regions (where search advertising expenditures remained unchanged). The **design** of the experiment also requires further details, such as precisely when, where, and to whom it administers the intervention. Thus, in addition to choosing the Midwestern region, Macy's might decide to focus its search advertising expenditures on Google instead of Bing. It also might define the length of the experiment as one month. The experimental group then would consist of all consumers exposed to the chosen keywords through Google searches in Midwestern regions, and Macy's would need to track any increases in sales or website visits among these consumers during the month-long intervention. The findings reflect an experimental effect, namely, the lift in sales induced by a 10% increase in search advertising, all else being equal.

**Table 8.2** Components of Experimental Attribution

| Component | Definition |
|---|---|
| Intervention | A key marketing action whose effectiveness the firm seeks to document |
| Outcome | The key marketing gain for the firm implementing the experiment |
| Design | When, where, and to whom the firm administers the intervention |
| Control group | A region, customer, or situation similar to the experimental intervention that remains unchanged during the experimental process |

With this approach, all other factors (at least those under the firm's control) that can influence sales are purposefully kept constant. Thus, the firm deliberately generates a scenario that enables it to quantify the financial impact of the marketing resource that it alters through the experiment. Because external effects are always at play – perhaps Macy's sales generally increase month to month, such that any increase in sales in a particular month is not necessarily attributable to greater online search advertising – a **control condition** can be beneficial. The control would involve a region similar to the experimental region for which the search advertising levels remain constant over the month. Then, a control group exists, comprised of all consumers who were not exposed to the intensified search advertising through Google. If sales increase among the control group, but by less than the increase among the experimental group, Macy's would have evidence of the incremental effect of its increased search advertising expenditures, for a group that is similar in all other respects.

This method offers many advantages over an anchoring and adjustment approach. By allowing the manager to control for factors that otherwise could influence outcomes, experiments help isolate the impact of the specific marketing instrument being studied. Experiments also are useful when managers have not tried something before and want to test out its impact for the first time. For example, for decades, conventional wisdom indicated that customers would round prices down and ignore the right-most digits of a price – such that they read $3.99 as $3 instead of $4 – so marketers started implementing prices that ended in 9.[25] But this assumption went untested for a long time, which could have been very risky for firms. To test the assumption experimentally, researchers mailed three versions of a large US mail order catalog to different, randomly selected customer groups. In these catalogs, the prices of four dresses were manipulated to end in 9 in some catalogs but not in others. The 9 price ending consistently increased demand, especially among consumers who were less familiar with the product advertised.[26] In this case, the conventional wisdom proved right, but an experiment was necessary to confirm it.

> By allowing the manager to control for factors that otherwise could influence outcomes, experiments help isolate the impact of the specific marketing instrument being studied.

Not all experiments are so straightforward though. Deciding which factors to test is critical, and experiments can quickly grow very complex. For example, IKEA's website features about 12,000 products, nearly the entire IKEA product range. They vary by price, category, rating, design, and so on. If managers want to conduct an experiment across this vast product range, they need to confirm which factors are truly important to study and limit the experimental design to those factors for it to be viable.

Another element that defines the success of an experimental approach is its reliability, that is, its internal and external validity. **Internal validity** means that the experiment is well designed, and it reflects three key criteria:

1 The cause should precede the effect in time, known as a *temporal precedence check*. In our Macy's example, this temporal precedence is pretty clear. The retailer checks its online and offline sales in the period before it invested more in search advertising, then checks those values in the month after its investment. A poor design might take measures of the outcomes too soon after the intervention, without giving it time to take effect.
2 The cause and the effect must be related, according to a *covariation check*. In our Macy's example, if sales increase in the experimental group and the control group and the difference is not statistically significant, the firm cannot establish that its increased search advertising really prompted the sales bump.
3 The hardest criterion to achieve is the requirement that no plausible alternative explanations exist for the observed outcome, which can be determined with a *non-spuriousness check*. Macy's would need to establish, for example, that the experimental and control groups represent regions that are truly similar in terms of Macy's penetration, market attractiveness, sales growth, competition, and so on. In addition, the consumers in these treatment and control groups need to be similar in their demographics, preferences, lifestyles, and past purchases from Macy's. If the experiment passes all three of these checks, it is internally valid.

**External validity** depends on whether the conclusions drawn from an experiment can generalize to the overall business. For example, Macy's might confirm the results by running similar experiments across a few different regions, search engines, consumer groups, or search advertising levels. More generally, managers should replicate experiments to gain confidence that the experiment will consistently produce the same results. An externally valid experiment ultimately provides confidence in the results.

However, even with all these checks and sufficient validity, in some situations, experiments simply are not feasible or practical. Testing a new sales force compensation system or territory structure would not be fair or pragmatic in an experimental setting, because the experimental and control groups would receive different compensation for similar efforts. Similarly, if a franchisor wants to test the efficacy of its promotions, it cannot demand deep price cuts by some franchisees but not require them for others, for fairness and legal reasons. Instead, firms need alternative approaches to understand impacts such as these.

## Response Model Attribution

With improved computing power, more data and advances in statistics, firms are in an unprecedented position to mine their historical data to measure the impact of various marketing resources on outcomes. The explosion of data and improvements in statistical methods, as well as the stronger foundational backgrounds of marketing managers, have led to a surge in sophisticated *response model attribution* techniques. A **response model** is a statistical model that captures the relationship between past marketing resources and past outcomes. The underlying philosophy in response models is that historical data contain insightful information about whether and how much marketing resources truly increase outcomes, which is useful to know when deciding on future marketing actions. With the basic – and often reasonable – assumption that past outcomes relate to future outcomes, this approach leverages the past data to isolate the relationship between marketing resources and performance. For example, if a manager wants to understand the effects of pricing-based marketing decisions on sales, a response model might:

1 Collect data on sales and pricing over the past 52 weeks.
2 Build a statistical model that links pricing and sales.
3 Generate results that reveal the predicted effect of a 1% price change on sales.

Then, from the 53rd week onward, the manager can set prices that are informed by the likely impact of any increase or decrease on sales. By avoiding arbitrary prices, the manager knows that the firm is not losing out on sales by underpricing or overpricing.

> The underlying philosophy in response models is that historical data contain insightful information about whether and how much marketing resources truly increase outcomes, which is useful to know when deciding on future marketing actions.

Response models also offer four main advantages, in terms of their flexibility and usefulness. First, the use of response models enables managers to identify several important patterns by which marketing resources affect marketing outcomes. The *shape of the relationship* between marketing resources and outcomes captures the rate of change in outcomes stemming from increases in particular marketing resources. Figure 8.2 illustrates three possible shapes, although a linear relationship is not really realistic, in that it implies financial outcomes increase to infinity if marketing resources were to increase to infinity. Managers can usually expect a *concave relationship*. Outcomes increase with increases in marketing resources, but only at a diminishing rate (Figure 8.2, top line). That is, a firm that increases its product assortment from a very low level to a very high level should enjoy more sales, because consumers enjoy more choice and can buy more products from that firm. But this marginal improvement starts to diminish as the firm keeps expanding the assortment further, because there are only so many products the customer can evaluate. An overly large assortment even might feel overwhelming and cause the customer to shift purchases elsewhere. Finally, an *S-shaped relationship* is more rare but still possible; it implies that at very low levels, these marketing resources are not effective. They are insufficient to be competitive. And, at very high levels, these marketing resources also are ineffective, because the market has reached a saturation point. Identifying the accurate, nonlinear shape of the relationship is crucial for understanding the diminishing returns on marketing effectiveness.

Second, marketing managers can answer critical resource allocation questions by using response models, especially questions involving **marketing elasticity**, or how much outcomes would change if they increased their marketing efforts by 1%. In research that summarizes thousands of advertising elasticities obtained from response models in various market settings worldwide, over an extended period from 1960 to 2008, the results reveal that the average short-term advertising elasticity is 0.12 (i.e., sales increase by 12% when advertising increases by 1%). Advertising elasticity also is higher

• for durable rather than nondurable goods,
• in early rather than mature stages of the lifecycle, and
• when advertising is measured in gross rating points rather than monetary terms.[27]

Another study summarized more than 3,000 sales force elasticities obtained from response models in various market settings around the world, between 1960 and 2010. In this case, the short-term sales force elasticity was 0.31 (sales increase by 31% when the sales force increases by 1%). Personal selling elasticities are higher for products in the early stage of their lifecycles than for products in later stages

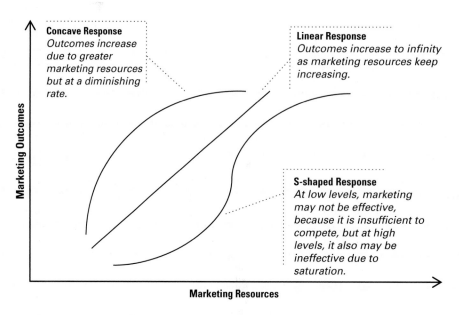

**Concave Response**
*Outcomes increase due to greater marketing resources but at a diminishing rate.*

**Linear Response**
*Outcomes increase to infinity as marketing resources keep increasing.*

**S-shaped Response**
*At low levels, marketing may not be effective, because it is insufficient to compete, but at high levels, it also may be ineffective due to saturation.*

Marketing Outcomes

Marketing Resources

**Benefits of Response Models**

- Provide insights into the shape of the relationship between marketing resources and marketing outcomes.

- Help managers understand the long-term impact of marketing outcomes.

- Capture the effects of competitive marketing efforts on firm outcomes.

**Figure 8.2** Response Model Shapes: Linear, Concave, and S-shaped

(by 0.26) and in Europe compared with the US (by 0.11).[28] Finally, sales force expenditures make advertising twice as effective, such that sales force and advertising exhibit synergistic effects on financial outcomes. All these findings would be impossible to discern without response models.

Third, marketing managers who use more than one marketing resource (as is almost always the case) can identify the relative impact of each resource with response models and thereby allocate these resources more optimally. Ideally, firms allocate their marketing resources in proportion to the effectiveness of those activities.

**Example:**  Samsung Electronics (South Korea)

In 1999, Samsung Electronics needed to allocate its corporate budget of $1 billion across 14 products, sold in more than 200 countries, with the goal of improving the returns on its marketing spending.[29] Before the reallocation exercise, Samsung had used an anchoring and adjustment method, such that it allocated resources to products and countries roughly in proportion to the sizes of their markets. However, when it adopted a response model approach, Samsung learned that it had overinvested in North America and Russia, compared with the profit potentials offered by those regions. It reduced spending in these regions substantially; and because another model pointed out that Samsung should invest more in Europe and China, it increased its spending in those areas from 31% to 42% of its budget. By 2002, Samsung had achieved significant market share gains in these countries, increased its brand value by 30% (to $8.3 billion), and grown its net income to $5.9 billion.

Fourth, response models help capture the effects of *competitive marketing efforts*. Competitive spending tends to clutter the market, reducing the salience and differentiation of the focal firm's products. For example, advertising recall is lower in countries where television advertising is more common. In Denmark, people receive an average of only 80 television exposures per week, and the Millward Brown advertising awareness index is 150 (cf. the UK benchmark of 100). In Italy, there are 300 average exposures per week per person, and the awareness index drops to 50.[30] With a response model, managers can gauge how increased spending on advertising by competitors will affect recall of their own advertising in the market.

Data Analytics Technique 8.1 details how response models inform the effectiveness of various marketing efforts. Recent versions even can help managers understand the *long-term impacts of marketing* rather than just its effect on the same or subsequent period outcomes. A promotion on select products might lead to increased sales in the same period; customers find the promoted price attractive. But the promotion also can induce long-term effects, such as when the promotion encourages trial, so that customers learn they like the product and possibly remain loyal to it.

Other updated versions of response models can capture *synergistic effects* across marketing efforts. With the growth in integrated marketing communications (IMC), marketing efforts began to spread over vast numbers of media channels – television, radio, online, mobile, outdoor, newspapers, magazines, and so on – in the hope that they would create synergies (or superadditive effects) and complementarities. As we discussed in Chapter 5, IMC aims to ensure consistency in marketing efforts to maximize effectiveness, such that the total impact exceeds the sum of each individual activity's impact. Thus, television should increase online advertising effectiveness, which should enhance promotion effectiveness, and so on. With response models, managers can assess the combined effects of their IMC efforts to ensure that their sum really is greater than the individual effects.[31]

## Framework for Managing Resource Trade-offs

The organizing framework for managing resource trade-offs (Figure 8.3) integrates the approaches and analyses described in this chapter. The three key inputs are the outputs of MPs#1–3. The two outputs of the framework for managing resource trade-offs are a description of the firm's resource plans and budgets and the key marketing metrics that the firm seeks to track in its efforts to validate its resource outlays. We conclude this chapter with a five-step process for using this framework to transform inputs into outputs.

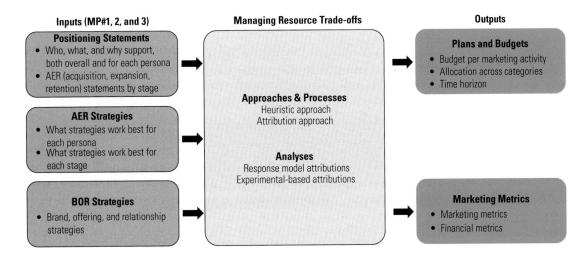

**Figure 8.3** Marketing Principle #4: All Resources Are Limited → Managing Resource Trade-offs

### Description

A response model is a mathematical model that captures the relationship between investments in marketing resources and outcomes to assist in optimally allocating resources.

### When to Use It

- To discover the shape of the relationship between marketing efforts and performance.
- To compare the effects of various marketing mix efforts on marketing outcomes.
- To capture the effects of competitive marketing efforts on a focal firm's outcomes.

### How It Works

Historical data contain insightful information about whether and how much marketing resources truly increase economic outcomes, which is useful to know when deciding on marketing actions in the future. A basic assumption is that past outcomes relate to future outcomes, which is reasonable most of the time, barring exceptions like recessionary periods. Using past data to uncover the relationship between marketing resources and performance, response models provide four main insights

1. They capture the shape of the relationship between marketing resources and outcomes, which is usually concave; financial outcomes increase with increases in marketing resources but at a diminishing rate.
2. They reveal exactly how much financial outcomes would change if marketing efforts increased by 1%, also known as marketing elasticity.
3. Marketing managers can figure out the relative impact of several resources and thereby allocate them optimally and in proportion to the effectiveness of the different activities.
4. They help managers capture the effect of focal marketing efforts on outcomes while controlling for competitive marketing efforts, which may increase the clutter in the market.

If the marketing outcome is given by Y, and we have two marketing efforts ($x_1$ and $x_2$) by the focal firm, as well as competitor spending ($Z_1$), the formula for a response model is given by

$$\ln(Y) = \beta_1 \ln(x_1) + \beta_2 \ln(x_2) + \beta_3 \ln(Z_1) + \varepsilon$$

Where the ln() term is the natural logarithm of all variables in the model, which captures the diminishing returns relationship between the outcome and the covariates, $\beta_1$ and $\beta_2$ are called the elasticities of marketing efforts, $\beta_1$ captures the % change expected in Y for a 1% change in $x_1$, $\beta_2$ captures the % change expected in Y for a 1% change in $x_2$, and captures the % change expected in Y for a 1% change in competitive efforts $Z_1$, and $\varepsilon$ is a random error term. With data about past outcomes and past marketing inventions, as well as confounds, software available from SAS or SPSS can determine the sign, strength, and statistical significance of the coefficients.

## Inputs to the Managing Resource Trade-offs Framework

The outputs of Marketing Principles #1–3 serve as the key inputs to the resource trade-off framework, such that each MP requires some initial trade-off decisions. Recall that the positioning statement attained through MP#1 answers key questions about who customers are, what needs the product or service can fulfill, and why this product/service is the best option to satisfy those customers' needs. To

Facing tough economic times, newspaper executives at XYZ company evaluated how much to spend on marketing investments in the newsroom (enhancing news quality by hiring more reporters, section editors, copy editors, and photographers) versus investing in the sales force to generate more advertising revenues. They decided to build an econometric model to study the revenue effects of these different marketing investments.

They collected monthly data for the previous 10 years, related to their investments in the newsroom and advertising sales force, their total revenues (outcomes), and the newsroom and sales force investments of other newspapers operating in the same city (competitive investments). The resulting response model captured the relationships among outcomes, marketing efforts, and competitive efforts, as estimated in the table.

| Variable | Coefficient Capturing Elasticity | $p$-Value for Statistical Significance |
|---|---|---|
| Ln(Newsroom investments) | 0.36 | 0.03 |
| Ln(Sales force investments) | 0.24 | 0.02 |
| Ln(Competitive newsroom investments) | −0.12 | 0.01 |
| Ln(Competitive sales force investments) | −0.08 | 0.02 |

With this model, XYZ determined that the elasticities of newsroom investments (0.36) and sales force investments were both positive and significant (0.24). Thus, $1 invested in the newsroom led to a 0.36% increase in sales, and $1 invested in the sales force led to a 0.24% increase. The magnitude of the elasticities revealed that newsroom investments were 1.5 times more effective than sales force investments. In XYZ's current plan, the company split its investments equally between the newsroom and sales force, so the response model estimates led the executives to make changes and invest more in the newsroom than in the sales force.

Adding in the effects of competitive efforts revealed that competitive newsroom investments hurt (−0.12) their revenues more than competitive sales force investments (−0.08). The overwhelming evidence pointed to XYZ's urgent need to commit strongly to investing in the newsroom, as the high quality of the newsroom would not only help it attract subscribers but also enable it to combat attacks on its revenue by competitors.

write a positioning statement, marketing managers must make multiple, relatively macro-level decisions about which customer segments to target (who), which needs the offering will satisfy (what), and how to achieve differentiation (why). Thus, each decision implies a trade-off. Sell to these customers but not those; satisfy these customer needs but not those; pursue a cost-based differentiation rather than a quality one. The output from MP#1 also serves as the starting point for subsequent resource allocation decisions, because it provides working boundaries for implementing marketing investment decisions.

The AER positioning statements, the output from MP#2, also are key inputs for the resource trade-off framework. These statements describe the who, what, why, and when answers for each key customer persona in the firm's customer portfolio and provide more detail about what the firm seeks to accomplish with existing customers over time or stages. The trade-offs associated with MP#2 involve how much to spend on acquisition versus expansion or retention strategies and which marketing investments are most effective in each stage. In combination, the outputs of MP#1 and MP#2 identify objectives and narrow the scope of allocation decisions (across customers and stages), by restricting them to strategies that are key to winning customers in the marketplace and managing those customers as they change over time.

Finally, the input derived from MP#3, which builds on MP#1 and MP#2, describes how to use BOR strategies to build SCA and erect strong barriers against competitive attacks. This MP also involves key trade-offs related to how much to allocate to brand, offering, and relationship-building efforts – often the largest marketing investments firms make.

In addition to the trade-offs they demand, MPs#1–3 inform the overall resource trade-off framework that can support aggregate-level optimization and improvement. Whereas Marketing Principles #1–3 require trade-off decisions for attracting, expanding, and maintaining customer markets, MP#4 focuses on optimally allocating resources to execute the related strategies while also tracking the firm's progress using appropriate metrics.

## Outputs of the Managing Resource Trade-offs Framework

A fundamental problem for effective resource allocation is identifying and measuring the best or most appropriate metrics. As a popular saying holds, a firm is only likely to achieve what it measures. Constant measures even might cause a particular metric to become more salient to the firm, with stronger influences on how the firm goes about achieving its goals.

For most marketing resource investments, financial and marketing metrics are necessary to capture the different aspects of the benefits earned from the investment. They also tend to respond at different rates to changes in investments levels. *Financial metrics* are monetarily based and entail ratios that can be easily converted to monetary outcomes, such as net profit, return on investment, or target sales volume.[32] *Marketing metrics* reflect customers' attitudes, behaviors, or mindsets, such as awareness, satisfaction, loyalty, or brand equity. These latter metrics offer a sense of why marketing might pay off. If a firm seeks to determine the effectiveness of its new products, measuring profits alone would not be sufficient, because profits can fluctuate for myriad reasons. But if it also tracks customers' perceptions of those new products – whether they realize the new products are available, whether they like them, whether they might repurchase them – the firm can determine if poor profits are due to low awareness, poor service performance, or low customer satisfaction scores. Intermediate metrics provide more insight than the ultimate financial outcome; they are "closer" to the customer. They also tend to change more quickly in response to resource changes, so managers can detect and adjust faster than if they had to wait for the financial metrics to become available. Table 8.3 offers a list of marketing and financial metrics related to various marketing functions.

Intermediate metrics provide more insight than the ultimate financial outcome; they are "closer" to the customer. They also tend to change more quickly in response to resource changes, so managers can detect and adjust faster than if they had to wait for the financial metrics to become available.

Another set of outputs pertains to the three components of each resource allocation decision:

• **Budget per marketing activity,** or the size of the commitment the firm makes to the marketing activity.

**Table 8.3** Types of Metrics

| Marketing Mix Functions | Marketing Terms | Close Financial Analogs |
|---|---|---|
| Customer Delight Metrics | Awareness | Return on marketing spending |
| | Interest | Return on marketing spending |
| | Desire | Return on marketing spending |
| | Sales | Sales return to marketing spending |
| | Loyalty | Projected sales |
| | Market share | Sales/total SIC sales |
| | Share of wallet | Customer sales/customer total SIC sales |
| | Social influence | Spillover sales |
| Advertising Metrics | Impressions/visits/page views | Cost per lead |
| | Click-through rate | Cost per click |
| | Media impressions | Cost per impression |
| | Recall | Cost per recall |
| Pricing Metrics | Price premium | Unit margin/margin percentage |
| | Price elasticity | Marginal price effect x (price/sales) |
| | Brand equity | Revenue premium |
| Sales force | Leads | Cost per lead |
| | Conversions | Cost per conversion |
| | Winbacks | Cost per winback |
| Distribution | Stock-keeping unit growth | Total inventory |
| | Same store sales | Sales per store/previous year sales |
| | Passthrough | Net margin |

*Note:* SIC = Standard Industry Classification.

*Source:* Inspired by Mintz, O. and Currim, I.S. (2013) 'What drives managerial use of marketing and financial metrics and does metric use affect performance of marketing-mix activities?,' *Journal of Marketing*, 77(2), pp. 17–40.

- **Allocation across categories**, which reflects the percentage split of the marketing budget for a specific activity across underlying categories.
- **Time horizon** of the budget, involving the timespan for which the firm commits to this marketing budget.

So, when choosing its advertising budget, for example, a firm would determine how many total dollars to spend (budget) on different forms of advertising (e.g., print and online), as well as how long to run the advertising campaigns (e.g., two months).

## Process for Managing Resource Trade-offs

Although we distinguish MP#4 as a separate Marketing Principle, as this chapter makes clear, all four MPs require some resource trade-offs, so the resource allocation techniques we describe here can apply to MPs#1–3. For example, when deciding whether to focus on brands, offerings, or relationships as the tools to build strong SCA, managers might use experimental and response attribution models. Beyond applying the allocation techniques to address specific marketing issues, most firms also generate annual marketing plans and budgets that capture how it is spending all its resources to achieve its overall strategy. In the simplified, step-by-step process we outline next, we provide a map for how to make resource trade-offs, one marketing activity at a time. Then, once all the marketing activities have been optimized, the last step is to build complex models that ensure their simultaneous optimization. The output of this process typically includes the total marketing budget for each specific marketing activity, the allocation of the budget to different spending categories within this activity, and the horizon for the budget (usually one year).

## Step 1: Identify Strategically Relevant Metrics

The three inputs of positioning statements, AER strategies, and BOR strategies result from a variety of analyses. They also need to be combined, synthesized, and focused to make an overall resource allocation decision. The positioning statement for an automobile firm might reveal that it is strongly competitive in the high-end segment; and its AER statements could suggest that it needs to focus on increasing the number of younger consumers it attracts. Finally, it may have determined that its SCA comes from its brand, which prompts a cutting-edge automotive technology image. Assume then that its strategic decision is to conduct a focused television and online advertising campaign, targeted at younger consumers, to increase their interest in its high-end cars. The car company needs to identify which marketing and financial metrics will enable it to track the payoff of its resource allocation decision. In this example, awareness among the target segment of young consumers is a likely marketing metric; profits probably offer the best financial metric. Its goal is to determine how much to invest in television and online advertising to increase awareness and profits to desired levels.

## Step 2: Assess the Relationship between Metrics and Marketing Resources

Can the automotive company's marketing resources actually increase awareness and profits, and if so, by how much? To answer these questions, the firm must investigate how much a dollar investment in television advertising affects awareness and profits, as well as how much a dollar investment in online advertising affects awareness and profits. This firm might use experimental or attribution methods. In an experimental approach, it could run a set of controlled field experiments to isolate the separate impacts of television and online advertising on awareness and profits. Alternatively, it could build a response model to capture the economic relationship between past uses of its marketing resources and outcomes.

## Step 3: Assess the Optimality of the Resource Allocation Decisions

The results from Step 2 provide an understanding of the payoff of the marketing resource. With this information, the firm can determine what amount represents an optimal resource allocation. Theory predicts a "sweet spot" in profit functions, that is, a point at which firms should invest neither more nor less. When choosing marketing investments with the goal of improving profits, managers need to know whether they are above or below this sweet spot – often described as "uphill" or "downhill" in the profit function, as in Figure 8.4. If the firm is on the uphill side, it needs to increase its investments to reach the sweet spot at the top. If it is on the downhill side, it needs to decrease its investments. The problem arises when a firm mischaracterizes its position. If, in reality, it is on the downhill side but believes it is on the uphill side, or vice versa, the firm would exacerbate its spending problems. Such spending errors can have serious consequences. To avoid them, managers should combine various analytical tools (experiments, response models) to justify any changes in investments as more likely to move the company to the area of the profit function that represents the sweet spot or its neighborhood.

## Step 4: Finalize Resource Allocation Decisions

The three preceding steps allow the firm to finalize its resource allocation decision: identify the total marketing budget for the activity, allocate this budget across categories, and select the budget horizon. Thus, our car company might decide to spend $500,000 on its advertising campaign – $350,000 on television advertising that will run over the course of two weeks, and $150,000 on online communications that it will maintain for a full month.

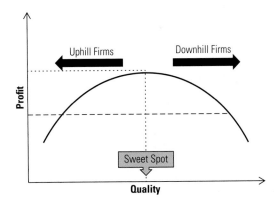

**Figure 8.4** Optimal Resource Allocation (Uphill/Downhill)

*Note:* The authors describe the curve as follows. If a firm located on the uphill side of the profit function (a Type U firm) believes incorrectly that it is located on the downhill side (a Type D firm) that generates the same amount of profit. Then, it will disinvest in quality and thus earn less profit (because it is really a Type U firm) rather than more profit. A Type U firm that makes the same profit would invest more in quality, again resulting in a profit reduction, which may induce a debilitating cycle of disinvestments in quality, falling revenues, and profits. So, it is crucial for managers to be able to determine whether their company is Type U or Type D with respect to each marketing effort before they implement an appropriate course of action.

*Source:* Adapted from Mantrala, M.K., Naik, P.A., Sridhar, S. and Thorson, E. (2007) 'Uphill or downhill? Locating the firm on a profit function,' *Journal of Marketing*, 71(2), pp. 26–44.

### Step 5: Integrate Across Different Marketing Activities

Steps 1–4 must be repeated for each marketing activity. The firm's overall plan and budget represent the sum of all these marketing activity (e.g., advertising, promotion, salesforce). Once the firm has developed effective allocation models for each marketing activity, it also should apply more sophisticated response models to optimize the resource allocations across its multiple marketing activities simultaneously.

## Summary

The most basic, yet perennial, issue facing managers making strategic marketing decisions for their firms is that *all resources are limited*. Understanding the performance impacts of investing in various marketing resources is critical; it provides insights into how firms should allocate their resources. After evaluating various options – whether consumer segments, product categories, or marketing activities – a firm decides how much to invest in each. Identifying the returns on the various marketing resources is key to developing effective marketing strategies and ensuring that the outputs of Marketing Principles #1–3 are implemented effectively.

Many factors contribute to *resource trade-offs*. Resources are limited, but *resource slack*, which refers to available resources that can be diverted or redeployed to achieve organizational goals, captures the amount of resources a firm has to allocate. The firm's customer segments are constantly changing, as are the lifecycle stages represented in a firm's product portfolio and the product market landscape as competitors enter and exit. All these changes require new and revised resource trade-offs. Finally, resource trade-offs need to reflect revisions in the effectiveness of marketing activities. Therefore, all resources are limited, and an effective marketing strategy must manage the ever-present resource constraint, which constitutes our fourth and final Marketing Principle (MP#4).

Two approaches for managing resource trade-offs are available to managers. With an *anchoring and adjustment heuristics approach*, managers rely on a heuristic, or anchor, that reflects some base decision rule they use to allocate marketing resources. Then, they can choose to adjust their decisions every period. For example, if the firm spends 1% of sales on advertising every period, in each decision situation, it can conduct business as usual and keep advertising as 1% of sales or else adjust the amount upward or downward. Common anchoring methods include the percentage of sales, percentage of profits, historical, and competitive parity methods. These heuristic approaches are simple to implement but lack any strong scientific basis. They mainly rely on tradition or managers' gut feelings about what the right resource allocations are.

An *attribution approach* links past decisions and past outcomes to derive mathematical assessments of impacts on outcomes. With an experimental attribution approach, the manager identifies an outcome and an intervention of interest, then administers that intervention to a chosen group, while holding the intervention for another, similar group constant. By controlling for factors that otherwise might influence the outcomes, such experiments reveal the isolated impact of the marketing instrument being studied. The *response model* attribution approach relies on a statistical model to capture the relationship between past marketing resources and past outcomes. These historical data generally provide insights into whether and how much each marketing resource truly increases different economic outcomes, which is useful to know when selecting marketing actions for the future.

The framework for managing resource trade-offs relies on the three key inputs from MP#1–3, namely, understanding what customers want and how the firm should position itself to give it to them, which AER strategies are most effective as customers change, and how to build and maintain strong barriers around customers using BOR strategies. The two outputs of this framework are descriptions of the firm's resource plans and budgets, together with metrics that enable the firm to track and validate its resource outlays. The process for using this framework and transforming the inputs into outputs consists of five steps.

## Takeaways

- All resources are limited. Managers must manage resource trade-offs to develop an effective marketing strategy. Most marketing decisions require trade-offs across multiple objectives, because resources are constrained and often interdependent.

- Several factors increase the need for ongoing resource trade-offs, including limited resources (resource slack), changes in the composition of consumer segments, changes in the lifecycle stages of the product portfolio, changes in the market landscape due to competitive actions, and changes in the effectiveness of marketing activities.

- Approaches to managing resource trade-offs have evolved from an exclusively heuristic-based era, in which managers solved resource allocation problems using simple rules of thumb, intuition, and judgment, to a data-based era, in which managers rely on statistical models and detailed information.

- The heuristics approach relies on anchors, often related to spending in the previous period, which managers use to make marketing resource allocation decisions. Then, managers may adjust their decisions every period, after observing the prior outcomes.

- An attribution approach asks: How does a specific (e.g., 1%) increase in a resource option affect a particular outcome, keeping all else constant? The model integrates past decisions and past outcomes, then produces a mathematical assessment of how much impact each resource trade-off truly has for generating outcomes.

- A response model-based attribution approach captures the relationship between past marketing resources and past outcomes. A basic assumption is that past outcomes relate to future outcomes, which is usually reasonable. The use of past data then can uncover the relationship between marketing resources and performance.

- There are three key inputs and two key outputs of the framework for managing resource trade-offs. The inputs are the outputs of MPs#1–3. The outputs are a description of the firm's resource plans and budgets and the use of key marketing metrics that can effectively validate these resource outlays.

## Analytics Driven Case

# Allocating Dollars Wisely at BRT Tribune[1]

## Problem Background

### Newspaper Industry

The near-monopolistic newspaper industry had enjoyed high profits for decades, with a high return on sales of 15–20% compared to pharmaceuticals (9%), metals (7–8%), aircraft (6%), auto (4%) and groceries (2.3%).[2] Moreover, as newspapers derive revenues from readers and advertisers, a local monopoly in print readership meant that local newspapers could derive the lion's share of print advertising dollars in the local market. However, over the past four decades, but most dramatically between 2000 and 2010, slowdowns and shifts (from print to free online news) in news consumption patterns, printing capacity constraints, circulation price ceilings, declining retail advertising revenues, and increasing competition from Internet advertising meant that the near-monopolistic newspaper industry had suffered in all possible ways. These trends impacted subscriptions and advertising revenue. The average daily circulation of local US newspapers has declined from 55,000 in 2001 to 44,000 in 2011, a drop of 20%; see Figure 1(a). Even more dramatically, advertising revenues for the industry dropped from $46 billion in 2003 to $24 billion in 2011, a nearly 50% drop; see Figure 1(b).[3]

### BRT Tribune's Troubles

For BRT's executives, the notion that the US print newspaper industry was in trouble was not news, but the *speed* at which the print newspaper industry had suffered in the past 15 years had been a huge setback. They looked across at some of their peers. For example, while in 1999, the *Minneapolis Star Tribune* sold for $1.2 billion, in 2009, it declared bankruptcy. Similarly, the *Rocky Mountain News* closed in March, 2009, and the *Seattle Post-Intelligencer* went to online only in the same month.

BRT was facing similar problems with its revenues and profits. On the circulation side, BRT had lost 18% in print circulation from 2001 to 2010, and about 7% in print circulation revenue. The only reason that print circulation revenue was not down as badly as circulation was that BRT had chosen to increase prices almost every year, to offset losses in print circulation. Print advertising, which contributed nearly 85% of its overall revenue, had decreased more dramatically, down 38% from 2001 to 2010, and the number was large enough for BRT to not draw solace from the fact that its drop looked smaller than the industry drop of 50%. Its online newspaper advertising was indeed a silver lining, having increased by 300% from 2001, but online advertising constituted only 3% of its overall revenue. Thus, the largest losses to overall revenue and profits came from losses in print advertising revenue.

### An Issue of Resource Allocation

BRT convened a meeting of its chief marketing office, vice president of sales, and strategic research director to address the issue of dropping print advertising. Historically, the main marketing instrument BRT used to maintain and grow its advertising was its field sales force. BRT's sales force was among the best in the US industry, and had been for decades. Media selling requires the sales force to call on local and national advertisers with current figures of subscriber numbers, buying power, compositional makeup, and projected revenue. As BRT was effectively the monopoly print newspaper in the city, its field sales force had built up good relationships with local advertisers, knowing exactly what advertisers in each industry wanted with their print advertising, and when they were likely to buy.

---

[1] Based on research by Shrihari Sridhar, Murali Mantrala, and Esther Thorson.
[2] Bogart, L. (2004) 'Reflections on content quality in newspaper,' *Newspaper Research Journal*, 25(1), pp. 40–53.
[3] Mitchell, A. (2015) 'State of the news media 2015.' Available at: www.journalism.org/2015/04/29/state-of-the-news-media-2015/ (accessed 6 June, 2016).

(a) Trends in Subscription

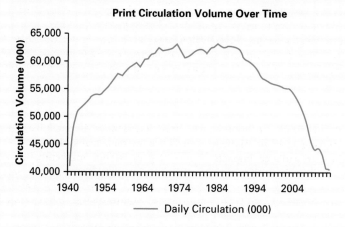

**Print Circulation Volume Over Time**

(b) Trends in Advertising Revenue

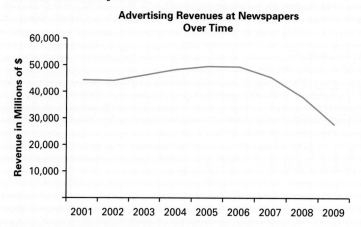

**Figure 1** Industry Trends in Subscription and Advertising Revenue

BRT's field sales force was split up into six divisions, separated along two strategic segments. The first segment was whether an advertiser was local or national. Local advertisers tended to rely more heavily on local newspapers, since local newspapers captured the main market of consumers for the advertisers. National advertisers occasionally used newspapers for advertising events (e.g., movies) or specials (e.g., a large-scale promotional event by Toyota), and bought ad space in larger amounts when they did. The second segment was defined based on the geographic location of the advertiser, that is, whether they mainly wanted to attract consumers from the newspaper's designated market (NDM) area, or the two neighboring outside newspaper designated market (ONDM1 and ONDM2) areas. Thus, the sales force constituted six divisions based on the advertisers they were targeting: Local and NDM, Local and ONDM1, Local and ONDM2, National and NMD, National and ONDM1, and National and ONDM2.

The tricky issue was one of how to allocate salespeople to each of the six divisions. BRT had traditionally used a combination of *percentage of sales* and *historical methods*. In the *percentage of sales method*, BRT determined the amount to spend on the sales force in each division by choosing a fixed percentage of sales revenue that should go towards each division. This method was simple to implement, and it prevented BRT from overspending, but with no strong industry standards on what the ratio is, BRT was beginning to doubt the efficacy of the method. It also used a *historical method* to decide resource allocations to a level very close to the previous year's spending. But BRT knew that this heuristic assumed that there are virtually no changes in the market, and market growth is slow, and with the newspaper industry going through volatile times, there was a need to change the method as well.

## Problem Statement

BRT's problem of sales force allocation across the six divisions is the most basic, yet perennial, issue facing managers making strategic marketing decisions for their firms, that is, *all resources are limited*. Understanding the performance impacts of investing in various marketing resources is critical; it provides insights into how firms should allocate their resources. After evaluating various options, BRT needs to decide how much to invest in each option. Thus, all resources are limited, and an effective marketing strategy must manage the ever-present resource trade-offs representing Marketing Principle #4.

   BRT's resource trade-offs came from a number of reasons. BRT's resource slack generally depended heavily on the economy and the state of the market. Organic downturns in the economy and the newspaper industry had contracted demand, reducing its marketing-related investments. So, BRT had to work with the same sales force budget, but learn how to redeploy dollars more wisely across the six divisions. On the issue of redeployment, BRT had to acknowledge that resource trade-offs stem from the *changes in advertiser needs*. BRT knew that the size and attractiveness of each of its six advertiser segments was changing; so, it could only allocate as many sales force dollars to each of the six divisions as was economically warranted. Thus, the fundamental issues of interest to BRT are:

- Does an increase in sales force size contribute to increase in advertising revenues?
- How many salespeople should be allocated to each of the six divisions to maximize profits?
- Assuming no more salespeople can be employed, how should BRT redistribute its sales force across the six divisions to maximize profits?

## Data[4]

BRT decided to shift from the heuristic-based methods of resource allocation to the more analytical, response model method to allocate sales force dollars. The philosophy of using a response model approach is that a marketer should only allocate resources to a segment/product/division in proportion to the profit-generating potential of the segment/product/division.

### Intuition of a Response Model

To understand the benefits of allocating additional sales force resources to each division, BRT first needed to know the marginal importance of adding a salesperson to each division. So, its first job was to estimate a sales force response model. As explained earlier in the chapter, a response model captures the relationship between marketing resources and outcomes mathematically. Using a response model for each division, BRT could estimate the shape of the relationship between sales force dollars and revenues, and capture the rate of change in outcomes stemming from increases in particular marketing resources. Next, it could ask the question: How much would revenue increase in each division if it increased sales force efforts by 1%? Knowing this answer for each of the six divisions, it could then decide the relative impact of adding sales force dollars to each of the six divisions, and redeploy the dollars optimally, that is, in a manner that would be profit maximizing for all six divisions combined.

---

[4] These analyses were performed using MEXL software as described in Data Analytics Technique 9.1 using data from the BRT Case dataset.

So, the first step would be to identify a response model that needed to be calibrated for each of the six divisions. Based on past practice, BRT knew that the mathematical model had to capture the following institutional characteristics:

- If the sales force was cut to zero, advertising revenue would decrease, but there is a floor (min) on how much advertising revenue would fall from its initial value by the end of a period.
- If the sales force is increased a great deal, say, to something that could be called "saturation," advertising revenue will increase but there is a ceiling (max) on how much can be achieved by the end of one period.
- There is some sales force rate that will maintain initial advertising revenue in each division.

Based on precedence and tradition in marketing analytics, BRT chose the following mathematical function:

$$Y = b + (a - b)\frac{X^c}{d + X^c}$$

where $Y$ is advertising revenue, $X$ is sales force effort in each division, $b$ is the minimum revenue with zero effort, $a$ is the maximum (saturation-level revenue), and $c$ and $d$ are response parameters that capture the relationship between sales force and revenue. The relationship that the response model would capture (between sales force effort and revenue) in each of the six divisions is shown in Figure 2. Depending on the coefficients $a$, $b$, $c$, and $d$ associated with each division, BRT could observe various S-shaped patterns in the relationship between effort and outcomes, and use that information to assess resource trade-offs across the six divisions.

## Calibration of Six Response Models

The next issue was how to obtain the coefficients $a$, $b$, $c$, and $d$ for each division. One method to obtain these parameters could stem from nonlinear regressions using past historical data on sales force efforts and revenues, which would provide the estimates of the four coefficients (and confidence bands) for each of the six divisions. In fact, using past data to uncover the relationship between marketing resources and performance and response models was the norm rather than the exception in many industries like the consumer packaged goods where such practices had seen adoption.

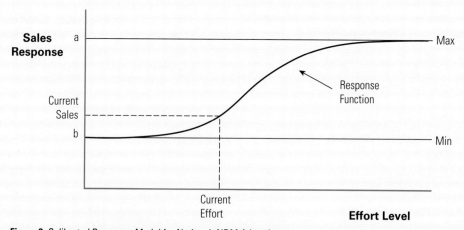

**Figure 2**  Calibrated Response Model for National_NDM Advertisers

For BRT, though, the managers wanted to implement something simple, just to see that "analytics works." In such a situation, note that the equation has four unknowns, which can be calculated by using four data points of $Y$ and $X$. Particularly, if BRT could understand how much revenue would increase when sales force was set at 10% of its current level (lowest effort), 50% of current levels (low effort), 150% of current levels (high effort), and 500% of current levels (saturation), it would be able to obtain the four most extreme $X$ and $Y$ data points in the sales response model defining each division.

BRT reasoned, who better to answer what the revenue levels would be for each of the four scenarios, than BRT's own sales force. Thus, BRT called a conference of five sales managers from each division. Together with the chief marketing office, vice president of sales, and strategic research director, the sales team in each division provided managerial estimates of expected revenue levels when sales effort levels were set to at 10% of its current level (lowest effort), 50% of current levels (low effort), 150% of current levels (high effort), and 500% of current levels (saturation). Using these four estimates of revenues and efforts, BRT calculated the coefficients $a$, $b$, $c$, and $d$ for each division, thus enabling the calibration of six response models, one for each sales force division.

## Results

### Sales Response Model Graphs

The calibrated data for each of the six divisions is presented in Table 1. For the National_NDM division (i.e., the division targeting national advertisers in the newspaper's designated market area), one can see that the sales force felt that the lowest effort would reduce revenues from the current levels (set as 100%) to 47%, while low efforts would reduce revenues from the current levels to 68%. Increasing sales force efforts to high levels would increase revenue to 126%, and the highest sales force efforts would yield 152% of sales respectively. The same exercise was repeated for the other five divisions, and the calibrated data are summarized in Table 1.

**Table 1** Calibrated Data

| Effort levels | Sales reps for National_NDM | Sales in $ for National_NDM | Sales reps for National_ONDM1 | Sales in $ for National_ONDM1 | Sales reps for National_ONDM2 | Sales in $ for National_ONDM2 |
|---|---|---|---|---|---|---|
| Lowest effort | None | 47% | None | 15% | None | 31% |
| Low effort | 50% | 68% | 50% | 48% | 50% | 63% |
| Current effort | Current effort | 100% | Current effort | 100% | Current effort | 100% |
| Higher effort | 150% | 126% | 150% | 120% | 150% | 115% |
| Highest effort | Saturation | 152% | Saturation | 135% | Saturation | 125% |

| Effort levels | Sales reps for Local_NDM | Sales in $ for Local_NDM | Sales reps for Local_ONDM1 | Sales in $ for Local_ONDM1 | Sales reps for Local_ONDM2 | Sales in $ for Local_ONDM2 |
|---|---|---|---|---|---|---|
| Lowest effort | None | 45% | None | 56% | None | 59% |
| Low effort | 50% | 70% | 50% | 80% | 50% | 76% |
| Current effort | Current effort | 100% | Current effort | 100% | Current effort | 100% |
| Higher effort | 150% | 105% | 150% | 111% | 150% | 107% |
| Highest effort | Saturation | 110% | Saturation | 120% | Saturation | 111% |

For the calibrated data, BRT calculated the coefficients $a$, $b$, $c$, and $d$ for each division, thus enabling the calibration of six response models, one for each sales force division. The sales response models were subsequently plotted for each division. Figure 3(a) depicts the sales response model for National_NDM, while Figure 3(b) depicts the sales response model for National_ONDM1. As we can see, both graphs depict an S-shaped relationship between revenue and sales force efforts. However, the graph of National_ONDM1 appears to be steeper than National_NDM indicating that the National_ONDM1 division is potentially able to generate more advertising revenue per unit of sales force effort than the National_NDM division.

In all, the graphing procedure is repeated for each of the six divisions. In sum, the answer to the question: "Does an increase in sales force size contribute to increase in advertising revenues?" appeared to meet resounding approval.

## Allocation Decisions

The next question facing BRT was: "How many salespeople should be allocated to each of the six divisions to maximize profits?" The intuition to solve this problem is as follows. As the response model calibrated earlier showed, the addition of a salesperson in each division did have revenue benefits, albeit different across each division based on the response graphs in each division. The addition of a salesperson also has a cost in terms of compensating the salesperson. The addition of salespeople in each division is permissible up to the point where the incremental profitability of adding salespeople in each division becomes zero. Thus, an optimal recommendation would be to add or subtract a certain number of salespeople from each division such that the marginal benefit of adding and subtracting salespeople across all six divisions is exactly equal to the marginal cost.

BRT calculated the exact mathematical addition or subtraction of salespeople needed in each division, based on this intuition. BRT first investigated the solution in the ideal scenario, where it could hire as many salespeople as the model recommended, even though this might be infeasible in reality. The results are presented in Table 2. First, it found that it was underspending on the total sales force; the model recommended that the optimal number of salespeople required to maximize profitability would be 69, as against the 37 that BRT was currently employing. Moreover, the addition of 32 extra salespeople would contribute to a 34% increase in profits (from $22,019 to $24,408). The model recommended adding salespeople across the board (except for Local_ONDM2), with the largest recommended increase in National_NDM.

However, it viewed the question: "Assuming no more salespeople can be employed, how should BRT redistribute its sales force across the six divisions to maximize profits?" as the most critical, since it represented the best use of its current resources. The results for such a profit optimization model, which constrained the total number of reps to 37, are presented in Table 3. As one can see in Table 3, the total number of recommended sales reps remains unchanged at 37, but the model recommends several reallocations, such as increasing the number of reps in the National_NDM division from 9 to 21, and reducing the number of reps in the National ONDM1 division from 14 to 6. With the redeployment and the same overall budget, BRT could potentially improve its profits by nearly 16%, from $22,019 to $26,481. Thus, the constrained solution, which simply involved redistributing the same resources to areas that promised better financial rewards, yielded significant upside potential for BRT.

BRT was energized by the solution since it could achieve potentially large gains without hiring any new salespeople. However, it had a limited budget with which it could hire new salespeople, even if not being able to hire a total of 69, as in the unconstrained model's case. It thus reviewed Figure 4, which plotted the profitability attainable against the total number of salespeople across all six divisions, and learnt that it could get almost 93% of the maximum profitability by simply reallocating salespeople as per the optimal ratio recommended by the constrained solution; and it could get 96% of the maximum profitability by hiring 5 more salespeople, but allocating the same way as the constrained solution recommended.

**Table 2** Unconstrained Allocation Recommendation

### Base Scenario

Enter effort and outcome values for the base scenario, which will be used for calibration first, and as a benchmark later.

| Efforts and outcomes | National_ NDM | National_ ONDM1 | National_ ONDM2 | Local_NDM | Local_ ONDM1 | Local_ ONDM2 | Total costs/ Total gross margins | Total net margins | Total reps | Total Sales |
|---|---|---|---|---|---|---|---|---|---|---|
| Sales reps | 9 | 14 | 5 | 3 | 3 | 3 | $2,331 | | 37 | |
| Sales in $ | $21,440 | $3,650 | $2,120 | $3,720 | $3,800 | $1,460 | $24,350 | $22,019 | | $36,190 |
| | | | | | | | | | | |
| | | | | | | | | | | |

### Recommended Scenario

This area will contain recommended effort and predicted outcome values.

| Efforts and outcomes | National_ NDM | National_ ONDM1 | National_ ONDM2 | Local_NDM | Local_ ONDM1 | Local_ ONDM2 | Total costs/ Total gross margins | Total net margins | Total reps | Total Sales |
|---|---|---|---|---|---|---|---|---|---|---|
| Sales reps | 32.4371353 | 16.74136127 | 6.950220919 | 4.271907343 | 5.54539663 | 3.048353986 | $4,347 | | 69 | |
| Sales in $ | $32,201 | $4,040 | $2,379 | $3,942 | $4,296 | $1,466 | $32,754 | $28,408 | | $48,324 |
| | | | | | | | | | | |
| | | | | | | | | | | |

### Costs and Gross Margins

Enter observations id (e.g., respondent's name), choice and independent variables.

| Efforts and outcomes | National_ NDM | National_ ONDM1 | National_ ONDM2 | Local_NDM | Local_ ONDM1 | Local_ ONDM2 |
|---|---|---|---|---|---|---|
| Sales reps | $63 | $63 | $63 | $63 | $63 | $63 |
| Unit Margin | 0.7 | 0.55 | 0.72 | 0.72 | 0.62 | 0.53 |
| | | | | | | |

**Table 3** Constrained Allocation Recommendation

*Base Scenario*

Enter effort and outcome values for the base scenario, which will be used for calibration first, and as a benchmark later.

| Efforts and outcomes | National_NDM | National_ONDM1 | National_ONDM2 | Local_NDM | Local_ONDM1 | Local_ONDM2 | Total costs/Total gross margins | Total net margins | Total reps | Total Sales |
|---|---|---|---|---|---|---|---|---|---|---|
| Sales reps | 9 | 14 | 5 | 3 | 3 | 3 | $2,331 | | 37 | |
| Sales in $ | $21,440 | $3,650 | $2,120 | $3,720 | $3,800 | $1,460 | $24,350 | $22,019 | | $36,190 |

*Recommended Scenario*

This area will contain recommended effort and predicted outcome values.

| Efforts and outcomes | National_NDM | National_ONDM1 | National_ONDM2 | Local_NDM | Local_ONDM1 | Local_ONDM2 | Total costs/Total gross margins | Total net margins | Total reps | Total Sales |
|---|---|---|---|---|---|---|---|---|---|---|
| Sales reps | 20.96740258 | 6.131264338 | 3.889555241 | 3.037558819 | 2.982920577 | 0 | $2,332 | | 37 | |
| Sales in $ | $30,248 | $1,475 | $1,850 | $3,732 | $3,794 | $861 | $28,812 | $26,481 | | $41,959 |

*Costs and Gross Margins*

Enter observations id (e.g., respondent's name), choice and independent variables.

| Efforts and outcomes | National_NDM | National_ONDM1 | National_ONDM2 | Local_NDM | Local_ONDM1 | Local_ONDM2 |
|---|---|---|---|---|---|---|
| Sales reps | $63 | $63 | $63 | $63 | $63 | $63 |
| Unit Margin | 0.7 | 0.55 | 0.72 | 0.72 | 0.62 | 0.53 |

(a) Response Model for National_NDM Advertisers

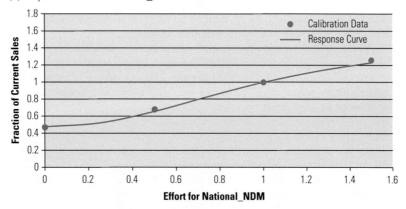

(b) Response Model for National_ONDM1 Advertisers

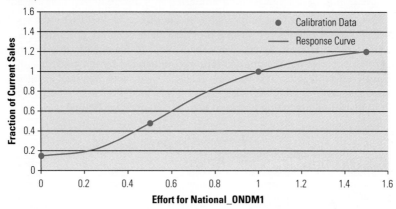

**Figure 3**  Calibrated Response Models

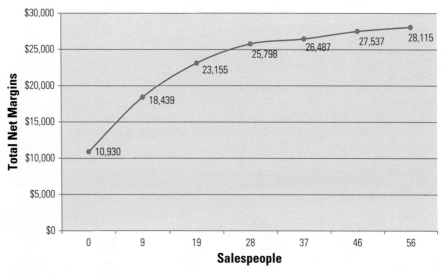

**Figure 4**  Opportunity Costs

## Summary of Solution

The analytics exercise enabled BRT to obtain a better view of its current standing in the marketplace, by better understanding how to allocate resources accurately.

1 By using a scientific, attribution-based approach to budgeting, it learnt that its marketing strategy is formed out of goals (profit maximization), rationale (sales response models), actions (budgets and reallocation) rather than just a gut-based decision (i.e. percentage of sales). This helped it feel more confident about its resource allocation policies, and arrive at a common language with which to discuss strategic advancements.

2 By using a sales response model, it learnt that in all six divisions, its salespeople were indeed adding value by bringing in more revenues, but that the responsiveness of each division to the addition of salespeople was mixed, that is, not all divisions were equally receptive to the addition of salespeople.

3 By using an optimization procedure to allocate salespeople across the division, it learnt that the addition of salespeople in each division is permissible up to the point where the incremental profitability of adding salespeople in each division becomes zero. Thus, an optimal recommendation would be to add or subtract a certain number of salespeople from each division such that the marginal benefit of adding and subtracting salespeople across all six divisions is exactly equal to the marginal cost.

4 BRT learnt that while it could not double its sales force, it could view the results from the unconstrained allocation with interest since it provided the benchmark profit figure that it could aim for in the ideal scenario. However, it could get almost 93% of the maximum profitability by simply reallocating salespeople as per the optimal ratio recommended by the constrained solution. Thus, BRT felt more confident going into the new financial year, with the dual emphasis on allocation and increased resources (adding five salespeople). Thus, analytics-oriented efforts helped BRT solve the fourth fundamental marketing problem, that all resources are limited.

## Appendix: Dataset Description

### General Description of the Data

The dataset is a simulated dataset, aimed at mimicking similar datasets that the authors have used in the past while working with companies. The data contain two Excel sheets. The first Excel sheet ("Scenario") provides data on the effort–outcome relationship under the base and recommended scenarios, and associated profit implications. The second Excel sheet ("Calibration") contains the calibration data obtained from salespeople.

### Description of Variables in the Data

Executing the analysis involves understanding two points. First, the students should observe that the "Calibration sheet" has data pertaining to effort and outcomes for each of the six sales regions. For each region, salespeople were asked to guess how much sales would be generated with the lowest effort, low effort, current effort, higher effort, and highest effort. The effort levels and outcomes for one district are shown below.

| Effort levels | Sales reps for National_NDM | Sales in $ for National_NDM |
|---|---|---|
| Lowest effort | None | 47% |
| Low effort | 50% | 68% |
| Current effort | Current effort | 100% |
| Higher effort | 150% | 126% |
| Highest effort | Saturation | 152% |

To obtain the calibration model results, the student can directly load the data in Excel, and use the MEXL add-in pertaining to resource allocation and choose "calibrate response models" as the option. They will get the response model results as shown in Figure 3.

The second part of the study involves using the "Scenario sheet." After calibrating the response model, the scenario presents the sales outcomes and profitability associated with the current vs. optimal efforts, and the optimal level of allocations needed to generate the optimal profits. To obtain the optimal allocations and view the optimal profits, students should go to the MEXL add-in pertaining to resource allocation and choose "run analysis." Here, they should choose to maximize net margins (same as profits) in cell J13. The software will calculate the optimal efforts and the optimal profits thereof. They could choose an unconstrained scenario and obtain results as shown in Table 2, or a constrained one where they restrict the total budget to the existing budget, and obtain the optimal reallocation results as shown in Table 3.

# References

1  Mantrala, M.K. (2002) 'Allocating marketing resources,' in Weitz, B. and Wensley, R. (eds) *Handbook of Marketing*. London: Sage.

2  Procter & Gamble (n.d.) *P&G's Billion Dollar Brands: Trusted, Valued, Recognized*. Available at: www.pg.com/en_US/downloads/media/Fact_Sheets_BDB.pdf (accessed 27 July, 2015).

3  Nerney, C. (2010) 'Is it too late for Microsoft in the smartphone market?,' 11 October. Available from: www.itworld.com/article/2749561/business/is-it-too-late-for-microsoft-in-the-smartphone-market-.html (accessed 5 August, 2016).

4  Kharpal, A. (2015) 'Can Microsoft make a smartphone comeback?,' 8 May. Available from: www.cnbc.com/2015/05/08/a-microsoft-flagship-smartphone-is-coming-but-is-it-too-late.html (accessed 5 August, 2016).

5  Moorman, C. (2011) 'Integrating social media,' *Marketing Management*, 20(4), pp. 16–18.

6  George, G. (2005) 'Slack resources and the performance of privately held firms,' *Academy of Management Journal*, 48(4), pp. 661–76.

7  Ryan, B. (1991) *Advertising in a Recession*. New York: American Association of Advertising Agencies.

8  Scanlon, J. (2010) 'Is recession the time to boost ad spending?,' *Businessweek*, 4 May.

9  Capozzi, C. (n.d.) 'Consumer segments in the hotel industry.' Available at: http://smallbusiness.chron.com/consumer-segments-hotel-industry-13764.html (accessed 7 March, 2016).

10  Grant, T. and Beer, T. (2008) 'Life cycle assessment of greenhouse gas emissions from irrigated maize and their significance in the value chain,' *Australian Journal of Experimental Agriculture*, 48, pp. 375–81.

11  Brownswell, A. (2012) 'HSBC's Chris Clark on a new era for the bank's marketing,' 31 May. Available at: www.campaignlive.co.uk/article/1134018/hsbcs-chris-clark-new-era-banks-marketing (accessed 5 August, 2016).

12  Albers, S., Mantrala, M.K. and Sridhar, S. (2010) 'Personal selling elasticities: A meta-analysis,' *Journal of Marketing Research*, 47(5), pp. 840–53.

13  Sethuraman, R., Tellis, G.J. and Briesch, R.A. (2011) 'How well does advertising work? Generalizations from meta-analysis of brand advertising elasticities,' *Journal of Marketing Research*, 48(3), pp. 457–71.

14  Garfield, B. (2009) 'Future may be brighter, but it's apocalypse now,' *Advertising Age*, 80(10), pp. 1, 26–7.

15  Weaver, D.H., Beam, R.A., Brownlee, B.J., Voakes, P.S. and Wilhoit, G.C. (2014) *The American Journalist in the 21st Century: US News People at the Dawn of a New Millennium*, 2nd edn. New York: Taylor & Francis.

16  Lacy, S., Thorson, E. and Russial, J. (2004) 'Special issue editors' comments,' *Newspaper Research Journal*, 25(1), pp. 1–5.

17  Mantrala, M.K., Naik, P.A., Sridhar, S. and Thorson, E. (2007) 'Uphill or downhill? Locating the firm on a profit function,' *Journal of Marketing*, 71(2), pp. 26–44.

18  Farris, P.W. (2015) 'How advertising budgets are like fly balls,' *Darden Ideas to Action*, 10 April.

19  Israel, S. (2013) 'How Walmart and Heineken will use Shopperception to put your in-store experience in context,' 27 January. Available at: www.forbes.com/sites/shelisrael/2013/01/27/how-walmart-and-heineken-will-use-shoppercetion-to-put-your-in-store-experience-in-context/#531b3761fb76 (accessed 5 August, 2016).

20  Baker, B.J., Fang, Z. and Luo, X. (2014) 'Hour-by-hour sales impact of mobile advertising,' 30 April. Available at: http://dx.doi.org/10.2139/ssrn.2439396 (accessed 5 August, 2016).

21  Germann, F., Lilien, G.L. and Rangaswamy, A. (2013) 'Performance implications of deploying marketing analytics,' *International Journal of Research in Marketing*, 30(2), pp. 114–28.

22  Chand, S. (n.d.) *15 Methods for Setting up of Advertisement Budget under Top down Budgeting Method*. Available at: www.yourarticlelibrary.com/advertising/15-methods-for-setting-up-of-advertisement-budget-under-top-down-budgeting-method/22291/ (accessed 22 February, 2016).

23  Fischer, M., Albers, S., Wagner, N. and Frie, M. (2011) 'Dynamic marketing budget allocation across countries, products, and marketing activities,' *Marketing Science*, 30(4), pp. 568–85.

24  Kerin, R., Hartley, S. and Rudelius, W. (2012) *Marketing*, 12th edn. New York: McGraw-Hill Education.

25  Gabor, A. and Granger, C.W.J. (1964) 'Price sensitivity of the consumer,' *Journal of Advertising Research*, 4, pp. 40–4.

26  Anderson, E.T. and Simester, D.I. (2003) 'Effects of $9 price endings on retail sales: Evidence from field experiments,' *Quantitative Marketing and Economics*, 1(1), pp. 93–110.

27  Sethuraman, R., Tellis, G.J. and Briesch, R.A. (2011) 'How well does advertising work? Generalizations from meta-analysis of brand advertising elasticities,' *Journal of Marketing Research*, 48(3), pp. 457–71.

28  Albers, S., Mantrala, M.K. and Sridhar, S. (2010) 'Personal selling elasticities: A meta-analysis,' *Journal of Marketing Research*, 47(5), pp. 840–53.

29  Corstjens, M. and Merrihue, J. (2003) 'Optimal marketing,' *Harvard Business Review*, 81(10), pp. 114–21.

30  Danaher, P.J., Bonfrer, A. and Dhar, S. (2008) 'The effect of competitive advertising interference on sales for packaged goods,' *Journal of Marketing Research*, 45(2), pp. 211–25.

31  Naik, P.A. and Raman, K. (2003) 'Understanding the impact of synergy in multimedia communications,' *Journal of Marketing Research*, 40(4), pp. 375–88.

32  Mintz, O. and Currim, I.S. (2013) 'What drives managerial use of marketing and financial metrics and does metric use affect performance of marketing-mix activities?,' *Journal of Marketing*, 77(2), pp. 17–40.

## Companion website

Please visit the companion website, **www.palgravehighered.com/palmatier-ms**, to access summary videos from the authors, and full-length cases with datasets and step-by-step solution guides.

Chapter **9**

# Marketing Strategy: Implementing Marketing Principles and Data Analytics

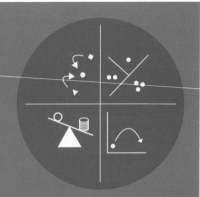

## Learning objectives

- Explain the importance of an overarching framework to drive marketing strategy decisions and the trends supporting its need.
- Describe evolutions in data, analytic tools, and targeting approaches over the past few decades.
- Review the logic and complexity behind each of the four Marketing Principles.
- Outline the keys success factors to executing a marketing strategy.
- Discuss the need to obtain or improve data and methodological capabilities to successfully implement marketing strategies.
- Understand and describe the role that the micro–macro duality plays in a successful marketing strategy.
- Critically discuss the benefits of using a customer-centric approach to implement marketing strategies.
- Highlight and analyze the salient data sources and important analytic techniques for marketing strategy.
- Elucidate the payoffs to successfully executing data analytics marketing strategies.

# Introduction

The marketing discipline and its approach to strategy have evolved dramatically over the past six decades: from a peripheral function that managed discretionary spending and outside vendors to a key component of a firm's overall business strategy, responsible for billion dollar budgets. The increasing importance and spending in the marketing domain have produced a wealth of new marketing strategies, approaches, and techniques, whether to find the best way to drive a company's performance or to address a range of specific marketing decisions. Business managers encounter vast numbers of buzzwords and consulting fads associated with new marketing approaches.

For example, in the 1970s and 1980s, the availability of scanner data enabled marketers to use databases to track sales and marketing efforts. A surge of new approaches and techniques followed, related to how to segment and target customers, as well as position products in competitive marketplaces. Most marketing firms employed basic marketing research techniques, such as focus groups, surveys, or cross-tabs of sales, but this era also led to the growth of direct marketing and targeted television advertising, because marketers were gaining more granular views of their customers' needs.[1]

In the 1990s and 2000s, the availability of customer relationship marketing (CRM) databases, clickstream data on customers' online searches, and the boom in syndicated data enabled marketers to use databases to observe micro-level data about every potential customer. The new approaches and techniques that arose as a result included online adword pricing, analyses of online product reviews, and Bayesian modeling, all infused with new marketing techniques such as online targeting and retargeting and micro-targeted television campaigns.[2]

Today, we have entered the "big data plus" era, such that marketers have data from smartphones and other Internet-enabled devices. The arrival of the Internet of things (IoT) means that the data available to marketers, including customer preferences and behaviors, doubles nearly every year. Thus, marketers have turned to mobile targeting and use day-to-day field experiments to make sense of the burgeoning data. They also are trying to create a coherent narrative across all marketing channels, to engage their customers more consistently.[3] Figure 9.1 summarizes the evolutions of marketing data, analytics techniques, and targeting approaches, which have significantly influenced marketing practice and strategies over the past six decades. In many markets, building data and analysis capabilities are becoming key to marketing success and superior financial performance.

> The arrival of the Internet of things (IoT) means that the data available to marketers, including customer preferences and behaviors, doubles nearly every year.

**Example:** Keytrade Bank (Belgium)

Belgium-based Keytrade Bank had the first Belgian online investment website. Priding itself on its customer loyalty, Keytrade Bank boasts a high Net Promoter Score, where 55% of its customers score it at a 9 or 10. The marketing department, inspired by its exceptionally high loyalty score, sought to create a loyalty rewards program. This program, called "Member Get Member" (MGM), rewarded customers who referred new customers with a cash incentive of €30 paid out to the recommender and the new customer. For years, this system was working well for Keytrade Bank, keeping the acquisition cost of new customers low. In the "ninth wave" of the program, Keytrade Bank implemented a new customer relationship management (CRM) system that helped it capture nearly every customer action. Through the use of a custom CRM tool, Keytrade Bank was able to send personalized reminder emails, integrate into customer's address books to ease referring, spread through easy social media integration, and automate the rewards processing system. With a well-built CRM, Keytrade Bank's MGM program was able to achieve 35% growth and attract over 5,000 new customers.[4]

Marketing decisions have become more complex. Take the phenomenon of pricing. A simple Google search of the term "pricing methods" yields at least eight major techniques: cost-based pricing, activity-based pricing, price customization, value pricing, freemium pricing, name your own price, pay what you please pricing, and adword pricing.

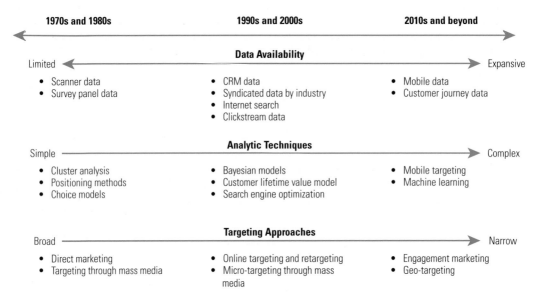

**Figure 9.1** Evolution of Marketing Data, Analytic Techniques, and Targeting Approaches

Such developments suggest an exciting future, but the exponential expansion of approaches and techniques also presents a dilemma to managers. It is hard to know which approach or method is most applicable in any specific situation. Worse, managers face an "over-choice" condition, such that their vast consideration sets can lead to decision-making paralysis. Marketers must address difficult questions in this complex environment, which undermines the effectiveness of their ultimate marketing strategies, including:

1  *When* should I use each specific approach or analysis tool?
2  *How* does each new marketing approach or tool improve my firm's performance?
3  *Which* approaches and tools are worth my firm's time and investment to implement?

Marketing textbooks or volumes targeted to marketing professionals now offer expanded content, reflecting these new approaches and methods. But this expanded provision of information just aggravates the situation. Organizing a book around specific approaches or techniques does not help resolve the over-choice issues, because managers simply confront more and more content that they must dig through to design and implement marketing strategy. New developments in marketing and research techniques also appear likely to continue to increase in number; the decision-making paralysis problem is only going to get worse.

This book takes a different approach to marketing strategy. Rather than adding to its complexity, we attempt to simplify it by arguing that managers' marketing decisions should focus on solving four underlying issues that come along with efforts to design any specific marketing initiative or develop their overall marketing strategies. When a marketing manager is sitting in a conference room, faced with the need to make a marketing decision (e.g., increase customer acquisition rates or retention, expand profit margins, strengthen brand equity), rather than trying to identify the one unique approach or consulting book to use, instead they should deconstruct the marketing decision into the four Principles and attack it, one Marketing Principle at a time. First Principles – "fundamental concepts or assumptions on which a theory, system, or method is based" – represent the most critical hurdles to marketing success, and they provide a structured approach to developing a marketing strategy.[5] By addressing each principle in turn, using analysis tools, processes, and research techniques that align with each fundamental marketing complexity, a manager gains a structured, robust way to address the vast plethora of marketing issues. For example, Chapter 2 offers a range of approaches and analysis tools focused on managing customer heterogeneity, to address the issue of *all customers differ*. Organizing the varied approaches, tools, processes, and discussions around these four fundamental principles means that every marketing decision appears within a meaningful context. The processes in each framework are designed to enable data-driven, rather than gut-based, decisions. Specifically, each Marketing Principle has an overall framework that reflects the data input needs, relevant approaches, processes, and analyses required to address these four underlying complexities:

1 All customers differ.
2 All customers change.
3 All competitors react.
4 All resources are limited.

This chapter therefore begins with a short discussion of historical trends that increase the relevance and need for a First Principles approach to marketing strategy. We synthesize the underlying problem and offer an overarching solution approach. Within this overview, we remind readers of concepts, analyses, and decisions addressed in the rest of this book. Finally, this chapter integrates the key implementation processes and techniques necessary to integrate the Marketing Principles; we also offer a discussion of how to build data analytics capabilities that enable firms to execute their marketing strategies successfully.

When a marketing manager is sitting in a conference room, faced with the need to make a marketing decision (e.g., increase customer acquisition rates or retention, expand profit margins, strengthen brand equity), rather than trying to identify the one unique approach or consulting book to use, instead they should deconstruct the marketing decision into the four Principles and attack it, one Marketing Principle at a time.

## Trends Increasing the Importance of the First Principles Approach to Marketing Strategy

Several business and marketing trends make it critical for firms to address each of the First Principles if they hope to succeed. In particular:

1 Firms are focusing on smaller customer segments in their move toward one-to-one customer marketing and their attempts to exploit natural differences in customers' needs.
2 Customers, products, and markets are changing faster than they did in the past, which requires managers to identify the change and respond quickly.
3 Competitive rivalry is increasing due to greater globalization, the increased ease of reaching customers through the Internet, and the entry of many new firms from emerging markets (e.g., China, India), which is making it more critical to build sustainable competitive advantages (SCAs) to maintain a leadership position.
4 The increase in the amount of data throughout the business and ease of making data-driven decisions increases the viability and impact of data analytical over gut-based marketing decisions.

We detail how each of these trends is enhancing the importance of using First Principle and data analytical approaches to developing marketing strategies.

First, firms are focusing on smaller and smaller customer segments in their move toward one-to-one customer marketing, thereby exploiting the natural differences in customer needs. As stated in Chapter 2, marketing has moved from a mass marketing era (firms use mass media to appeal to an entire market with a single message), to a niche marketing era (firms apply marketing efforts to well-defined, narrow segments of consumers), to a *one-to-one marketing era* (firms attempt to apply marketing strategies directly to specific consumers). These trends have continued largely because they lead to the delivery of products or services that better match a customer's intrinsic preferences (i.e., gives customers what they want). All else being equal, the smaller the segment, the more closely a targeted offering will match the needs of the members of that segment. By focusing on a subsample of the overall market with mostly homogeneous customers, firms also can better anticipate future needs and detect emerging trends, which allows them to respond with well-targeted solutions before their more broadly focused competitors do. To compete, it is critical for a firm to have a process to manage customer heterogeneity (MP#1). Having a framework that allows a firm to continually and deliberately address the preferences of a micro-segment makes the process of managing customer heterogeneity more efficient. Across all three eras, the underlying method for dealing with customer heterogeneity is the same: focus on smaller groups of customers, such that the needs of each group are more similar as they are subdivided into smaller units, until the focus reaches an individual customer.

Second, customers, products, and markets are changing faster than in the past, which requires managers to identify and respond quickly to these dynamic changes. As stated in Chapter 3, to manage dynamics, marketing has moved from a lifecycle approach (in a customer lifecycle, across multiple products and firms, customers can be aggregated to identify an average change or migration that they follow as they age) to a *dynamic customer segmentation approach* (segmenting a firm's existing customers according to a criterion that defines migration patterns expected to be similar). This persistent trend allows firms to manage market dynamics by focusing on smaller and smaller groups of customers, either by assimilating them into small segments with similar trends or by projecting the trends in each individual's behavior. All else being equal, the smaller the target segment and the clearer the projected needs, the more closely a targeted offering will match the needs of the members of that segment. Without being equipped to deal with customer dynamics (MP#2) in the marketplace, firms cannot accurately project what their customer (or industry) will prefer in the future. With a framework for focusing on smaller groups of customers, firms get to know the projected needs of each customer group precisely, until their focus reaches future projects for each individual customer.

Third, competitive rivalry is increasing in conjunction with increased globalization, ease of reaching customers via the Internet, and entry of new firms from emerging markets. As Chapter 4 establishes, to manage competitive attacks, marketing has moved from a product equity to a customer equity perspective. The customer equity perspective recommends regarding customers as financial assets, such that they can be measured, managed, and maximized, similar to any other firm asset. To manage competitor reactions, firms must build and maintain strong barriers to withstand competitive attacks, by building brand, offering, and relationship equities. A firm's barriers to competition, or SCAs, must meet these three requirements:

1 Customers care about what the firm offers.
2 They do it better than competitors.
3 Their offerings are hard to duplicate.

Having a framework that allows a firm to build and maintain barriers (MP#3) makes the process of managing competitive rivalry more efficient. This framework also generates descriptions of the firm's SCAs, now and in the future, and the strategies it should use to build and maintain these SCAs as outputs. The outputs aggregate insights gained from more fine-grained analyses, in an effort to support more effective macro-level decision making.

Fourth, the increase in the amount of data across all aspects of business and the ability to make data-driven decisions more easily increases the viability and impact of data analytical rather than gut-based marketing decisions. As stated in Chapter 8, marketing has moved from a gut feeling or heuristic era (managers solved the resource allocation problem using simple rules of thumb, driven by intuition and judgment) to a data era (the firm attempts to use historical data about resource trade-offs and past outcomes to determine marketing decisions). Firms perennially trade off among a variety of marketing alternatives, and they always face resource constraints. Having a framework that allows the firm to make resource trade-offs optimally (MP#4) makes the process of managing resource constraints more efficient. The framework also enables the firm to develop and track key metrics of marketing effectiveness, as well as a set of approaches for allocating resources optimally.

# Overview of the Four Marketing Principles: Problems and Solutions

## MP#1: All Customers Differ → Managing Customer Heterogeneity

### Problem

The basic phenomenon that motivates the first Marketing Principle is that *all customers differ*. Customer needs emerge from a variety of sources, including: basic, personal differences; varying life experiences;

unique functional needs for the product; distinct aspirational self-identities; and previous persuasion-based activities focused on changing their preferences. These changes vary so widely that a firm could be faced with the task of catering to two diametrically opposite consumer segments, and the need to satisfy both of them, within its cost constraints. If a firm sells products or services that ignore the differences across consumer segments and tries to reach the "average" between these two segments, it will lose both. Other firms targeting each separate segment can better satisfy that segment's needs, and no customers want the average product. Thus, the main challenge is evident: What is the best way to sell to customers when they all have varying needs?

### Solution

The solution lies in selecting a *specific* segment of customers whose preferences match very closely with the firm's selected set of offerings, then targeting them by positioning the selected offering in a way that highlights why it is the best solution for a subsegment (i.e., why the firm's offering is better than any offering competitors might provide). This is broadly known as the STP (segmentation, targeting, and positioning) approach.

*Segmenting* is the process of dividing the overall market into groups, such that potential customers in each group have similar needs and desires for a particular product or service (e.g., high preference for quality and service warranties, low need for large assortments), but the differences across groups (based on customer characteristics) are maximal. *Targeting* involves deciding which segment(s) to go after, based on the market attractiveness and competitive strength of each subsegment. *Positioning* refers to the process of improving a firm's relative advantage in the minds of its targeted customers, by emphasizing the key attributes of its offerings for the right subsegments. We discuss several techniques for performing segmentation in Chapter 2. For example, cluster analysis uses survey data about customers' needs and desires, as well as their characteristics, to classify a large set of heterogeneous consumers or companies into a few homogeneous segments. Often used in combination with a customer-centric approach or strategy, STP helps the firm recognize the long-term value of its core customer segment and makes it central to all its major internal business processes and decisions.

## MP#2: All Customers Change → Managing Customer Dynamics

### Problem

The phenomenon that motivates the second Marketing Principle is that *all customers change.* Customers' changing needs arise from several sources, including: discrete life events; typical lifecycle choices; learning effects; product lifecycle effects; or changing environmental contexts. How do these changes challenge firms? When changes are rapid and diverse, even firms that have done a good job of selecting the right subsegments face a constantly moving target. If a firm underestimates the problem and expects that changes in customers' proclivities over time are minor (compared with their stable differences), they will always be following dominant trends in the marketplace. Instead, competitors might strategically anticipate customer changes and adjust their value proposition to target customers proactively. Thus, the main challenge is finding out how to sell to customers whose preferences constantly change.

### Solution

The solution lies in applying STP solutions to a customer dynamic problem, that is, segmenting the firm's existing customers according to similarities in their migration patterns, then developing customized strategies for the distinct patterns. We discuss three approaches associated with this solution. The first, *the AER (acquisition, expansion, retention) approach*, assumes that customers in each of three different AER stages are similar, so it develops specific strategies to deal with customers in each stage. In a second approach, *lost customer analysis*, firms set regular intervals for contacting lost customers to identify the causes of their transition, where they went, and potential recovery strategies. The firm takes appropriate corrective action depending on whether the lost customer was in the firm's target segment and the root cause. *Choice models* offer a way to understand customer AER decisions, as we discuss in Chapter 3. Finally, a *hidden Markov model (HMM) approach* uses the changes in past customer behavior to identify customer "states" (or dynamic segments) and model the probability of transitioning among those various states. The dynamic segments can be defined in terms of their economic value to the firm and their probabilities of switching from state to state, which is useful for firms that seek to understand the importance of anticipated changes in customer behavior. When AER approaches combine with individual-level approaches like lost customer analysis, the firm can develop a detailed picture of how past or anticipated changes in customer behaviors are likely to change the composition of their target segments.

## MP#3: All Competitors React → Managing Sustainable Competitive Advantage

### Problem

The third Marketing Principle is motivated by the knowledge that *all competitors react.* Firms see their competitors attack from several sides, including technical innovations that make their own products and services obsolete, as well as cultural, environmental, or random factors that suddenly sway customers away from loyalty to a firm and toward seeking out another firm's products. The entrepreneurship and creativity of diverse actors also can disrupt the very nature of the business in the firm's industry. Intense competitive rivalry then challenges even the most prepared firms, which already selected the right subsegments of the market and continue to do a good job of managing existing and anticipated trends in customers' migration patterns. But still, competitors persistently try to copy their success or innovate business processes and offerings to match customers' needs and desires better. If a firm underestimates competitive reactions, it lacks suitably strong barriers to withstand attacks, which cause it to lose its dominant market position. Thus, the main challenge is learning how to manage the ever-present competitive actions and reactions.

### Solution

The solution entails building and maintaining strong barriers, or SCAs, to withstand competitive attacks. A firm has SCA when it is able to generate more customer value than competitive firms in its industry for the same set of products and service categories. In other words, customers care about what this SCA offers, the firm does it better than competitors (which generates a relative advantage), and the SCA is hard to duplicate or substitute, even with significant resources. Most firms build SCA by building *brand, offering, and relationship (BOR) equities.* Building brand equities entails strong brand positioning (whether a brand captures the firm's desired place in the customer's mind), brand architecture (rationale and structure among the firm, its products, and brand/product extensions), and brand extensions (the approach the firm uses to launch a new offering by leveraging an existing brand). In Chapter 5, we discuss surveys as a tool to conduct brand audits, which help establish the brand's positioning, architecture, and extension strategies. To build offering equity, a firm should invest in research and development (R&D) so that it can introduce the newest, most innovative products, reduce costs, expand supplementary services, or fundamentally alter the customer experience. To the extent that these new offerings meet customers' needs better than existing offerings, and customers care about the new features, a firm possesses high offering equity. Another strategy is to reposition an existing product dramatically, such as by removing some features and adding others so that the total offering appeals to a different customer segment with a "new" value proposition. In Chapter 6, we discuss conjoint analysis as a way for a firm to redesign its product offerings. Finally, to build relationship equity, a firm can use social programs (e.g., meals, sporting events) to convey the customer's special status, structural programs (e.g., electronic order processing interfaces, customized packaging) that provide investments that customers might not make themselves, or financial programs that provide economic benefits (e.g., special discounts, giveaways, free shipping, extended payment terms). In Chapter 7, we discuss regression analysis as a way for a firm to gauge the effectiveness of its relationship marketing efforts.

## MP#4: All Resources Are Limited ➔ Managing Resource Trade-offs

### Problem

The fourth and final Marketing Principle deals with the issue that *all resources are limited*. Resource constraints could emerge from different sources, including: a firm's resource slack (usable resources that change with the health of the economy); changes in the composition of a firm's segments; variations in the competitiveness of a firm's product portfolio and landscape; and differences in the effectiveness of a firm's current marketing activities. How does this situation complicate firms' marketing problems? Resource constraints mean that even if firms are excellent at selecting the right subsegments (MP#1), managing existing and anticipated trends in customers' migration patterns (MP#2), and developing SCA through brand, offering, and relationships equities (MP#3), they must constantly adjust their marketing budgets and reallocate them in a manner commensurate with market conditions. Thus, the main challenge surrounds the question: How can a firm effectively manage resource trade-offs when executing its marketing strategy?

### Solution

The solution to managing resource trade-offs is understanding the marginal benefit and cost of every incremental dollar devoted to a segment or product, such that the ultimate allocation decision is proportional to the marginal benefit and cost trade-off associated with each segment or product. This proportionality can be accomplished by two approaches. The first is to create, measure, and monitor performance at every turn, using a *metrics-driven approach*. Firms often use financial metrics, typically based on financial ratios, which easily can be converted into monetary outcomes, such as the net profit return on investment, and thus link to the firms' overall accounting measures. They also use marketing metrics, based on values related to consumers' attitudes, behaviors, and mindsets about a firm's products. These metrics include awareness, satisfaction, loyalty, and brand equity. Intermediate marketing metrics are faster at detecting change and allow for more diagnostics related to the effects of marketing expenditures than the more aggregated financial metrics.

A second approach is to validate the effectiveness of each marketing dollar using the same metrics, which reflects an *attribution-based allocation approach*. In Chapter 8, we recommend that firms use *attribution-based models* to review their historical data and measure the impacts of various marketing activities using mathematical models. Historical data contain insightful information about whether and how much marketing resources truly increase outcomes. With a well-executed attribution approach, marketing managers can discern the relative impact of each resource, which is crucial to their optimal allocation. This step ensures that the firm manages its resource trade-offs effectively, to fund each initiative based on its expected benefit and cost.

The Marketing Principles, solutions, and supporting analytical techniques are summarized in Table 9.1.

## Synergistic Integration of the Four Marketing Principles

A precursor to successfully utilizing the Marketing Principles' approach to marketing strategy is understanding how they fit together, so that the collective lessons learned are greater than the learning from each principle individually. The MPs work together synergistically to improve the effectiveness of a marketing strategy in two ways, namely, *temporal interconnections* that allow the output of one MP to provide key input data to another MP, and *micro–macro duality*, which supports a deep understanding of customers at micro levels (avoiding aggregation bias) while also supporting strategic and resource-oriented decisions at macro levels.

### Temporal Interconnections

The four Marketing Principles are noteworthy for their hierarchical nature. Figure 9.2 illustrates how the MPs are temporally connected in practice. The gray boxes represent the overarching marketing principle, and the blue ovals represent the solution, or output, of each principle. For example, solving

**Table 9.1** Summary of First Principles, Solutions, and Supporting Analytical Techniques

| First Principles | Solutions | Supporting Analytical Techniques |
|---|---|---|
| All customers differ | The solution to the managing customer heterogeneity lies in selecting a specific segment of customers whose preferences match very closely with the firm's selected set of offerings, and targeting them by positioning the selected offering in a way that highlights why it is the best solution for a subsegment | Cluster analysis uses survey data on customers' needs and desires, and their characteristics to classify a large set of heterogeneous consumers or companies into a few homogeneous segments |
| All customers change | The solution to managing customer dynamics lies in applying strategies similar to MP#1, but to the customer dynamic problem, i.e. segmenting a firm's existing customers according to a criterion that defines migration patterns that are expected to be similar | Using lost customer analysis, firms set regular intervals for contacting lost customers to identify the cause of their transition, where they went, and potential recovery strategies. The firm takes appropriate corrective action depending on whether the lost customer was in the firm's target segment, or not. Dynamic segmentation using cluster analysis, and choice models are used to understand customer changes and AER decisions |
| All competitors react | The solution to managing competitor reaction lies in building and maintaining strong barriers to withstand competitive attacks. These barriers are called sustainable competitive advantages (SCAs) | Regression analysis helps firms gauge the effectiveness of its brand, offering, and relationship marketing efforts. Conjoint analysis allows managers to understand the relative value across different product features |
| All resources are limited | The solution to limited resources lies in understanding the marginal benefit and costs of every incremental dollar across segments and products, such that the ultimate allocation decision made by the firm is proportional to the marginal benefit and cost trade-off associated with each segment or product | With response models, firms use historical data to measure the impacts of various marketing investments using mathematical models. Experimental and attributional models allow managers to understand the exact quantitative effectiveness of different marketing resources |

MP#3 requires output from the first and second principles; solving MP#4 requires outputs from the first, second, and third principles.

Suppose that a manufacturer of roofing solutions seeks to develop a new product that will appeal to its customer base of industrial contractors. As we read in Chapter 4, this firm will try to develop a new product that represents an SCA (MP#3). This new offering must provide something new that customers care about, the firm can design and manufacturer better than competitors, and is hard to duplicate. However, the firm will find it very difficult – if not impossible – to build an effective offering or positioning strategy without knowing which customer sub-segments it wants to target and how it can uniquely fulfill their needs and benefits (relative to other offerings). Should the new shingle be offered at a high price, with cutting-edge life expectancy, and aesthetics, and a reasonable installation speed? Or should it provide a medium price level, with average features, but rapid delivery? To answer these questions, the firm needs the outputs from MP#1 to even begin building its SCA (e.g., positioning statement in Figure 9.2). Moreover, to build an SCA that thwarts competitive attacks, the firm needs to account for how contractors might change over time and understand when these customers might start or stop buying specific product features. For example, have contractors' preferences for speed of installation changed over time? Do they change as the contractors gain more experience? The

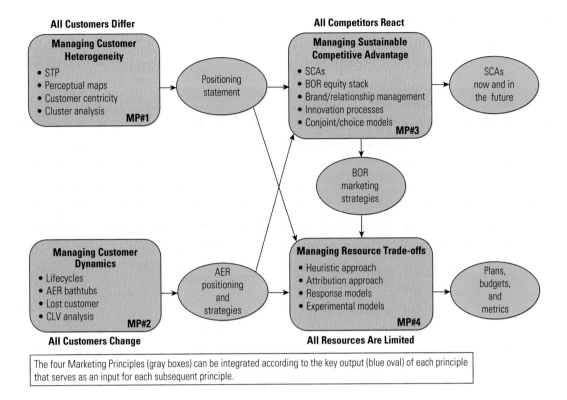

**Figure 9.2** Integrating the Four Marketing Principles

output of MP#2, capturing the triggers of migration across stages, thus represents further critical input to the problem of building SCA (e.g., AER positioning and strategies in Figure 9.2). The same intuition applies to the solution of MP#4, because making resource trade-offs requires a clear understanding of the first three principles.

To develop an effective marketing strategy requires the understanding that the four MPs are interconnected, in a natural sequence. Starting from the overall market in MP#1, then moving to the firm's own customer base in MP#2 and building a barrier around these segments and customers using BOR strategies (MP#3), only with the outputs of these three MPs can a firm allocate its resources in an efficient manner (MP#4).

> To develop an effective marketing strategy requires the understanding that the four MPs are interconnected, in a natural sequence.

## Micro–Macro Duality

The First Principle approach to marketing strategy also represents a **micro–macro duality**, such that it identifies insights at the micro level while supporting macro-level marketing decisions. This process is critical. If a firm only averages the available data and studies them at the macro level, it will overlook many deep insights and trends. In particular, newly emerging customer trends get hidden when they are averaged in with the mass of mainstream customers. Even worse, two very different segments might be merged inaccurately, which would provide misleading insights into what these smaller groups of customers really want.

A micro–macro duality is especially pertinent to MP#3, for which the AER strategy grid captures acquisition, expansion, and retention strategies (i.e., microanalysis of customer dynamics) across customer personas (i.e., microanalysis of customer heterogeneity). When a manager uses the AER strategy grid to populate the BOR equity grid, the firm gains a macro perspective on market-based sources of SCA. This micro–macro duality also provides two key macro outputs: descriptions of the firm's SCAs now and in the future and the BOR strategies that the firm should use to build and maintain these SCAs. Both outputs aggregate insights gained from more fine-grained analyses, in an effort to support more effective macro decision making. This micro–macro duality also is critical to a successful marketing strategy, because true understanding of customers and markets occurs at the micro level, but strategic and resource decisions take place at the macro level.

## Building Marketing Analytics Capabilities

Another precursor to implementing the four principles framework successfully is for a firm to develop customer analytics capabilities. **Customer analytics** can be broadly defined as a technology-enabled, model-supported approach to harnessing customer and market data to understand and serve customers. Firms using customer analytics rely on data and methods (rather than gut feelings) to test and improve their marketing decision frameworks. Why exactly does the use of customer analytics help a firm? Firms deploying customer analytics solutions use a scientific, data-driven approach to understand their customer base, so they improve their overall market-sensing capabilities. *Market sensing* includes all the activities involved in gathering market data or intelligence, disseminating these data throughout the organization, analyzing the data from different perspectives, and acting on the information gleaned. It also prepares and emboldens firms in the marketplace. In B2C and B2B markets, rapid technological advances in customer data collection, data concatenation (linking), and data analysis abilities help firms differentiate themselves according to their ability to acquire, cross-sell, upsell, and retain customers.[6] Accordingly, the resources that firms devote to customer analytics have grown exponentially in recent years. Market reports in 2009 indicated that only 10% of firms regularly employed customer analytics,[7] but that number grew to more than 80% by 2013, with firms spending nearly one-quarter (21%) of their marketing budgets on customer analytics projects.[8] Thus, the vendor market for customer analytics is burgeoning; for example, the worldwide customer analytics software market, consisting of data ware-housing software and analytics tools, grew 8.7% to reach $34.9 billion in 2012, with a projected growth rate of 9.7% through to 2017.[9] So, it is no surprise that numerous consulting companies actively promote customer analytics tools and skills to their clients to aid in identifying business opportunities.

**Example:** Anomaly (Australia)

Anomaly is a boutique consulting company in Australia tasked with enhancing acquisition efficiencies for a major entertainment retailer, while increasing its market share. By leveraging the client's customer data and conducting a series of detailed profiling and segmentation analyses, it was able to achieve 34% savings in the cost per acquisition and a 14% decline in customer churn rate. Driven by the analytics data, hot/cold maps of customer traffic were created for the client's local marketing as well.[10]

Firms deploying analytics perform better than those that do not adopt such practices, because they are better prepared to understand what customers want and react to changes in customer and environmental trends.[11] Thus, we expect that firms with analytics capabilities can better implement the Marketing Principles. They can manage customer heterogeneity, manage customer change, respond to competitors by building a sustainable competitive advantage, and manage resource trade-offs. The effective use of customer analytics requires building data capabilities and methodological capabilities.

Firms deploying analytics perform better than those that do not adopt such practices, because they are better prepared to understand what customers want and react to changes in customer and environmental trends.

## Data Capabilities

A firm can increase its **data capabilities** by building databases that improve three forms of intelligence:

- *economic:* helps understand the trading environment and relationship partners
- *customer:* clarifies customers' needs and behaviors
- *competitive:* reveals the competitive landscape in terms of threats and opportunities.

Data specific to each of these areas are becoming more widely available, with firms beginning to invest in internal databases to link their marketing efforts to financial outcomes. Technological advances like the Internet and social media are profoundly affecting these trends too. Broadly, such data sources can be classified into structured versus unstructured data. Structured data include information on customers' identities, purchase histories, and preferences, as are typically available in customer relationship management (CRM) databases. Unstructured data extend beyond the customer–firm exchange and include messages that customers post on social media or information about friends with similar tastes. Firms should strive to match their structured and unstructured data to maximize their data capabilities.

## Methodological Capabilities

A firm can build **methodological capabilities** by mastering the analytical tools that we describe in detail in the Data Analytics Techniques and more generally in each chapter, which outline the most critical analytical tools relevant to marketing strategy. There are three main purposes of the analyses we describe in this book (see Table 9.2): simplification through data reduction; linking variables to outcomes by identifying causality; and finding trade-offs among variables through resource optimization:

1 **Data simplification methods** allow a firm to simplify large amounts of data into smaller, more meaningful, more actionable insights. Factor analysis provides a means to find common factors in a dataset and group variables that are highly correlated; cluster analysis helps the firm group similar customers into customer segments.
2 **Linking methods** support cause-and-effect investigations of marketing interventions. Experiments enable firms to link a marketing treatment to an outcome and identify the causal effects of a marketing action. Multiple regression allows firms to link multiple marketing predictors to a continuous marketing outcome. Choice models reveal links between multiple marketing predictors and a discrete marketing outcome.
3 **Optimization methods** help firms trade off among multiple marketing variables. For example, conjoint analysis helps determine individual-level trade-offs across dissimilar product features, such as size and price. Response models allow a firm to find the dollar impact of spending on different marketing interventions, and customer lifetime value analysis accounts for customer, time, and dynamic differences to make trade-offs across customers whose predicted future levels of profitability for the firm vary.

**Table 9.2** Building Methodological Capabilities across Three Key Purposes

| Analysis Purpose | Description | Analytical Techniques |
|---|---|---|
| Data simplification | Allows a firm to simplify large amounts of data into smaller, more meaningful and more actionable insights | Factor analysis, cluster analysis, multidimensional scaling, principal components analysis, hidden Markov models |
| Linking variables to outcomes | Allows a firm to perform cause-and-effect studies of their marketing interventions | Experiments, multivariate regression analysis, choice models |
| Resource optimization | Allows a firm to find trade-offs among multiple marketing variables | Conjoint analysis, response models, customer lifetime analysis |

Various analysis tools are available to help students and firms improve their methodological capabilities. Readers would do well to consider Marketing Engineering by Decision Pro, marketing analytics software that is designed to work as a "plug-in" to Microsoft Excel (a cloud-based version is also forthcoming). More popularly known as MEXL, this software allows managers to use Microsoft Excel and bring in relevant add-ins to a variety of analyses, as required. The software solutions include factor and cluster analyses that underlie data reduction capabilities to simplify large amounts of data into smaller, more meaningful, and more actionable insights. They also include regression, choice models, and diffusion models to build data-linking capabilities and perform cause-and-effect studies. Finally, the software solutions include response models, conjoint models, and optimization models that improve firms' marketing resource optimization capabilities.

In Data Analytics Technique 9.1, we list the different models available in MEXL, for each of the four MPs. Although this software is an excellent cost-effective companion to this book, many other data analysis packages are available, including SAS, IBM's SPSS, open source software such as R, and visual packages such as JMP. We focus on MEXL because of its simplicity and resonance with our approach for this book. But this focus is not meant to ignore other packages that are effective for integrating the concepts, approaches, and techniques offered here.

# Executing Marketing Strategies

To enjoy the benefits of following a First Principle approach, firms also must undertake the effective execution of their marketing strategy. Data and methodological capabilities are the first tools to put in the toolbox that is needed to build research processes and create the analytical models that underlie data-based decisions. Two additional factors also can improve the effective implementation of a firm marketing strategy:

1 Instituting a *customer-centric approach* across the organization to ensure an external customer focus in decisions and to better motivate employees to satisfy customer needs.
2 Continuously *iterating* and *improving* each aspect of the marketing strategy, with the recognition that an effective marketing strategy is a process, not an endpoint, and requires continuous adaption.

## Customer-centric Approach

In Chapter 2, we described the customer-centric approach as a company-wide philosophy that places customers' needs at the center of an organization's strategic process and uses the resultant insights to make decisions. Being customer centric requires a firm to align multiple aspects of its organization to be consistent with this perspective, such as leadership, structure, culture, metrics, processes, and strategy. Senior management typically needs to adopt this philosophy first, to make customer-centric decisions. Then, the customer-centric approach can function as an enabler, promoting customer preferences throughout the organization in the implementation of a marketing strategy.[12] It promotes *internal* alignment. A customer-centric approach also increases the firm's knowledge of and commitment to focal customer segments. This focus positions the firm favorably to identify any unmet needs and enables it to adapt quickly and effectively to changing needs.[13] Furthermore, a customer-centric approach offers execution and adaptation benefits that improve the overall effectiveness of a firm's marketing strategies.

Successful customer centricity depends on a strong *market orientation*, defined as the organization-wide generation of market intelligence, dissemination of that intelligence across departments, and organization-wide responsiveness. A market orientation can capture an aspect of a firm's customer centricity that enhances its performance.[14] It involves three dimensions: intelligence generation, intelligence dissemination, and responsiveness.[15] Thus, a market orientation implies that a firm can capture customer preferences, communicate these needs throughout the organization, and use the information to target their needs, all of which allows the firm to match customer needs better and implement and adapt its marketing strategies on an ongoing basis.

# MEXL: Using Data Analytics to Implement Marketing Principles

## Description

Marketing Engineering (MEXL), an add-on to Microsoft Excel, contains mathematical tools that enable data analytic implementation of the four marketing principles.

## When to Use It

- To practice implementing the four marketing principles and developing effective marketing strategies.
- To enable data analytics techniques that can reveal insights about marketing strategic choices, before their actual implementation.

## How It Works

We present an overview of the analyses associated with each of the marketing principles detailed in this book, along with the MEXL models that enable these analytic processes. Notably, MEXL contains almost all the analyses we recommend in our input-process-output approach to each marketing principle (presently MEXL is an add-on to Excel but a cloud-based version is being launched soon). MEXL is accessible online for a fee at www.decisionpro.biz/business-users/software/marketing-engineering-for-excel.

**MP#1:** Target products to meet the needs of different customer segments and manage customer heterogeneity.

| Recommended Approaches | MEXL Models/Analyses |
|---|---|
| Segmenting | Factor analysis, cluster analysis, discriminant analysis |
| Targeting | GE matrix |
| Positioning | Perceptual maps, positioning maps |

**MP#2:** Adjust strategies over time to adapt to changing customer needs.

| Recommended Approaches | MEXL Models/Analyses |
|---|---|
| Lifecycle approach | Bass diffusion models |
| Acquisition, expansion, retention model | Choice models |
| Dynamic segmentation | Customer lifetime value calculator |

**MP#3:** Introduce new products to create a sustainable competitive advantage as a barrier to other firms attacking the position.

| Recommended Approaches | MEXL Models/Analyses |
|---|---|
| Brand, offering, relationship equity grids | Multiple regression, choice models |
| Innovation process | Conjoint models |

**MP#4:** Manage limited resources by making resource trade-offs among marketing mix categories and brands.

| Recommended Approaches | MEXL Models/Analyses |
|---|---|
| Attribution approach | Response models, choice models, multiple regression |

Customer centricity grants an organization deep knowledge about and commitment to its focal customers, supporting faster detection and responses to changing market conditions. This continuous, real-time responsiveness is built into the organization's structure, culture, and processes. Customer-centric metrics also provide quick feedback on any misalignments, such that any strategy the firm adopts becomes more effective.

Customer centricity grants an organization deep knowledge about and commitment to its focal customers, supporting faster detection and responses to changing market conditions.

## Continuously Iterating and Improving

Sustainable offerings that stand the test of time require recognition that the firm cannot solve all the Marketing Principles simultaneously, because of their complex and interrelated nature. Instead, firms need an **iterative approach** to integrate and execute the principles.[16] An ideal solution might optimize all the MPs simultaneously, but firms likely lack the required time, resources, and skills to implement any such solution. Instead, they can gradually improve their overall marketing functions by improving one MP at a time, while maintaining their existing (even if suboptimal) approach to the other three MPs. In Figure 9.2 above, for any given time period (e.g., 6–12 months), a firm might focus on improving the processes associated with one MP (gray box) and the related macro output (blue oval), while continuing with "business as usual" in other areas. Then, in the next period, it can improve the second MP, having already improved the first one, and follow the same process for the third and fourth MPs. With this approach, the firm can cycle through all four MPs in four planning periods, thereby gradually improving through its focus on one principle at a time, so that it can collect and analyze data effectively to make significant improvements.

Consider an example. A firm might conduct a deep segmentation analysis of its customers and define them better, on the basis of their current needs and product uses. While conducting this study, the firm would maintain its current focus regarding the other three MPs. In the next quarter, this firm can refocus to determine where the newly defined customer segments migrate when they undergo changes. By dedicating its resources to one MP at a time, it gains the best chance to maximize its outputs in a complex environment.

## Executing a Marketing Strategy Using Marketing Principles and Data Analytics

Firms that adopt a well-planned marketing strategy based on the Marketing Principles and data analytics have great potential to reap financial rewards. We illustrate this claim with Best Buy's efforts between 2001 and 2015. In 2001, Best Buy was still a dominant electronics retailer, but it was starting to see slower growth in business and profitability drops. By careful reasoning, Best Buy deduced that the slowdown was due to specialty retailers (e.g., RadioShack), the growth of the powerful and low-cost retailer Walmart, and the boom in electronic retailing induced by e-commerce. Even more important, it recognized that it seemed stuck in the "unprofitable middle": not good enough to cater to specialty shoppers who offered high margins, or to low-margin value shoppers who provided attractively high volume. Thus, it faced the fundamental marketing problem of managing customer heterogeneity (MP#1). To better position its products in the marketplace, Best Buy assimilated a massive database of more than 500 million sales transactions across its stores and began to analyze shopping patterns. A segmentation exercise classified shoppers in five segments, with specific names: upper-income men, suburban mothers, small-business owners, young family men, and technology enthusiasts, where "high-income men, referred to internally as Barrys, tend to be enthusiasts of action movies and cameras. Suburban moms, called Jills, are busy but usually willing to talk about helping their families. Male technology enthusiasts, nicknamed Buzzes, are early adopters, interested in buying and showing off the latest gadgets."[17]

Through this data analytics exercise, Best Buy then designated each of its stores according to the one or two segments it catered to, for the most part. Thus, it could eliminate redundant inventory, save costs, train staff to identify shoppers by segments, serve each shopper more efficiently, and increase revenues. These efforts improved profitability on the revenue and cost sides, while also enabling Best Buy to position each of its stores according to the target market in that geographic area. Moreover, it could track the sales of each store running this new segmentation strategy and build response models that linked marketing investments in each store to its profitability. In turn, Best Buy could manage resource trade-offs better (MP#4) and allocate extra marketing dollars only to those stores that showed the promise of profitability.

However, by 2004, Best Buy realized that its competitors all were adopting similar strategies, even as target consumers' preferences were evolving rapidly to expect every store in their geographic area (including competitors) to cater specifically to their tastes. The fundamental marketing problem of managing customer change thus arose (MP#2). To manage changing preferences and cater to only the most profitable customers, Best Buy shifted its analysis from the store to the customer level. Specifically, it assimilated longitudinal data about each customer's transaction history, then built models to estimate the lifetime value of each customer. This exercise helped the company take its segmentation strategy to the next, individual level. For example, Best Buy could tailor marketing communication messages specifically to each customer in a geographic area, as well as mail promotional coupons to customers according to their expected or forecasted profitability. With this approach, Best Buy could track, manage, and maximize profitability at the customer level, staying ahead of competitors that continued to manage their businesses at the store level. The data analysis also could forecast the future profitability of each customer (in each store), creating a view of each customer as a profit center. The resulting individual-level response models helped connect marketing investments (e.g., promotional coupons) in each customer to that customer's future sales and profitability – that is, helped manage resource trade-offs (MP#4) at the customer level. By providing the right coupon to the right customers (i.e., those most profitable to Best Buy), the company outcompeted online retailers that provided deep price promotions to all customers.

Then, between 2008 and 2010, as online and mobile retailing expanded exponentially, firms such as Apple and Amazon made severe inroads into Best Buy's top and bottom lines. Online retailers do not have the burden of inventory costs, and they can capitalize on lower prices, no sales tax, and convenient ordering and return policies. As result, Amazon's revenue grew from $6.9 billion in 2004 to nearly $50 billion in 2011, while Best Buy's revenue stayed stagnant at $50 billion between 2009 and 2011.[18] Thus, Best Buy faced the fundamental marketing problem of ever-present competitive reactions (MP#3). At first, it sought to match Amazon's prices, but this competitive strategy could not work, because Amazon would always have a cost advantage due to its lower inventory carrying costs. Researchers suggested that "Best Buy should be looking for opportunities to optimize their business model around the jobs that Amazon can't do for customers," by building its own sustainable competitive advantage rather than reacting with price cuts.[19] Accordingly, in the fall of 2012, Best Buy launched a data analytics-driven "Renew Blue" strategy. The idea was to build on Best Buy's strengths – a unique bricks-and-mortar shopping environment, helpful service staff, and the convenience of touching and feeling products – while also maintaining low inventory costs. The program first gathered sales transaction data to identify which segments and stores were not profitable; these were closed down. Then, using consumer-level data, Renew Blue sought to offer unique "purchase online, pick-up in-store" programs that enabled profitable customers to buy online, while still encouraging them to visit the store and engage in cross-shopping. The program also aimed to increase store inventory in select stores, to encourage consumers to stay engaged with the retailer. Thus, Best Buy refined its segmentation and customer-level strategies, formulated a decade prior, to compete better in the digital era. By 2014, the Renew Blue plan appeared to be working. Best Buy could report increased online sales, from 7% to nearly 10% of its total sales, together with a $1 billion cost reduction.[20] As this real-world example shows, a data analytic, process-driven marketing strategy framework can help a firm reap financial rewards, even in highly competitive marketplaces.

# Summary

As the marketing function has grown to be more legitimate, credible, and accountable, an explosion of new marketing techniques and buzzwords prescribe various paths to financial success. Most accounts take a functional perspective and update readers about the latest tools; instead, we adopt a simplifying, customer-centric perspective and aim to provide an overarching framework of marketing strategy to support a portable, generalizable input-process-output approach to all marketing problems. With this framework, marketing managers can avoid process and method paralysis and rely on strong fundamentals that they can revisit and tweak, in their efforts to understand and solve four fundamental marketing problems or First Principles: MP#1 All customers differ, MP#2 All customers change, MP#3 All competitors react, and MP#4 All resources are limited.

The need for an overarching framework is more pronounced than ever, considering three marketing trends:

1 Firms are moving from mass to one-to-one marketing, serving the needs of smaller groups of customers.
2 Firms manage dynamics in their markets by transforming lifecycle approaches into dynamic customer segmentation approaches, as well as managing anticipated changes at the customer level.
3 Managers have more data and techniques than ever before, necessitating prioritization in terms of which techniques to use, to solve what problems, in which situations.

Managing these three trends requires managers to develop core skills and processes to address the four fundamental problems.

The motivation for MP#1 is that *all customers differ*, and the main challenge is managing *customer heterogeneity*. The solution requires selecting a *specific* segment of customers whose preferences match closely with the firm's offerings and targeting them by positioning the selected offerings to highlight what makes them the best solutions for that subsegment (i.e., why the firm's offerings are better than any offerings competitors might provide). It is also called the STP (i.e., segmentation, targeting, positioning) approach.

The problem driving MP#2 is that *all customers change*, creating the challenge of managing *customer dynamics*. The solution lies in applying solutions similar to MP#1 (i.e., STP), but to the problem of customer dynamics, by segmenting existing customers according to some criterion that can define similar migration patterns. For example, customers in each of three different stages of dealing with a firm – acquisition, expansion, and retention (AER) stages – may be similar, so specific strategies can be developed to deal with customers in each stage. Two methods help with dynamic customer segmentation: lost customer analysis and hidden Markov models.

Underlying MP#3 is the recognition that *all competitors react*. The main challenge then is *building barriers to withstand competitive attacks*, or *sustainable competitive advantages* (SCAs). A firm with SCAs can generate more customer value than competitive firms in its industry for the same set of products and service categories. Most firms build SCA through brand, offering, and relationship (BOR) equities. To build brand equities, a firm can invest in advertising, public relations, or celebrity sponsorships, which enhance brand awareness and brand images that match the focal positioning strategies. To build offering equities, a firm can invest in R&D and introduce the newest or most innovative products, reduce costs, add supplementary services, or fundamentally alter the customer experience. Finally, to build relationship equities, a firm should invest in efforts to build strong relationships between customers and the firm's salespeople or other boundary-spanning employees. These efforts can create especially powerful barriers to customer defection, prompting customer loyalty and superior financial performance.

The problem leading to MP#4 is that *all resources are limited*. The main challenge is *managing resource trade-offs*, and the solution entails understanding the marginal benefits and marginal costs of every incremental dollar devoted to a segment or product. The ultimate allocation decision thus is in proportion to the marginal benefit and cost trade-off associated with each segment or product. It involves the creation, measurement, and monitoring of appropriate performance metrics, using appropriate methods to measure the impact of each resource allocation activity on key metrics of interest.

Four implementation tips for successfully executing the four MPs support seamless integration:

1 Solving MP#2 requires output from MP#1, solving MP#3 requires outputs from MP#1 and MP#2, and solving MP#4 requires outputs from MP#1, MP#2, and MP#3. Thus, fully applying and leveraging the framework requires an understanding that all four principles are interconnected.
2 We stress the importance of a micro–macro duality in executing the framework, which identifies insights at the micro level while also supporting macro-level marketing decisions.
3 Each firm needs to build data and methodology capabilities.
4 The firm cannot solve all the Marketing Principles simultaneously, because of their complex and interrelated nature. Instead, it needs an iterative approach to integrate the principles.

We close by noting the importance of an analytical approach to the framework. *Customer analytics* reflect a technology-enabled, model-supported approach to harnessing customer and market data to understand and serve customers. Firms can rely on customer analytics to embed data and methods (rather than gut feelings) in their marketing decision frameworks. Both data capabilities and methodological capabilities contribute to competence in such analytics. A firm can build data capabilities by collecting data related to customer, economic, and competitive intelligence. It might build methodological capabilities by mastering techniques to perform *data reduction* (find common factors in a data set and group variables), *linking* (perform cause-and-effect studies of marketing interventions), and *optimization* (find trade-offs among multiple marketing variables) functions.

## Takeaways

- Most approaches to marketing strategy take a functional perspective and update readers about the latest tools. Instead, we adopt a simplifying, customer-centric perspective to provide an overarching framework of marketing strategy, with a portable, generalized input-process-output approach to all marketing problems.
- Firms are moving from mass marketing to one-to-one marketing and thus serving the needs of smaller and smaller groups of customers. To manage dynamics and respond to changes at the customer level, firms also are moving from lifecycle approaches to dynamic customer segmentation approaches. Managers have more data and techniques, which requires them to prioritize techniques, problems, and situations. In turn, managers need well-developed core skills and processes, which is why we propose an overarching, generalized framework.
- *All customers differ:* The main challenge of MP#1 is managing customer heterogeneity, which can be achieved though segmentation, targeting, and positioning. Cluster analysis supports segmentation; positioning analyses rely on techniques such as multidimensional scaling.
- *All customers change:* The main challenge of MP#2 is managing customer dynamics, which requires an AER (acquisition, expansion, retention) strategy. Methods that enable AER approaches include lost customer analysis, dynamic segmentation, and hidden Markov models.
- *All competitors react:* The main challenge of MP#3 is managing competitor reactions and building sustainable competitive advantages, using brand, offering, and relationship (BOR) equities. Surveys are a tool for conducting brand audits and revealing the brand's positioning, architecture, and extension strategies. Conjoint analysis offers a way for a firm to redesign its product offerings. Regression analysis enables the firm to gauge the effectiveness of its relationship marketing efforts.
- *All resources are limited:* The main challenge of MP#4 is managing resource trade-offs, by ensuring that allocations to marketing activities are based on a scientific analysis of their benefits and costs. Response models using historical data can measure the impacts of various marketing efforts, according to marketing and financial metrics.
- Several tips can support the successful implementation of the four Marketing Principles. Each of the principles is temporally interconnected with the others, it is important to take advantage of the

micro–macro duality of each principle, firms need to develop data and methodological capabilities, and firms should not solve all principles simultaneously but rather attempt to do so iteratively.

- An analytical approach is important to the successful implementation of our framework. Data capabilities and methodological capabilities contribute to analytical competence. A firm can build data capabilities by collecting data about customer intelligence, economic intelligence, and competitive intelligence. It can build methodological capabilities by mastering the techniques required to perform data reduction, linking, and optimization functions.

# References

1   Leeflang, P.S.H. and Olivier, A.J. (1985) 'Bias in consumer panel and store audit data,' *International Journal of Research in Marketing*, 2(1), pp. 27–41.
2   Chintagunta, P.K., Gopinath, S. and Venkataraman, S. (2010) 'The effects of online user reviews on movie box office performance: Accounting for sequential rollout and aggregation across local markets,' *Marketing Science*, 29(5), pp. 944–57.
3   Xueming, L., Andrews, M., Fang, Z. and Phang, C.W. (2014) 'Mobile targeting,' *Management Science*, 60(7), pp. 1738–56.
4   Real Dolmen CRM (2013) '35% more new customers for Keytrade Bank, with Microsoft Dynamics CRM as driving force of Member Get Member project,' 12 November. Available at: www.slideshare.net/TraviataCRM/case-story-keytrade-bank-member-get-member-project (accessed 9 August, 2016).
5   Stevenson, A. (ed.) (2010) *Oxford Dictionary of English*, 3rd edn. Oxford: Oxford University Press.
6   Davenport, T.H. (2006) 'Competing on analytics,' *Harvard Business Review*, 84(1), pp. 98–110.
7   McKinsey and Co. (2009) 'McKinsey global survey results: Measuring marketing,' *McKinsey Quarterly*, pp. 1–8.
8   Parenteau, J., Sallam, R.L., Howson, C., Tapadinhas, J., Schlegel, K. and Oestreich, T.W. (2016) 'Magic quadrant for business intelligence and analytics platforms.' Available at: www.microstrategy.com/us/company/analyst-reviews/gartner-magic-quadrant (accessed 3 March, 2016).
9   IDC Report (2013) 'IDC forecasts business analytics software market to continue on its strong growth trajectory through 2017,' 25 June. Available at: www.businesswire.com/news/home/20130625005448/en/IDC-Forecasts-Business-Analytics-Software-Market-Continue (accessed 3 March, 2016).
10  Anomaly (2014) 'Case studies: Customer analytics.' Available at: https://weareanomaly.com/portfolio/customer-analytics/ (accessed 10 August, 2016).

11  Germann, F., Lilien, G.L. and Rangaswamy, A. (2012) 'Performance implications of deploying marketing analytics,' *International Journal of Research in Marketing*, 30(2), pp. 114–28.
12  Sheth, J.N., Sisodia, R.S. and Sharma, A. (2000) 'The antecedents and consequences of customer-centric marketing,' *Journal of the Academy of Marketing Science*, 28(1), pp. 55–66.
13  Lee, J.Y., Kozlenkova, I.V. and Palmatier, R.W. (2015) 'Structural marketing: Using organizational structure to achieve marketing objectives,' *Journal of the Academy of Marketing Science*, 43(1), pp. 73–99.
14  Kohli, A.K. and Jaworski, B.J. (1990) 'Market orientation: The construct, research propositions, and managerial implications,' *Journal of Marketing*, 54(2), pp. 1–18.
15  Jaworski, B.J. and Kohli, A.K. (1993) 'Market orientation: Antecedents and consequences,' *Journal of Marketing*, 57(3), pp. 53–70.
16  Martin, R. (2014) 'Strategy is iterative prototyping,' 6 June. Available at: https://hbr.org/2014/06/strategy-is-iterative-prototyping (accessed 10 August, 2016).
17  McWilliams, G. (2004) 'Analyzing customers, Best Buy decides not all are welcome,' 8 November. Available at www.wsj.com/articles/SB109986994931767086 (accessed 10 August, 2016).
18  Frommer, D. (2012) 'Amazon vs. Best Buy: A tale of two retailers,' 18 April. Available at: http://readwrite.com/2012/04/18/amazon_vs_best_buy_a_tale_of_two_retailers (accessed 10 August, 2016).
19  Wessel, M. (2012) 'Best Buy can't match Amazon's prices, and shouldn't try,' 10 December. Available at: https://hbr.org/2012/12/best-buy-cant-match-amazons-pr (accessed 10 August, 2016).
20  Page, V. (2015) 'Is Amazon killing the Best Buy business model?,' 20 July. Available at: www.investopedia.com/articles/personal-finance/072015/amazon-killing-best-buy-business-model.asp (accessed 10 August, 2016).

# Companion website

Please visit the companion website, **www.palgravehighered.com/palmatier-ms**, to access summary videos from the authors, and full-length cases with datasets and step-by-step solution guides.

# Glossary

**acquisition, expansion, retention (AER) approach** An approach that groups existing customers into three stages – those recently acquired, longer-term customers, and those lost or at risk of being lost – can offer some insights into customer dynamics.

**acquisition stage** A stage where customers first evaluate and begin to deal with a firm, at or before first contact, where they start to learn about the firm's offerings and how to transact with the firm.

**adoption lifecycle** A model that describes the timeline and pattern of adoption of a new product, service or innovation that generally follows a normal distribution.

**anchoring and adjustment heuristics** A decision-making process where an individual generally uses a prior expectation (anchor) with which to form beliefs, and updates the belief (adjustment) based on new data that changes the prior expectation.

**attribution-based processes** A method for gauging marketing effectiveness that attributes causal economic effect to a marketing investment, in environments where multiple marketing and confounds events may shape an economic outcome.

**Bass model** A model that uses social contagion theories to predict adoption rates of new products, also capturing product-based factors such as pricing and advertising levels.

**brand** a name, term, design, symbol, or any other feature that identifies one seller's good or service as distinct from those of other sellers.

**brand architecture** The rationale and structure among the firm, its products, and brand/product extension.

**brand associations** The specific words, colors, logo, fonts, emotions, features, music, smells, people, animals, or symbols that are linked to a brand.

**brand audit** An evaluation of the brand's health to understand its strengths and weaknesses.

**brand awareness or familiarity** The ability of a customer to identify a brand indicated by how recognizable the elements associated with the brand are.

**brand category extensions** The new offering moves to a completely different product category.

**branded house architecture** A branding style that uses a single set of brand elements for all products and services provided by the firm.

**brand elements** The elements used to identify a brand, including its name, symbol, package design, and any other features that serve to differentiate that brand's offering from competitors'.

**brand equity** A set of brand assets and liabilities linked to a brand, its name, and symbol that add to or subtract from the economic value provided by a firm's offering and relationships.

**brand extensions** The approach the firm uses to launch new offerings by leveraging an existing brand, whether through line or category extensions.

**brand image** Customers' perceptions and associations with the brand are represented by the links of brand name node to other informational nodes in the model.

**brand line extensions** A new brand offering that is in the same product category but targets a different segment of customers, usually with a slightly different set of attributes (often termed "line extensions").

**brand metrics** A measure that provides a nuanced way to measure brand characteristics.

**brand, offering, relationship (BOR) equity stack** A stack of brand, offering, and relationship equities that represents the firm's overall customer equity.

**bystanders** The customers not targeted by a firm's marketing or loyalty program.

**choice model** A model that predicts the likelihood of observed customer choices/responses (e.g., joining, cross-buying, leaving), using data about that customer's characteristics and past behaviors, as well as the firm's marketing interventions.

**classification analysis** A technique that reports a percentage accuracy at predicting a customer segment for a given set of demographic variables in order to apply a segment prediction to a group of non-surveyed customers.

**cluster analysis** A technique that uses customer preferences to cluster individual customers into a given number of groups.

**commitment** An enduring desire to maintain a valued relationship.

**communication** The amount, frequency, and quality of information shared by exchange partners.

**competitive strength** A measurement that captures the relative strength of a firm versus competitors at securing and maintaining market share in a given segment.

**conflict** A serious disagreement or ongoing argument among relational partners.

**conjoint analysis** A modelling methodology with which marketers can design and develop new products by thinking of products as bundles of attributes, and then determining which combination of attributes is best suited to meet the preferences of customers.

**cooperative behaviors** Coordinated, complementary actions between partners to achieve a mutual goal.

**corporate strategy** The direction and scope of an organization over the long term, to achieve some well-defined objectives.

**crossing the chasm** Label given to the process of a new firm successfully moving from early adopters to majority groups.

**customer analytics** A technology-enabled, model-supported approach to harnessing customer and market data to understand and serve customers.

**customer-centric approach** A company-wide philosophy that places customers' needs at the center of an organization's strategic process and uses the resultant insights to make decisions.

**customer dynamics** The processes by which customers' desires and needs change over time.

**customer equity** The total lifetime values of all current and future customers, which is the sum of a firm's brand, offering, and relational equities.

**customer heterogeneity** The variation among customers in terms of needs, desires, and subsequent behaviors.

**customer learning effect** The process where users of a particular product or service become more familiar with the product, and thus are more likely to repurchase the same product in the future.

**customer lifecycle** The average change or migration among customers as they age, independent of any product or industry differences.

**customer lifetime value (CLV)** An approach that attempts to capture the financial contribution of each customer by determining the discounted value of the sales and costs.

**customer onboarding** The planned process of introducing new customers to a firm to improve their long-term satisfaction and loyalty.

**customer relationship management (CRM)** The managerially relevant, organization-wide, customer-focused application of relationship marketing, using IT to achieve performance objectives.

**data capabilities** The ability of a firm to measure, monitor, and manage its marketing function's effectiveness in an objective, fact-based manner.

**data era** A period in which firms start using historical data that reveal the link between their past resource trade-off decisions and outcomes, such that they could determine the actual effects of certain resources on specific outcomes.

**decline or recovery stage** A stage in response to specific events (conflict, unfairness, betrayal) or passive neglect (failure to communicate, ending investments).

**dependence** Customers work to maintain relationships with sellers on which they depend.

**designers' curse** A bias that once developers or designers accept some new feature, they perceive its great value – far more than would be assigned the feature by non-users.

**discrete life events** Events that have immediate impacts on many aspects of customers' purchase decisions.

**disruptive technologies** Technologies that present highly different price and performance characteristics or value propositions.

**empathic behaviors** The impact on a customer or relational partner's behavior based on their sensitivity to the seller's situation.

**endorsed brand strategy** A strategy that suggests the approval and imprimatur of the brand.

**expansion stage** A stage where firms are trying to upsell or cross-sell in order to expand sales and engagement with existing customers, in addition to predicting and adapting to customers' future migrating paths

**experiment** A scientific procedure undertaken by managers to discover, test, or demonstrate a marketing hypothesis.

**exploratory or early stage** A stage most relationships begin with, featuring limited confidence in the partner's ability and trustworthiness.

**factor analysis** A way to meaningfully reduce the number of variables being investigated in a research study. An important preceding step for any cluster analysis, depending on the number of items included in a research study.

**First Principles** The fundamental concepts or assumptions on which a theory, system, or method is based.

**free will** The freedom or power to act without constraints or regulations.

**GE matrix** An analysis tool designed to helps managers visualize and select target segments.

**growth or developing stage** A stage where the escalation of reciprocated transactions and increased affective attachment produce trust, commitment, and satisfaction.

**heuristic-based processes** A decision-making process where an individual uses lay theories or common beliefs (heuristics) to make decisions with uncertain outcomes.

**heuristics era** A period in which firms constantly decide how to allocate resources across different customer segments, different customer stages, different offerings, different regions, and different marketing communication formats.

**hidden Markov model (HMM)** A statistical model that can uncover "states" of customer behaviors, as well as how those states evolve.

**house of brand architecture** A branding style where a firm focuses on branding each major product with its own unique set of brand elements.

**individual differences** A person's stable and consistent way of responding to the environment in a specific domain.

**innovation** Creation of substantial new value for customers and the firm by creatively changing one or more dimensions of the business.

**integrated marketing communications (IMC)** The process of designing and delivering marketing messages to customers while ensuring that they are relevant and consistent over time and channels.

**interaction frequency** The number of interactions per unit of time between exchange partners.

**iterative approach** A decision-making process where an individual takes multiple related steps to make and improve decisions, wherein the decision in each step is informed by the outcome of the previous step.

**latent customer heterogeneity** Potential differences in desires that are unobserved and have not manifested in different customer purchases or behaviors.

**latent loyalty** Loyalty generated when customers express positive attitudes but fail to actually buy a firm's products.

**learning effect** The process by which customers become familiar with the product by using it, which changes their weighting of the relative importance of different attributes due to their enhanced knowledge and experience.

**market attractiveness** A measurement that captures the external market characteristics that make a given segment strategically and financially valuable to serve, such as size, growth rate, and price sensitivity.

**marketing elasticity** A unit-free measure of the percentage change in a marketing outcome, due to a one percent increase in marketing efforts or investment.

**Marketing Principle** A First Principle or underlying assumption, when matched with its associated managerial decisions.

**marketing strategy** A collection of decisions and actions focused on building a sustainable differential advantage, relative to competitors, in the minds of customers, in order to create value for stakeholders.

**market orientation** The organization-wide generation of market intelligence, dissemination of that intelligence across departments, and organization-wide responsiveness to it.

**mass marketing (undifferentiated marketing)** A marketing strategy that utilizes mass media to appeal to an entire market with a single message; where a firm mostly ignores customer heterogeneity based on the assumption that reaching the largest audience possible will lead to the largest sales revenue.

**maturity or maintaining stage** A stage where the partners' calculative trust gets replaced by knowledge- and affective-based trust, communication, and other relational norms that reinforce their common goals.

**methodological capabilities** Abilities built by mastering the analytical tools.

**micro–macro duality** A process that allows deep understanding of customers at micro levels (avoiding aggregation bias) and supports strategic and resource decisions at macro levels (advertising, R&D, and sales force strategies).

**motives** The desire or need that incites action.

**multiple discriminant analysis (MDA)** A technique to classify research respondents into appropriate segments using a set of demographic characteristics as the predictors.

**natural experiments** Experiments that purposefully (rather than randomly) apply a marketing treatment to one group, then compare the effects of different marketing strategies.

**need** A condition in which a person requires or desires something.

**niche marketing** A marketing strategy that focuses marketing efforts on well-defined, narrow segments of consumers in hopes of gaining a competitive advantage through specialization.

**offering** A purposely broad term that captures tangible products and intangible services provided by firms.

**offering equity** The core value that the performance of the product or service offers the customer.

**one-to-one marketing** A marketing strategy that attempts to market directly to a specific consumer; where a firm attempts to tailor one or more aspects of the firm's marketing mix to the individual customer, segmenting a population to the extreme by having a single customer in the target segment.

**perceptual maps** Maps that depict customer segments, competitors, and a firm's own position in a multidimensional space, defined by the purchase attributes identified during the segmentation process.

**points of difference** The key ways a brand differs from its competition.

**points of parity** The aspects of the brand that may not be unique but still are required by customers in the target market.

**positioning statement** Words that capture the key marketing decisions, internal and external, needed to effectively appeal to customers in the firm's target segment that include the who, what, and why the firm is targeting.

**product or industry lifecycle** Typical user experiences and industry developmental effects that can be observed as the product category matures.

**product lifecycle** A well-recognized phenomenon that captures prototypical changes in customers' purchase criteria and marketers' actions as the product category matures.

**qualitative analysis** A method that helps the firm refine its ideas with smaller samples.

**quantitative analysis** A method designed to test theories and ideas, using data and specific analysis techniques.

**relational loyalty** Customers provide benefits due to their relational attitudes and ties with the seller or seller's employees.

**relationship breadth** A measure of the number of relational bonds with an exchange partner.

**relationship composition** A diverse, authoritative contact portfolio that increases a seller's ability to make decisions and effect change in its customers' organizations.

**relationship duration** The length of the relationship between exchange partners.

**relationship equity** The aggregation of relational assets and liabilities, associated with the firm's boundary-spanning employees and social networks linked to the offering or experience.

**relationship investment** The time, resource, and effort investments, such as preferential treatment, gifts, or loyalty programs.

**relationship marketing (RM)** The process of building and maintaining strong customer relationships which can produce relationship equity.

**relationship orientation** Desire to engage in a strong relationship.

**relationship quality** Diverse interaction characteristics.

**repositioning** The process by which a firm shifts its target market.

**resource slack** The potentially utilizable resources a firm possesses that it could divert or redeploy to achieve organizational goals.

**resource trade-offs** A situation under which firms combine all of the marketing mix allocation decisions.

**response model** A mathematical model that tracks the relationship between a firm's marketing efforts and economic outcomes.

**retention stage** A stage that deals with customers that are migrating due to a basic propensity to switch.

**risk** The possibility that the investment fails to prompt reciprocated behavior.

**segmenting** The process of dividing the overall market into groups where the potential customers in each group have similar needs and desires for a particular category of product or service while also maximizing the differences among groups.

**seller expertise** A seller who can be relied upon to provide knowledgeable and credible information.

**similarity** The parties share common cultures, values, and goals.

**spurious loyalty** Loyalty that is manifested in ambivalent or negative feelings.

**stage-gate development process** The process that most firms rely on to increase the speed of their offering development and enhance their likelihood of success, while also reducing development costs.

**STP (segmentation, targeting, positioning) analysis** The general approach of grouping customers into segments, selecting target segments, and using marketing activities to improve a firm's positioning in the target segment.

**sub-branding strategy** A strategy that assigns some major product categories.

**sustainable competitive advantage (SCA)** An advantage that a firm has when it is able to generate more customer value than the other firms in its industry and when these other firms are unable to duplicate its effective strategy.

**sustaining technologies** Technologies exploited by market leaders, which produce continuous, incremental improvements over time.

**SWOT analysis** Analysis of strengths, weaknesses, opportunities, and threats.

**true loyalty** Loyalty that is manifested in consumers' positive feelings and actions.

**trust** Confidence in a relationship partner's reliability and integrity.

**vertical extensions** The planned process where a firm changes an offering's price and performance positioning over time (moving up or down market).

**word of mouth (WOM)** Communication by a customer about a seller to others, which can be positive or negative.

# Index

Entries for figures are in **bold**. Entries for tables are in *italics*.